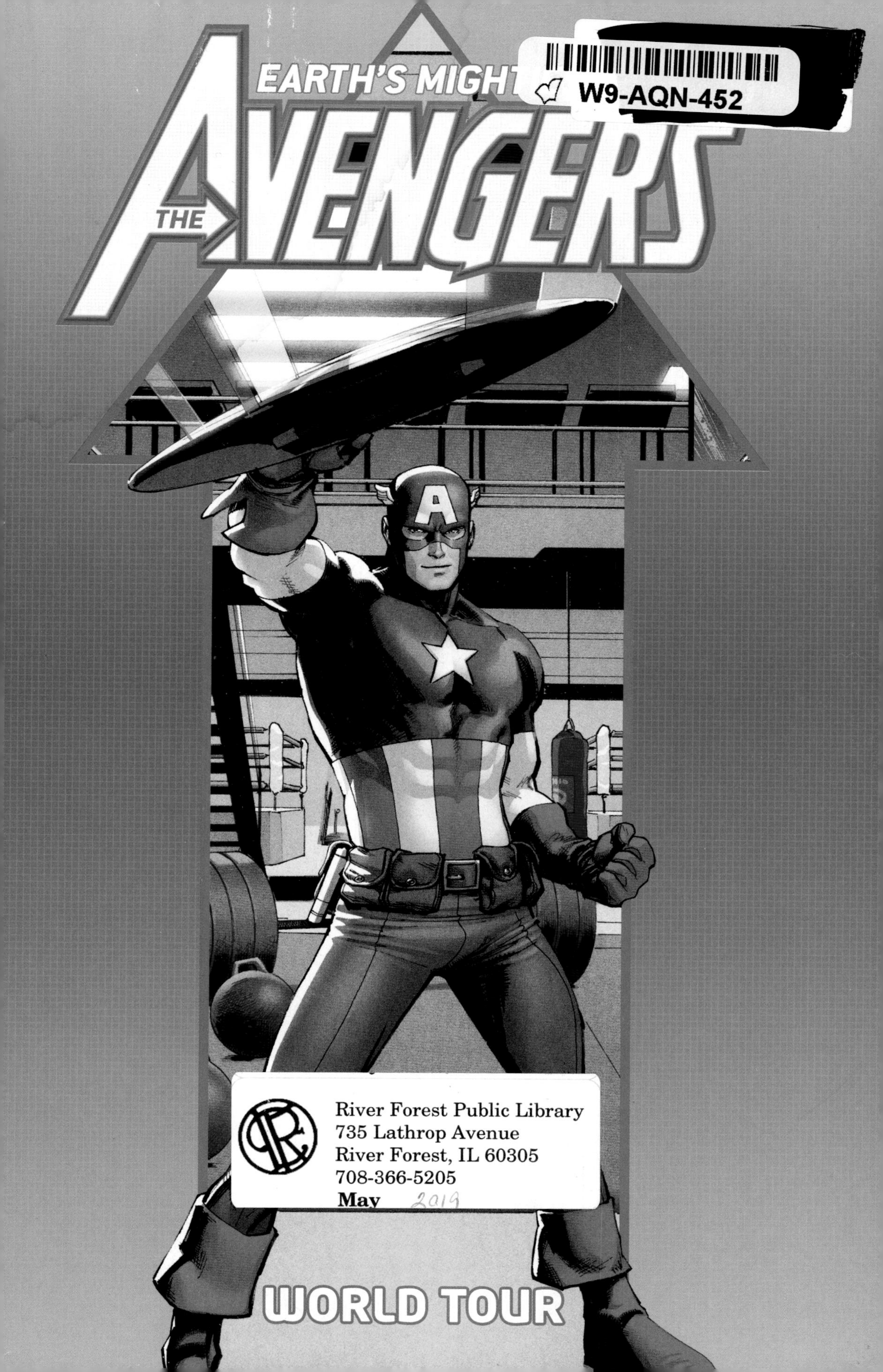
EARTH'S MIGHT
THE AVENGERS
WORLD TOUR

ON A DAY UNLIKE ANY OTHER, A DARK CELESTIAL INVASION LED IRON MAN, THOR AND CAPTAIN AMERICA TO RE-FORM THE AVENGERS, ADDING BLACK PANTHER, CAPTAIN MARVEL, SHE-HULK AND GHOST RIDER TO THEIR RANKS. NOW THEY PROTECT THE WORLD AS THE MIGHTY AVENGERS!

AVENGERS BY JASON AARON VOL. 2: WORLD TOUR. Contains material originally published in magazine form as AVENGERS #7-12. First printing 2019. ISBN 978-1-302-91188-1. Published by MARVEL WORLDWIDE, INC., a subsidiary of MARVEL ENTERTAINMENT, LLC. OFFICE OF PUBLICATION: 135 West 50th Street, New York, NY 10020. Copyright © 2019 MARVEL No similarity between any of the names, characters, persons, and/or institutions in this magazine with those of any living or dead person or institution is intended, and any such similarity which may exist is purely coincidental. **Printed in the U.S.A.** DAN BUCKLEY, President, Marvel Entertainment; JOHN NEE, Publisher; JOE QUESADA, Chief Creative Officer; TOM BREVOORT, SVP of Publishing; DAVID BOGART, SVP of Business Affairs & Operations, Publishing & Partnership; DAVID GABRIEL, SVP of Sales & Marketing, Publishing; JEFF YOUNGQUIST, VP of Production & Special Projects; DAN CARR, Executive Director of Publishing Technology; ALEX MORALES, Director of Publishing Operations; DAN EDINGTON, Managing Editor; SUSAN CRESPI, Production Manager; STAN LEE, Chairman Emeritus. For information regarding advertising in Marvel Comics or on Marvel.com, please contact Vit DeBellis, Custom Solutions & Integrated Advertising Manager, at vdebellis@marvel.com. For Marvel subscription inquiries, please call 888-511-5480. Manufactured between 1/11/2019 and 2/12/2019 by LSC COMMUNICATIONS INC., KENDALLVILLE, IN, USA.

10 9 8 7 6 5 4 3 2 1

COLLECTION EDITOR
JENNIFER GRÜNWALD
ASSISTANT EDITOR
CAITLIN O'CONNELL
ASSOCIATE MANAGING EDITOR
KATERI WOODY
EDITOR, SPECIAL PROJECTS
MARK D. BEAZLEY
VP PRODUCTION
& SPECIAL PROJECTS
JEFF YOUNGQUIST
SVP PRINT, SALES & MARKETING
DAVID GABRIEL
BOOK DESIGNER
ADAM DEL RE

EDITOR IN CHIEF
C.B. CEBULSKI
CHIEF CREATIVE OFFICER
JOE QUESADA
PRESIDENT
DAN BUCKLEY
EXECUTIVE PRODUCER
ALAN FINE

EARTH'S MIGHTIEST HEROES
THE AVENGERS
WORLD TOUR

JASON AARON
WRITER

AVENGERS #7

SARA PICHELLI
PENCILER

SARA PICHELLI
WITH **ELISABETTA D'AMICO**
INKERS

JUSTIN PONSOR
COLOR ARTIST

GEOFF SHAW & **JASON KEITH**
COVER ART

AVENGERS #8-9

DAVID MARQUEZ
ARTIST

JUSTIN PONSOR
COLOR ARTIST

DAVID MARQUEZ WITH **JUSTIN PONSOR** [#8] & **MARCIO MENYZ** [#9]
COVER ART

AVENGERS #10

DAVID MARQUEZ &
ED McGUINNESS
PENCILERS

DAVID MARQUEZ &
MARK MORALES
INKERS

**FRAZER IRVING,
ADAM KUBERT** &
ANDREA SORRENTINO
GUEST ARTISTS

**JUSTIN PONSOR,
ERICK ARCINIEGA, FRAZER
IRVING, MATTHEW WILSON** &
GIADA MARCHISIO
COLOR ARTISTS

DAVID MARQUEZ & **MARTE GRACIA**
COVER ART

AVENGERS #11-12

ED McGUINNESS
& **CORY SMITH**
PENCILERS

**MARK MORALES,
SCOTT HANNA** & **KARL KESEL**
INKERS/FINISHERS

ERICK ARCINIEGA
COLOR ARTIST

ED McGUINNESS
& **MARTE GRACIA** [#8]
AND **ALAN DAVIS, MARK FARMER**
& **JIM CAMPBELL** [#12]
COVER ART

VC's CORY PETIT
LETTERER

ALANNA SMITH
ASSOCIATE EDITOR

TOM BREVOORT
EDITOR

AVENGERS CREATED BY
STAN LEE & **JACK KIRBY**

7 FIRE AND BONE

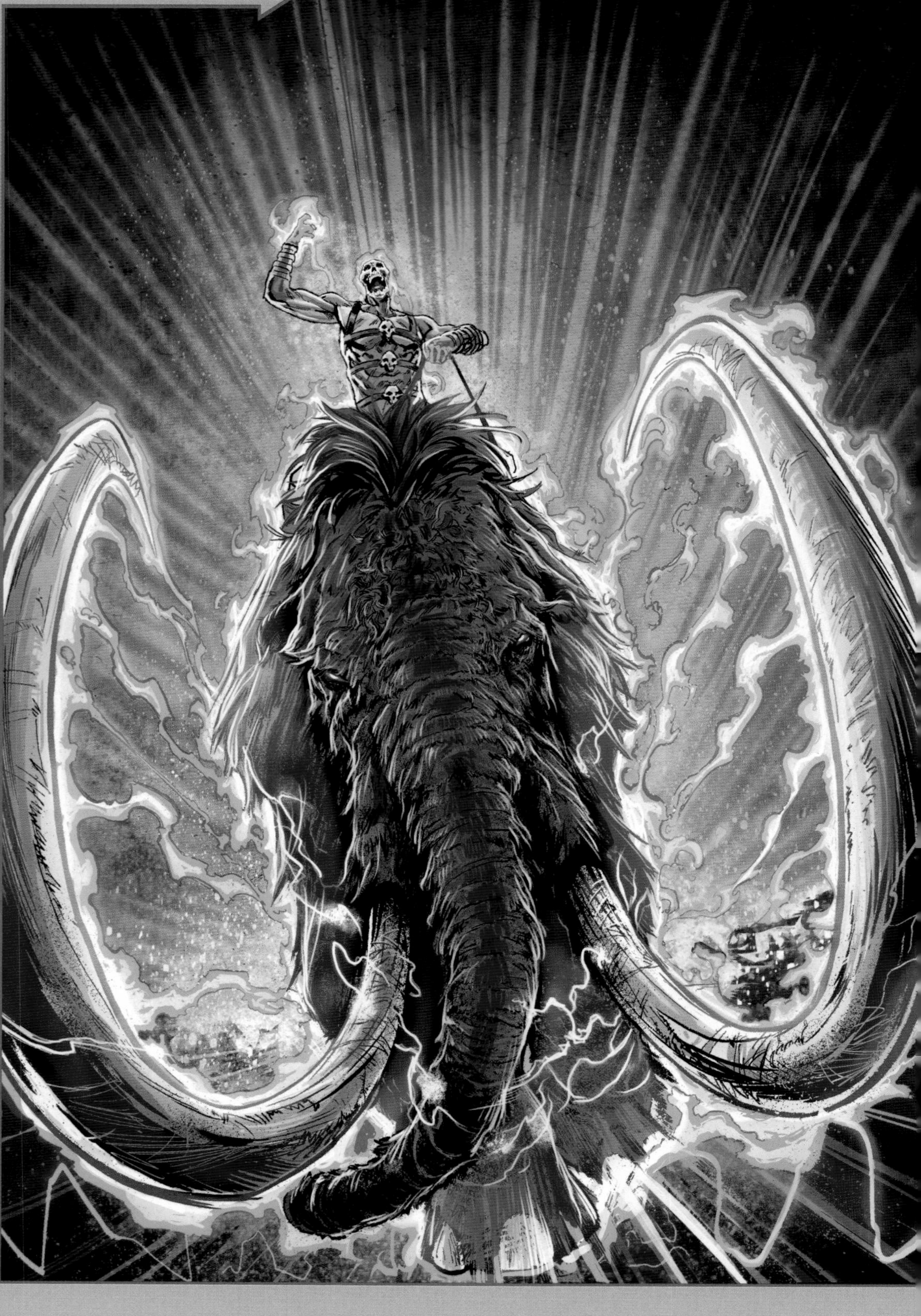

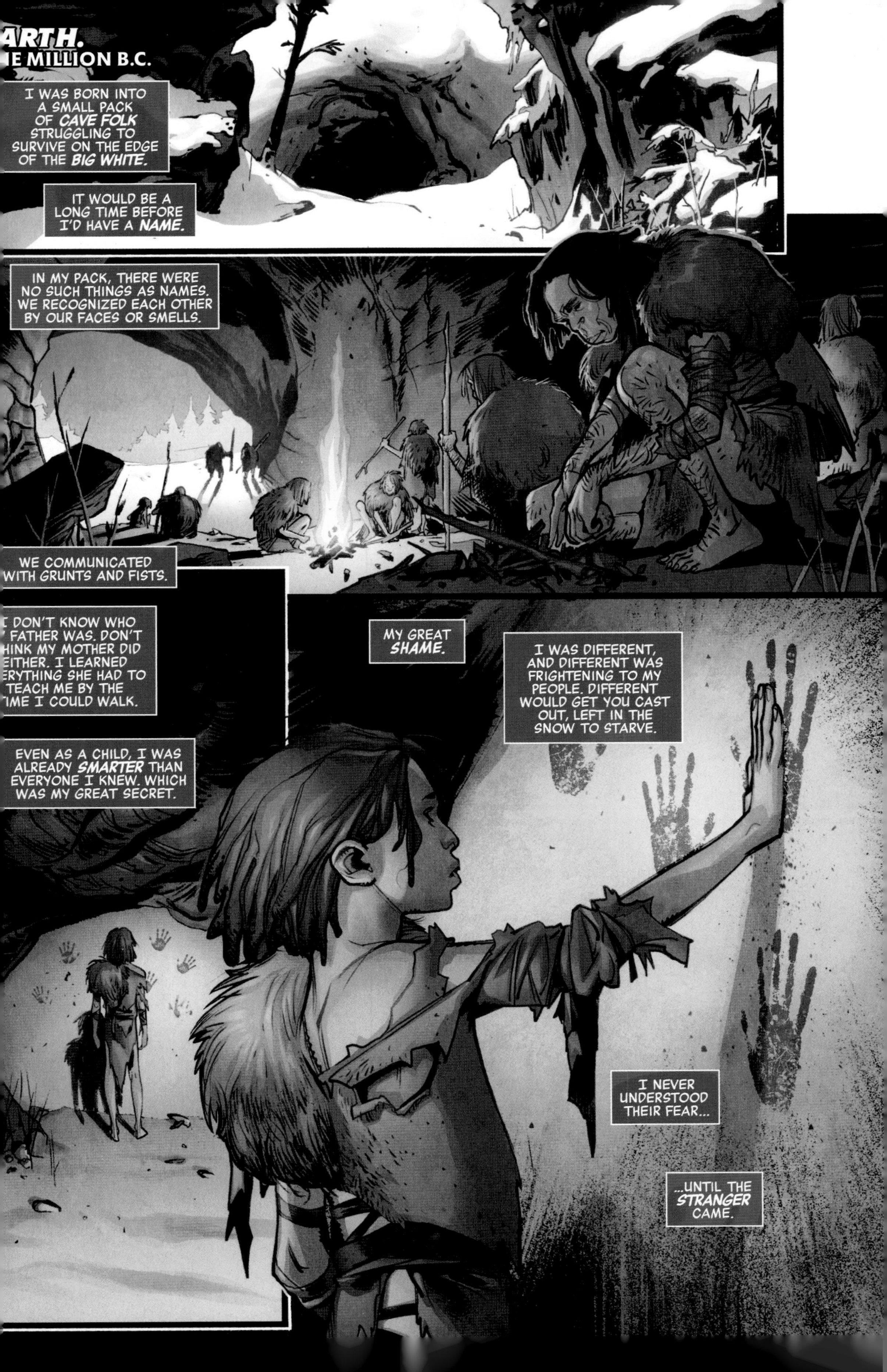

ARTH.
E MILLION B.C.
I WAS BORN INTO A SMALL PACK OF CAVE FOLK STRUGGLING TO SURVIVE ON THE EDGE OF THE BIG WHITE.
IT WOULD BE A LONG TIME BEFORE I'D HAVE A NAME.
IN MY PACK, THERE WERE NO SUCH THINGS AS NAMES. WE RECOGNIZED EACH OTHER BY OUR FACES OR SMELLS.
WE COMMUNICATED WITH GRUNTS AND FISTS.
DON'T KNOW WHO FATHER WAS. DON'T HINK MY MOTHER DID EITHER. I LEARNED ERYTHING SHE HAD TO TEACH ME BY THE TIME I COULD WALK.
EVEN AS A CHILD, I WAS ALREADY SMARTER THAN EVERYONE I KNEW. WHICH WAS MY GREAT SECRET.
MY GREAT SHAME.
I WAS DIFFERENT, AND DIFFERENT WAS FRIGHTENING TO MY PEOPLE. DIFFERENT WOULD GET YOU CAST OUT, LEFT IN THE SNOW TO STARVE.
I NEVER UNDERSTOOD THEIR FEAR...
...UNTIL THE STRANGER CAME.

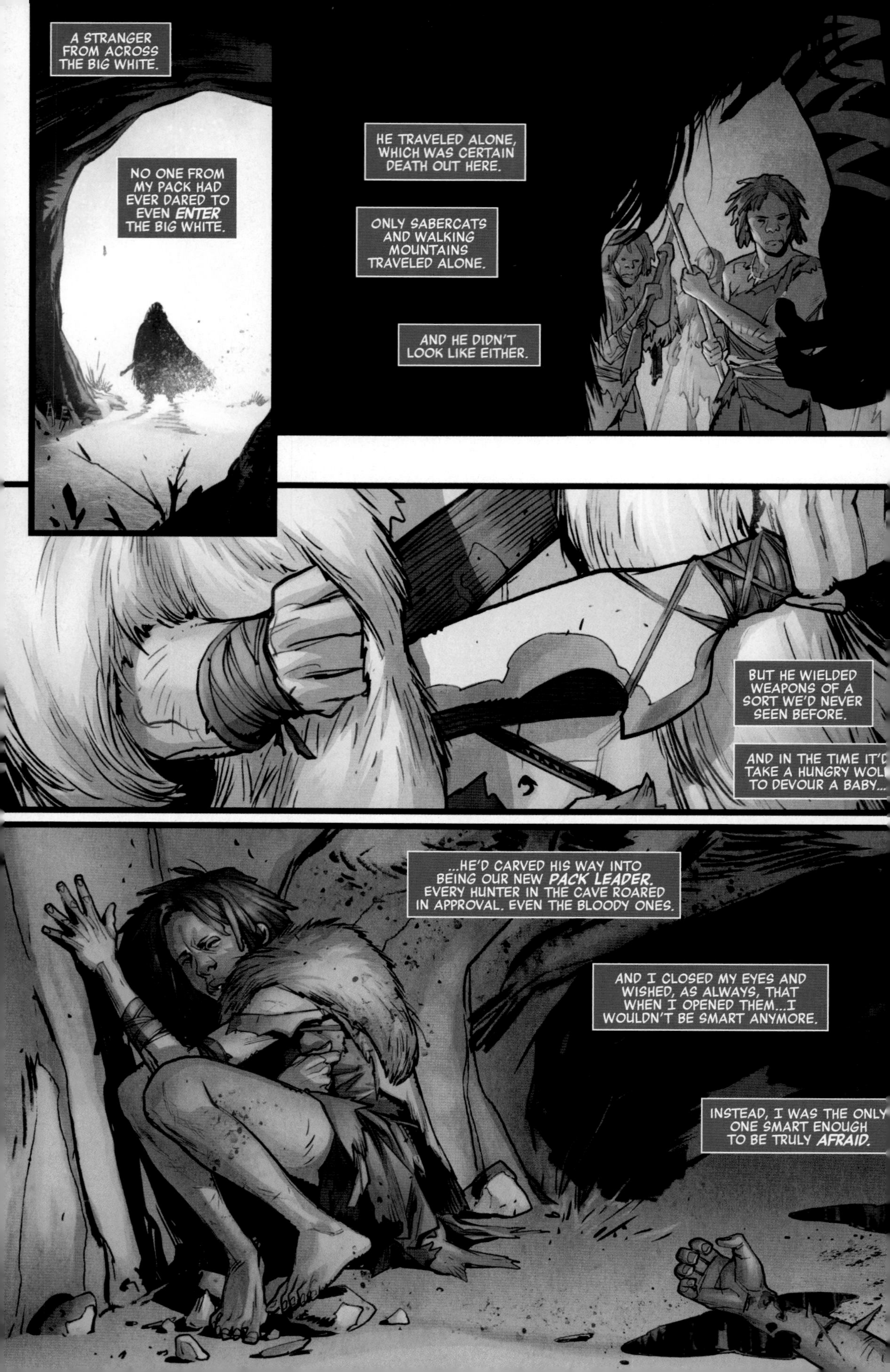
A STRANGER FROM ACROSS THE BIG WHITE.
NO ONE FROM MY PACK HAD EVER DARED TO EVEN *ENTER* THE BIG WHITE.
HE TRAVELED ALONE, WHICH WAS CERTAIN DEATH OUT HERE.
ONLY SABERCATS AND WALKING MOUNTAINS TRAVELED ALONE.
AND HE DIDN'T LOOK LIKE EITHER.
BUT HE WIELDED WEAPONS OF A SORT WE'D NEVER SEEN BEFORE.
AND IN THE TIME IT'D TAKE A HUNGRY WOLF TO DEVOUR A BABY...
...HE'D CARVED HIS WAY INTO BEING OUR NEW *PACK LEADER.* EVERY HUNTER IN THE CAVE ROARED IN APPROVAL. EVEN THE BLOODY ONES.
AND I CLOSED MY EYES AND WISHED, AS ALWAYS, THAT WHEN I OPENED THEM...I WOULDN'T BE SMART ANYMORE.
INSTEAD, I WAS THE ONLY ONE SMART ENOUGH TO BE TRULY *AFRAID.*

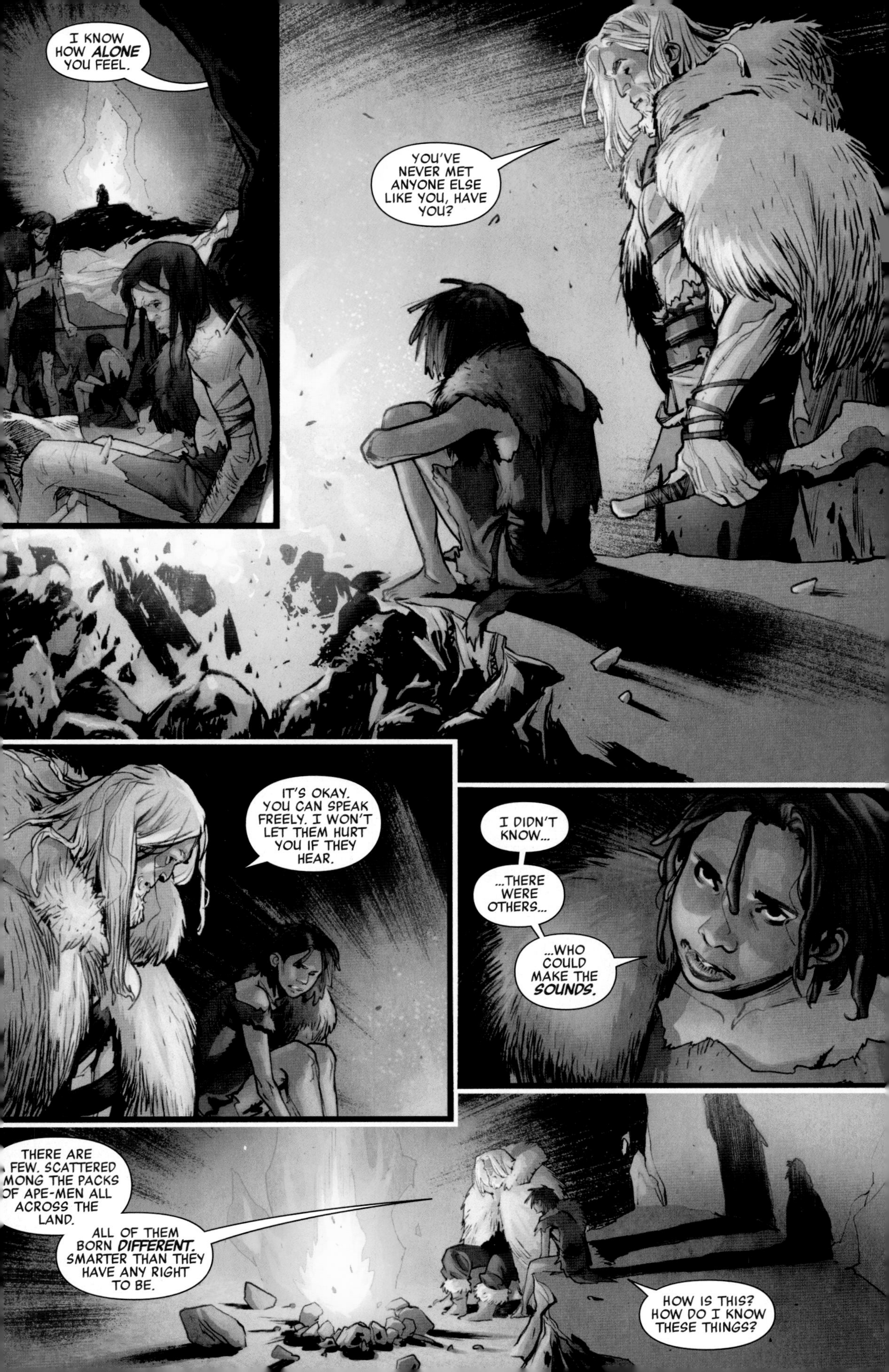
I KNOW HOW *ALONE* YOU FEEL.
YOU'VE NEVER MET ANYONE ELSE LIKE YOU, HAVE YOU?
IT'S OKAY. YOU CAN SPEAK FREELY. I WON'T LET THEM HURT YOU IF THEY HEAR.
I DIDN'T KNOW...
...THERE WERE OTHERS...
...WHO COULD MAKE THE *SOUNDS.*
THERE ARE FEW. SCATTERED MONG THE PACKS OF APE-MEN ALL ACROSS THE LAND.
ALL OF THEM BORN *DIFFERENT.* SMARTER THAN THEY HAVE ANY RIGHT TO BE.
HOW IS THIS? HOW DO I KNOW THESE THINGS?

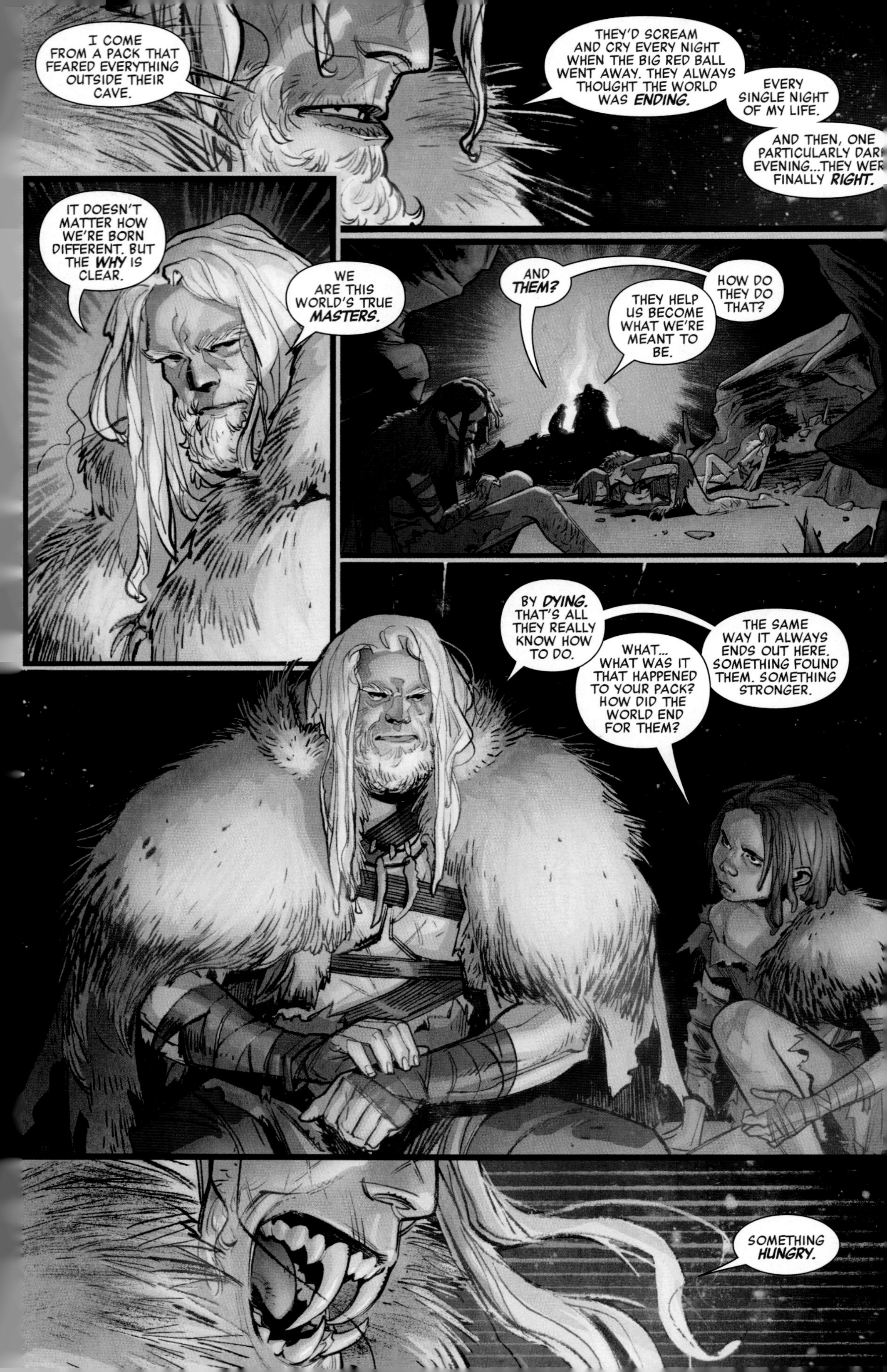
I COME FROM A PACK THAT FEARED EVERYTHING OUTSIDE THEIR CAVE.
THEY'D SCREAM AND CRY EVERY NIGHT WHEN THE BIG RED BALL WENT AWAY. THEY ALWAYS THOUGHT THE WORLD WAS ENDING.
EVERY SINGLE NIGHT OF MY LIFE.
AND THEN, ONE PARTICULARLY DARK EVENING...THEY WERE FINALLY RIGHT.
IT DOESN'T MATTER HOW WE'RE BORN DIFFERENT. BUT THE WHY IS CLEAR.
WE ARE THIS WORLD'S TRUE MASTERS.
AND THEM?
THEY HELP US BECOME WHAT WE'RE MEANT TO BE.
HOW DO THEY DO THAT?
BY DYING. THAT'S ALL THEY REALLY KNOW HOW TO DO.
WHAT... WHAT WAS IT THAT HAPPENED TO YOUR PACK? HOW DID THE WORLD END FOR THEM?
THE SAME WAY IT ALWAYS ENDS OUT HERE. SOMETHING FOUND THEM. SOMETHING STRONGER.
SOMETHING HUNGRY.

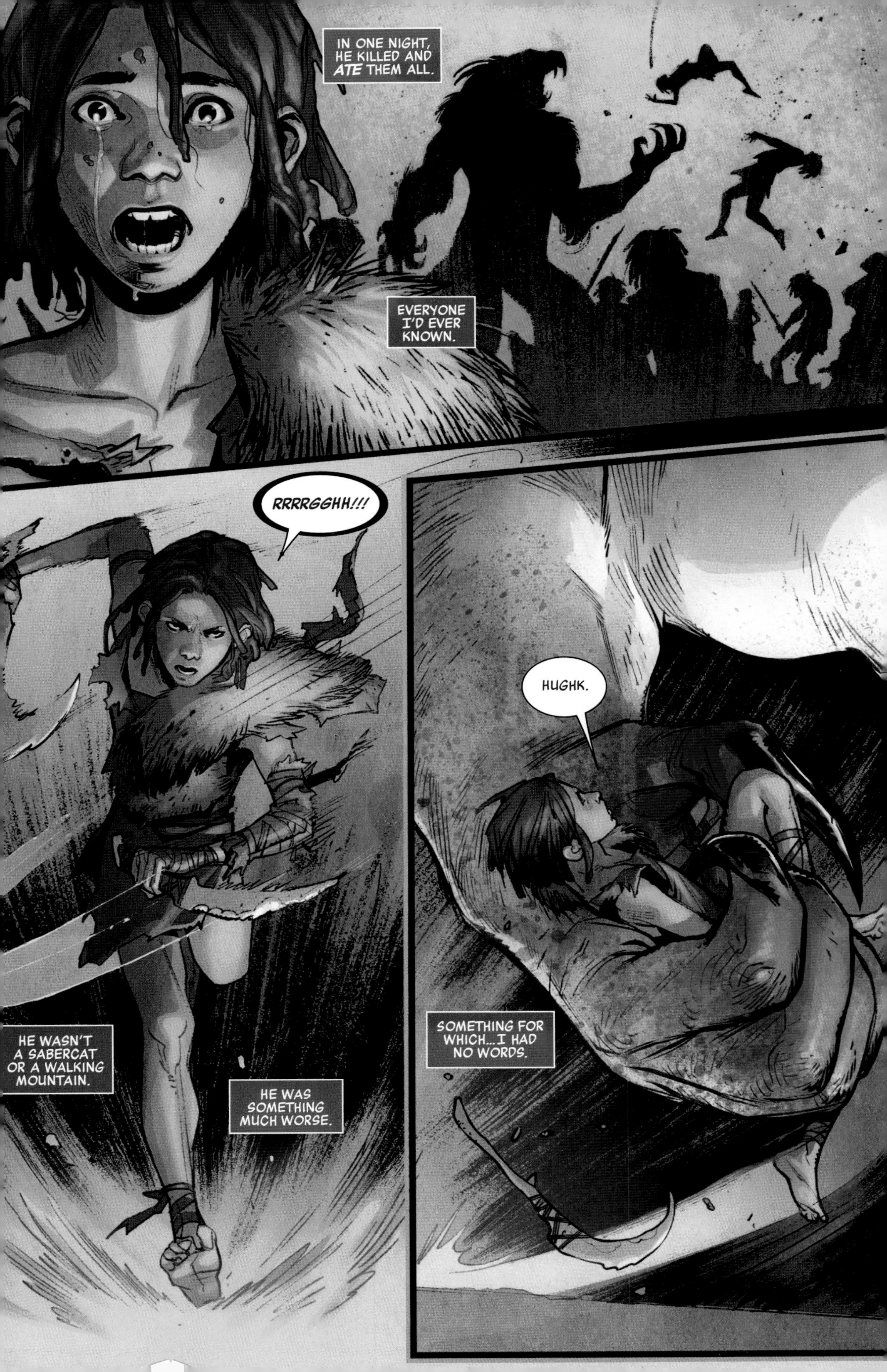
IN ONE NIGHT, HE KILLED AND ATE THEM ALL.
EVERYONE I'D EVER KNOWN.
RRRRGGHH!!!
HE WASN'T A SABERCAT OR A WALKING MOUNTAIN.
HE WAS SOMETHING MUCH WORSE.
HUGHK.
SOMETHING FOR WHICH... I HAD NO WORDS.

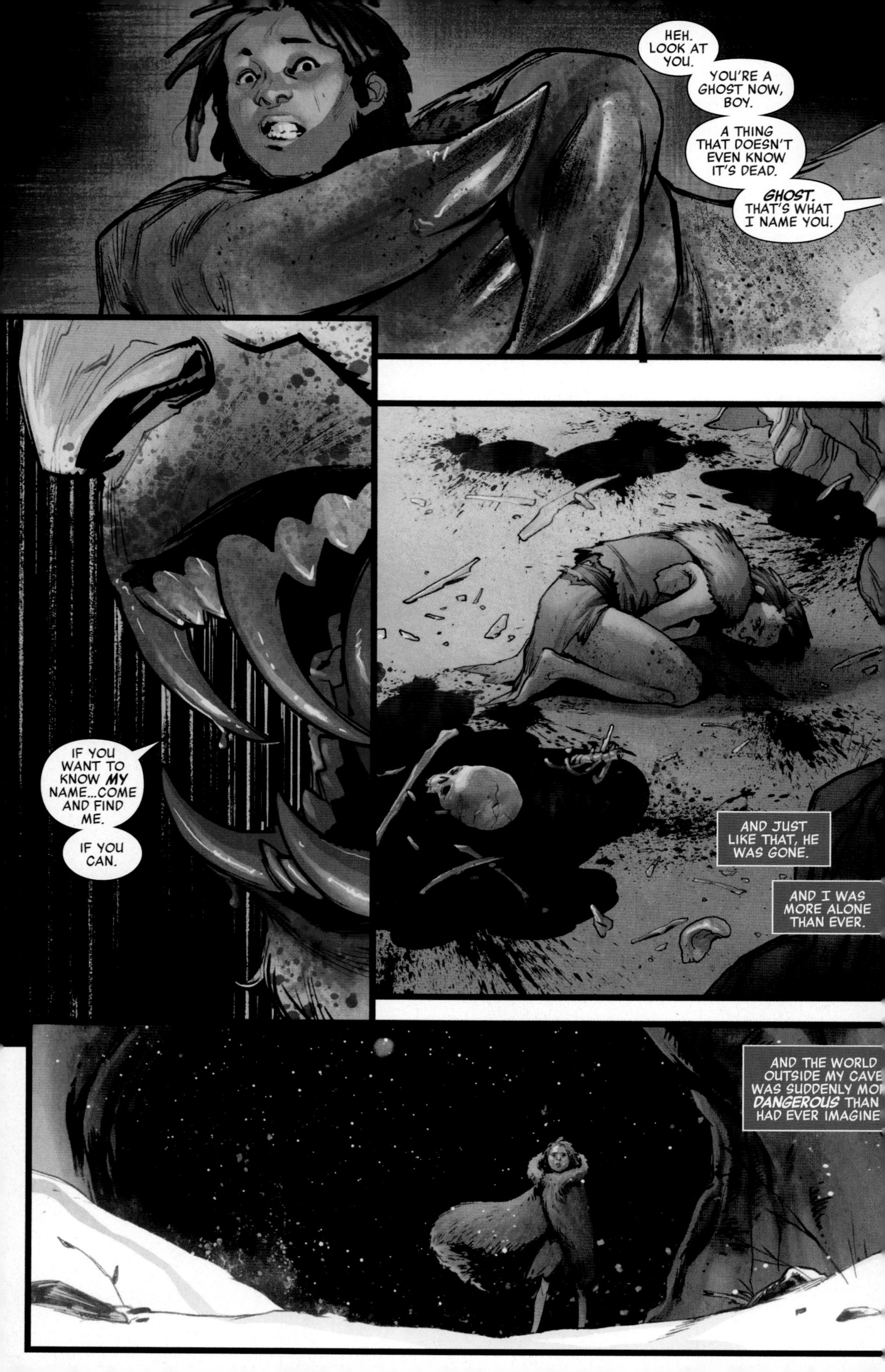
HEH. LOOK AT YOU.
YOU'RE A GHOST NOW, BOY.
A THING THAT DOESN'T EVEN KNOW IT'S DEAD.
GHOST. THAT'S WHAT I NAME YOU.
IF YOU WANT TO KNOW MY NAME...COME AND FIND ME.
IF YOU CAN.
AND JUST LIKE THAT, HE WAS GONE.
AND I WAS MORE ALONE THAN EVER.
AND THE WORLD OUTSIDE MY CAVE WAS SUDDENLY MO DANGEROUS THAN HAD EVER IMAGINE

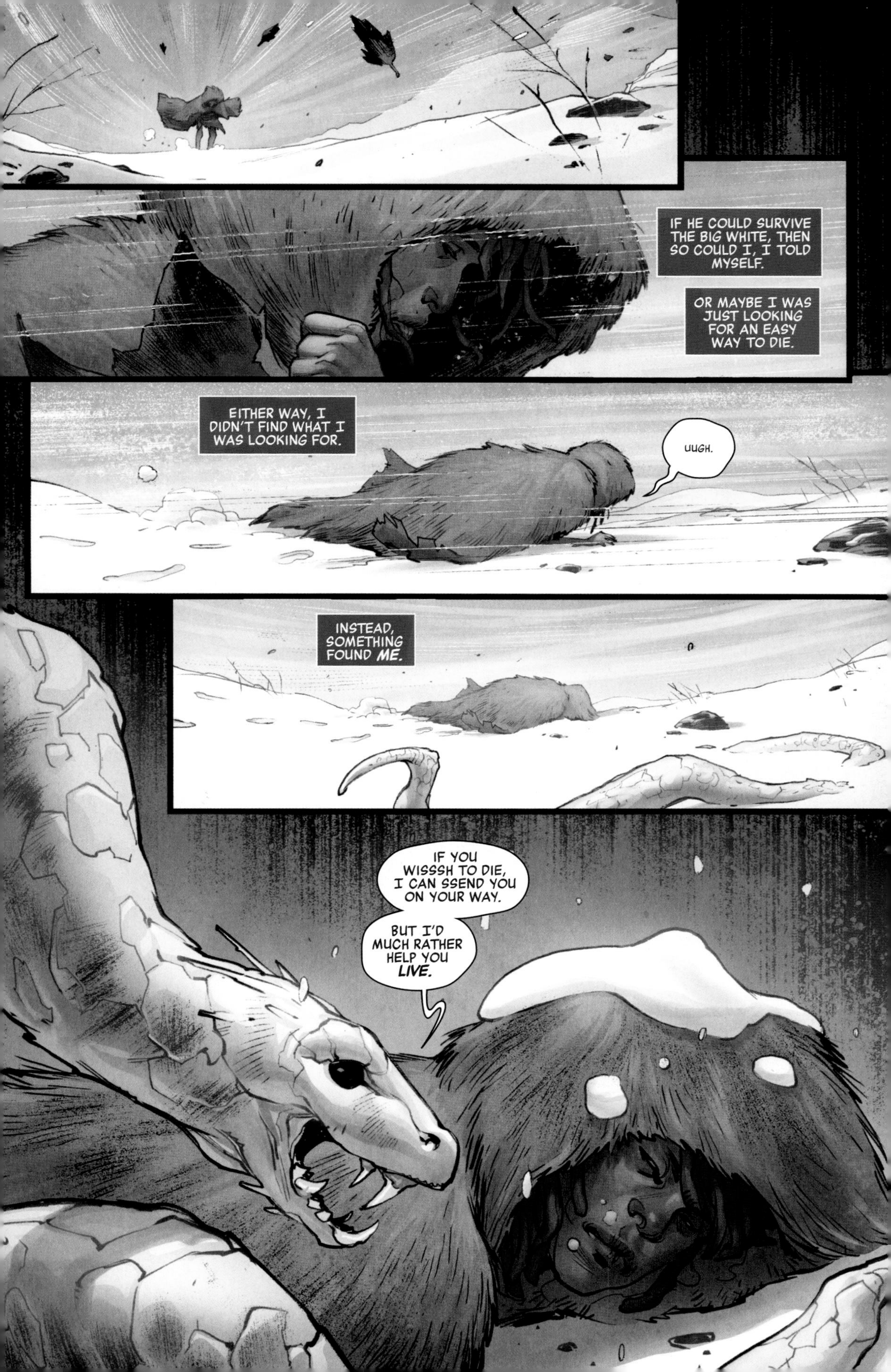
IF HE COULD SURVIVE THE BIG WHITE, THEN SO COULD I, I TOLD MYSELF.
OR MAYBE I WAS JUST LOOKING FOR AN EASY WAY TO DIE.
EITHER WAY, I DIDN'T FIND WHAT I WAS LOOKING FOR.
UUGH.
INSTEAD, SOMETHING FOUND ***ME.***
IF YOU WISSSH TO DIE, I CAN SSEND YOU ON YOUR WAY.
BUT I'D MUCH RATHER HELP YOU ***LIVE.***

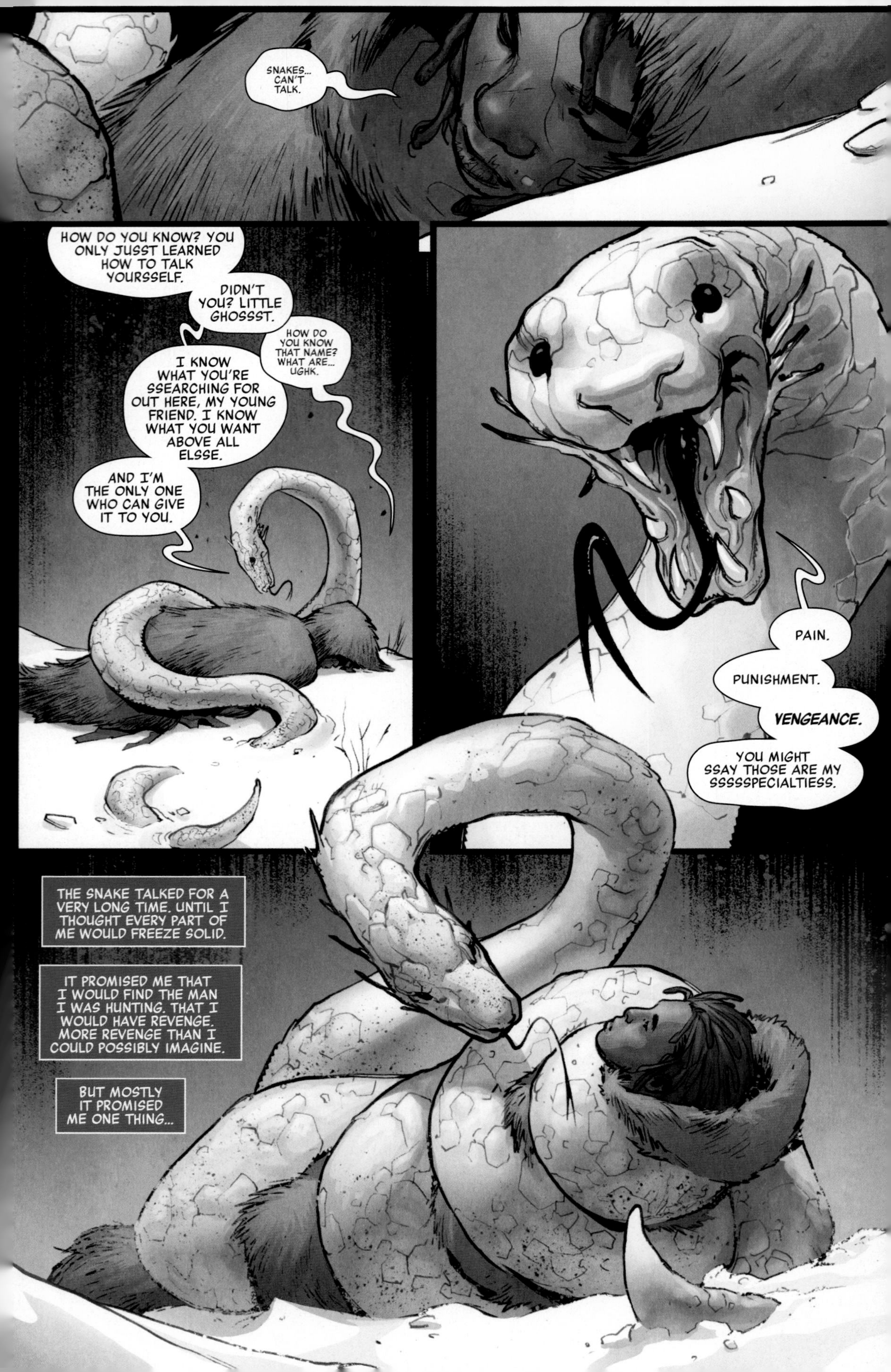
SNAKES... CAN'T TALK.
HOW DO YOU KNOW? YOU ONLY JUSST LEARNED HOW TO TALK YOURSSELF.
DIDN'T YOU? LITTLE GHOSSST.
HOW DO YOU KNOW THAT NAME? WHAT ARE... UGHK.
I KNOW WHAT YOU'RE SSEARCHING FOR OUT HERE, MY YOUNG FRIEND. I KNOW WHAT YOU WANT ABOVE ALL ELSSE.
AND I'M THE ONLY ONE WHO CAN GIVE IT TO YOU.
PAIN.
PUNISHMENT.
VENGEANCE.
YOU MIGHT SSAY THOSE ARE MY SSSSSPECIALTIESS.
THE SNAKE TALKED FOR A VERY LONG TIME. UNTIL I THOUGHT EVERY PART OF ME WOULD FREEZE SOLID.
IT PROMISED ME THAT I WOULD FIND THE MAN I WAS HUNTING. THAT I WOULD HAVE REVENGE. MORE REVENGE THAN I COULD POSSIBLY IMAGINE.
BUT MOSTLY IT PROMISED ME ONE THING...

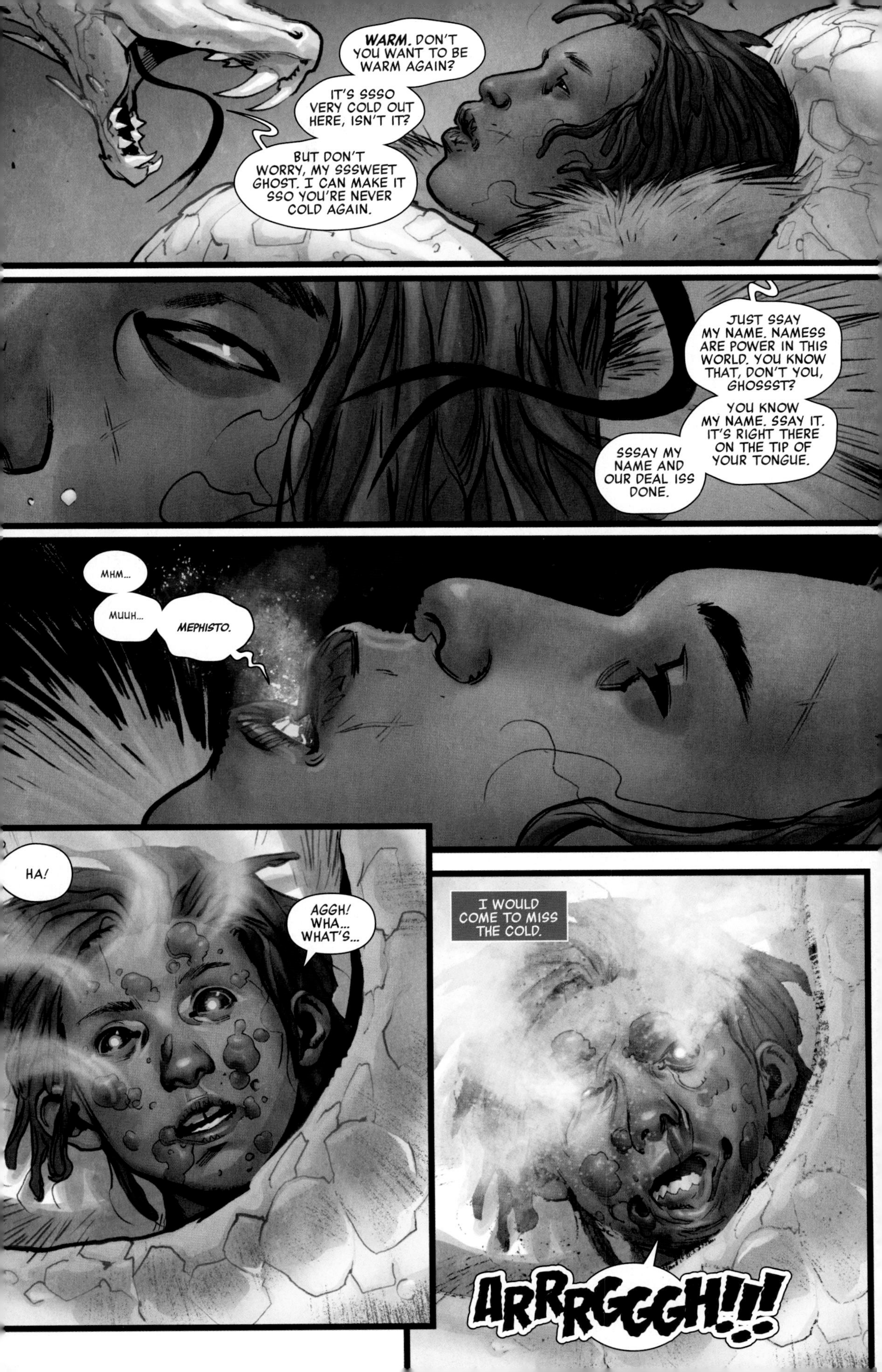
WARM. DON'T YOU WANT TO BE WARM AGAIN?
IT'S SSSO VERY COLD OUT HERE, ISN'T IT?
BUT DON'T WORRY, MY SSSWEET GHOST. I CAN MAKE IT SSO YOU'RE NEVER COLD AGAIN.
JUST SSAY MY NAME. NAMESS ARE POWER IN THIS WORLD. YOU KNOW THAT, DON'T YOU, GHOSSST?
YOU KNOW MY NAME. SSAY IT. IT'S RIGHT THERE ON THE TIP OF YOUR TONGUE.
SSSAY MY NAME AND OUR DEAL ISS DONE.
MHM...
MUUH...
MEPHISTO.
HA!
AGGH! WHA... WHAT'S...
I WOULD COME TO MISS THE COLD.
ARRRGGGH!!!

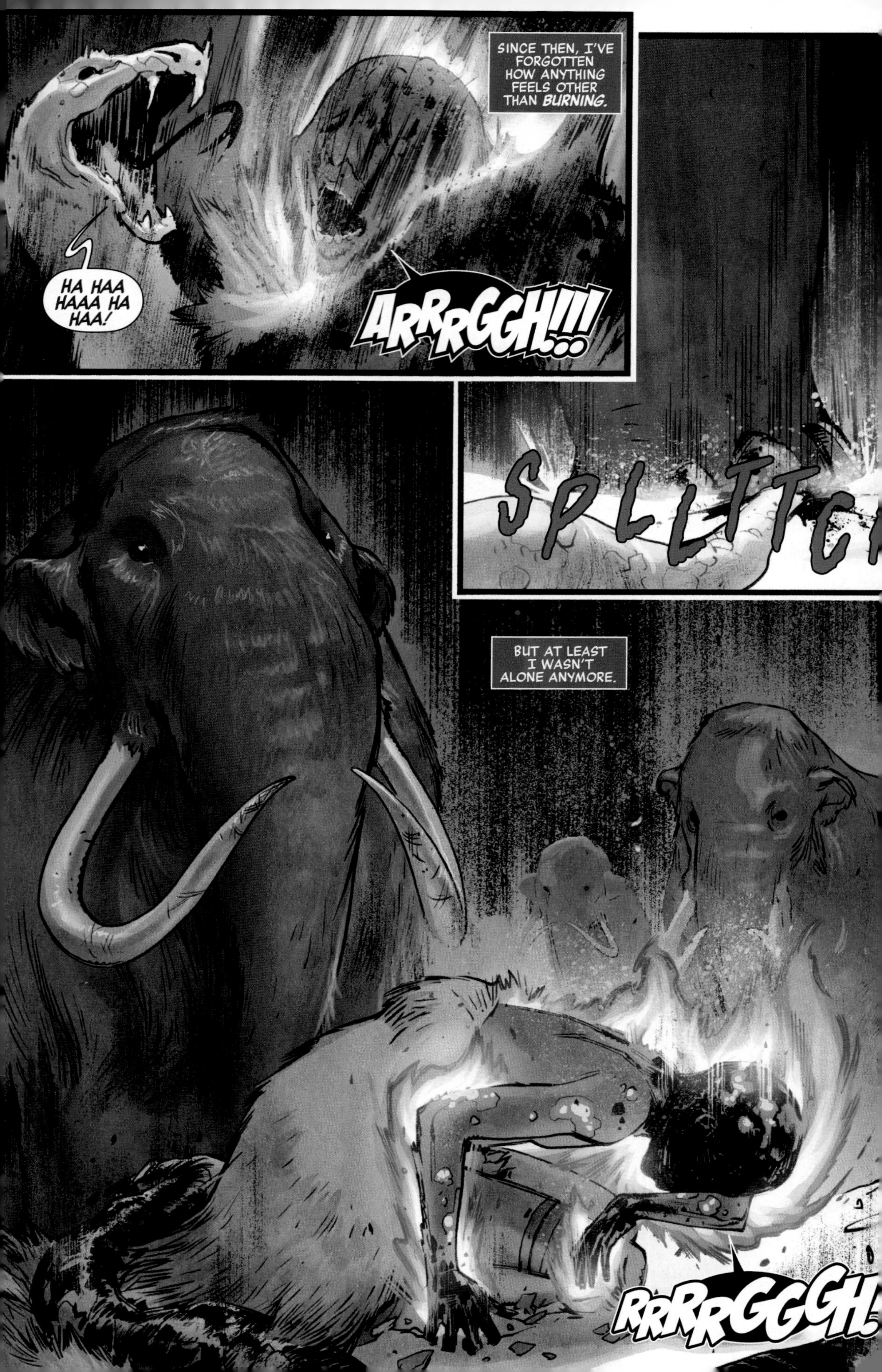

SINCE THEN, I'VE FORGOTTEN HOW ANYTHING FEELS OTHER THAN BURNING.
HA HAA HAAA HA HA HAA!
ARRRGGH!!!
SPLLTTC
BUT AT LEAST I WASN'T ALONE ANYMORE.
RRRRGGGH.

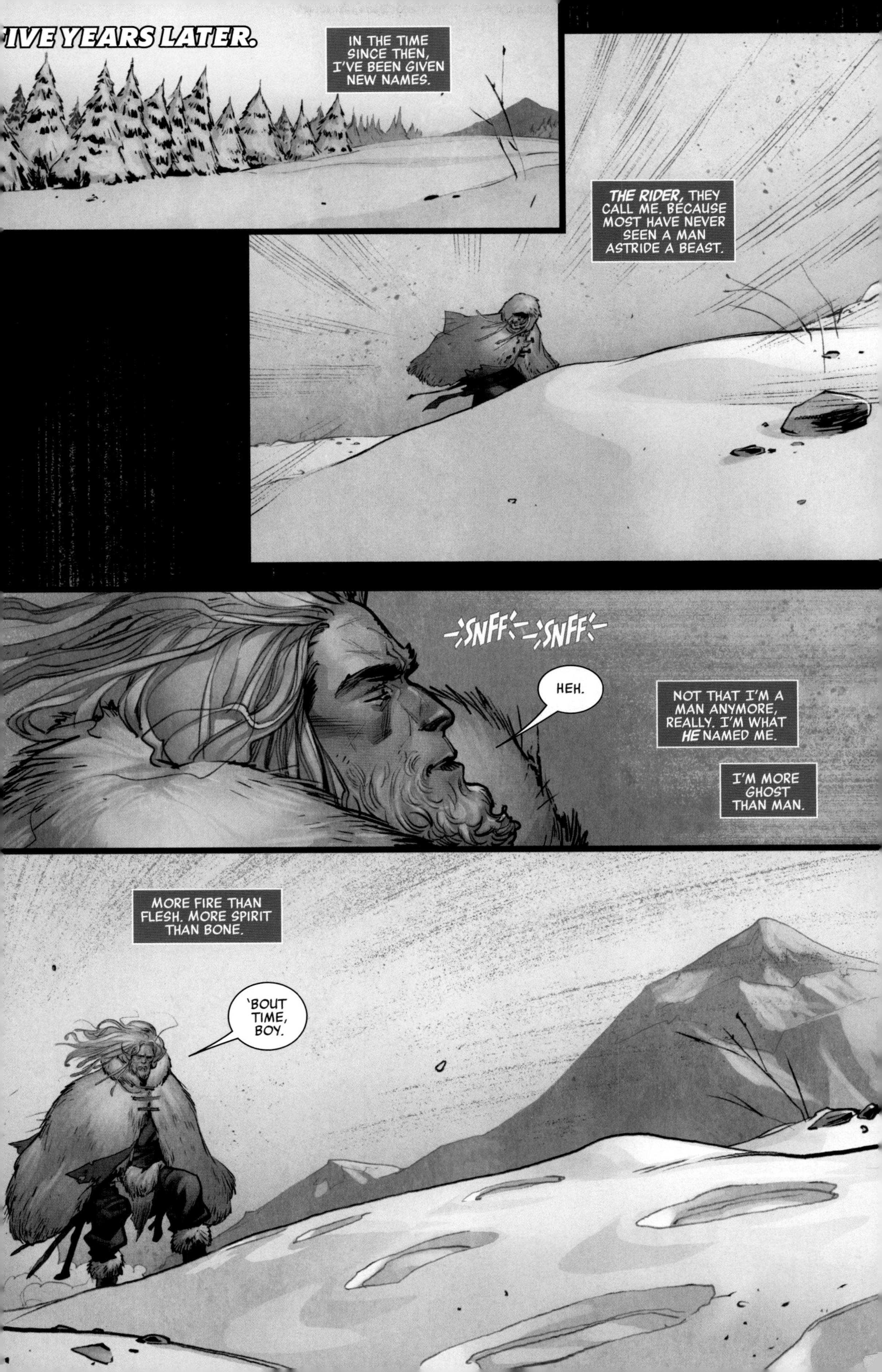
IVE YEARS LATER.
IN THE TIME SINCE THEN, I'VE BEEN GIVEN NEW NAMES.
THE RIDER, THEY CALL ME. BECAUSE MOST HAVE NEVER SEEN A MAN ASTRIDE A BEAST.
-SNFF- -SNFF-
HEH.
NOT THAT I'M A MAN ANYMORE, REALLY. I'M WHAT HE NAMED ME.
I'M MORE GHOST THAN MAN.
MORE FIRE THAN FLESH. MORE SPIRIT THAN BONE.
'BOUT TIME, BOY.

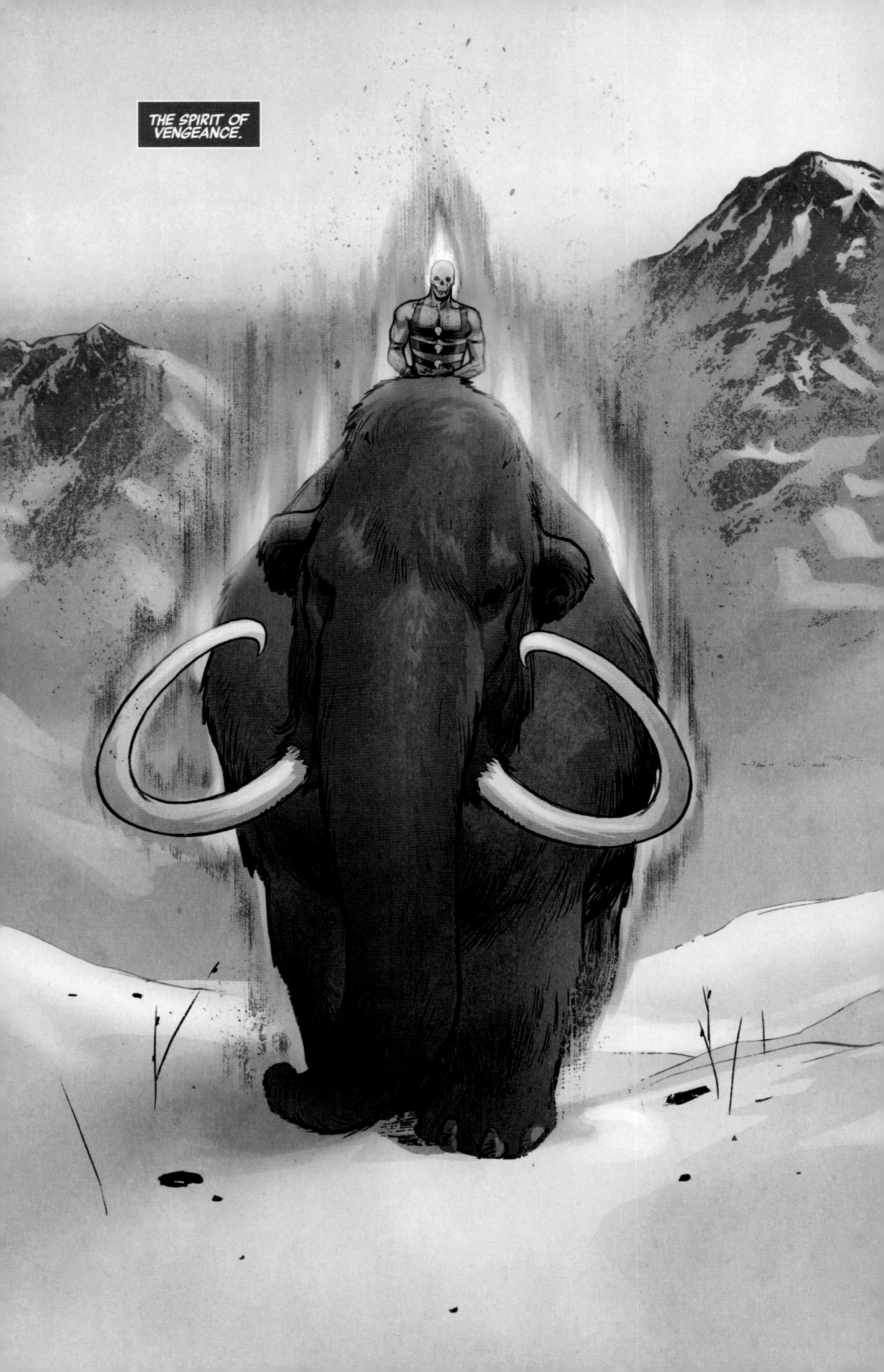
THE SPIRIT OF VENGEANCE.

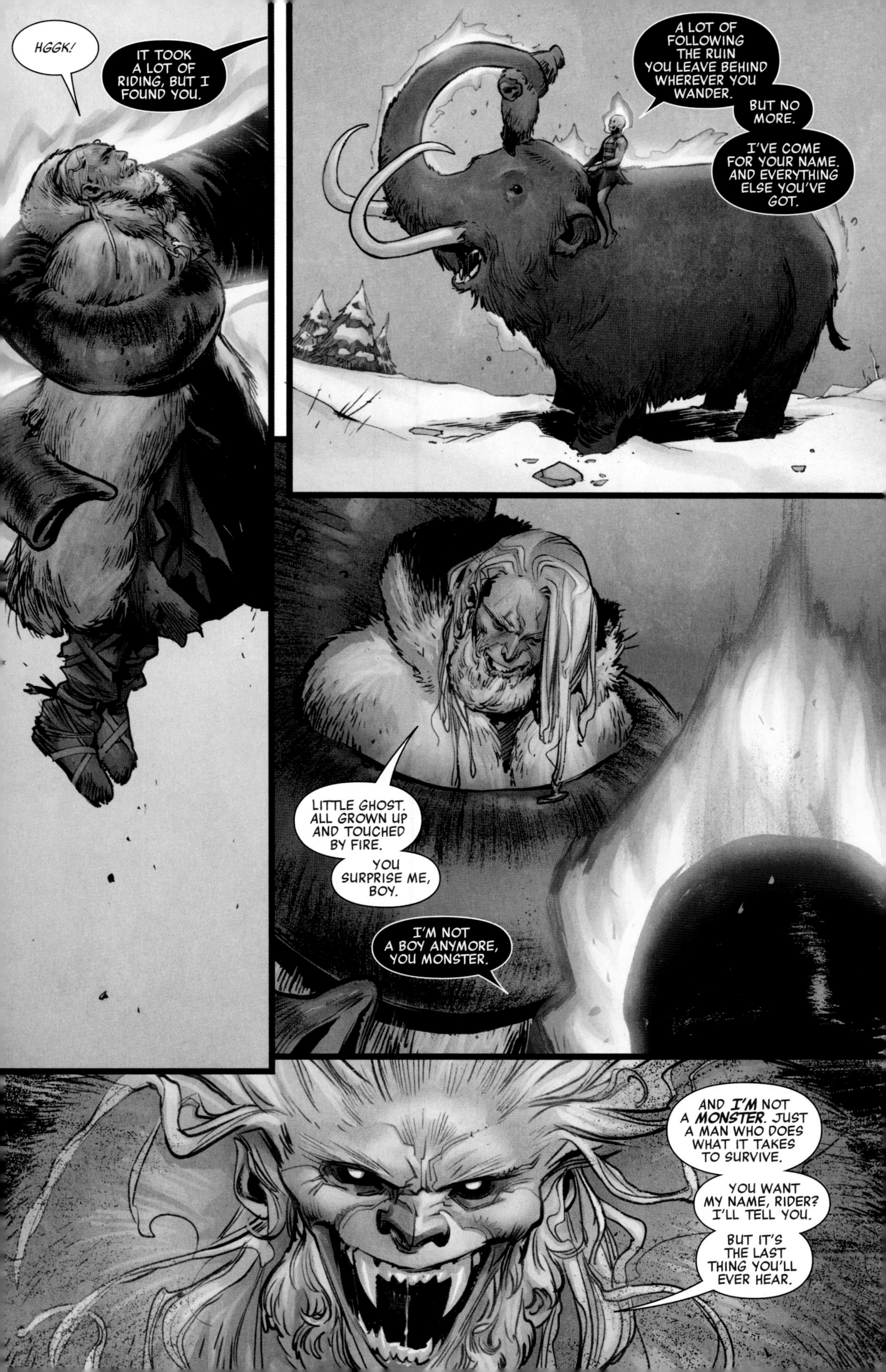
HGGK!
IT TOOK A LOT OF RIDING, BUT I FOUND YOU.
A LOT OF FOLLOWING THE RUIN YOU LEAVE BEHIND WHEREVER YOU WANDER.
BUT NO MORE.
I'VE COME FOR YOUR NAME. AND EVERYTHING ELSE YOU'VE GOT.
LITTLE GHOST. ALL GROWN UP AND TOUCHED BY FIRE.
YOU SURPRISE ME, BOY.
I'M NOT A BOY ANYMORE, YOU MONSTER.
AND *I'M* NOT A ***MONSTER***. JUST A MAN WHO DOES WHAT IT TAKES TO SURVIVE.
YOU WANT MY NAME, RIDER? I'LL TELL YOU.
BUT IT'S THE LAST THING YOU'LL EVER HEAR.

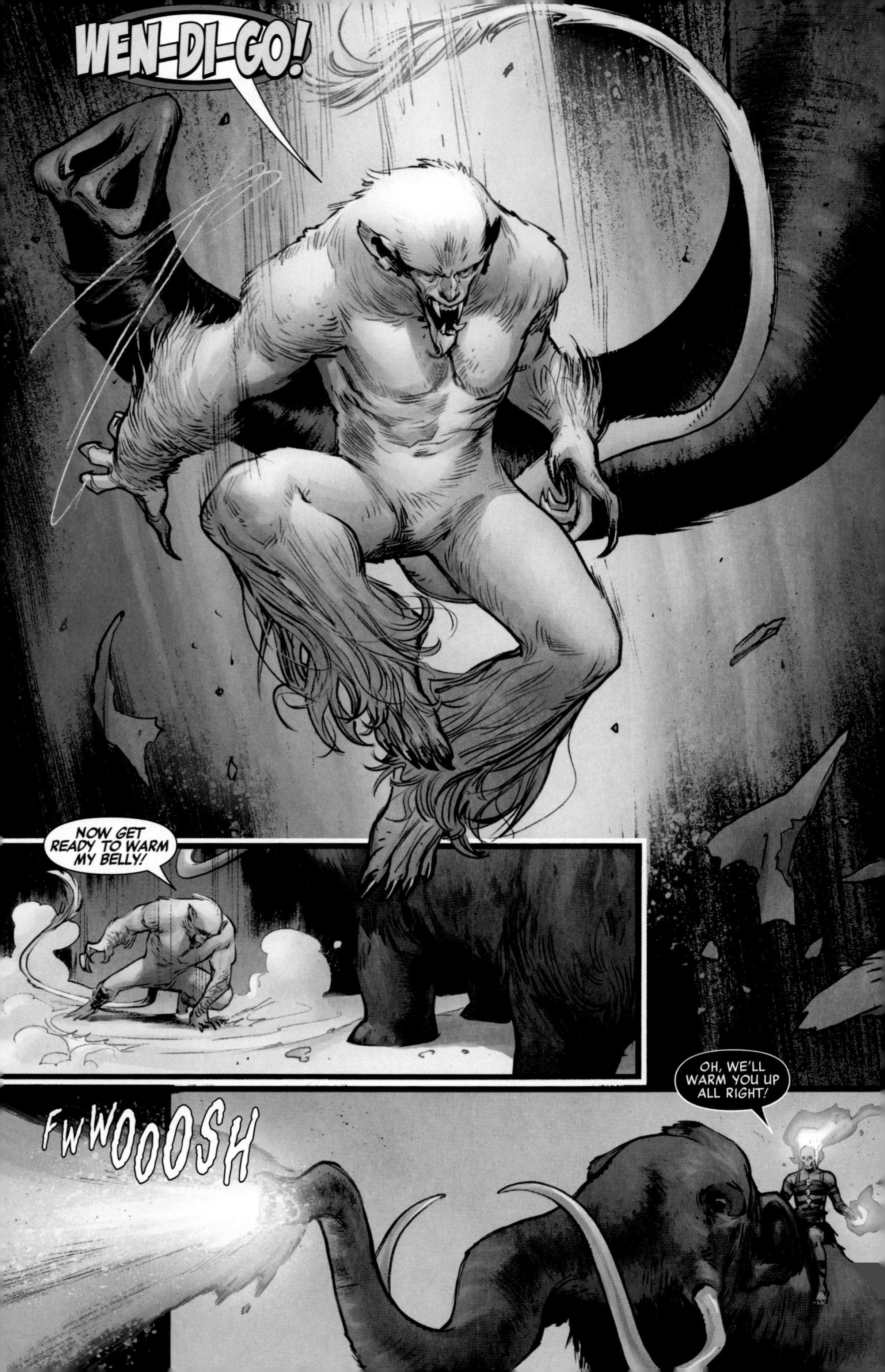
WEN-DI-GO!
NOW GET READY TO WARM MY BELLY!
OH, WE'LL WARM YOU UP ALL RIGHT!
FWWOOOOSH

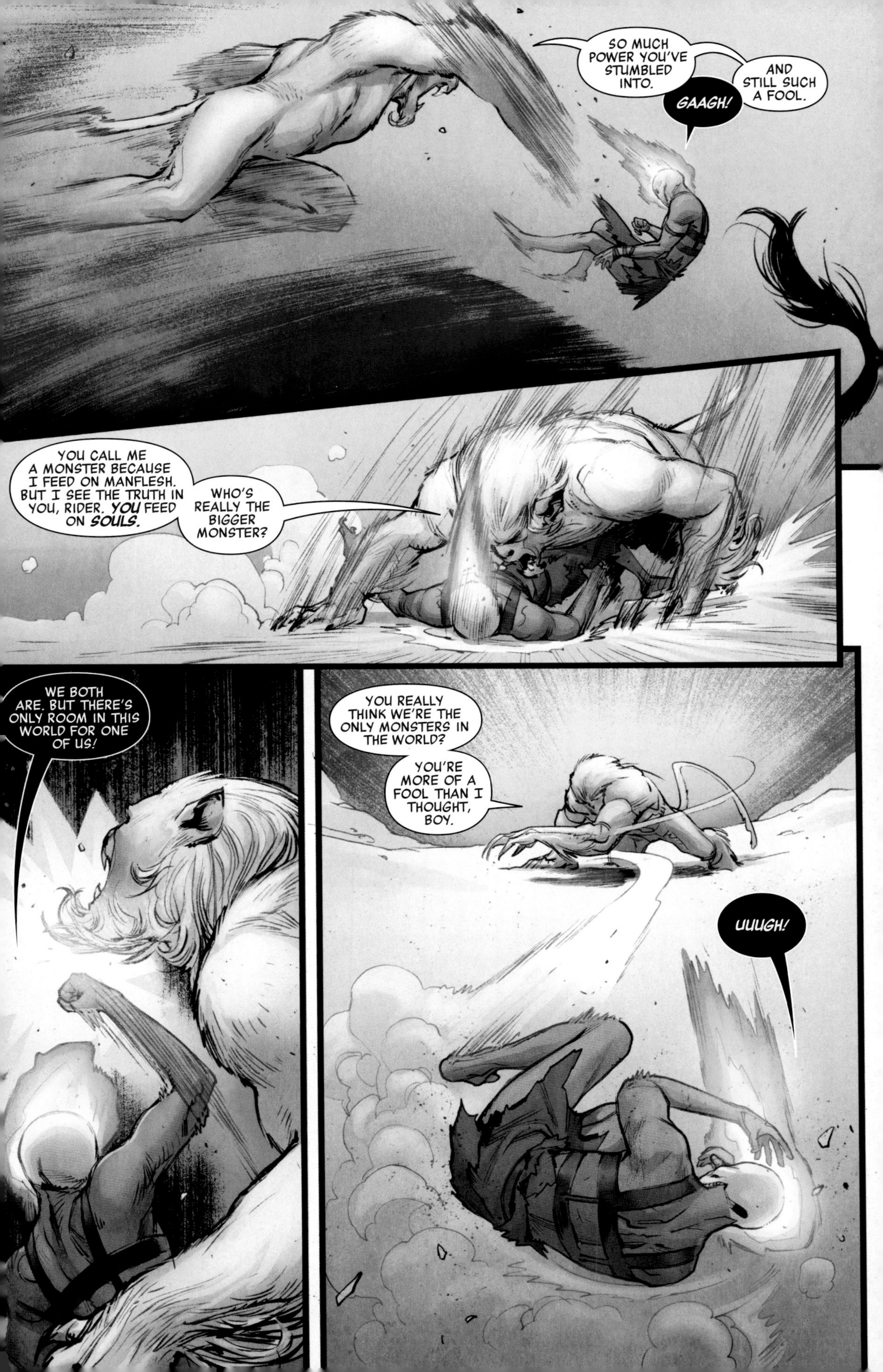
SO MUCH POWER YOU'VE STUMBLED INTO.
AND STILL SUCH A FOOL.
GAAGH!
YOU CALL ME A MONSTER BECAUSE I FEED ON MANFLESH. BUT I SEE THE TRUTH IN YOU, RIDER. YOU FEED ON SOULS.
WHO'S REALLY THE BIGGER MONSTER?
WE BOTH ARE. BUT THERE'S ONLY ROOM IN THIS WORLD FOR ONE OF US!
YOU REALLY THINK WE'RE THE ONLY MONSTERS IN THE WORLD?
YOU'RE MORE OF A FOOL THAN I THOUGHT, BOY.
UUUGH!

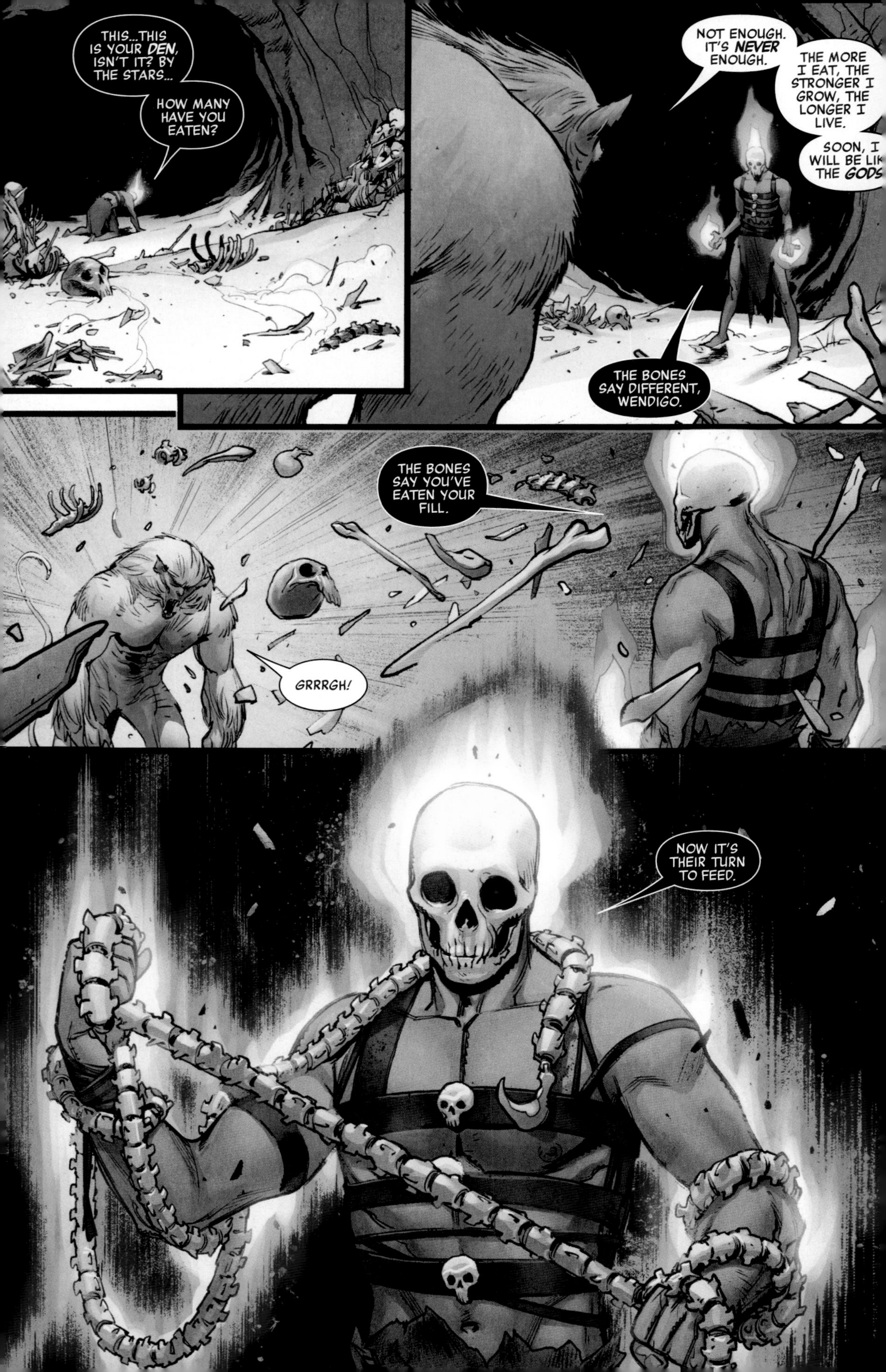
THIS...THIS IS YOUR *DEN*, ISN'T IT? BY THE STARS...
HOW MANY HAVE YOU EATEN?
NOT ENOUGH. IT'S *NEVER* ENOUGH.
THE MORE I EAT, THE STRONGER I GROW, THE LONGER I LIVE.
SOON, I WILL BE LIK THE *GODS*
THE BONES SAY DIFFERENT, WENDIGO.
THE BONES SAY YOU'VE EATEN YOUR FILL.
GRRRGH!
NOW IT'S THEIR TURN TO FEED.

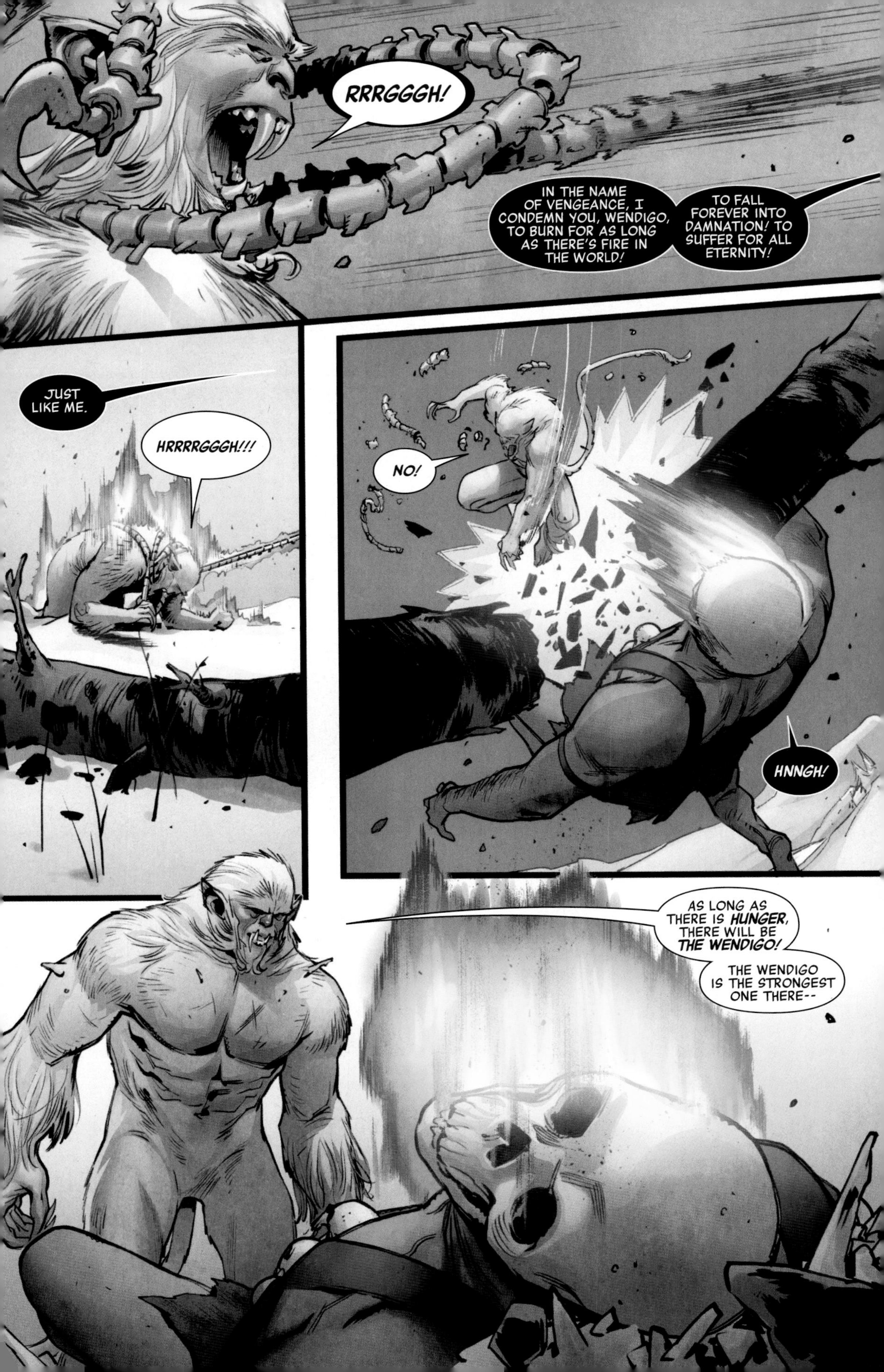
RRRGGGH!
IN THE NAME OF VENGEANCE, I CONDEMN YOU, WENDIGO, TO BURN FOR AS LONG AS THERE'S FIRE IN THE WORLD!
TO FALL FOREVER INTO DAMNATION! TO SUFFER FOR ALL ETERNITY!
JUST LIKE ME.
HRRRRGGGH!!!
NO!
HNNGH!
AS LONG AS THERE IS HUNGER, THERE WILL BE THE WENDIGO!
THE WENDIGO IS THE STRONGEST ONE THERE--

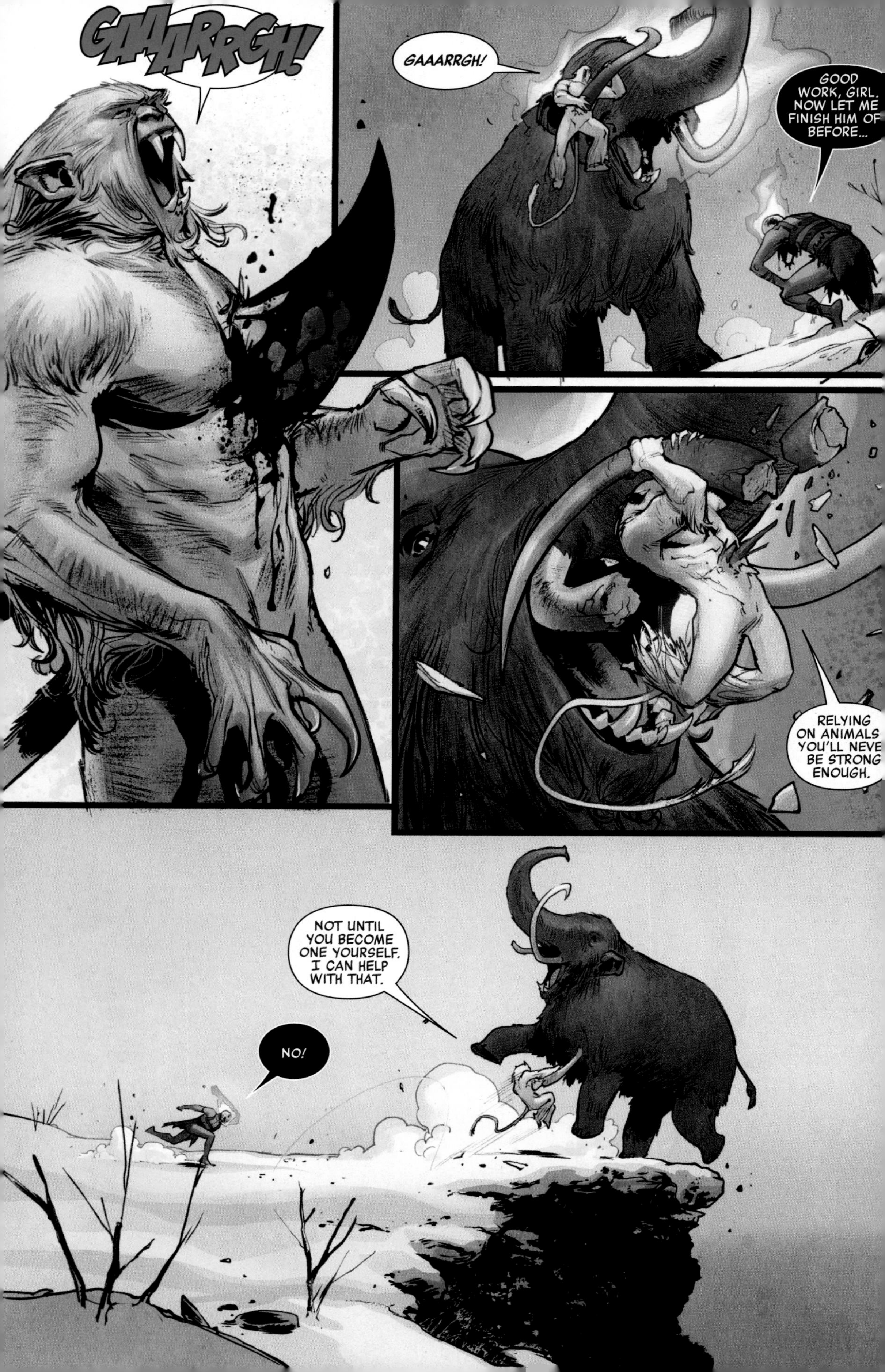
GAAARRGH!
GAAARRGH!
GOOD WORK, GIRL. NOW LET ME FINISH HIM OF BEFORE...
RELYING ON ANIMALS YOU'LL NEVE BE STRONG ENOUGH.
NOT UNTIL YOU BECOME ONE YOURSELF. I CAN HELP WITH THAT.
NO!

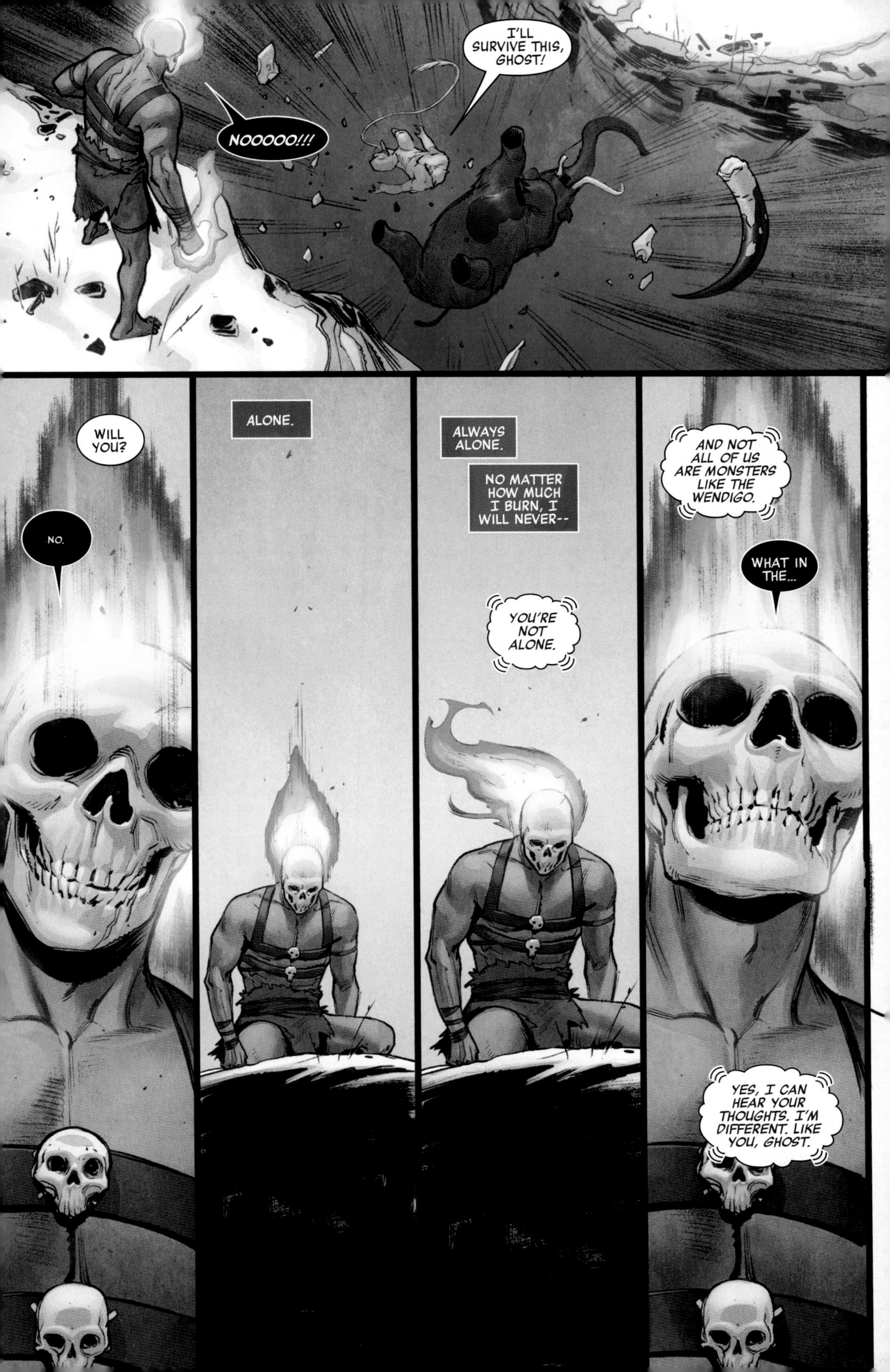
NOOOOO!!!
I'LL SURVIVE THIS, GHOST!
WILL YOU?
NO.
ALONE.
ALWAYS ALONE.
NO MATTER HOW MUCH I BURN, I WILL NEVER--
YOU'RE NOT ALONE.
AND NOT ALL OF US ARE MONSTERS LIKE THE WENDIGO.
WHAT IN THE...
YES, I CAN HEAR YOUR THOUGHTS. I'M DIFFERENT. LIKE YOU, GHOST.

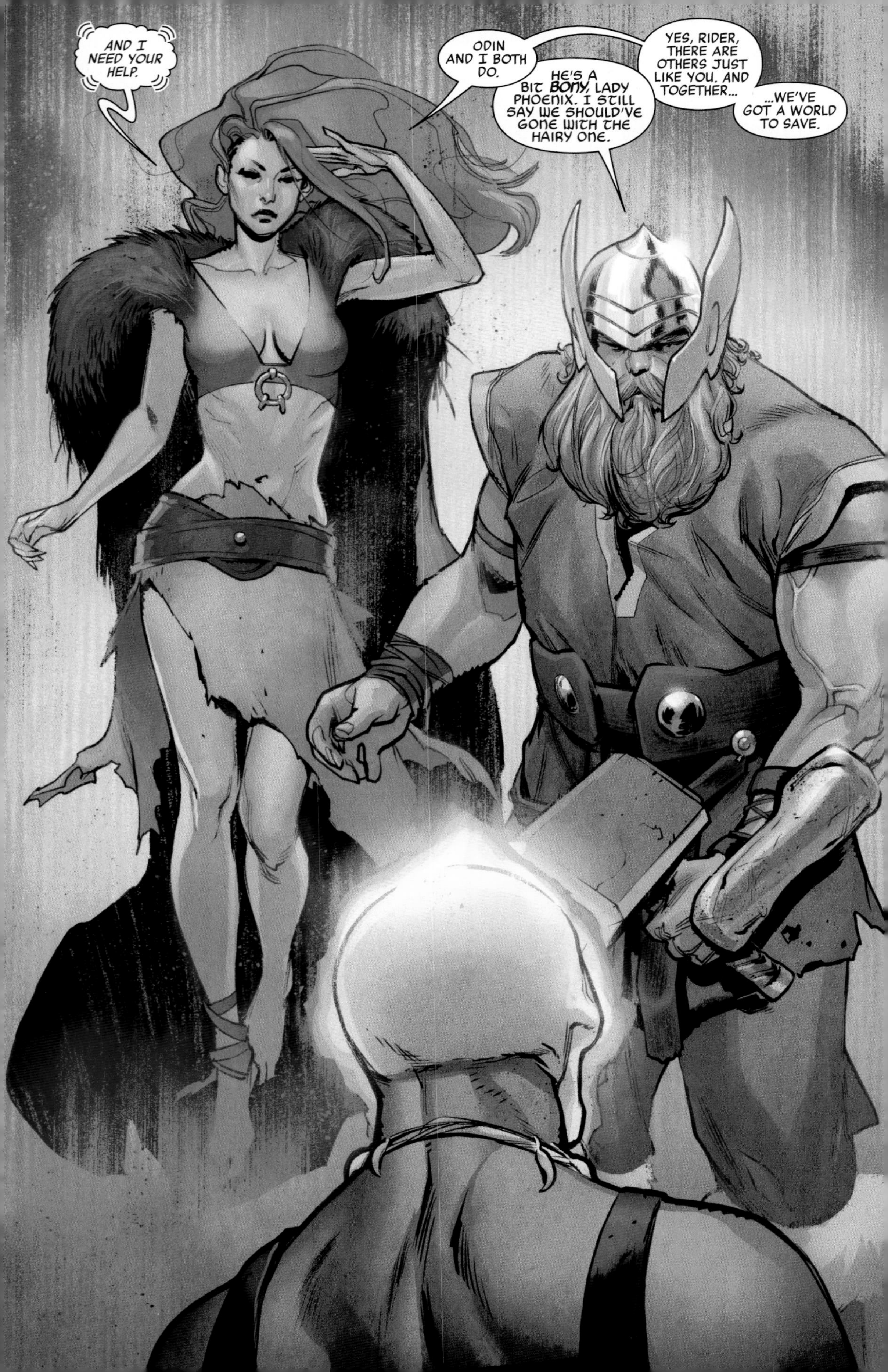
AND I NEED YOUR HELP.
ODIN AND I BOTH DO.
YES, RIDER, THERE ARE OTHERS JUST LIKE YOU. AND TOGETHER...
...WE'VE GOT A WORLD TO SAVE.
HE'S A BIT BONY, LADY PHOENIX. I STILL SAY WE SHOULD'VE GONE WITH THE HAIRY ONE.

8 INSIDE AVENGERS MOUNTAIN

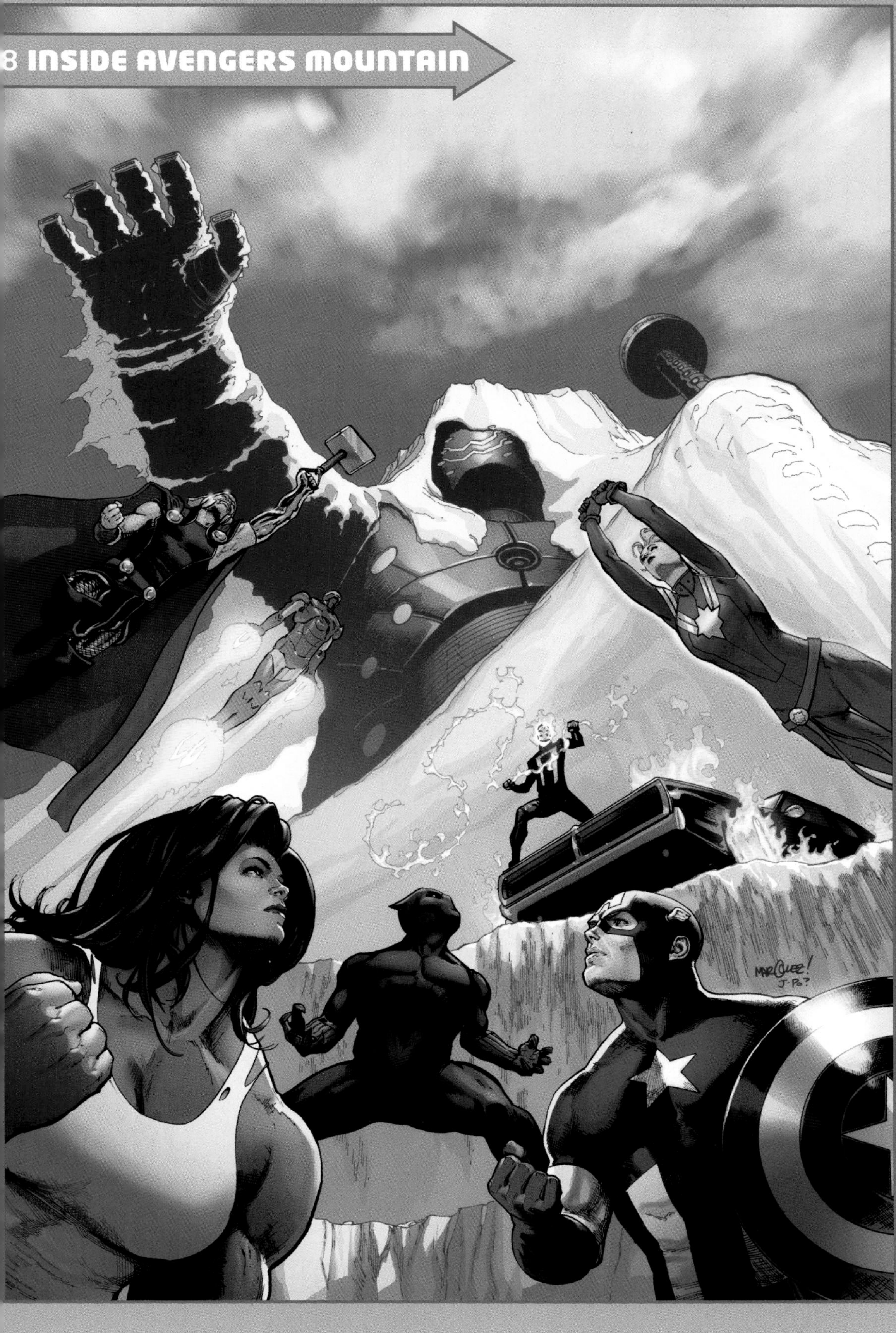
MARQUEZ!
J-Po?

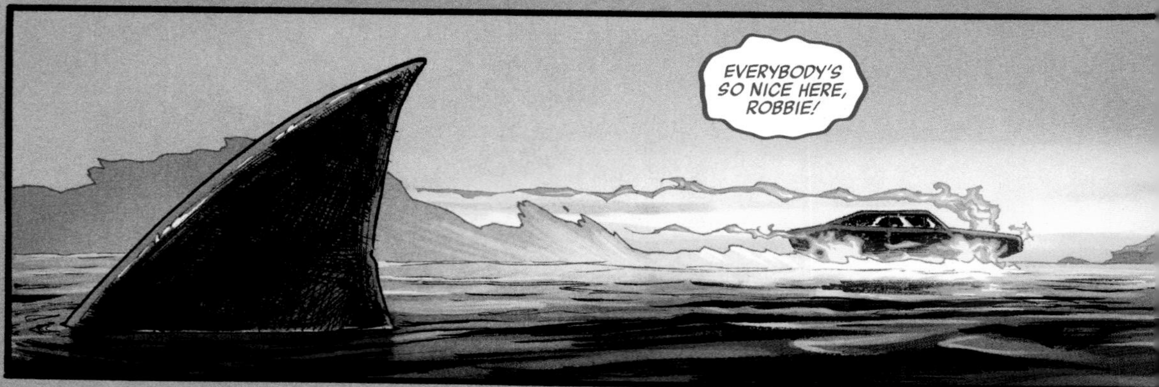
EVERYBODY'S SO NICE HERE, ROBBIE!

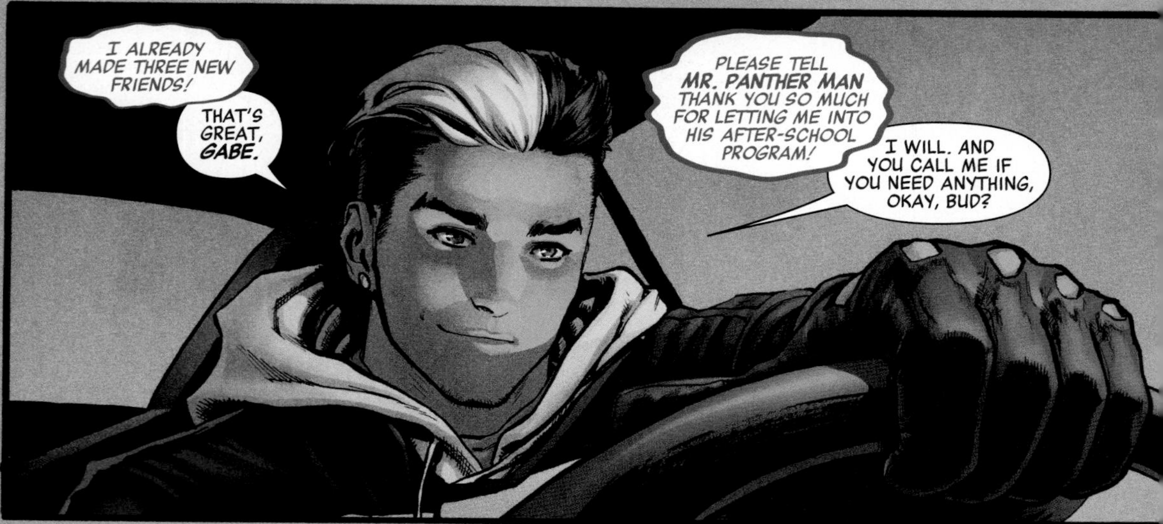
I ALREADY MADE THREE NEW FRIENDS!
THAT'S GREAT, **GABE.**
PLEASE TELL **MR. PANTHER MAN** THANK YOU SO MUCH FOR LETTING ME INTO HIS AFTER-SCHOOL PROGRAM!
I WILL. AND YOU CALL ME IF YOU NEED ANYTHING, OKAY, BUD?

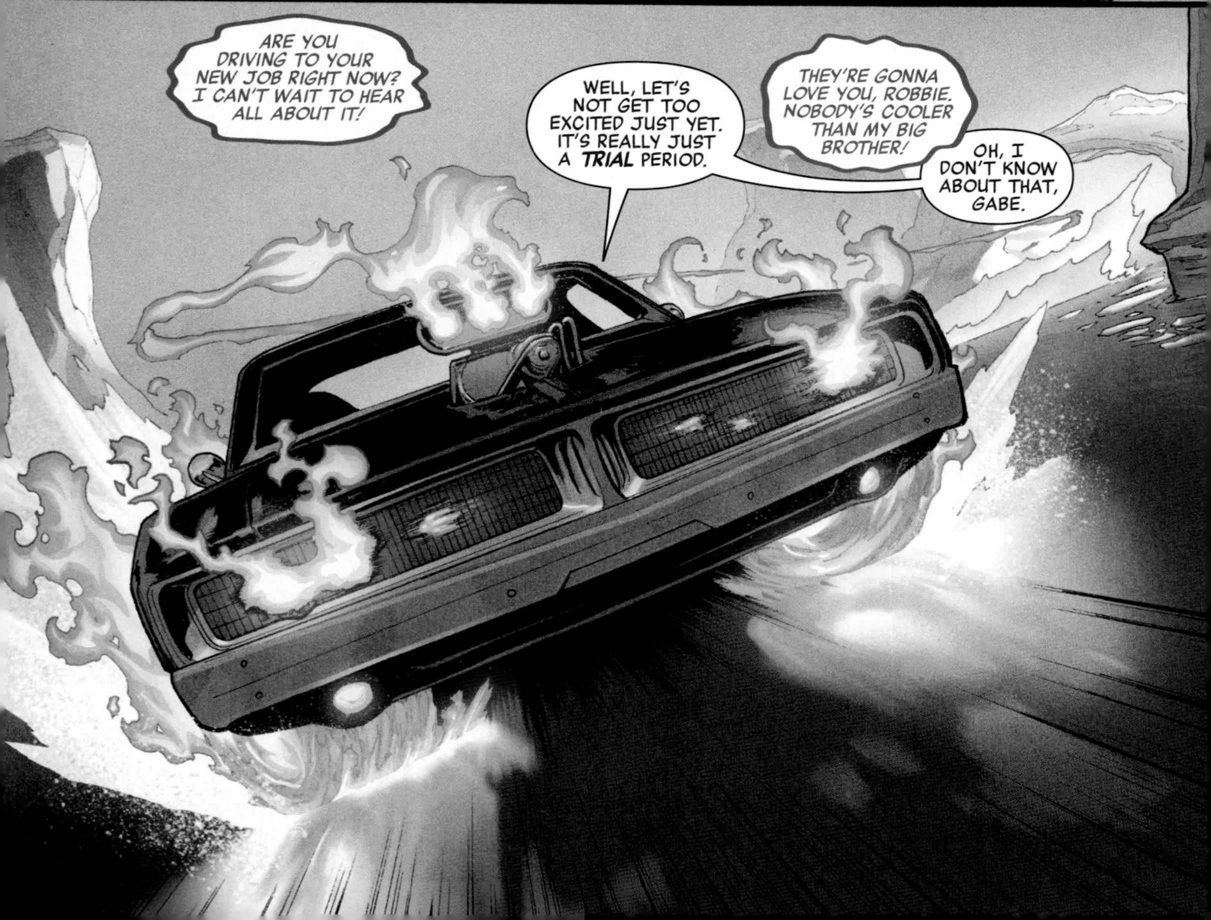
ARE YOU DRIVING TO YOUR NEW JOB RIGHT NOW? I CAN'T WAIT TO HEAR ALL ABOUT IT!
WELL, LET'S NOT GET TOO EXCITED JUST YET. IT'S REALLY JUST A **TRIAL** PERIOD.
THEY'RE GONNA LOVE YOU, ROBBIE. NOBODY'S COOLER THAN MY BIG BROTHER!
OH, I DON'T KNOW ABOUT THAT, GABE.

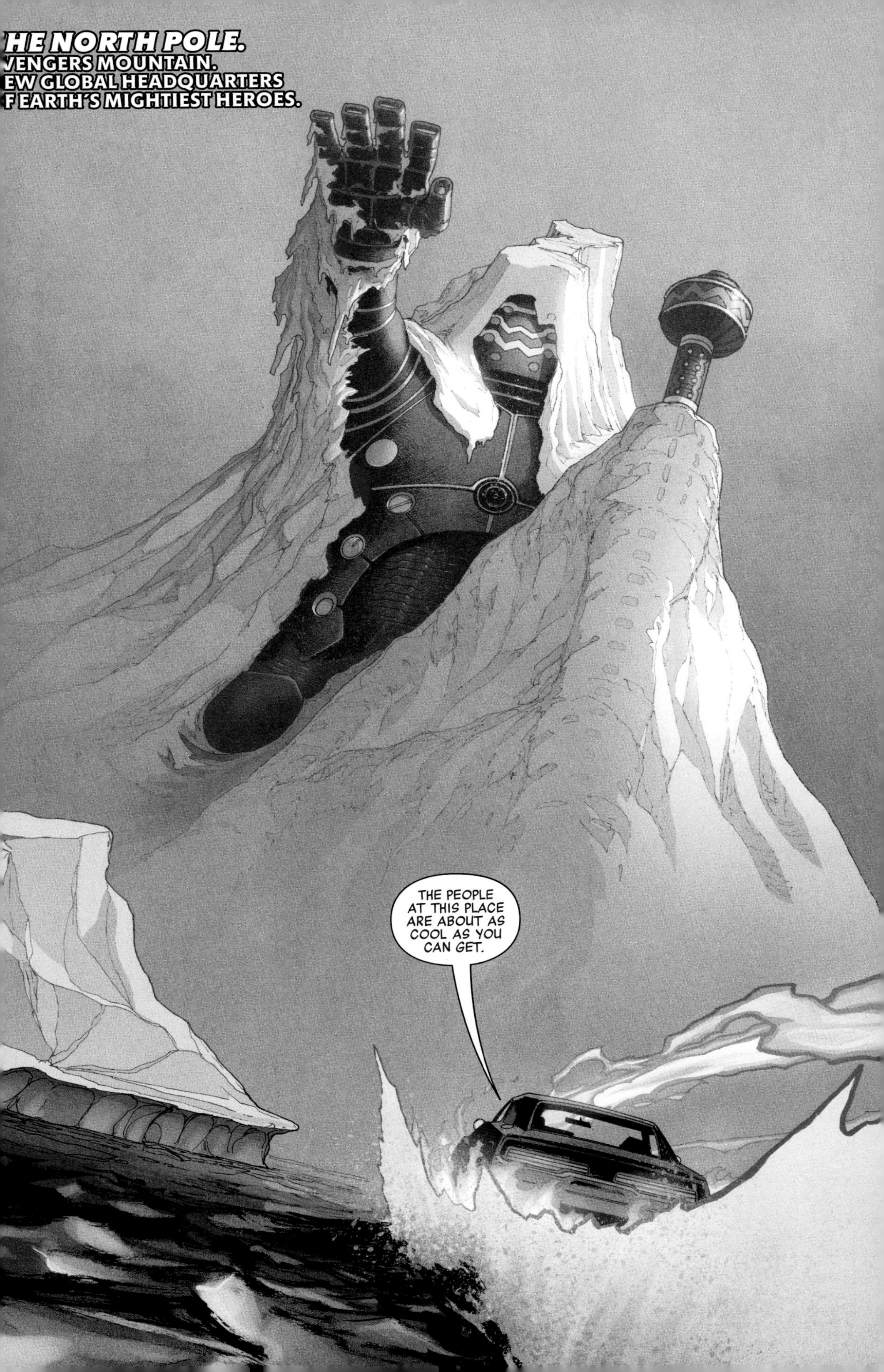

HE NORTH POLE.
VENGERS MOUNTAIN.
EW GLOBAL HEADQUARTERS
F EARTH'S MIGHTIEST HEROES.
THE PEOPLE AT THIS PLACE ARE ABOUT AS COOL AS YOU CAN GET.

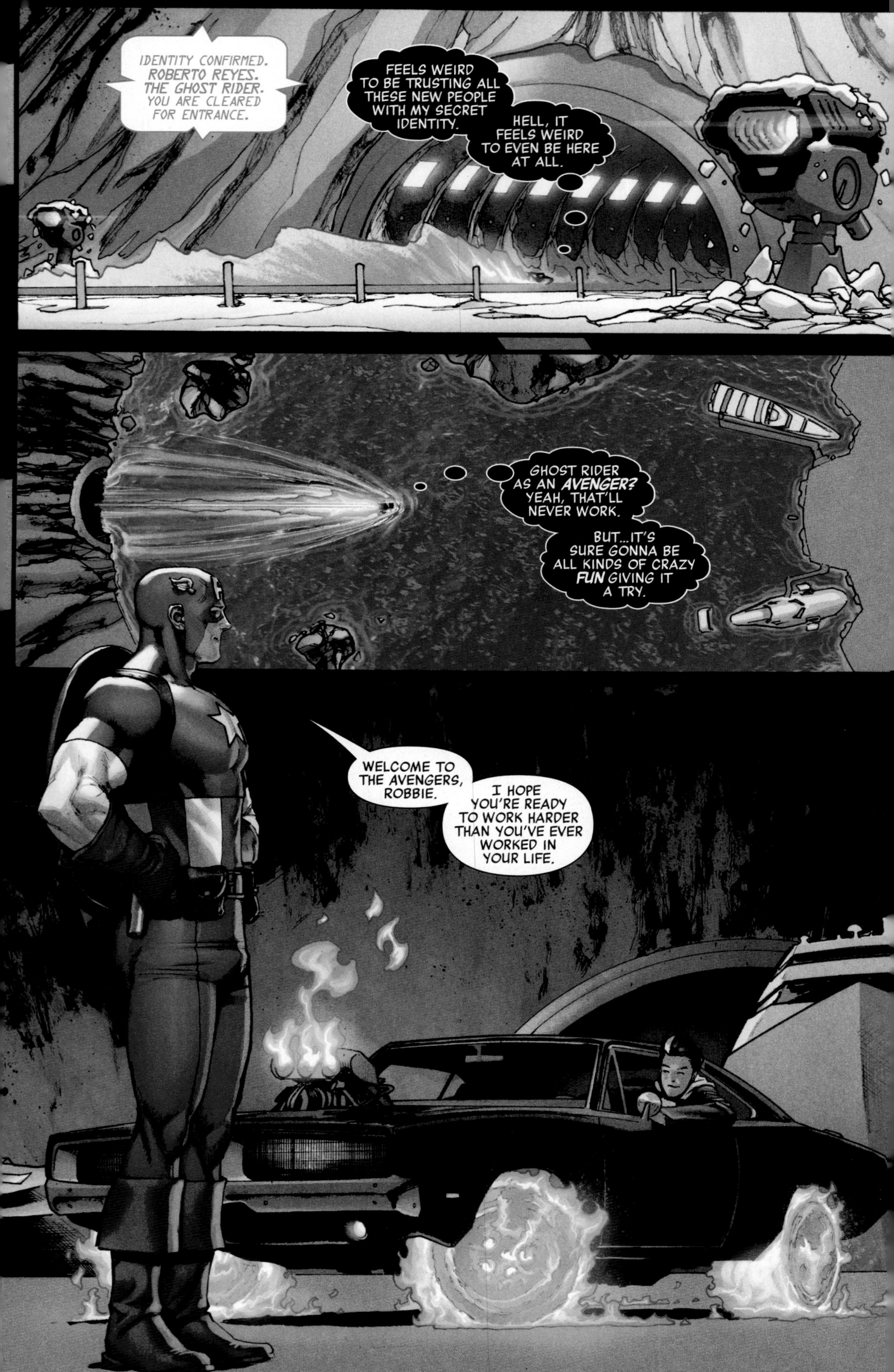
IDENTITY CONFIRMED. ROBERTO REYES. THE GHOST RIDER. YOU ARE CLEARED FOR ENTRANCE.
FEELS WEIRD TO BE TRUSTING ALL THESE NEW PEOPLE WITH MY SECRET IDENTITY.
HELL, IT FEELS WEIRD TO EVEN BE HERE AT ALL.
GHOST RIDER AS AN AVENGER? YEAH, THAT'LL NEVER WORK.
BUT...IT'S SURE GONNA BE ALL KINDS OF CRAZY FUN GIVING IT A TRY.
WELCOME TO THE AVENGERS, ROBBIE.
I HOPE YOU'RE READY TO WORK HARDER THAN YOU'VE EVER WORKED IN YOUR LIFE.

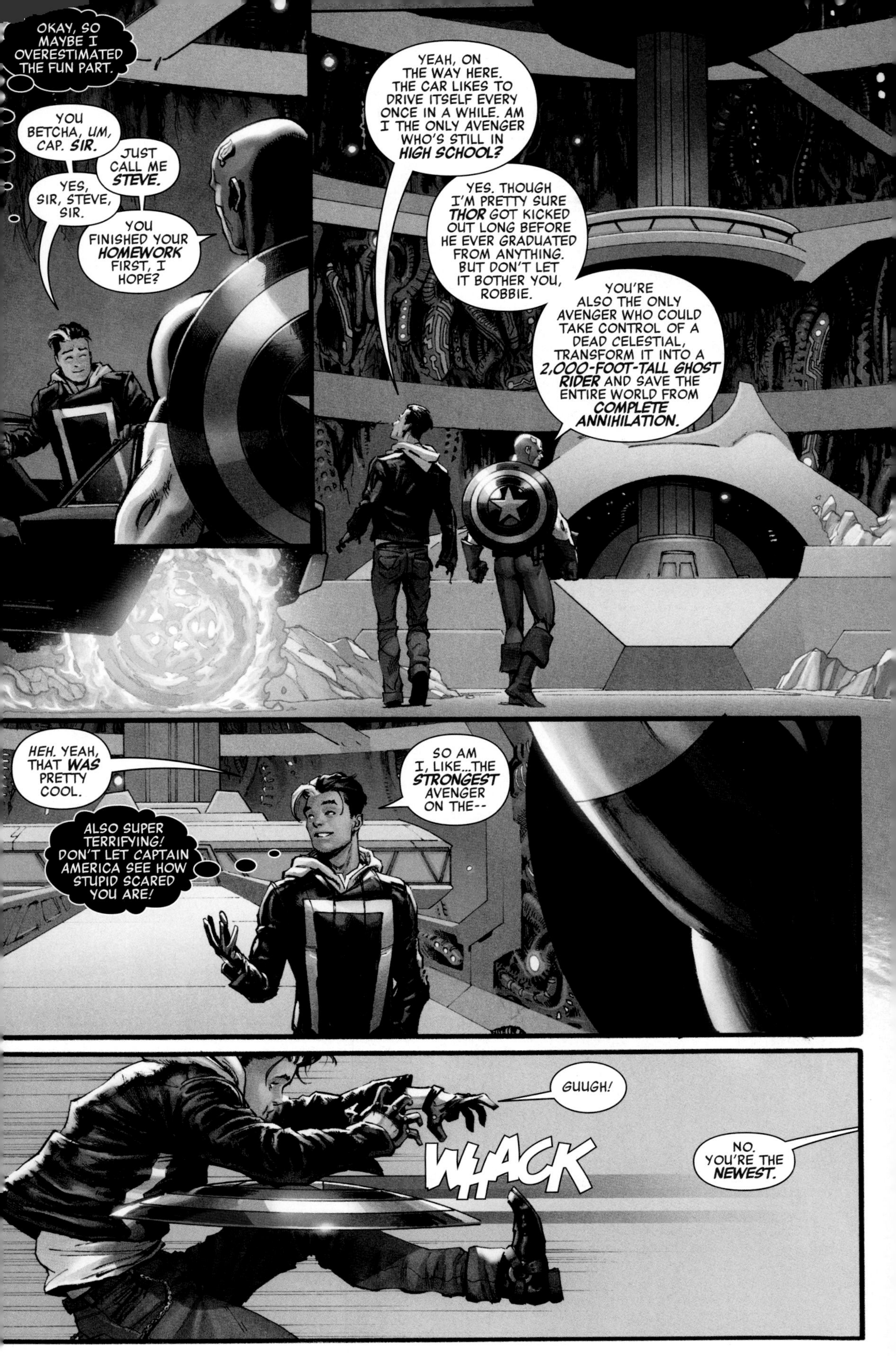
OKAY, SO MAYBE I OVERESTIMATED THE FUN PART.
YOU BETCHA, UM, CAP. SIR.
JUST CALL ME STEVE.
YES, SIR, STEVE, SIR.
YOU FINISHED YOUR HOMEWORK FIRST, I HOPE?
YEAH, ON THE WAY HERE. THE CAR LIKES TO DRIVE ITSELF EVERY ONCE IN A WHILE. AM I THE ONLY AVENGER WHO'S STILL IN HIGH SCHOOL?
YES. THOUGH I'M PRETTY SURE THOR GOT KICKED OUT LONG BEFORE HE EVER GRADUATED FROM ANYTHING. BUT DON'T LET IT BOTHER YOU, ROBBIE.
YOU'RE ALSO THE ONLY AVENGER WHO COULD TAKE CONTROL OF A DEAD CELESTIAL, TRANSFORM IT INTO A 2,000-FOOT-TALL GHOST RIDER AND SAVE THE ENTIRE WORLD FROM COMPLETE ANNIHILATION.
HEH. YEAH, THAT WAS PRETTY COOL.
ALSO SUPER TERRIFYING! DON'T LET CAPTAIN AMERICA SEE HOW STUPID SCARED YOU ARE!
SO AM I, LIKE...THE STRONGEST AVENGER ON THE--
GUUGH!
WHACK
NO. YOU'RE THE NEWEST.

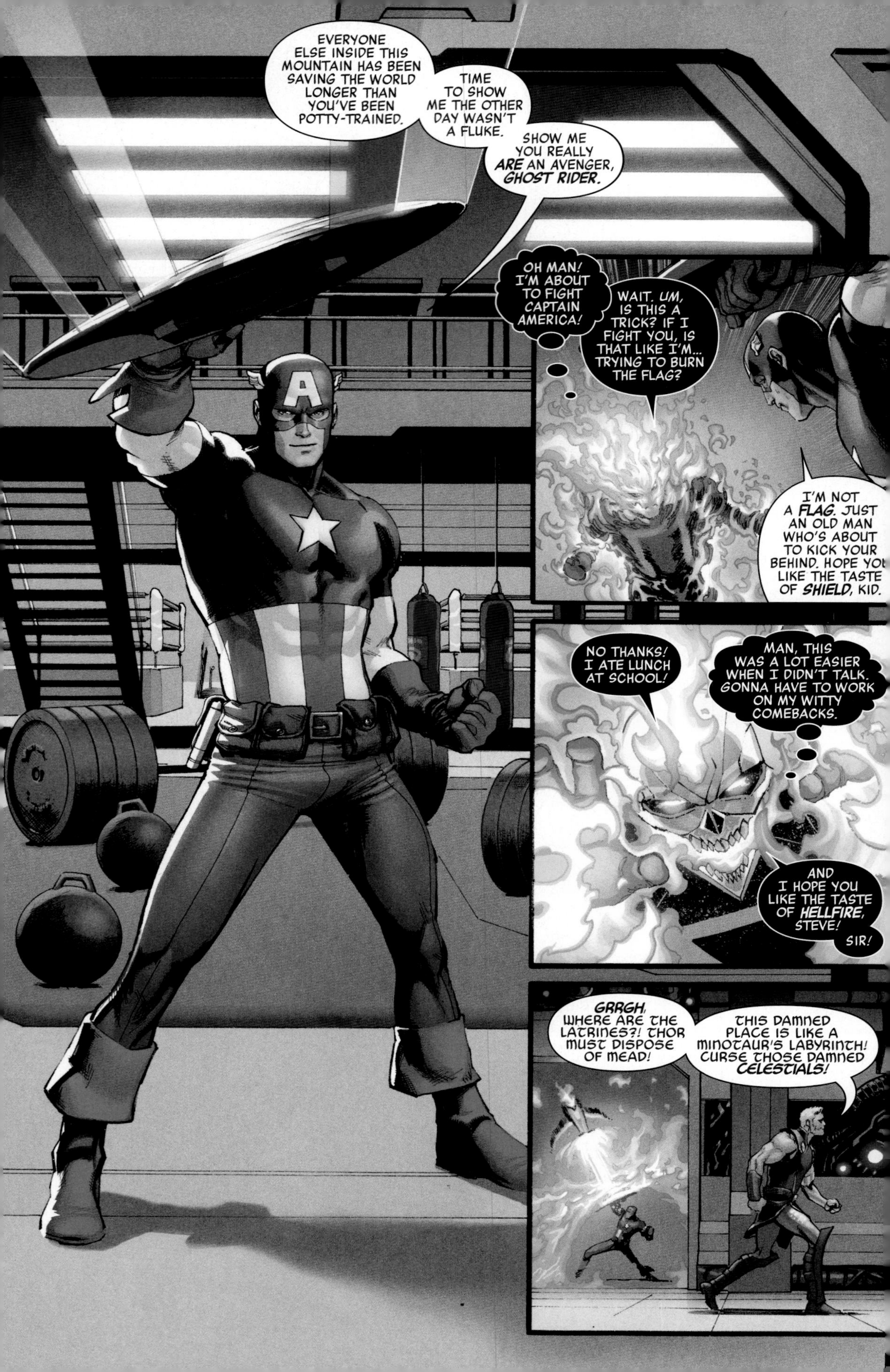
EVERYONE ELSE INSIDE THIS MOUNTAIN HAS BEEN SAVING THE WORLD LONGER THAN YOU'VE BEEN POTTY-TRAINED.
TIME TO SHOW ME THE OTHER DAY WASN'T A FLUKE.
SHOW ME YOU REALLY **ARE** AN AVENGER, **GHOST RIDER.**
OH MAN! I'M ABOUT TO FIGHT CAPTAIN AMERICA!
WAIT. *UM*, IS THIS A TRICK? IF I FIGHT YOU, IS THAT LIKE I'M... TRYING TO BURN THE FLAG?
I'M NOT A **FLAG**. JUST AN OLD MAN WHO'S ABOUT TO KICK YOUR BEHIND. HOPE YOU LIKE THE TASTE OF **SHIELD**, KID.
NO THANKS! I ATE LUNCH AT SCHOOL!
MAN, THIS WAS A LOT EASIER WHEN I DIDN'T TALK. GONNA HAVE TO WORK ON MY WITTY COMEBACKS.
AND I HOPE YOU LIKE THE TASTE OF **HELLFIRE**, STEVE!
SIR!
GRRGH, WHERE ARE THE LATRINES?! THOR MUST DISPOSE OF MEAD!
THIS DAMNED PLACE IS LIKE A MINOTAUR'S LABYRINTH! CURSE THOSE DAMNED **CELESTIALS!**

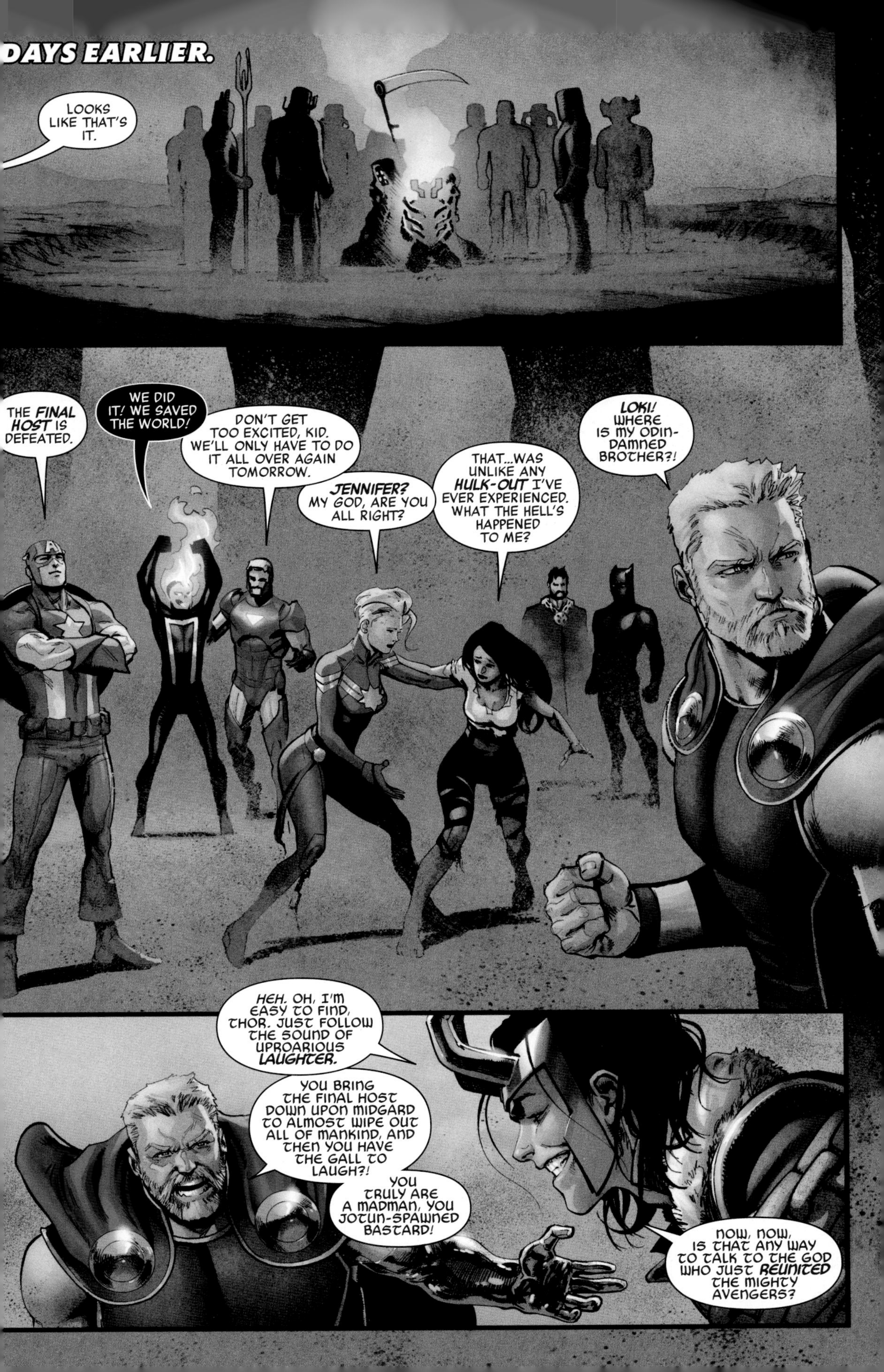
DAYS EARLIER.
LOOKS LIKE THAT'S IT.
THE FINAL HOST IS DEFEATED.
WE DID IT! WE SAVED THE WORLD!
DON'T GET TOO EXCITED, KID. WE'LL ONLY HAVE TO DO IT ALL OVER AGAIN TOMORROW.
JENNIFER? MY GOD, ARE YOU ALL RIGHT?
THAT...WAS UNLIKE ANY HULK-OUT I'VE EVER EXPERIENCED. WHAT THE HELL'S HAPPENED TO ME?
LOKI! WHERE IS MY ODIN-DAMNED BROTHER?!
HEH. OH, I'M EASY TO FIND, THOR. JUST FOLLOW THE SOUND OF UPROARIOUS LAUGHTER.
YOU BRING THE FINAL HOST DOWN UPON MIDGARD TO ALMOST WIPE OUT ALL OF MANKIND, AND THEN YOU HAVE THE GALL TO LAUGH?!
YOU TRULY ARE A MADMAN, YOU JOTUN-SPAWNED BASTARD!
NOW, NOW, IS THAT ANY WAY TO TALK TO THE GOD WHO JUST REUNITED THE MIGHTY AVENGERS?

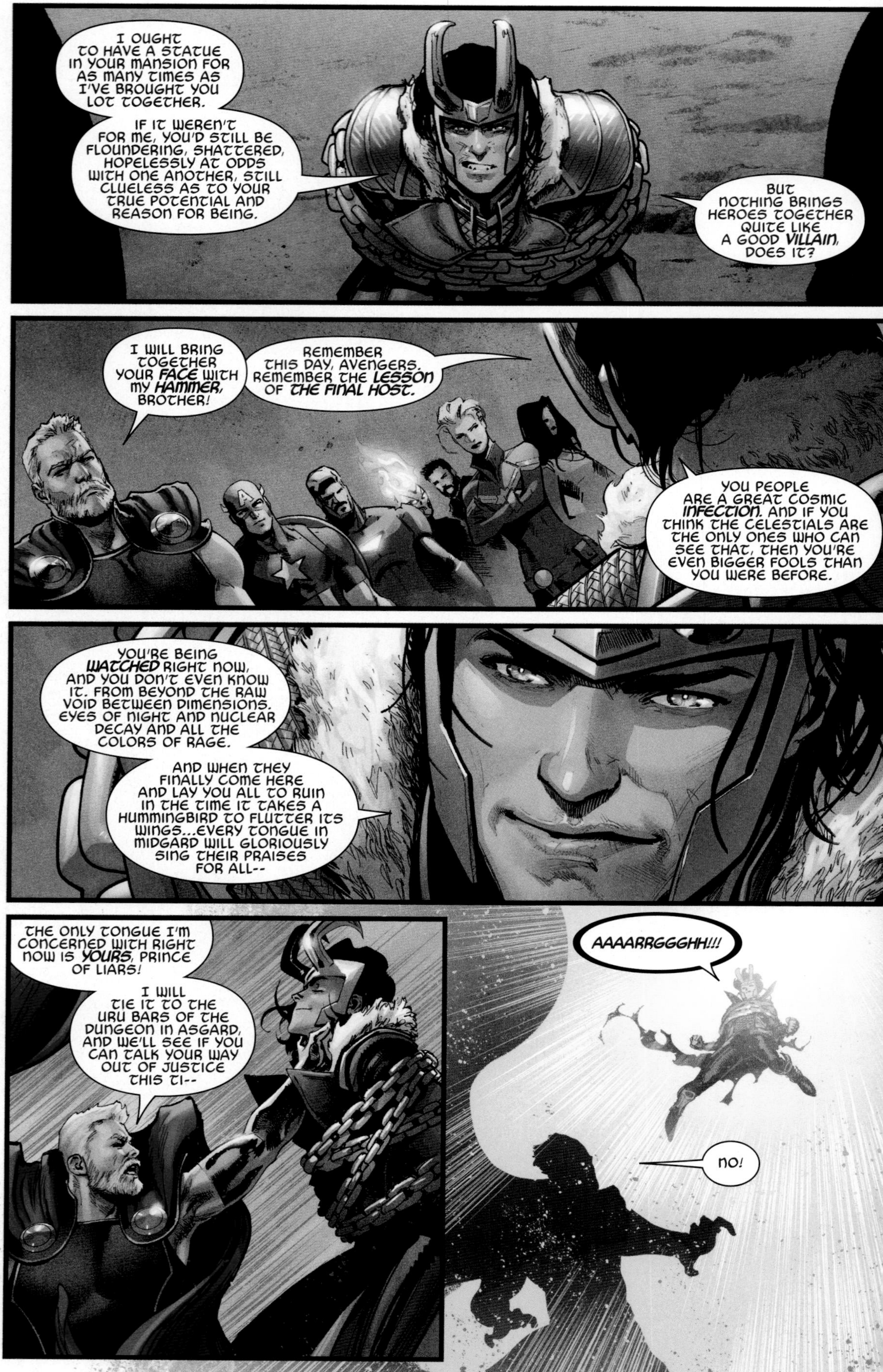
I OUGHT TO HAVE A STATUE IN YOUR MANSION FOR AS MANY TIMES AS I'VE BROUGHT YOU LOT TOGETHER.
IF IT WEREN'T FOR ME, YOU'D STILL BE FLOUNDERING, SHATTERED, HOPELESSLY AT ODDS WITH ONE ANOTHER, STILL CLUELESS AS TO YOUR TRUE POTENTIAL AND REASON FOR BEING.
BUT NOTHING BRINGS HEROES TOGETHER QUITE LIKE A GOOD VILLAIN, DOES IT?
I WILL BRING TOGETHER YOUR FACE WITH MY HAMMER, BROTHER!
REMEMBER THIS DAY, AVENGERS. REMEMBER THE LESSON OF THE FINAL HOST.
YOU PEOPLE ARE A GREAT COSMIC INFECTION. AND IF YOU THINK THE CELESTIALS ARE THE ONLY ONES WHO CAN SEE THAT, THEN YOU'RE EVEN BIGGER FOOLS THAN YOU WERE BEFORE.
YOU'RE BEING WATCHED RIGHT NOW, AND YOU DON'T EVEN KNOW IT. FROM BEYOND THE RAW VOID BETWEEN DIMENSIONS. EYES OF NIGHT AND NUCLEAR DECAY AND ALL THE COLORS OF RAGE.
AND WHEN THEY FINALLY COME HERE AND LAY YOU ALL TO RUIN IN THE TIME IT TAKES A HUMMINGBIRD TO FLUTTER ITS WINGS...EVERY TONGUE IN MIDGARD WILL GLORIOUSLY SING THEIR PRAISES FOR ALL--
THE ONLY TONGUE I'M CONCERNED WITH RIGHT NOW IS YOURS, PRINCE OF LIARS!
I WILL TIE IT TO THE URU BARS OF THE DUNGEON IN ASGARD, AND WE'LL SEE IF YOU CAN TALK YOUR WAY OUT OF JUSTICE THIS TI--
AAAARRGGGHH!!!
NO!

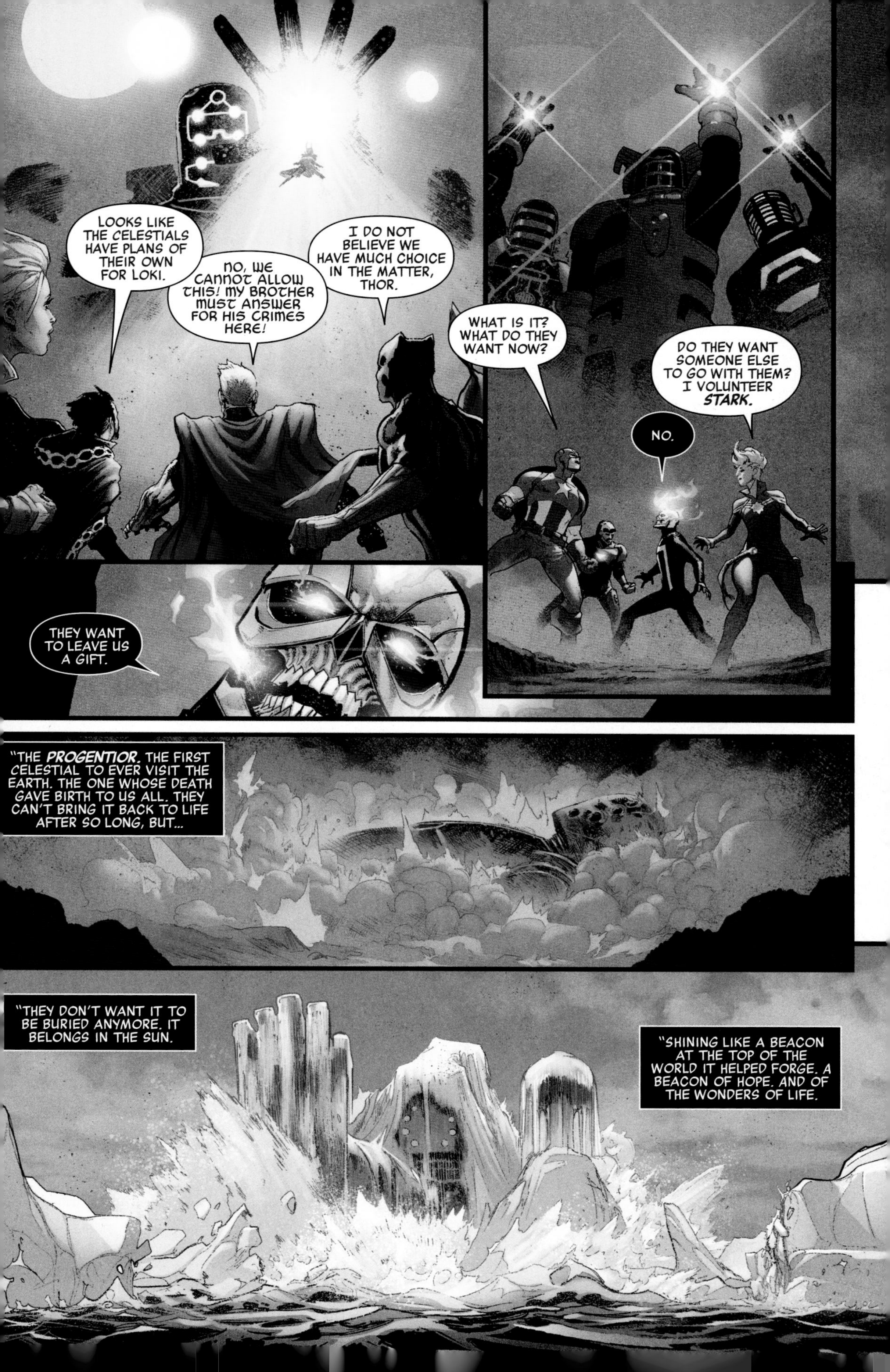
LOOKS LIKE THE CELESTIALS HAVE PLANS OF THEIR OWN FOR LOKI.
NO, WE CANNOT ALLOW THIS! MY BROTHER MUST ANSWER FOR HIS CRIMES HERE!
I DO NOT BELIEVE WE HAVE MUCH CHOICE IN THE MATTER, THOR.
WHAT IS IT? WHAT DO THEY WANT NOW?
DO THEY WANT SOMEONE ELSE TO GO WITH THEM? I VOLUNTEER STARK.
NO.
THEY WANT TO LEAVE US A GIFT.
"THE PROGENTIOR. THE FIRST CELESTIAL TO EVER VISIT THE EARTH. THE ONE WHOSE DEATH GAVE BIRTH TO US ALL. THEY CAN'T BRING IT BACK TO LIFE AFTER SO LONG, BUT...
"THEY DON'T WANT IT TO BE BURIED ANYMORE. IT BELONGS IN THE SUN.
"SHINING LIKE A BEACON AT THE TOP OF THE WORLD IT HELPED FORGE. A BEACON OF HOPE. AND OF THE WONDERS OF LIFE.

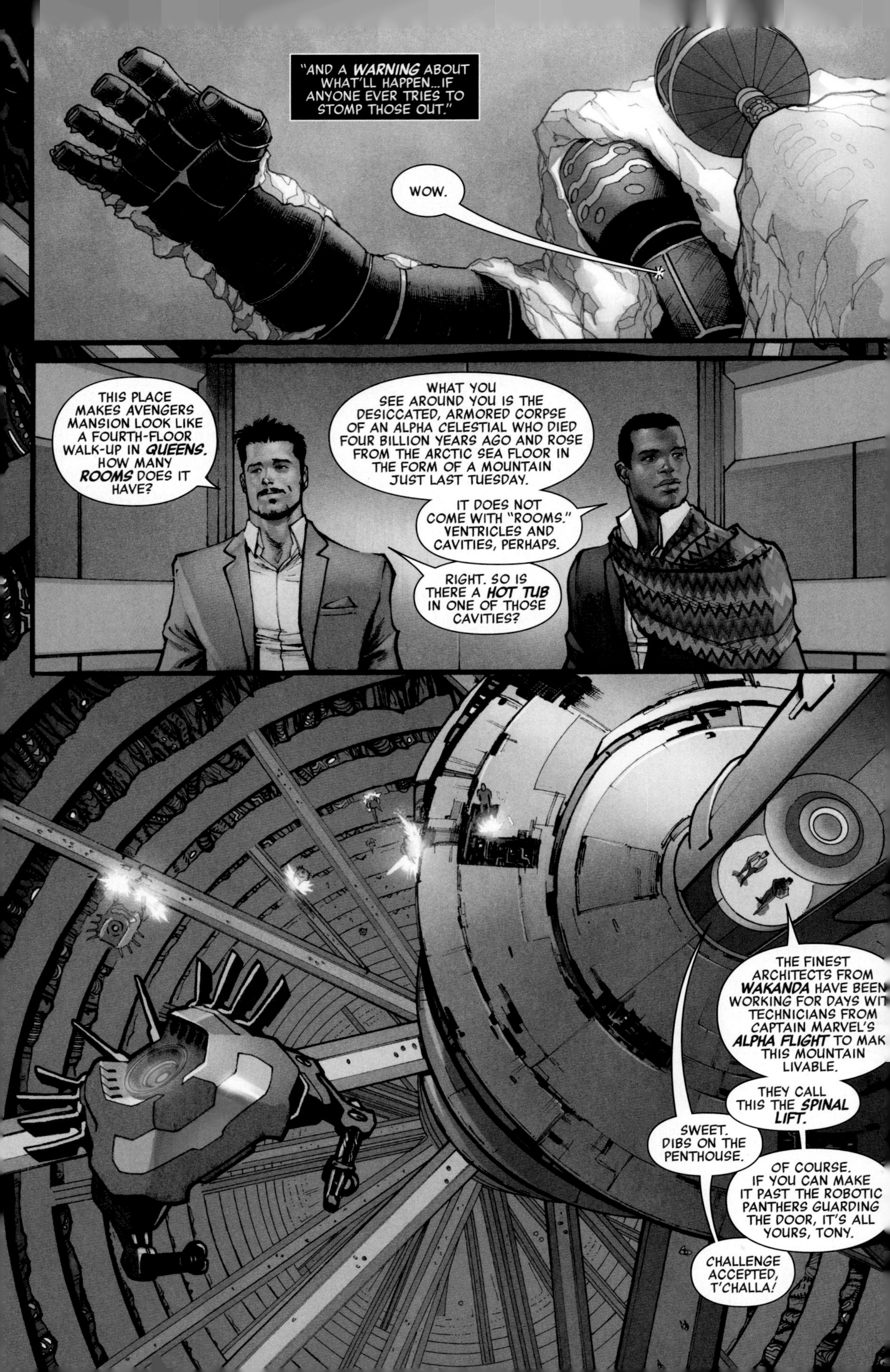
"AND A WARNING ABOUT WHAT'LL HAPPEN...IF ANYONE EVER TRIES TO STOMP THOSE OUT."
WOW.
THIS PLACE MAKES AVENGERS MANSION LOOK LIKE A FOURTH-FLOOR WALK-UP IN QUEENS. HOW MANY ROOMS DOES IT HAVE?
WHAT YOU SEE AROUND YOU IS THE DESICCATED, ARMORED CORPSE OF AN ALPHA CELESTIAL WHO DIED FOUR BILLION YEARS AGO AND ROSE FROM THE ARCTIC SEA FLOOR IN THE FORM OF A MOUNTAIN JUST LAST TUESDAY.
IT DOES NOT COME WITH "ROOMS." VENTRICLES AND CAVITIES, PERHAPS.
RIGHT. SO IS THERE A HOT TUB IN ONE OF THOSE CAVITIES?
THE FINEST ARCHITECTS FROM WAKANDA HAVE BEEN WORKING FOR DAYS WIT TECHNICIANS FROM CAPTAIN MARVEL'S ALPHA FLIGHT TO MAK THIS MOUNTAIN LIVABLE.
THEY CALL THIS THE SPINAL LIFT.
SWEET. DIBS ON THE PENTHOUSE.
OF COURSE. IF YOU CAN MAKE IT PAST THE ROBOTIC PANTHERS GUARDING THE DOOR, IT'S ALL YOURS, TONY.
CHALLENGE ACCEPTED, T'CHALLA!

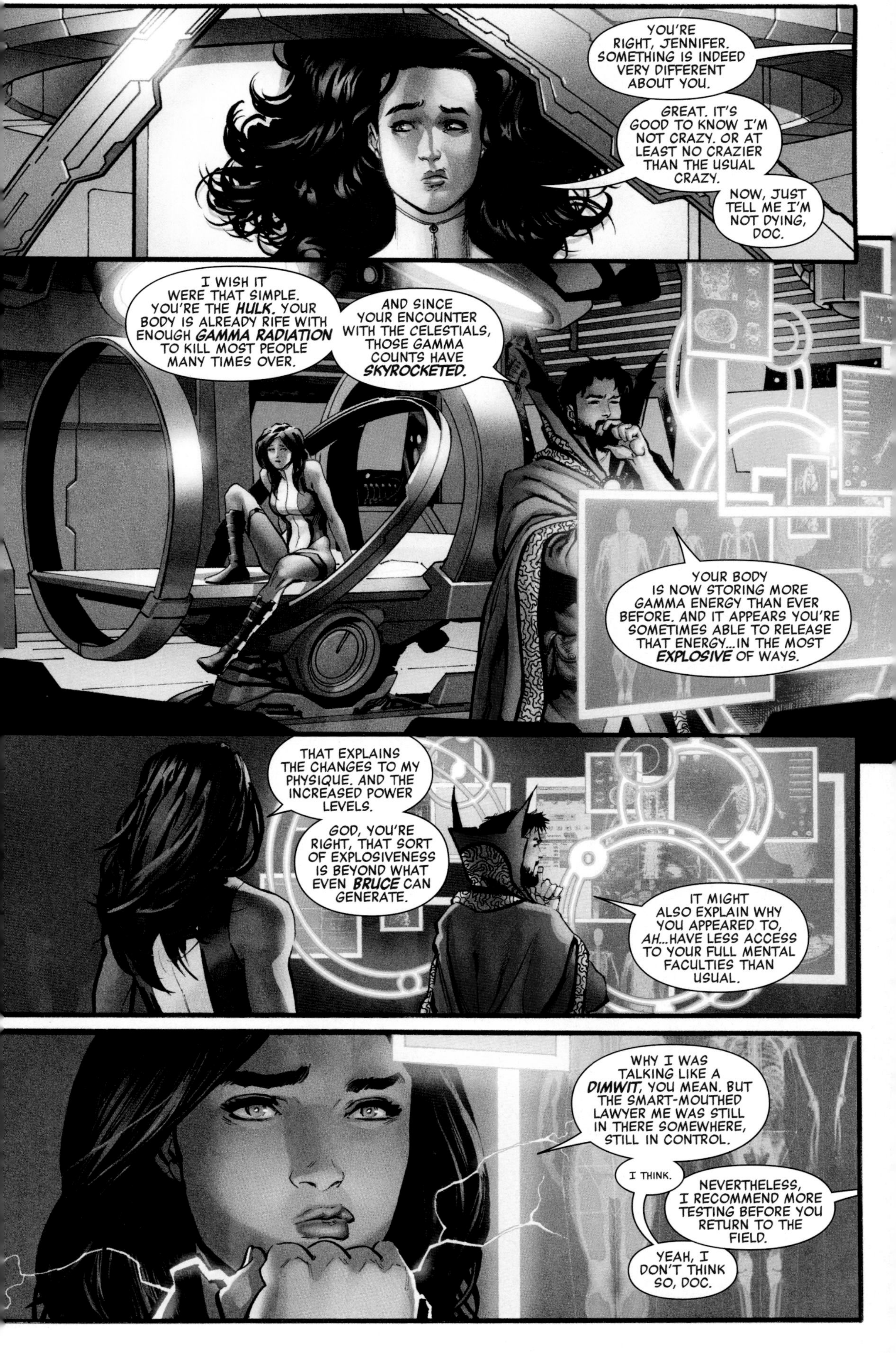
YOU'RE RIGHT, JENNIFER. SOMETHING IS INDEED VERY DIFFERENT ABOUT YOU.
GREAT. IT'S GOOD TO KNOW I'M NOT CRAZY. OR AT LEAST NO CRAZIER THAN THE USUAL CRAZY.
NOW, JUST TELL ME I'M NOT DYING, DOC.
I WISH IT WERE THAT SIMPLE. YOU'RE THE HULK. YOUR BODY IS ALREADY RIFE WITH ENOUGH GAMMA RADIATION TO KILL MOST PEOPLE MANY TIMES OVER.
AND SINCE YOUR ENCOUNTER WITH THE CELESTIALS, THOSE GAMMA COUNTS HAVE SKYROCKETED.
YOUR BODY IS NOW STORING MORE GAMMA ENERGY THAN EVER BEFORE. AND IT APPEARS YOU'RE SOMETIMES ABLE TO RELEASE THAT ENERGY...IN THE MOST EXPLOSIVE OF WAYS.
THAT EXPLAINS THE CHANGES TO MY PHYSIQUE. AND THE INCREASED POWER LEVELS.
GOD, YOU'RE RIGHT, THAT SORT OF EXPLOSIVENESS IS BEYOND WHAT EVEN BRUCE CAN GENERATE.
IT MIGHT ALSO EXPLAIN WHY YOU APPEARED TO, AH...HAVE LESS ACCESS TO YOUR FULL MENTAL FACULTIES THAN USUAL.
WHY I WAS TALKING LIKE A DIMWIT, YOU MEAN. BUT THE SMART-MOUTHED LAWYER ME WAS STILL IN THERE SOMEWHERE, STILL IN CONTROL.
I THINK.
NEVERTHELESS, I RECOMMEND MORE TESTING BEFORE YOU RETURN TO THE FIELD.
YEAH, I DON'T THINK SO, DOC.

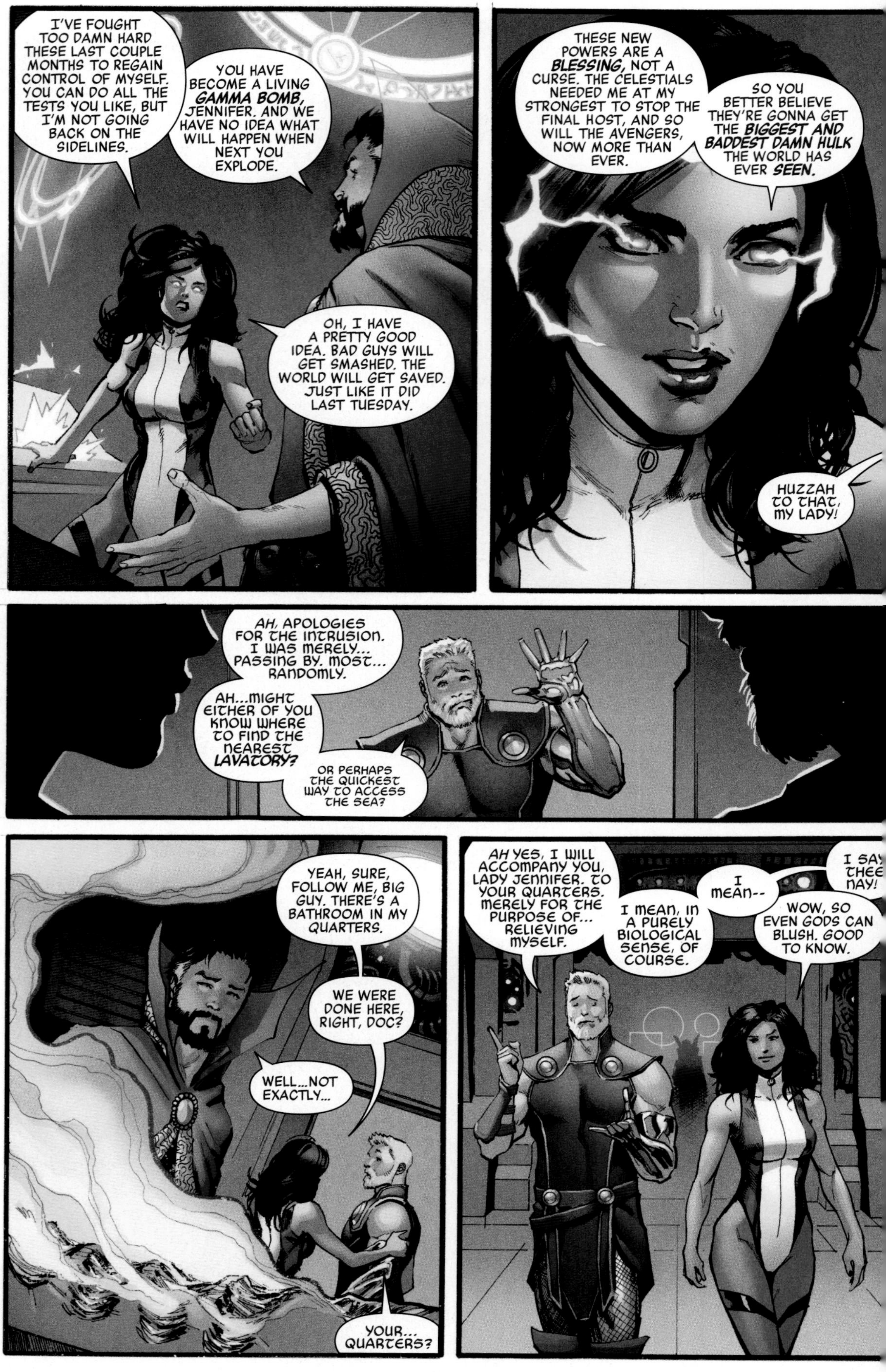
I'VE FOUGHT TOO DAMN HARD THESE LAST COUPLE MONTHS TO REGAIN CONTROL OF MYSELF. YOU CAN DO ALL THE TESTS YOU LIKE, BUT I'M NOT GOING BACK ON THE SIDELINES.
YOU HAVE BECOME A LIVING GAMMA BOMB, JENNIFER. AND WE HAVE NO IDEA WHAT WILL HAPPEN WHEN NEXT YOU EXPLODE.
OH, I HAVE A PRETTY GOOD IDEA. BAD GUYS WILL GET SMASHED. THE WORLD WILL GET SAVED. JUST LIKE IT DID LAST TUESDAY.
THESE NEW POWERS ARE A BLESSING, NOT A CURSE. THE CELESTIALS NEEDED ME AT MY STRONGEST TO STOP THE FINAL HOST, AND SO WILL THE AVENGERS, NOW MORE THAN EVER.
SO YOU BETTER BELIEVE THEY'RE GONNA GET THE BIGGEST AND BADDEST DAMN HULK THE WORLD HAS EVER SEEN.
HUZZAH TO THAT, MY LADY!
AH, APOLOGIES FOR THE INTRUSION. I WAS MERELY... PASSING BY. MOST... RANDOMLY.
AH...MIGHT EITHER OF YOU KNOW WHERE TO FIND THE NEAREST LAVATORY?
OR PERHAPS THE QUICKEST WAY TO ACCESS THE SEA?
YEAH, SURE, FOLLOW ME, BIG GUY. THERE'S A BATHROOM IN MY QUARTERS.
WE WERE DONE HERE, RIGHT, DOC?
WELL...NOT EXACTLY...
YOUR... QUARTERS?
AH YES, I WILL ACCOMPANY YOU, LADY JENNIFER. TO YOUR QUARTERS. MERELY FOR THE PURPOSE OF... RELIEVING MYSELF.
I MEAN, IN A PURELY BIOLOGICAL SENSE, OF COURSE.
I MEAN--
WOW, SO EVEN GODS CAN BLUSH. GOOD TO KNOW.

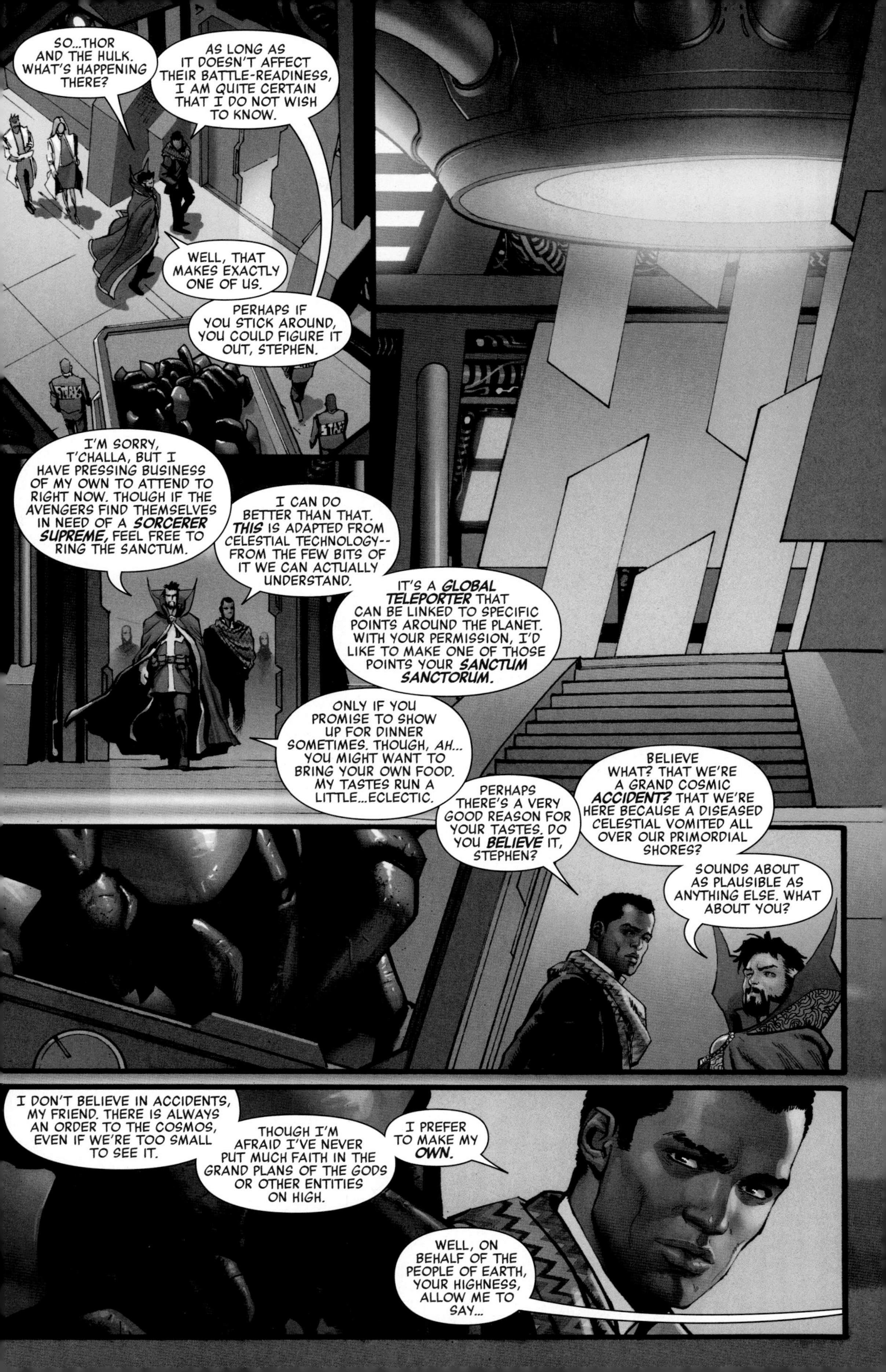
SO...THOR AND THE HULK. WHAT'S HAPPENING THERE?
AS LONG AS IT DOESN'T AFFECT THEIR BATTLE-READINESS, I AM QUITE CERTAIN THAT I DO NOT WISH TO KNOW.
WELL, THAT MAKES EXACTLY ONE OF US.
PERHAPS IF YOU STICK AROUND, YOU COULD FIGURE IT OUT, STEPHEN.
I'M SORRY, T'CHALLA, BUT I HAVE PRESSING BUSINESS OF MY OWN TO ATTEND TO RIGHT NOW. THOUGH IF THE AVENGERS FIND THEMSELVES IN NEED OF A SORCERER SUPREME, FEEL FREE TO RING THE SANCTUM.
I CAN DO BETTER THAN THAT. THIS IS ADAPTED FROM CELESTIAL TECHNOLOGY-- FROM THE FEW BITS OF IT WE CAN ACTUALLY UNDERSTAND.
IT'S A GLOBAL TELEPORTER THAT CAN BE LINKED TO SPECIFIC POINTS AROUND THE PLANET. WITH YOUR PERMISSION, I'D LIKE TO MAKE ONE OF THOSE POINTS YOUR SANCTUM SANCTORUM.
ONLY IF YOU PROMISE TO SHOW UP FOR DINNER SOMETIMES. THOUGH, AH... YOU MIGHT WANT TO BRING YOUR OWN FOOD. MY TASTES RUN A LITTLE...ECLECTIC.
PERHAPS THERE'S A VERY GOOD REASON FOR YOUR TASTES. DO YOU BELIEVE IT, STEPHEN?
BELIEVE WHAT? THAT WE'RE A GRAND COSMIC ACCIDENT? THAT WE'RE HERE BECAUSE A DISEASED CELESTIAL VOMITED ALL OVER OUR PRIMORDIAL SHORES?
SOUNDS ABOUT AS PLAUSIBLE AS ANYTHING ELSE. WHAT ABOUT YOU?
I DON'T BELIEVE IN ACCIDENTS, MY FRIEND. THERE IS ALWAYS AN ORDER TO THE COSMOS, EVEN IF WE'RE TOO SMALL TO SEE IT.
THOUGH I'M AFRAID I'VE NEVER PUT MUCH FAITH IN THE GRAND PLANS OF THE GODS OR OTHER ENTITIES ON HIGH.
I PREFER TO MAKE MY OWN.
WELL, ON BEHALF OF THE PEOPLE OF EARTH, YOUR HIGHNESS, ALLOW ME TO SAY...

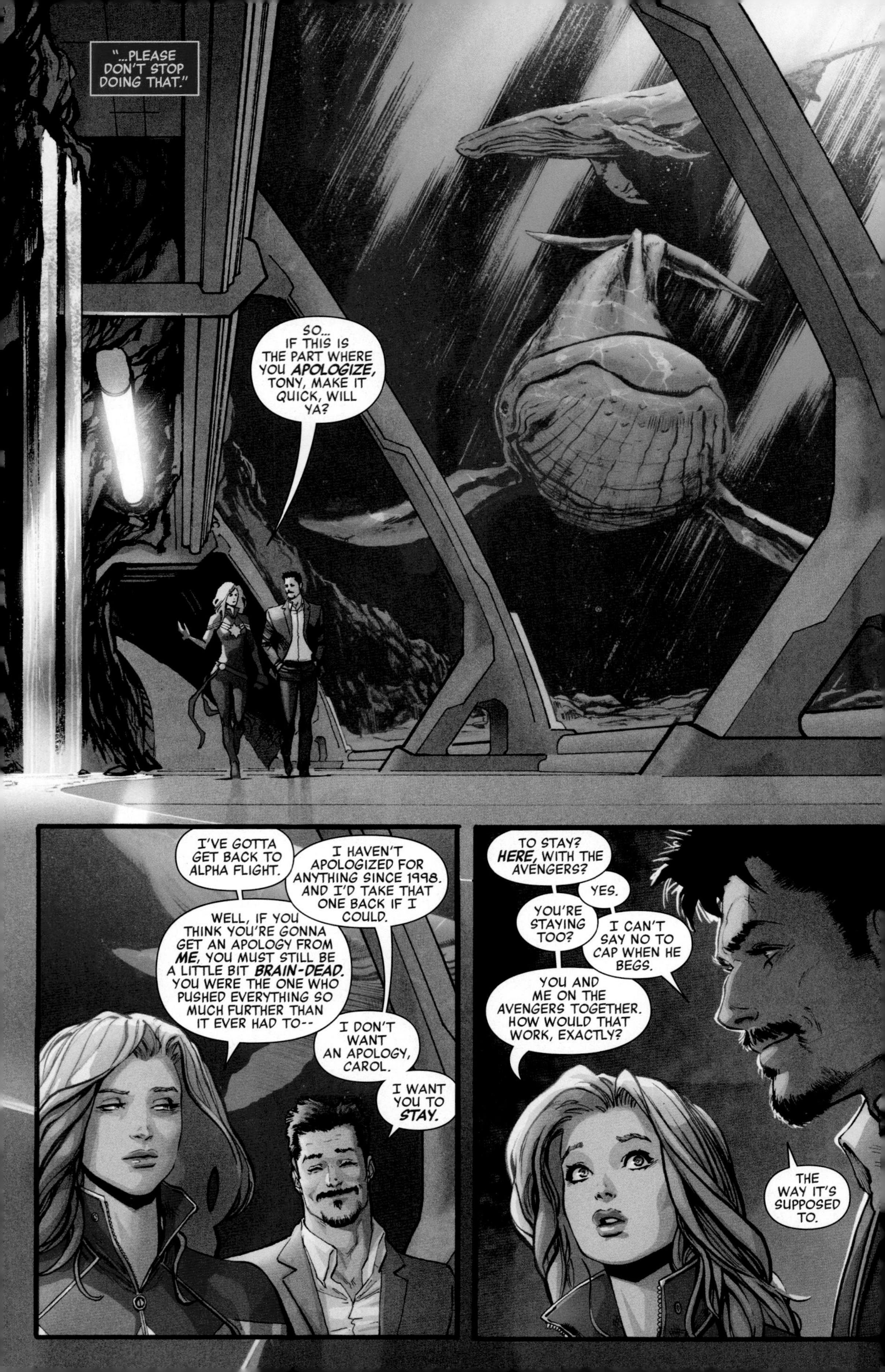
"...PLEASE DON'T STOP DOING THAT."
SO... IF THIS IS THE PART WHERE YOU APOLOGIZE, TONY, MAKE IT QUICK, WILL YA?
I'VE GOTTA GET BACK TO ALPHA FLIGHT.
I HAVEN'T APOLOGIZED FOR ANYTHING SINCE 1998. AND I'D TAKE THAT ONE BACK IF I COULD.
WELL, IF YOU THINK YOU'RE GONNA GET AN APOLOGY FROM ME, YOU MUST STILL BE A LITTLE BIT BRAIN-DEAD. YOU WERE THE ONE WHO PUSHED EVERYTHING SO MUCH FURTHER THAN IT EVER HAD TO--
I DON'T WANT AN APOLOGY, CAROL.
I WANT YOU TO STAY.
TO STAY? HERE, WITH THE AVENGERS?
YES.
YOU'RE STAYING TOO?
I CAN'T SAY NO TO CAP WHEN HE BEGS.
YOU AND ME ON THE AVENGERS TOGETHER. HOW WOULD THAT WORK, EXACTLY?
THE WAY IT'S SUPPOSED TO.

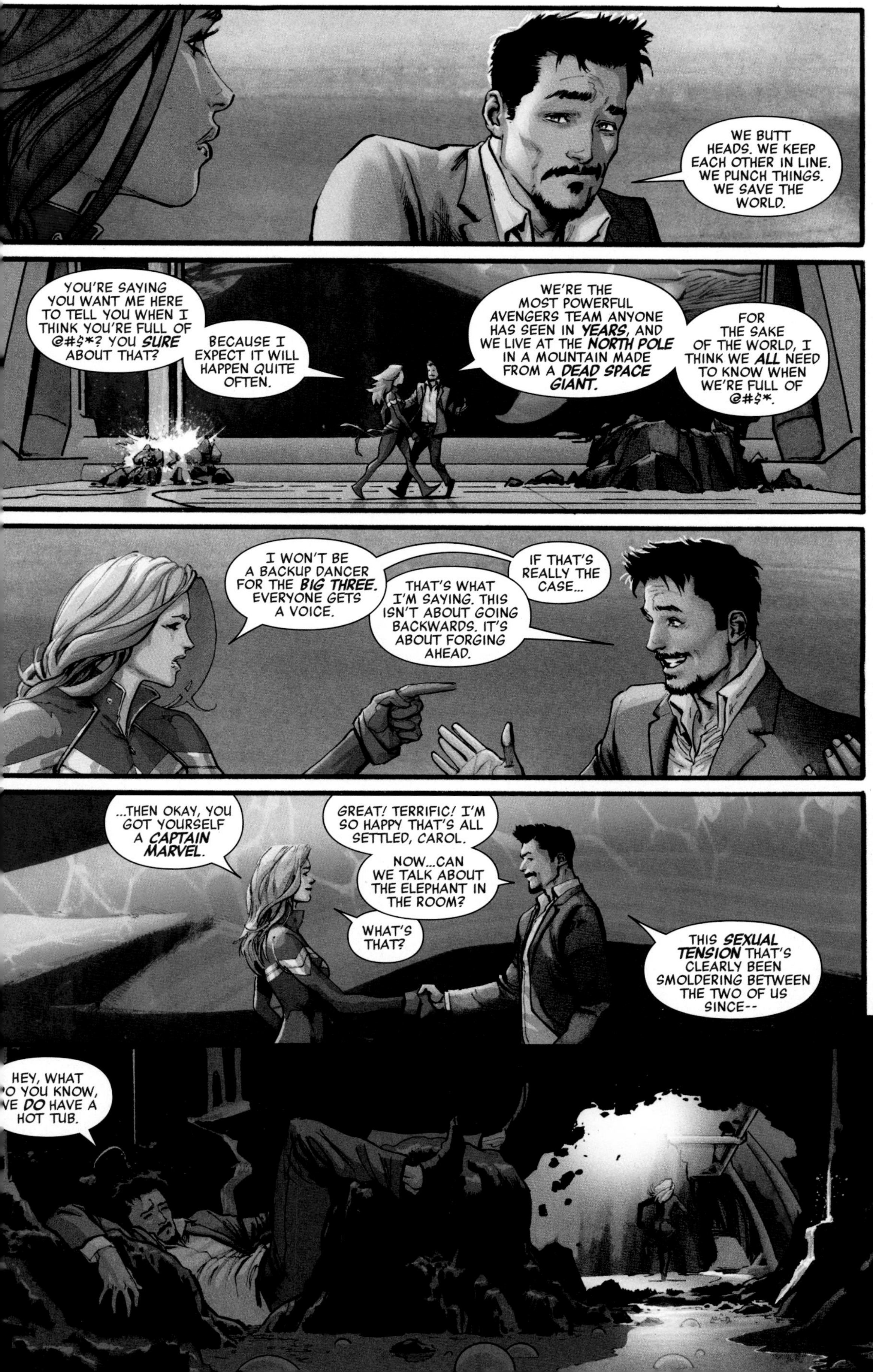
WE BUTT HEADS. WE KEEP EACH OTHER IN LINE. WE PUNCH THINGS. WE SAVE THE WORLD.
YOU'RE SAYING YOU WANT ME HERE TO TELL YOU WHEN I THINK YOU'RE FULL OF @#$*? YOU SURE ABOUT THAT?
BECAUSE I EXPECT IT WILL HAPPEN QUITE OFTEN.
WE'RE THE MOST POWERFUL AVENGERS TEAM ANYONE HAS SEEN IN YEARS, AND WE LIVE AT THE NORTH POLE IN A MOUNTAIN MADE FROM A DEAD SPACE GIANT.
FOR THE SAKE OF THE WORLD, I THINK WE ALL NEED TO KNOW WHEN WE'RE FULL OF @#$*.
I WON'T BE A BACKUP DANCER FOR THE BIG THREE. EVERYONE GETS A VOICE.
IF THAT'S REALLY THE CASE...
THAT'S WHAT I'M SAYING. THIS ISN'T ABOUT GOING BACKWARDS. IT'S ABOUT FORGING AHEAD.
...THEN OKAY, YOU GOT YOURSELF A CAPTAIN MARVEL.
GREAT! TERRIFIC! I'M SO HAPPY THAT'S ALL SETTLED, CAROL.
NOW...CAN WE TALK ABOUT THE ELEPHANT IN THE ROOM?
WHAT'S THAT?
THIS SEXUAL TENSION THAT'S CLEARLY BEEN SMOLDERING BETWEEN THE TWO OF US SINCE--
HEY, WHAT
O YOU KNOW,
VE DO HAVE A
HOT TUB.

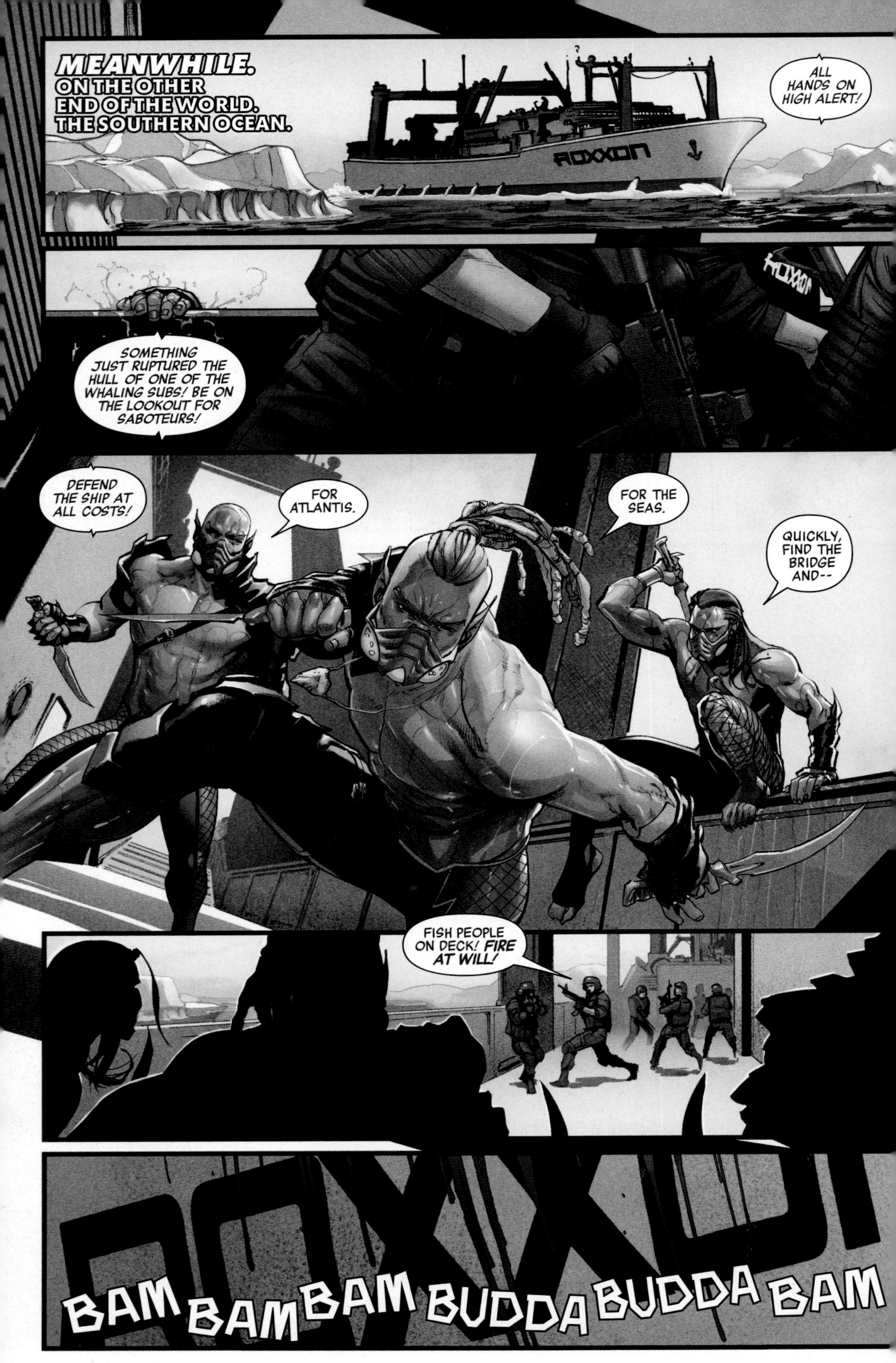
MEANWHILE. ON THE OTHER END OF THE WORLD. THE SOUTHERN OCEAN.
ROXXON
ALL HANDS ON HIGH ALERT!
ROXXON
SOMETHING JUST RUPTURED THE HULL OF ONE OF THE WHALING SUBS! BE ON THE LOOKOUT FOR SABOTEURS!
DEFEND THE SHIP AT ALL COSTS!
FOR ATLANTIS.
FOR THE SEAS.
QUICKLY, FIND THE BRIDGE AND--
FISH PEOPLE ON DECK! FIRE AT WILL!
BAM BAM BAM BUDDA BUDDA BAM

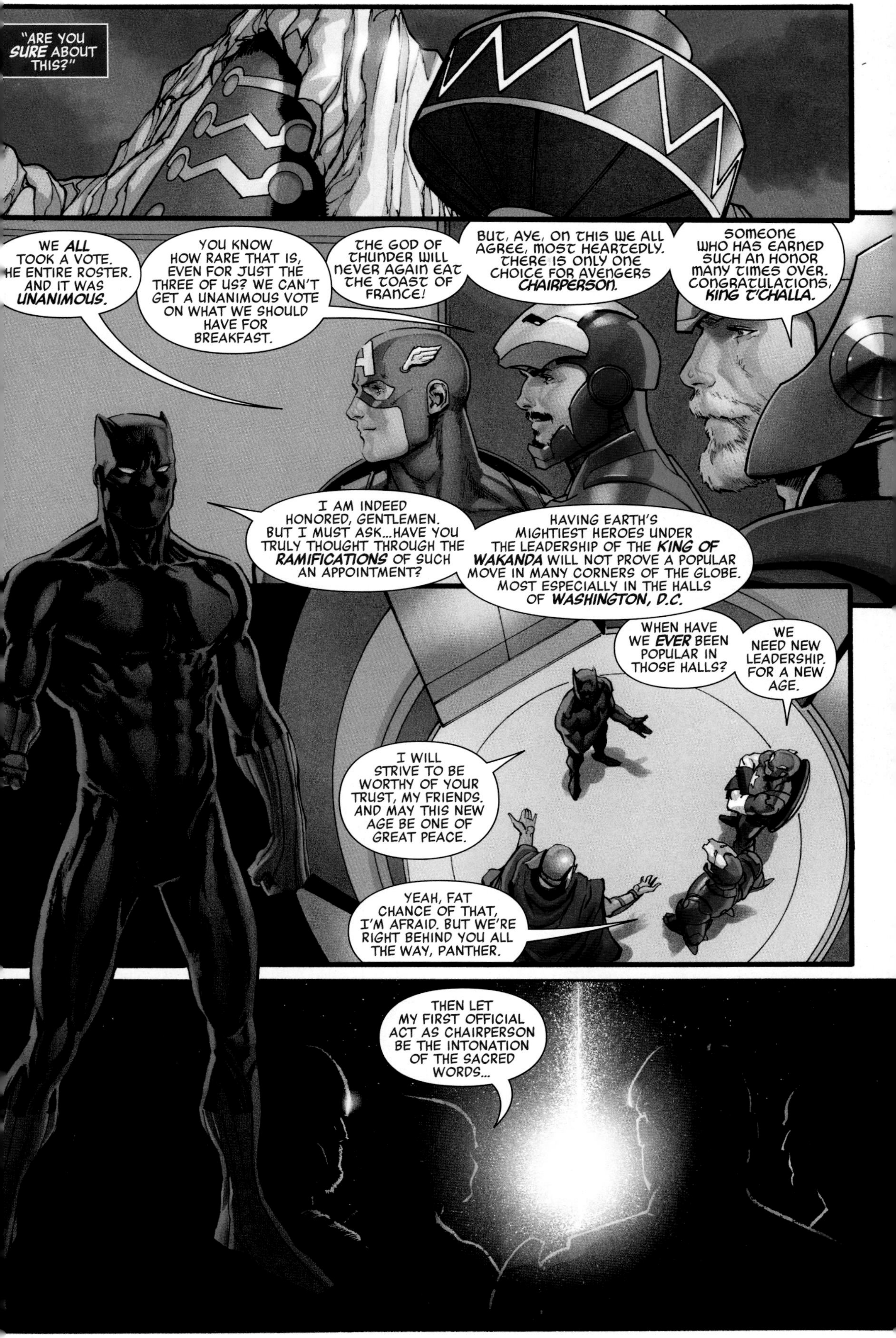
"ARE YOU SURE ABOUT THIS?"
WE ALL TOOK A VOTE. THE ENTIRE ROSTER. AND IT WAS UNANIMOUS.
YOU KNOW HOW RARE THAT IS, EVEN FOR JUST THE THREE OF US? WE CAN'T GET A UNANIMOUS VOTE ON WHAT WE SHOULD HAVE FOR BREAKFAST.
THE GOD OF THUNDER WILL NEVER AGAIN EAT THE TOAST OF FRANCE!
BUT, AYE, ON THIS WE ALL AGREE, MOST HEARTEDLY. THERE IS ONLY ONE CHOICE FOR AVENGERS CHAIRPERSON.
SOMEONE WHO HAS EARNED SUCH AN HONOR MANY TIMES OVER. CONGRATULATIONS, KING T'CHALLA.
I AM INDEED HONORED, GENTLEMEN. BUT I MUST ASK...HAVE YOU TRULY THOUGHT THROUGH THE RAMIFICATIONS OF SUCH AN APPOINTMENT?
HAVING EARTH'S MIGHTIEST HEROES UNDER THE LEADERSHIP OF THE KING OF WAKANDA WILL NOT PROVE A POPULAR MOVE IN MANY CORNERS OF THE GLOBE. MOST ESPECIALLY IN THE HALLS OF WASHINGTON, D.C.
WHEN HAVE WE EVER BEEN POPULAR IN THOSE HALLS?
WE NEED NEW LEADERSHIP. FOR A NEW AGE.
I WILL STRIVE TO BE WORTHY OF YOUR TRUST, MY FRIENDS. AND MAY THIS NEW AGE BE ONE OF GREAT PEACE.
YEAH, FAT CHANCE OF THAT, I'M AFRAID. BUT WE'RE RIGHT BEHIND YOU ALL THE WAY, PANTHER.
THEN LET MY FIRST OFFICIAL ACT AS CHAIRPERSON BE THE INTONATION OF THE SACRED WORDS...

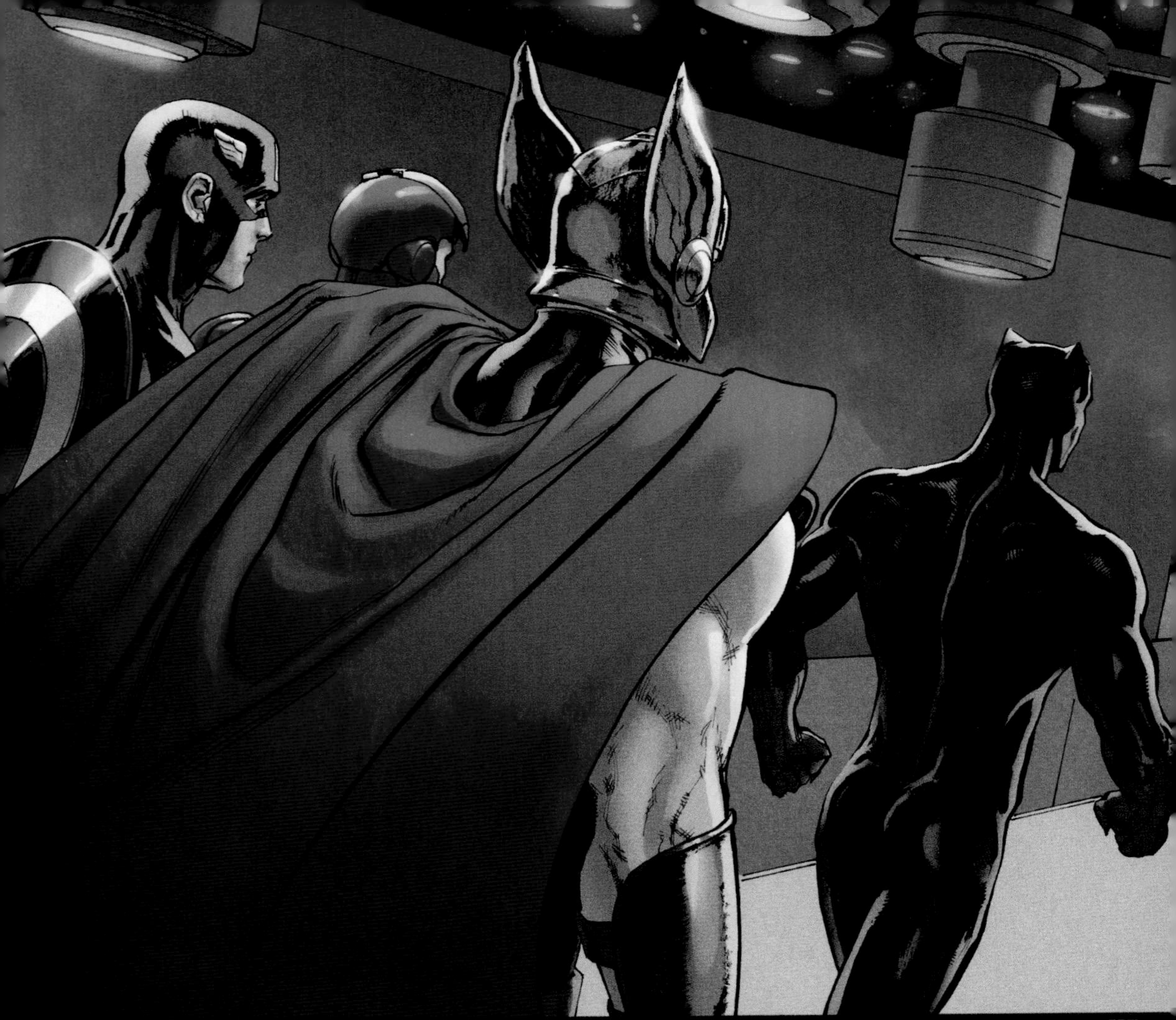

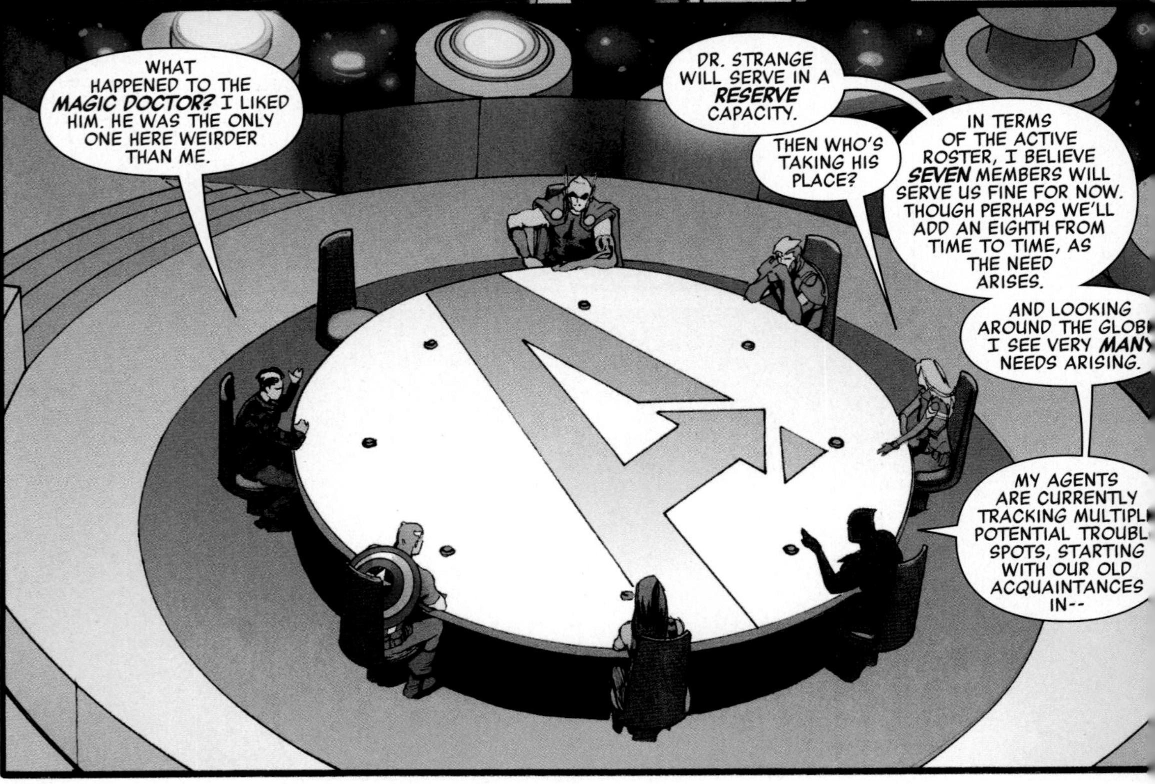

WHAT HAPPENED TO THE MAGIC DOCTOR? I LIKED HIM. HE WAS THE ONLY ONE HERE WEIRDER THAN ME.
DR. STRANGE WILL SERVE IN A RESERVE CAPACITY.
THEN WHO'S TAKING HIS PLACE?
IN TERMS OF THE ACTIVE ROSTER, I BELIEVE SEVEN MEMBERS WILL SERVE US FINE FOR NOW. THOUGH PERHAPS WE'LL ADD AN EIGHTH FROM TIME TO TIME, AS THE NEED ARISES.
AND LOOKING AROUND THE GLOB I SEE VERY MANY NEEDS ARISING.
MY AGENTS ARE CURRENTLY TRACKING MULTIPL POTENTIAL TROUBL SPOTS, STARTING WITH OUR OLD ACQUAINTANCES IN--

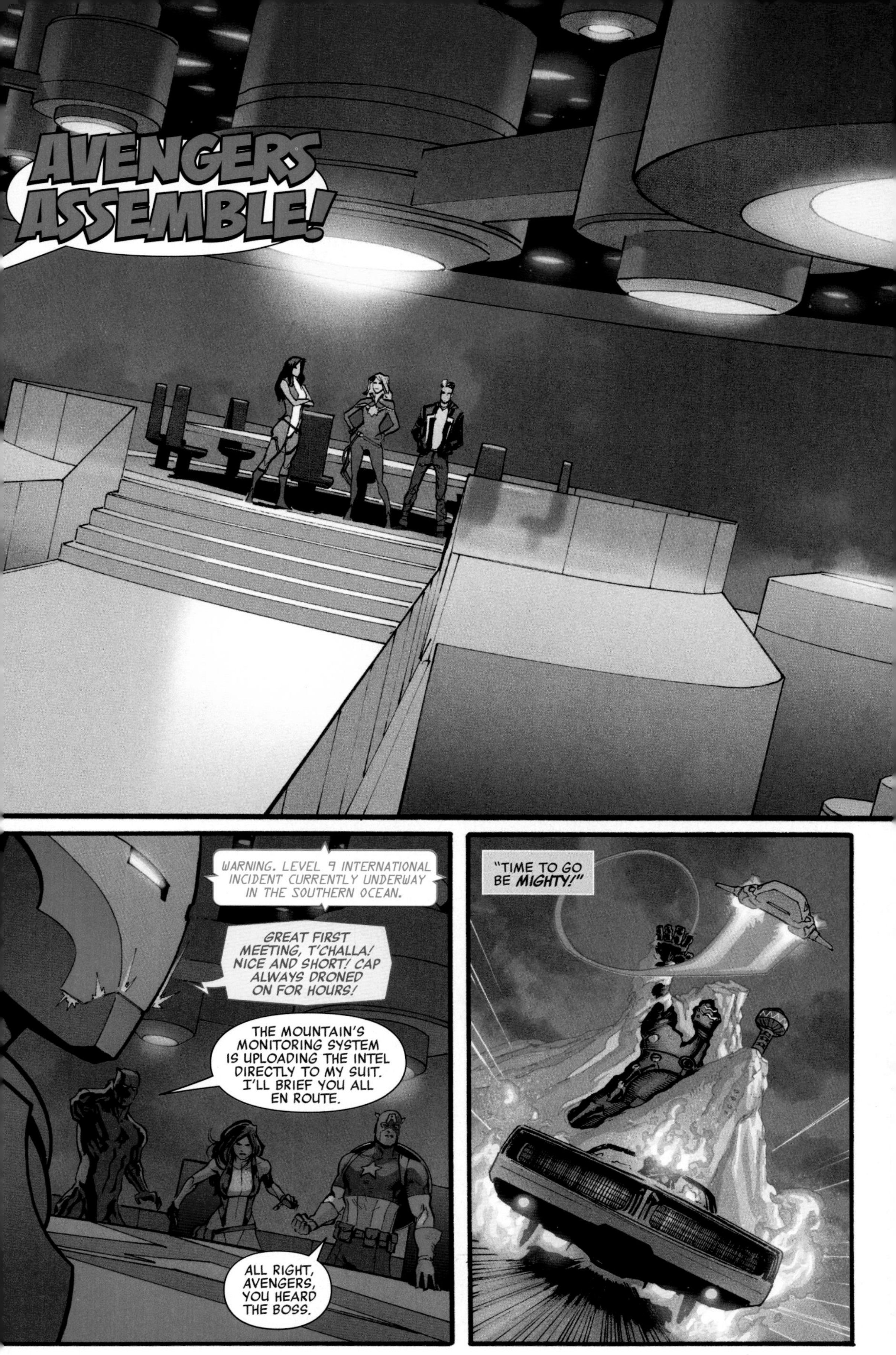
AVENGERS ASSEMBLE!
WARNING. LEVEL 9 INTERNATIONAL INCIDENT CURRENTLY UNDERWAY IN THE SOUTHERN OCEAN.
GREAT FIRST MEETING, T'CHALLA! NICE AND SHORT! CAP ALWAYS DRONED ON FOR HOURS!
THE MOUNTAIN'S MONITORING SYSTEM IS UPLOADING THE INTEL DIRECTLY TO MY SUIT. I'LL BRIEF YOU ALL EN ROUTE.
ALL RIGHT, AVENGERS, YOU HEARD THE BOSS.
"TIME TO GO BE MIGHTY!"

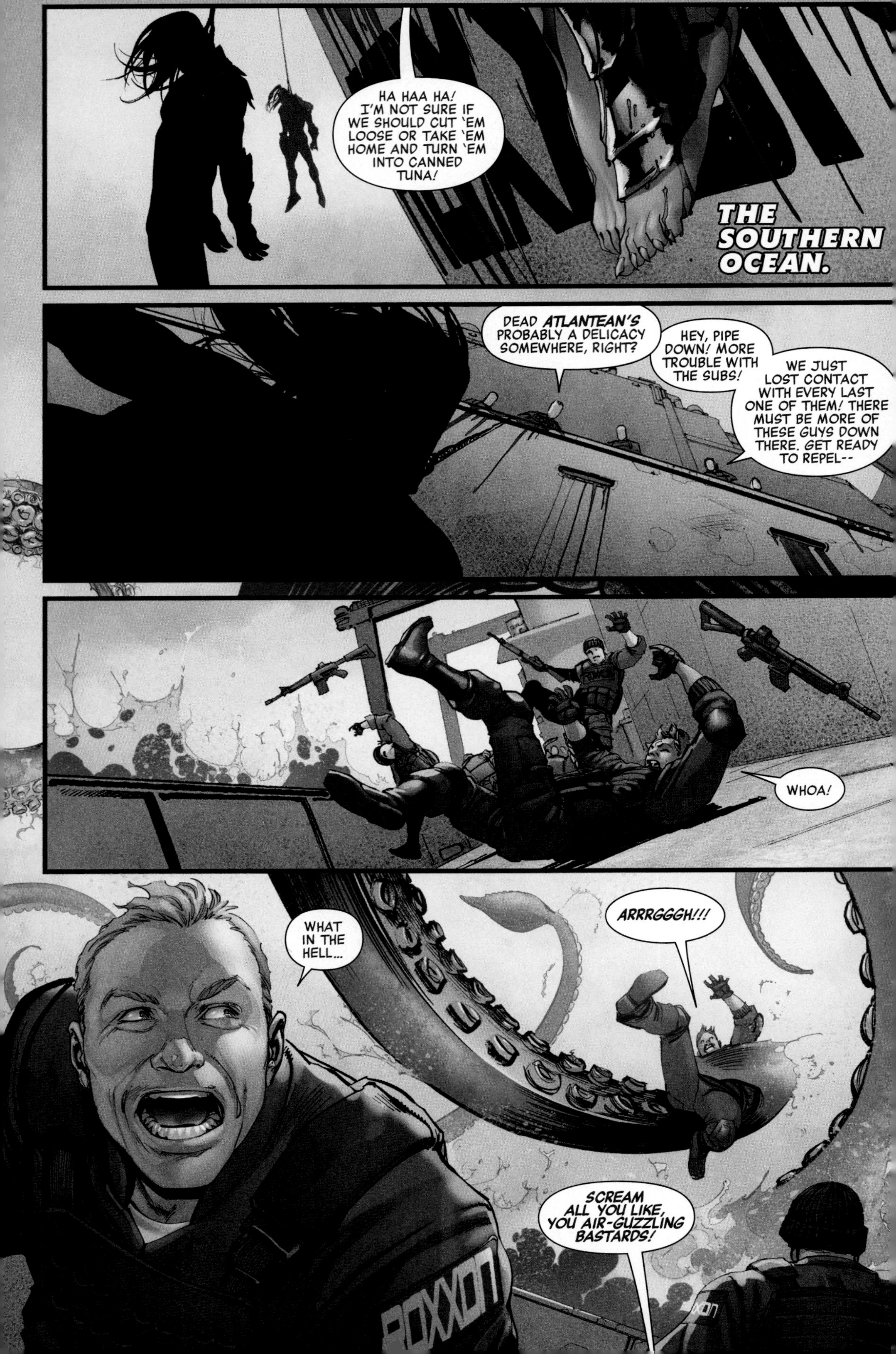
HA HAA HA! I'M NOT SURE IF WE SHOULD CUT 'EM LOOSE OR TAKE 'EM HOME AND TURN 'EM INTO CANNED TUNA!
THE SOUTHERN OCEAN.
DEAD ATLANTEAN'S PROBABLY A DELICACY SOMEWHERE, RIGHT?
HEY, PIPE DOWN! MORE TROUBLE WITH THE SUBS!
WE JUST LOST CONTACT WITH EVERY LAST ONE OF THEM! THERE MUST BE MORE OF THESE GUYS DOWN THERE. GET READY TO REPEL--
WHOA!
WHAT IN THE HELL...
ARRRGGGH!!!
SCREAM ALL YOU LIKE, YOU AIR-GUZZLING BASTARDS!
ROXXON

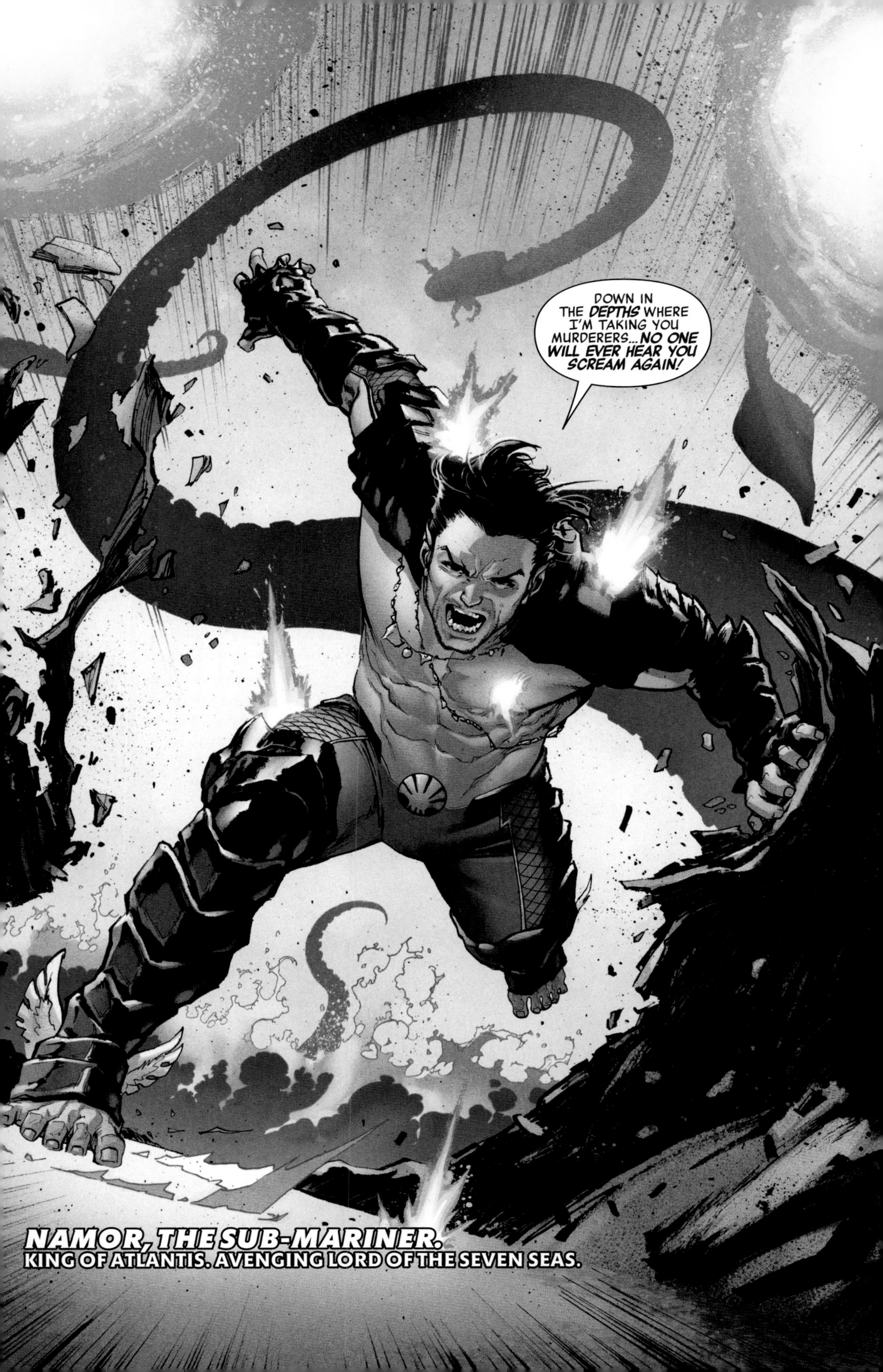
DOWN IN THE DEPTHS WHERE I'M TAKING YOU MURDERERS... NO ONE WILL EVER HEAR YOU SCREAM AGAIN!
NAMOR, THE SUB-MARINER.
KING OF ATLANTIS. AVENGING LORD OF THE SEVEN SEAS.

9 THE DEFENDERS OF THE DEEP

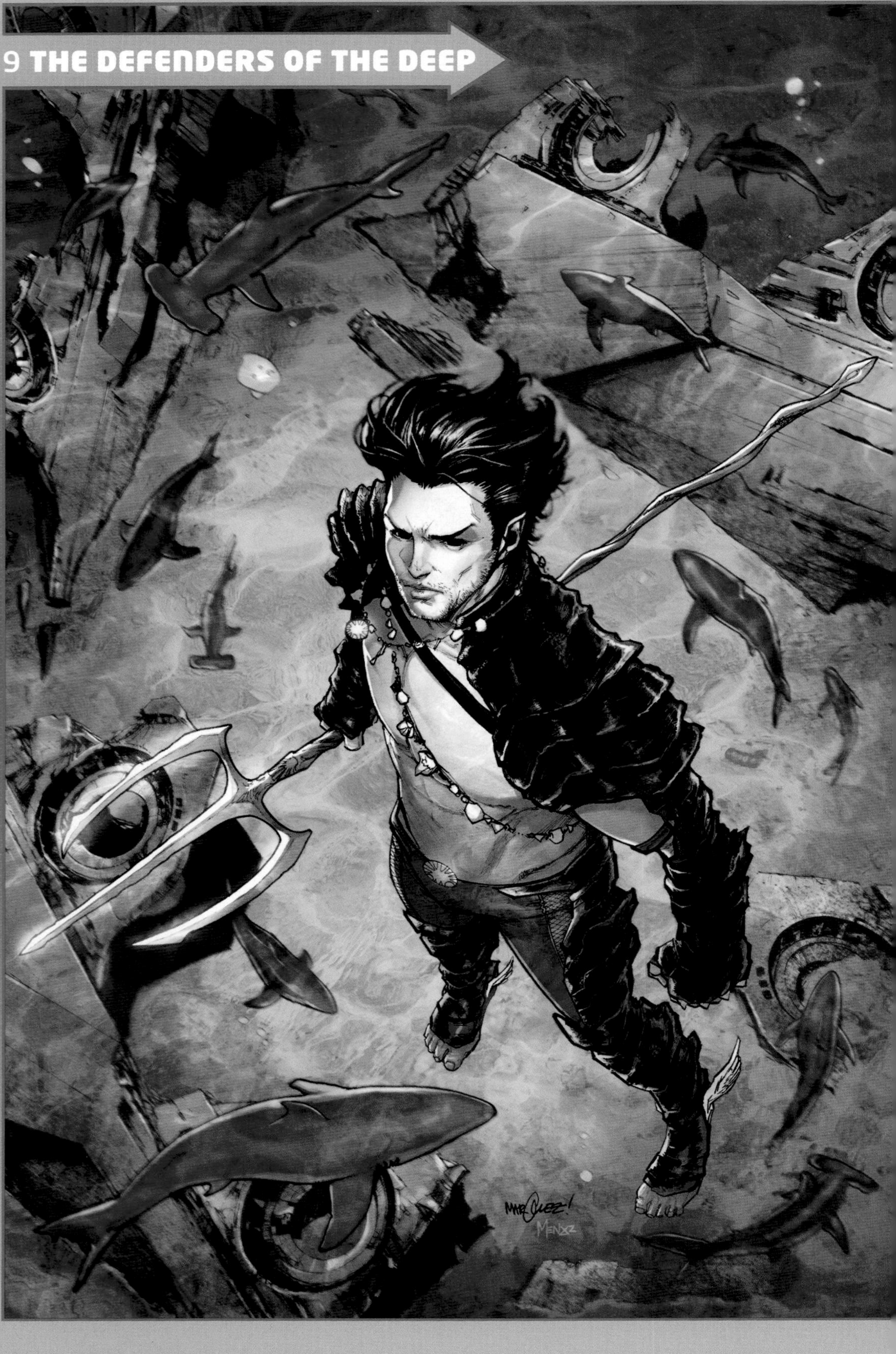

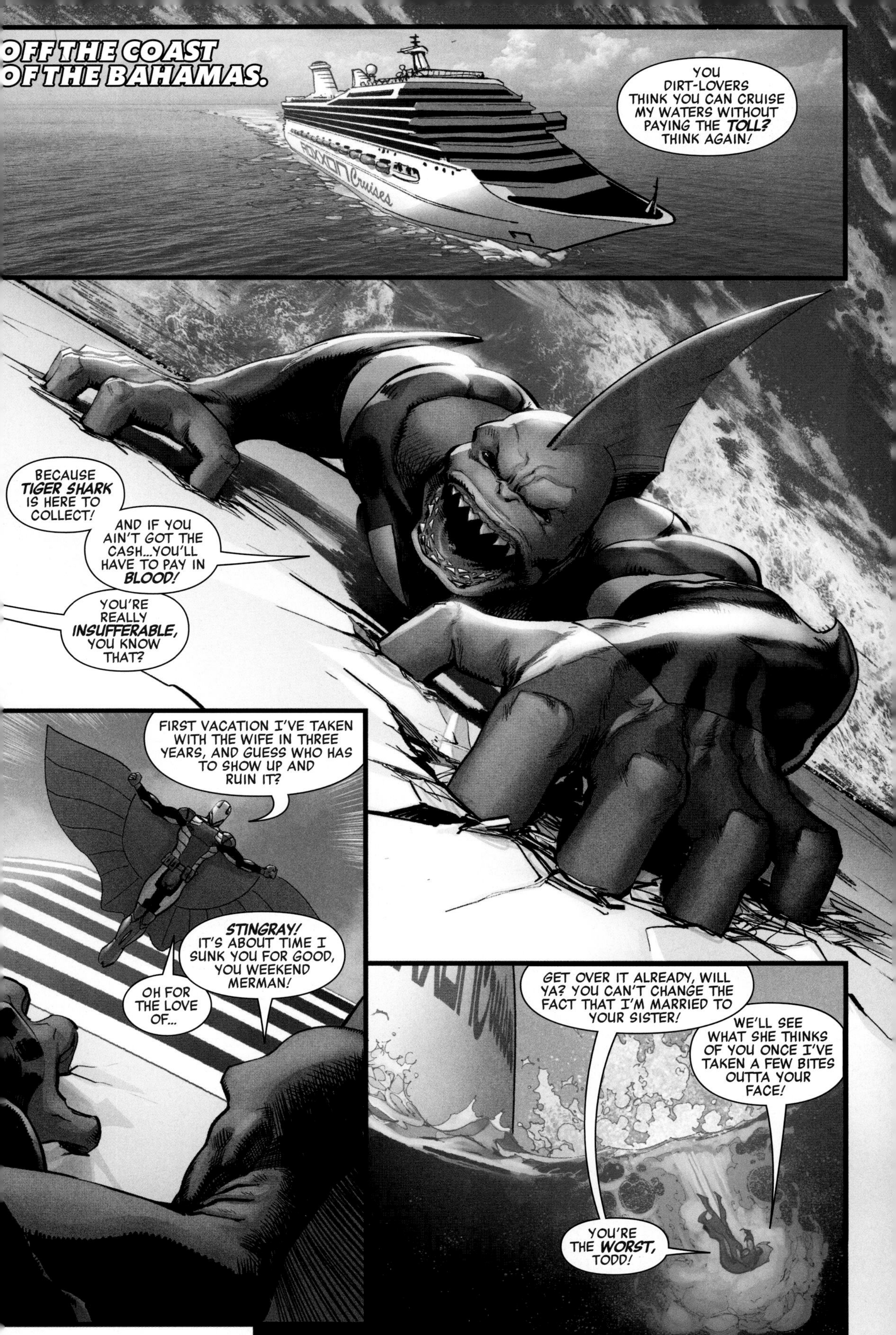
OFF THE COAST OF THE BAHAMAS.
YOU DIRT-LOVERS THINK YOU CAN CRUISE MY WATERS WITHOUT PAYING THE TOLL? THINK AGAIN!
ROXXON Cruises
BECAUSE TIGER SHARK IS HERE TO COLLECT!
AND IF YOU AIN'T GOT THE CASH...YOU'LL HAVE TO PAY IN BLOOD!
YOU'RE REALLY INSUFFERABLE, YOU KNOW THAT?
FIRST VACATION I'VE TAKEN WITH THE WIFE IN THREE YEARS, AND GUESS WHO HAS TO SHOW UP AND RUIN IT?
STINGRAY! IT'S ABOUT TIME I SUNK YOU FOR GOOD, YOU WEEKEND MERMAN!
OH FOR THE LOVE OF...
GET OVER IT ALREADY, WILL YA? YOU CAN'T CHANGE THE FACT THAT I'M MARRIED TO YOUR SISTER!
WE'LL SEE WHAT SHE THINKS OF YOU ONCE I'VE TAKEN A FEW BITES OUTTA YOUR FACE!
YOU'RE THE WORST, TODD!

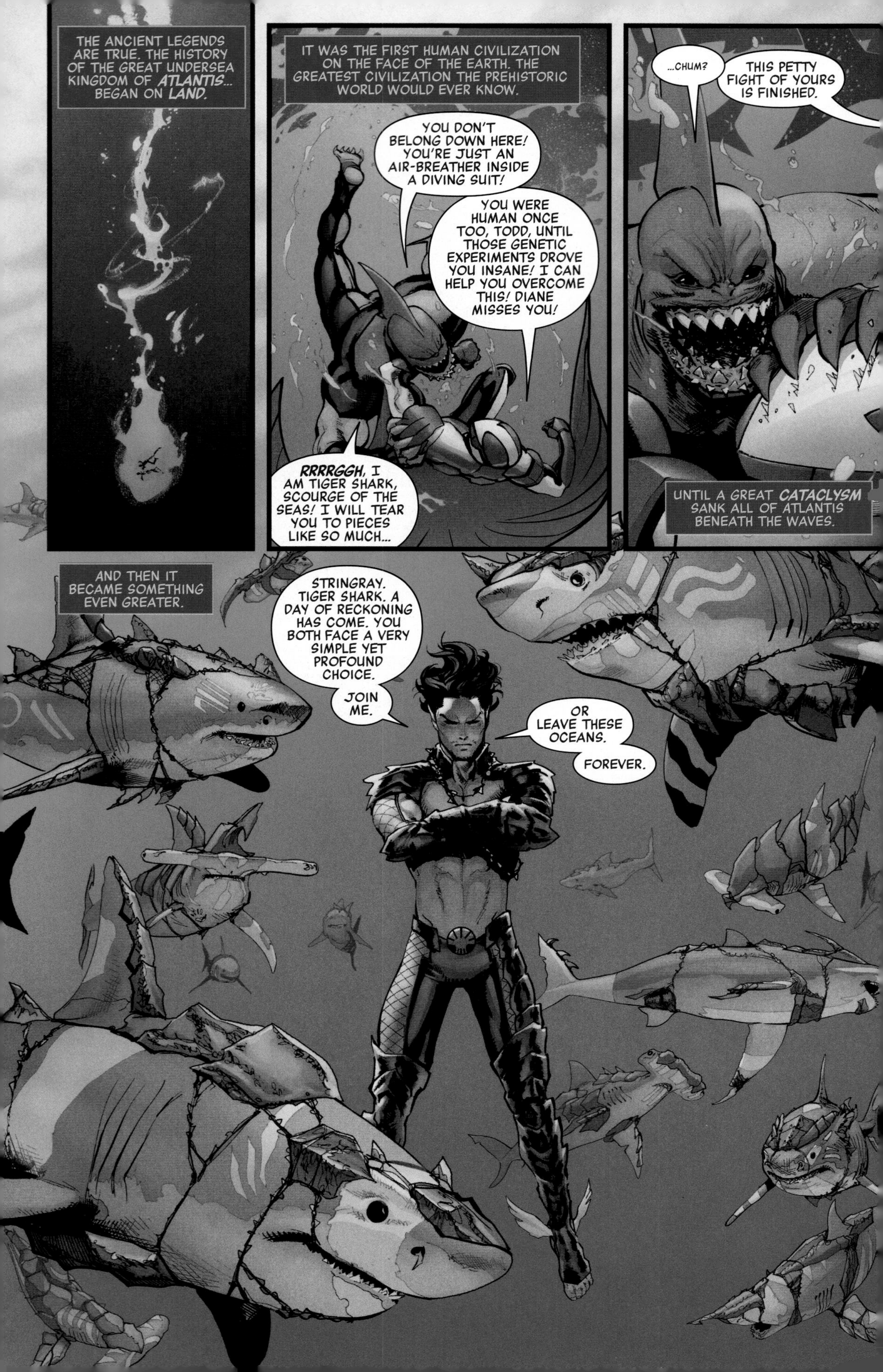
THE ANCIENT LEGENDS ARE TRUE. THE HISTORY OF THE GREAT UNDERSEA KINGDOM OF ATLANTIS... BEGAN ON LAND.
IT WAS THE FIRST HUMAN CIVILIZATION ON THE FACE OF THE EARTH. THE GREATEST CIVILIZATION THE PREHISTORIC WORLD WOULD EVER KNOW.
YOU DON'T BELONG DOWN HERE! YOU'RE JUST AN AIR-BREATHER INSIDE A DIVING SUIT!
RRRRGGH, I AM TIGER SHARK, SCOURGE OF THE SEAS! I WILL TEAR YOU TO PIECES LIKE SO MUCH...
YOU WERE HUMAN ONCE TOO, TODD, UNTIL THOSE GENETIC EXPERIMENTS DROVE YOU INSANE! I CAN HELP YOU OVERCOME THIS! DIANE MISSES YOU!
...CHUM?
THIS PETTY FIGHT OF YOURS IS FINISHED.
UNTIL A GREAT CATACLYSM SANK ALL OF ATLANTIS BENEATH THE WAVES.
AND THEN IT BECAME SOMETHING EVEN GREATER.
STRINGRAY. TIGER SHARK. A DAY OF RECKONING HAS COME. YOU BOTH FACE A VERY SIMPLE YET PROFOUND CHOICE.
JOIN ME.
OR LEAVE THESE OCEANS.
FOREVER.

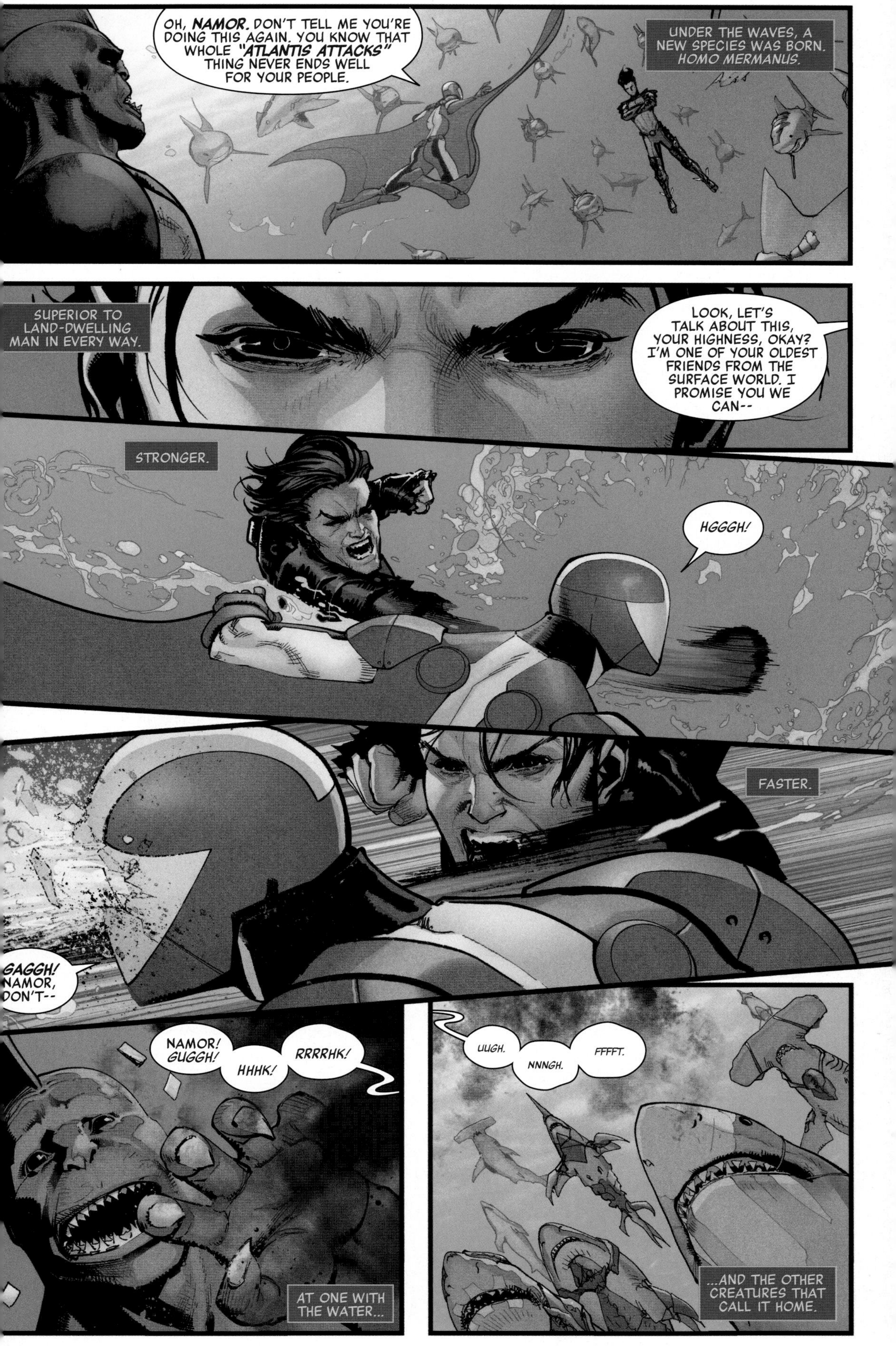
OH, NAMOR. DON'T TELL ME YOU'RE DOING THIS AGAIN. YOU KNOW THAT WHOLE "ATLANTIS ATTACKS" THING NEVER ENDS WELL FOR YOUR PEOPLE.
UNDER THE WAVES, A NEW SPECIES WAS BORN. HOMO MERMANUS.
SUPERIOR TO LAND-DWELLING MAN IN EVERY WAY.
LOOK, LET'S TALK ABOUT THIS, YOUR HIGHNESS, OKAY? I'M ONE OF YOUR OLDEST FRIENDS FROM THE SURFACE WORLD. I PROMISE YOU WE CAN--
STRONGER.
HGGGH!
FASTER.
GAGGH! NAMOR, DON'T--
NAMOR! GUGGH!
HHHK!
RRRRHK!
AT ONE WITH THE WATER...
UUGH.
NNNGH.
FFFFT.
...AND THE OTHER CREATURES THAT CALL IT HOME.

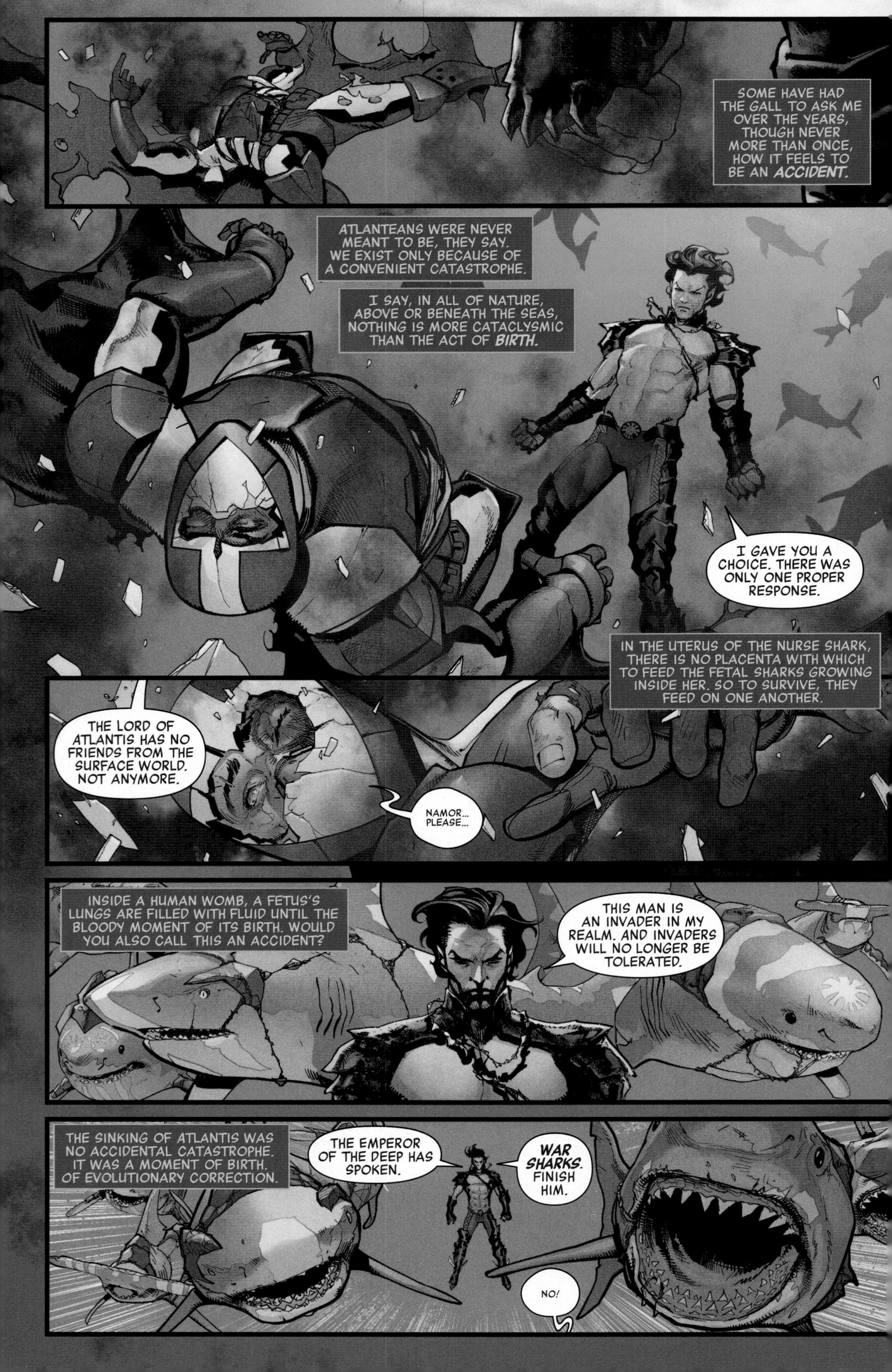
SOME HAVE HAD THE GALL TO ASK ME OVER THE YEARS, THOUGH NEVER MORE THAN ONCE, HOW IT FEELS TO BE AN ACCIDENT.
ATLANTEANS WERE NEVER MEANT TO BE, THEY SAY. WE EXIST ONLY BECAUSE OF A CONVENIENT CATASTROPHE.
I SAY, IN ALL OF NATURE, ABOVE OR BENEATH THE SEAS, NOTHING IS MORE CATACLYSMIC THAN THE ACT OF BIRTH.
I GAVE YOU A CHOICE. THERE WAS ONLY ONE PROPER RESPONSE.
IN THE UTERUS OF THE NURSE SHARK, THERE IS NO PLACENTA WITH WHICH TO FEED THE FETAL SHARKS GROWING INSIDE HER. SO TO SURVIVE, THEY FEED ON ONE ANOTHER.
THE LORD OF ATLANTIS HAS NO FRIENDS FROM THE SURFACE WORLD. NOT ANYMORE.
NAMOR... PLEASE...
INSIDE A HUMAN WOMB, A FETUS'S LUNGS ARE FILLED WITH FLUID UNTIL THE BLOODY MOMENT OF ITS BIRTH. WOULD YOU ALSO CALL THIS AN ACCIDENT?
THIS MAN IS AN INVADER IN MY REALM. AND INVADERS WILL NO LONGER BE TOLERATED.
THE SINKING OF ATLANTIS WAS NO ACCIDENTAL CATASTROPHE. IT WAS A MOMENT OF BIRTH. OF EVOLUTIONARY CORRECTION.
THE EMPEROR OF THE DEEP HAS SPOKEN.
WAR SHARKS. FINISH HIM.
NO!

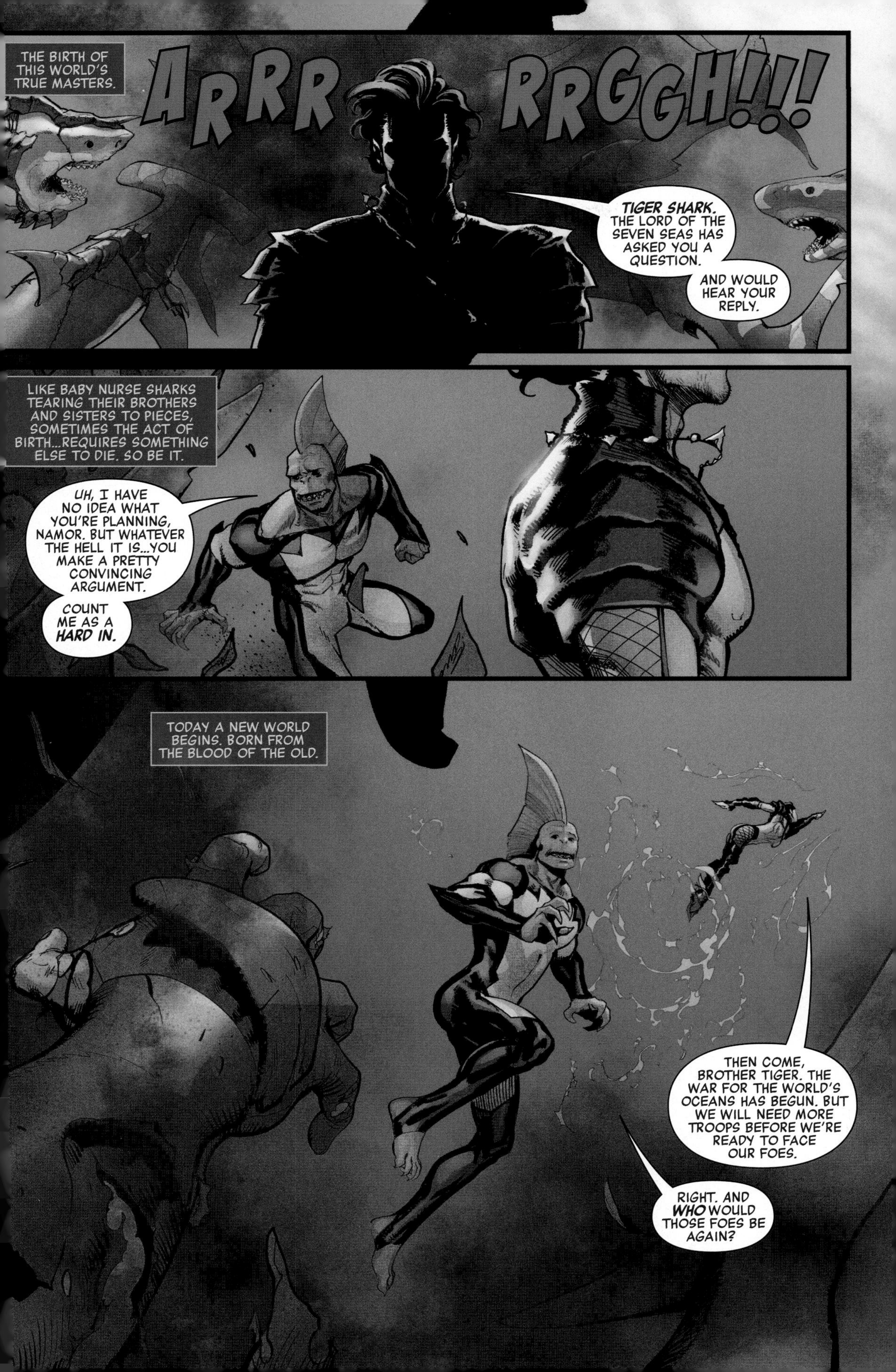
THE BIRTH OF THIS WORLD'S TRUE MASTERS.
ARRRRRGGH!!!!
TIGER SHARK. THE LORD OF THE SEVEN SEAS HAS ASKED YOU A QUESTION.
AND WOULD HEAR YOUR REPLY.
LIKE BABY NURSE SHARKS TEARING THEIR BROTHERS AND SISTERS TO PIECES, SOMETIMES THE ACT OF BIRTH...REQUIRES SOMETHING ELSE TO DIE. SO BE IT.
UH, I HAVE NO IDEA WHAT YOU'RE PLANNING, NAMOR. BUT WHATEVER THE HELL IT IS...YOU MAKE A PRETTY CONVINCING ARGUMENT.
COUNT ME AS A HARD IN.
TODAY A NEW WORLD BEGINS. BORN FROM THE BLOOD OF THE OLD.
THEN COME, BROTHER TIGER. THE WAR FOR THE WORLD'S OCEANS HAS BEGUN. BUT WE WILL NEED MORE TROOPS BEFORE WE'RE READY TO FACE OUR FOES.
RIGHT. AND WHO WOULD THOSE FOES BE AGAIN?

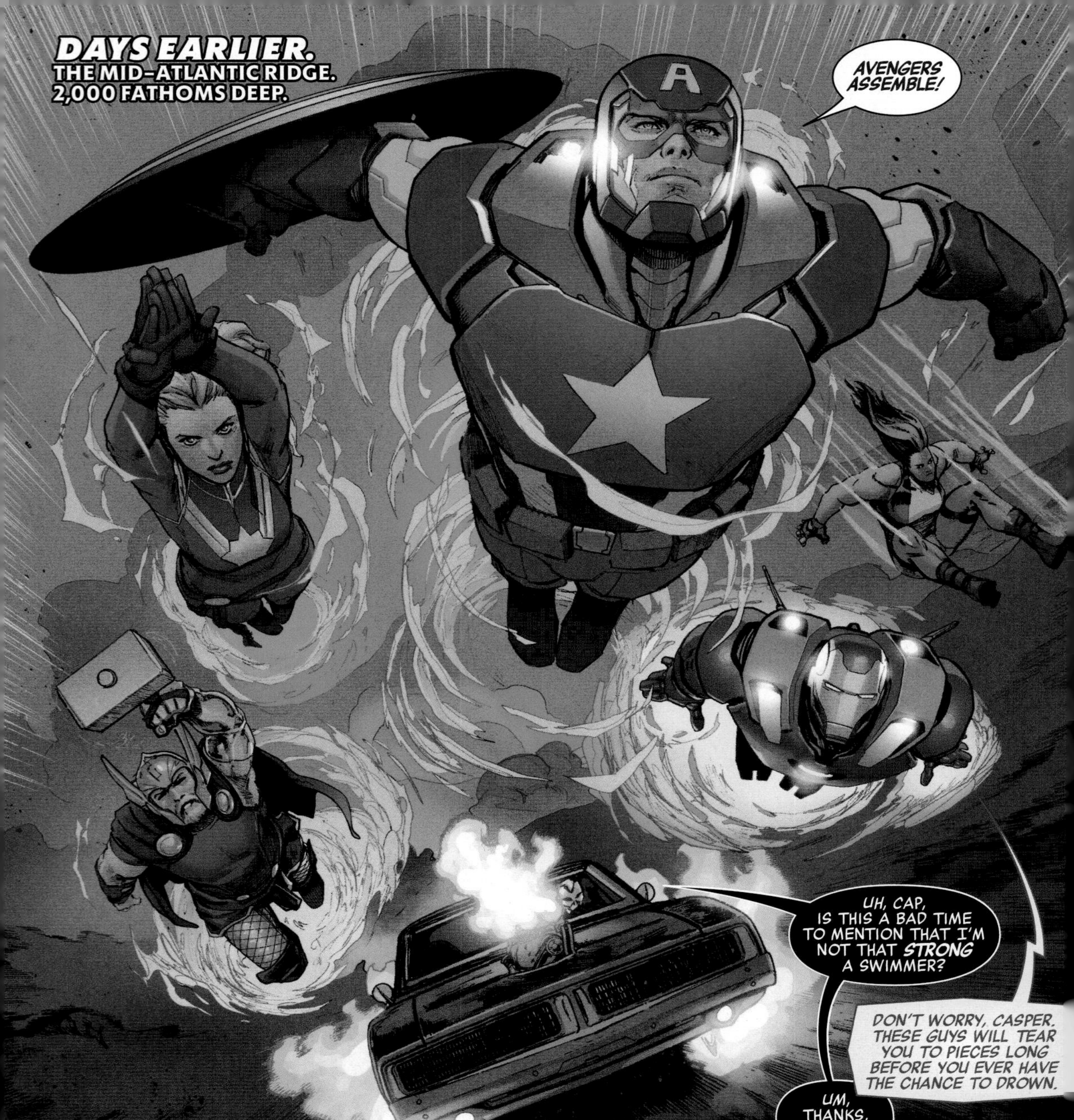
DAYS EARLIER.
THE MID-ATLANTIC RIDGE.
2,000 FATHOMS DEEP.
AVENGERS ASSEMBLE!
UH, CAP, IS THIS A BAD TIME TO MENTION THAT I'M NOT THAT STRONG A SWIMMER?
DON'T WORRY, CASPER. THESE GUYS WILL TEAR YOU TO PIECES LONG BEFORE YOU EVER HAVE THE CHANCE TO DROWN.
UM, THANKS, MR. STARK.

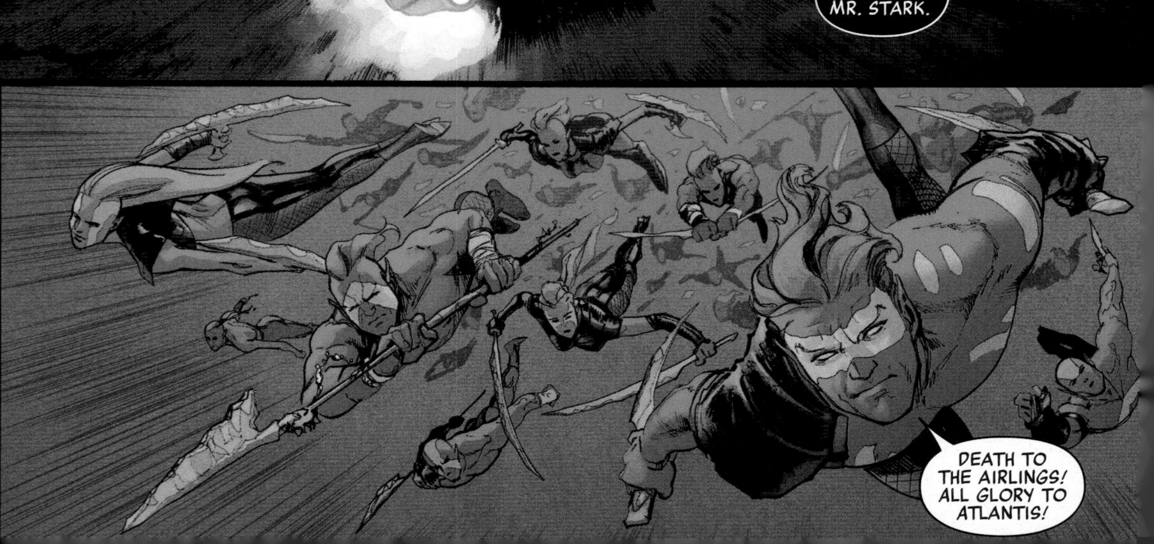
DEATH TO THE AIRLINGS! ALL GLORY TO ATLANTIS!

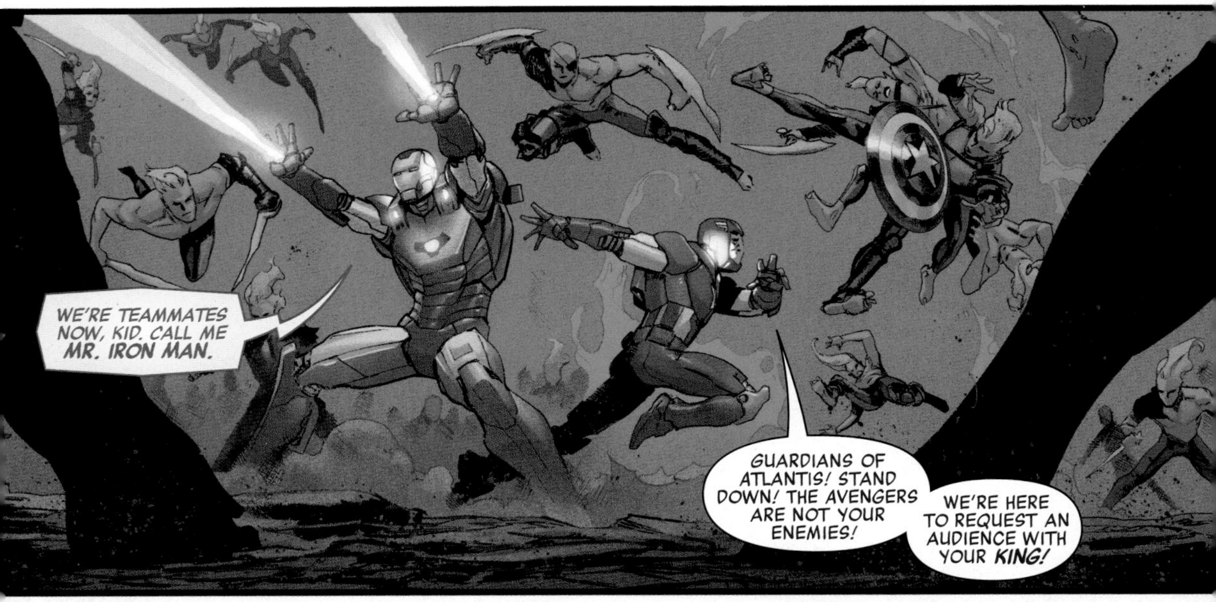
WE'RE TEAMMATES NOW, KID. CALL ME MR. IRON MAN.
GUARDIANS OF ATLANTIS! STAND DOWN! THE AVENGERS ARE NOT YOUR ENEMIES!
WE'RE HERE TO REQUEST AN AUDIENCE WITH YOUR KING!

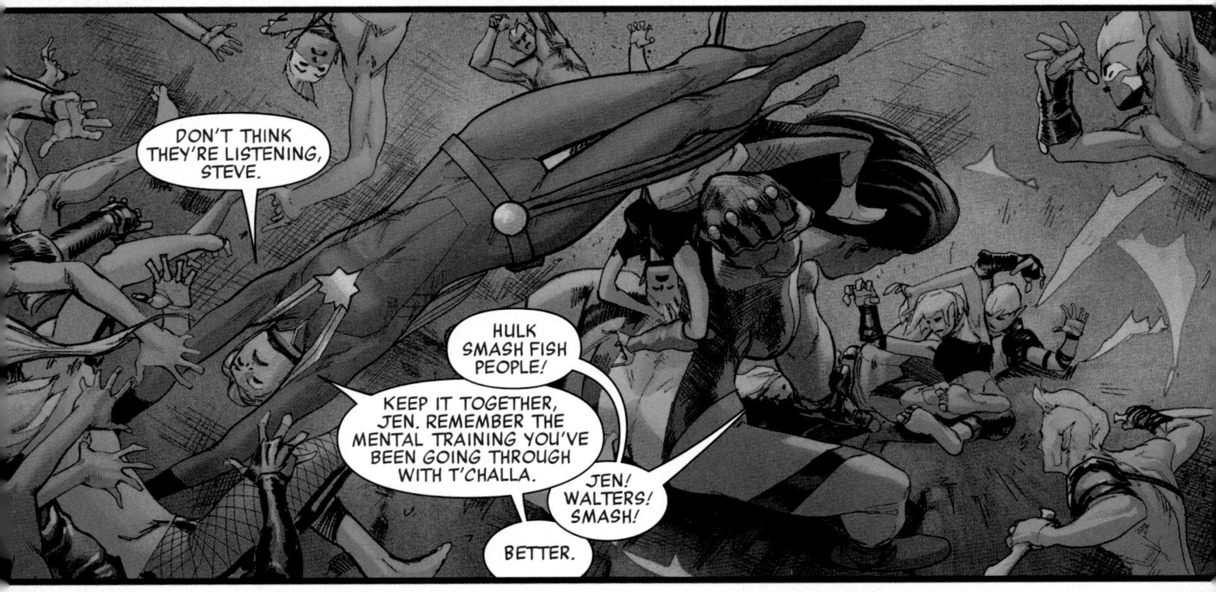
DON'T THINK THEY'RE LISTENING, STEVE.
HULK SMASH FISH PEOPLE!
KEEP IT TOGETHER, JEN. REMEMBER THE MENTAL TRAINING YOU'VE BEEN GOING THROUGH WITH T'CHALLA.
JEN! WALTERS! SMASH!
BETTER.

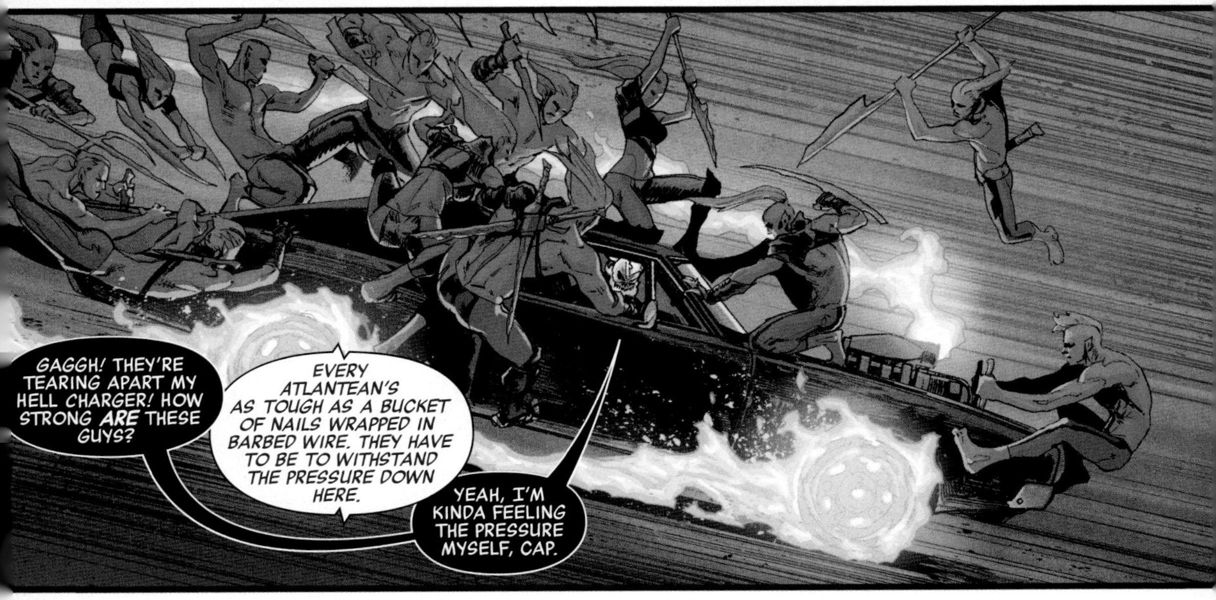
GAGGH! THEY'RE TEARING APART MY HELL CHARGER! HOW STRONG ARE THESE GUYS?
EVERY ATLANTEAN'S AS TOUGH AS A BUCKET OF NAILS WRAPPED IN BARBED WIRE. THEY HAVE TO BE TO WITHSTAND THE PRESSURE DOWN HERE.
YEAH, I'M KINDA FEELING THE PRESSURE MYSELF, CAP.

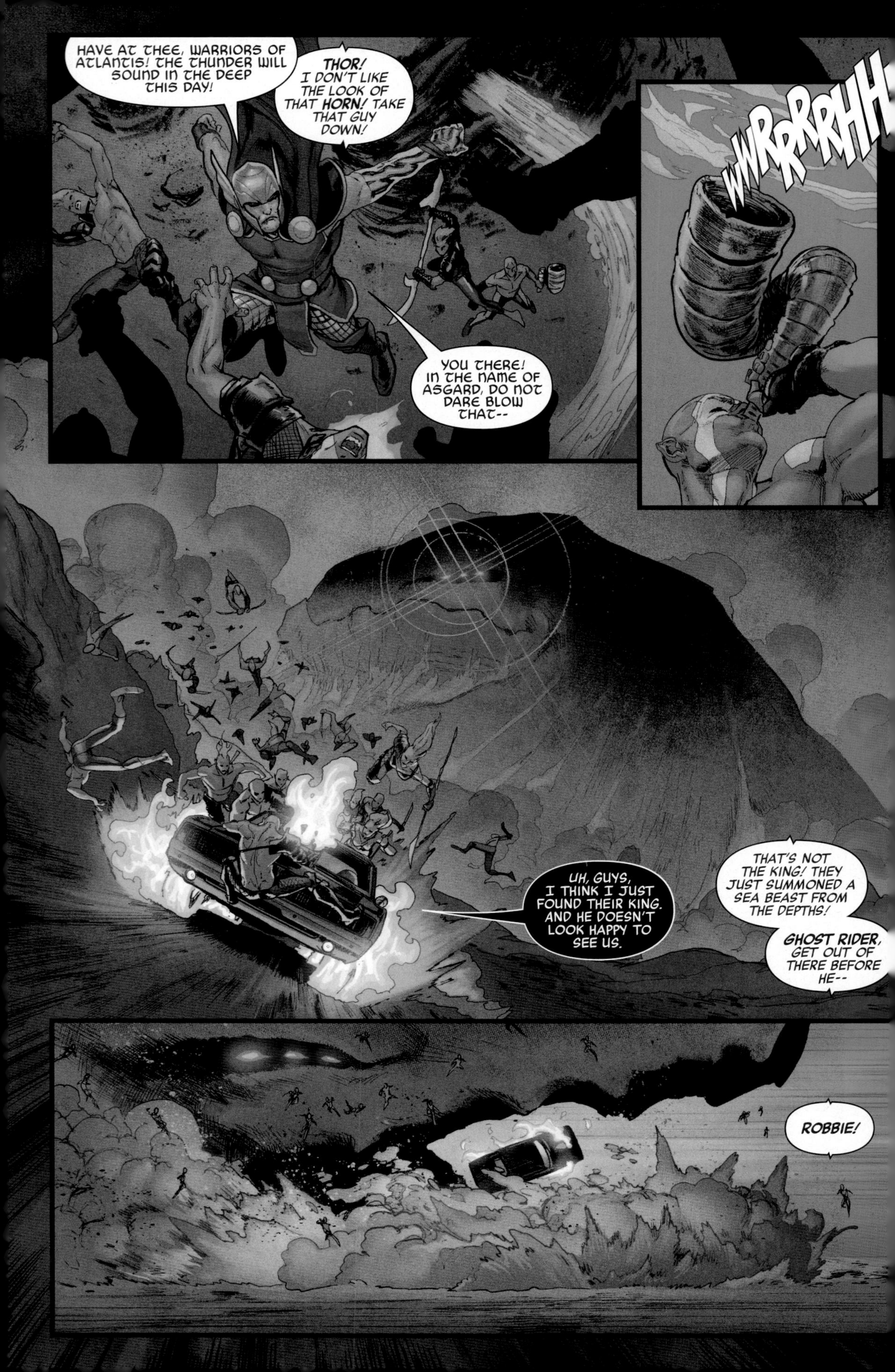
HAVE AT THEE, WARRIORS OF ATLANTIS! THE THUNDER WILL SOUND IN THE DEEP THIS DAY!
THOR! I DON'T LIKE THE LOOK OF THAT HORN! TAKE THAT GUY DOWN!
YOU THERE! IN THE NAME OF ASGARD, DO NOT DARE BLOW THAT--
WWRRRRHH
UH, GUYS, I THINK I JUST FOUND THEIR KING. AND HE DOESN'T LOOK HAPPY TO SEE US.
THAT'S NOT THE KING! THEY JUST SUMMONED A SEA BEAST FROM THE DEPTHS!
GHOST RIDER, GET OUT OF THERE BEFORE HE--
ROBBIE!

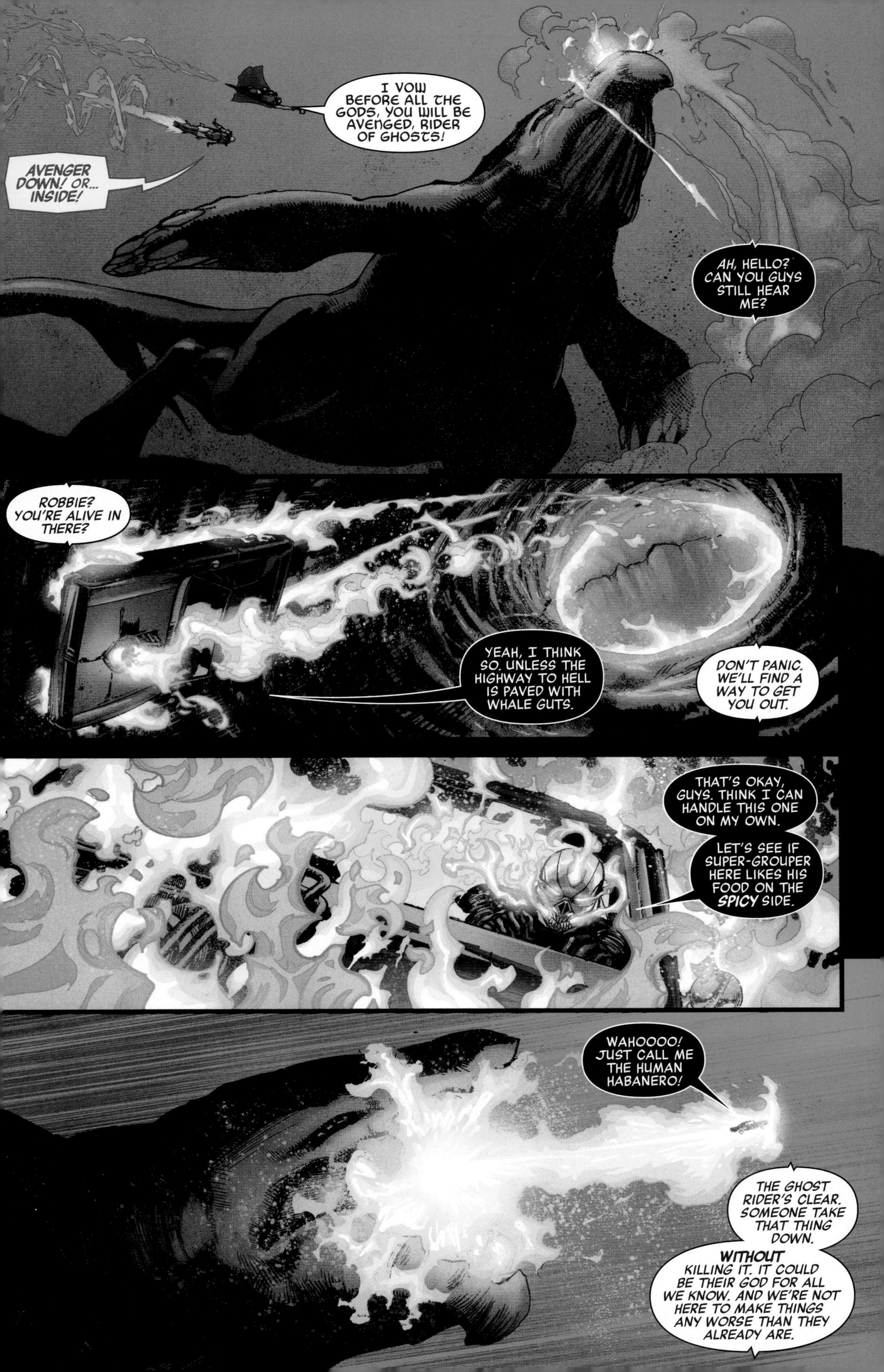
I VOW BEFORE ALL THE GODS, YOU WILL BE AVENGED, RIDER OF GHOSTS!
AVENGER DOWN! OR... INSIDE!
AH, HELLO? CAN YOU GUYS STILL HEAR ME?
ROBBIE? YOU'RE ALIVE IN THERE?
YEAH, I THINK SO. UNLESS THE HIGHWAY TO HELL IS PAVED WITH WHALE GUTS.
DON'T PANIC. WE'LL FIND A WAY TO GET YOU OUT.
THAT'S OKAY, GUYS. THINK I CAN HANDLE THIS ONE ON MY OWN.
LET'S SEE IF SUPER-GROUPER HERE LIKES HIS FOOD ON THE SPICY SIDE.
WAHOOOO! JUST CALL ME THE HUMAN HABANERO!
THE GHOST RIDER'S CLEAR. SOMEONE TAKE THAT THING DOWN.
WITHOUT KILLING IT. IT COULD BE THEIR GOD FOR ALL WE KNOW. AND WE'RE NOT HERE TO MAKE THINGS ANY WORSE THAN THEY ALREADY ARE.

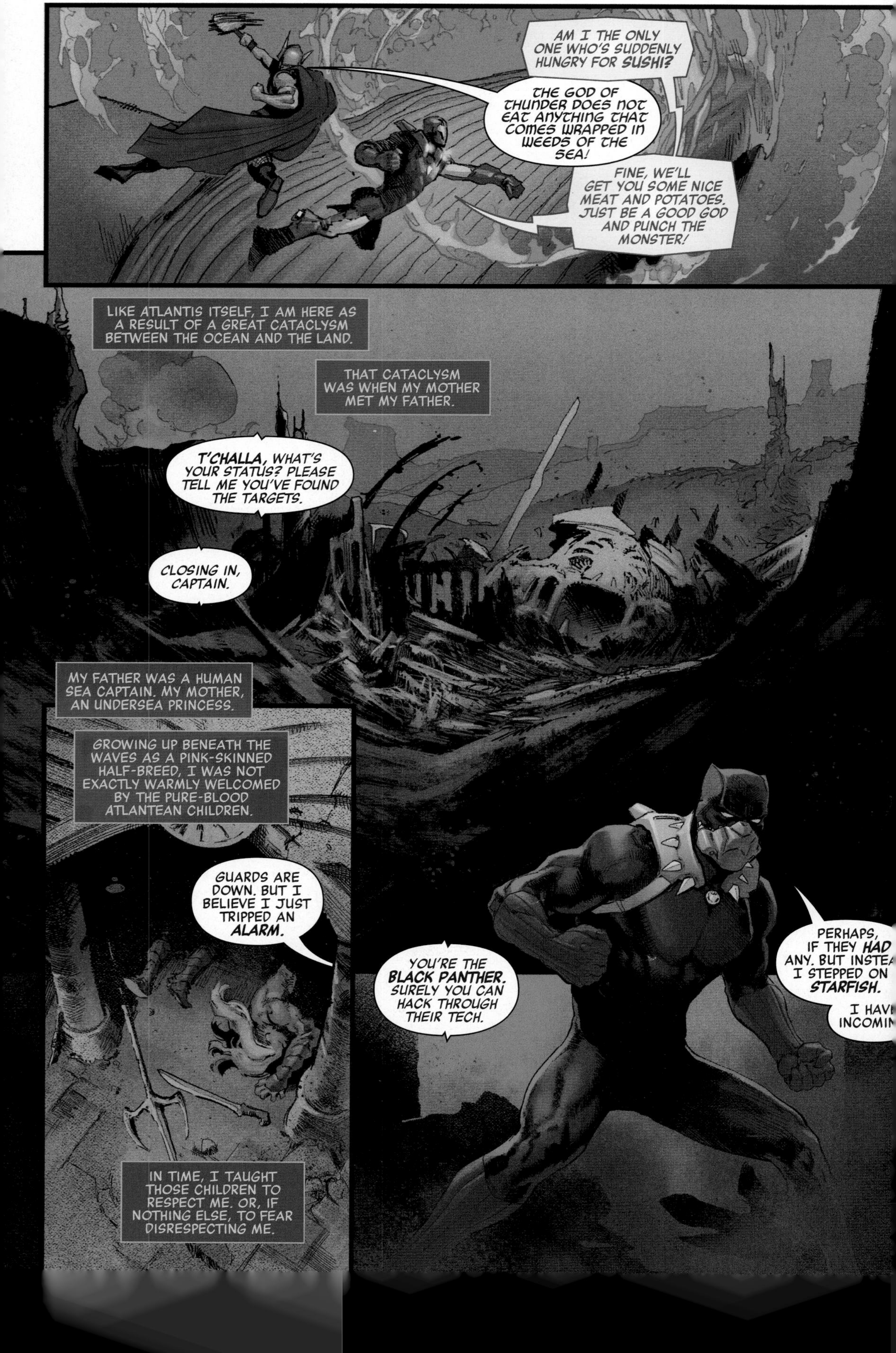
AM I THE ONLY ONE WHO'S SUDDENLY HUNGRY FOR SUSHI?
THE GOD OF THUNDER DOES NOT EAT ANYTHING THAT COMES WRAPPED IN WEEDS OF THE SEA!
FINE, WE'LL GET YOU SOME NICE MEAT AND POTATOES. JUST BE A GOOD GOD AND PUNCH THE MONSTER!
LIKE ATLANTIS ITSELF, I AM HERE AS A RESULT OF A GREAT CATACLYSM BETWEEN THE OCEAN AND THE LAND.
THAT CATACLYSM WAS WHEN MY MOTHER MET MY FATHER.
T'CHALLA, WHAT'S YOUR STATUS? PLEASE TELL ME YOU'VE FOUND THE TARGETS.
CLOSING IN, CAPTAIN.
MY FATHER WAS A HUMAN SEA CAPTAIN. MY MOTHER, AN UNDERSEA PRINCESS.
GROWING UP BENEATH THE WAVES AS A PINK-SKINNED HALF-BREED, I WAS NOT EXACTLY WARMLY WELCOMED BY THE PURE-BLOOD ATLANTEAN CHILDREN.
GUARDS ARE DOWN. BUT I BELIEVE I JUST TRIPPED AN ALARM.
YOU'RE THE BLACK PANTHER. SURELY YOU CAN HACK THROUGH THEIR TECH.
PERHAPS, IF THEY HAD ANY. BUT INSTEA I STEPPED ON STARFISH.
I HAV INCOMIN
IN TIME, I TAUGHT THOSE CHILDREN TO RESPECT ME. OR, IF NOTHING ELSE, TO FEAR DISRESPECTING ME.

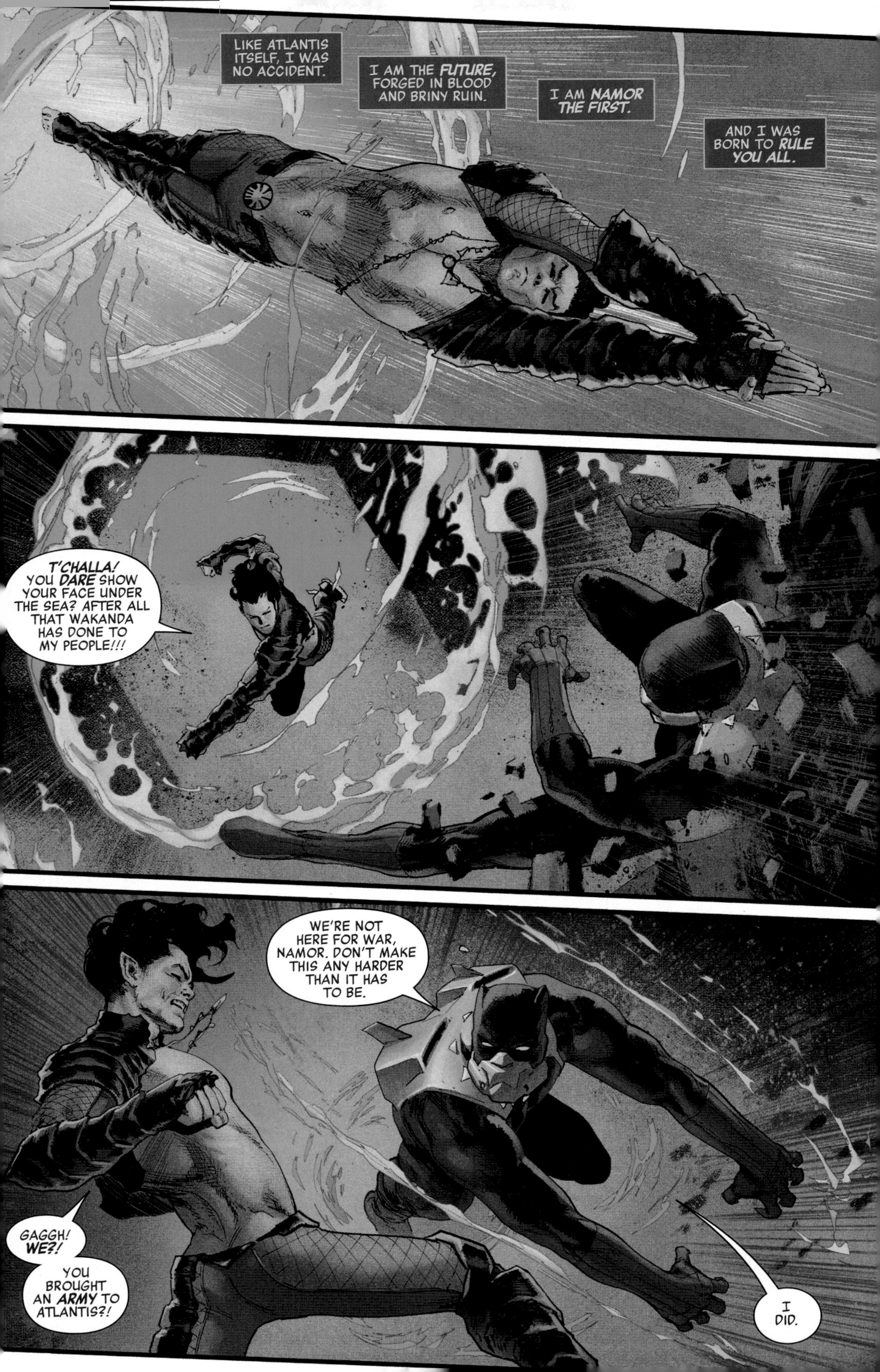
LIKE ATLANTIS ITSELF, I WAS NO ACCIDENT.
I AM THE FUTURE, FORGED IN BLOOD AND BRINY RUIN.
I AM NAMOR THE FIRST.
AND I WAS BORN TO RULE YOU ALL.
T'CHALLA! YOU DARE SHOW YOUR FACE UNDER THE SEA? AFTER ALL THAT WAKANDA HAS DONE TO MY PEOPLE!!!
WE'RE NOT HERE FOR WAR, NAMOR. DON'T MAKE THIS ANY HARDER THAN IT HAS TO BE.
GAGGH! WE?!
YOU BROUGHT AN ARMY TO ATLANTIS?!
I DID.

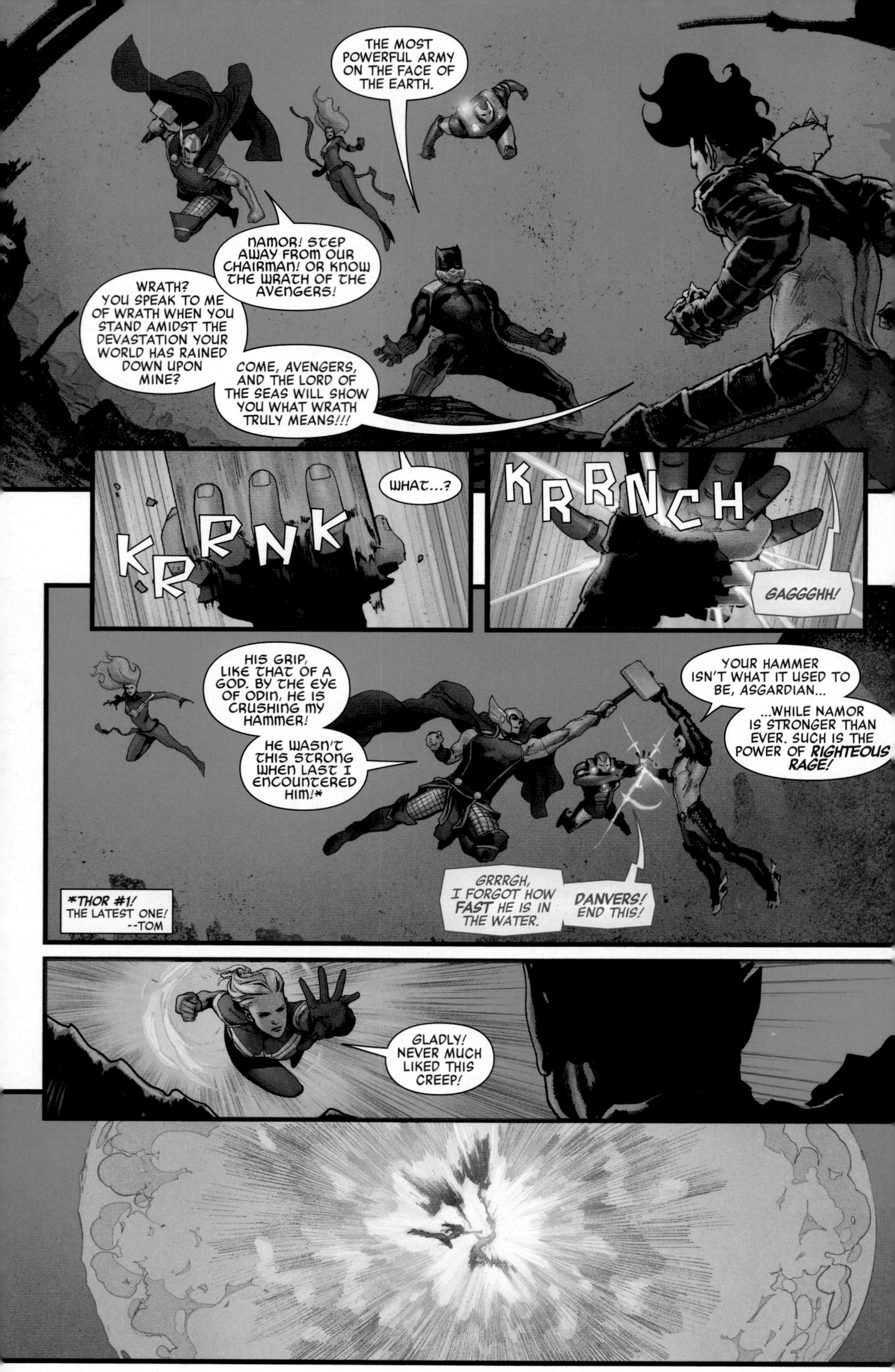
THE MOST POWERFUL ARMY ON THE FACE OF THE EARTH.
NAMOR! STEP AWAY FROM OUR CHAIRMAN! OR KNOW THE WRATH OF THE AVENGERS!
WRATH? YOU SPEAK TO ME OF WRATH WHEN YOU STAND AMIDST THE DEVASTATION YOUR WORLD HAS RAINED DOWN UPON MINE?
COME, AVENGERS, AND THE LORD OF THE SEAS WILL SHOW YOU WHAT WRATH TRULY MEANS!!!
WHAT...?
KRRNK
KRRNCH
GAGGGHH!
HIS GRIP, LIKE THAT OF A GOD. BY THE EYE OF ODIN, HE IS CRUSHING MY HAMMER!
HE WASN'T THIS STRONG WHEN LAST I ENCOUNTERED HIM!*
YOUR HAMMER ISN'T WHAT IT USED TO BE, ASGARDIAN...
...WHILE NAMOR IS STRONGER THAN EVER. SUCH IS THE POWER OF RIGHTEOUS RAGE!
*THOR #1! THE LATEST ONE! --TOM
GRRRGH, I FORGOT HOW FAST HE IS IN THE WATER.
DANVERS! END THIS!
GLADLY! NEVER MUCH LIKED THIS CREEP!

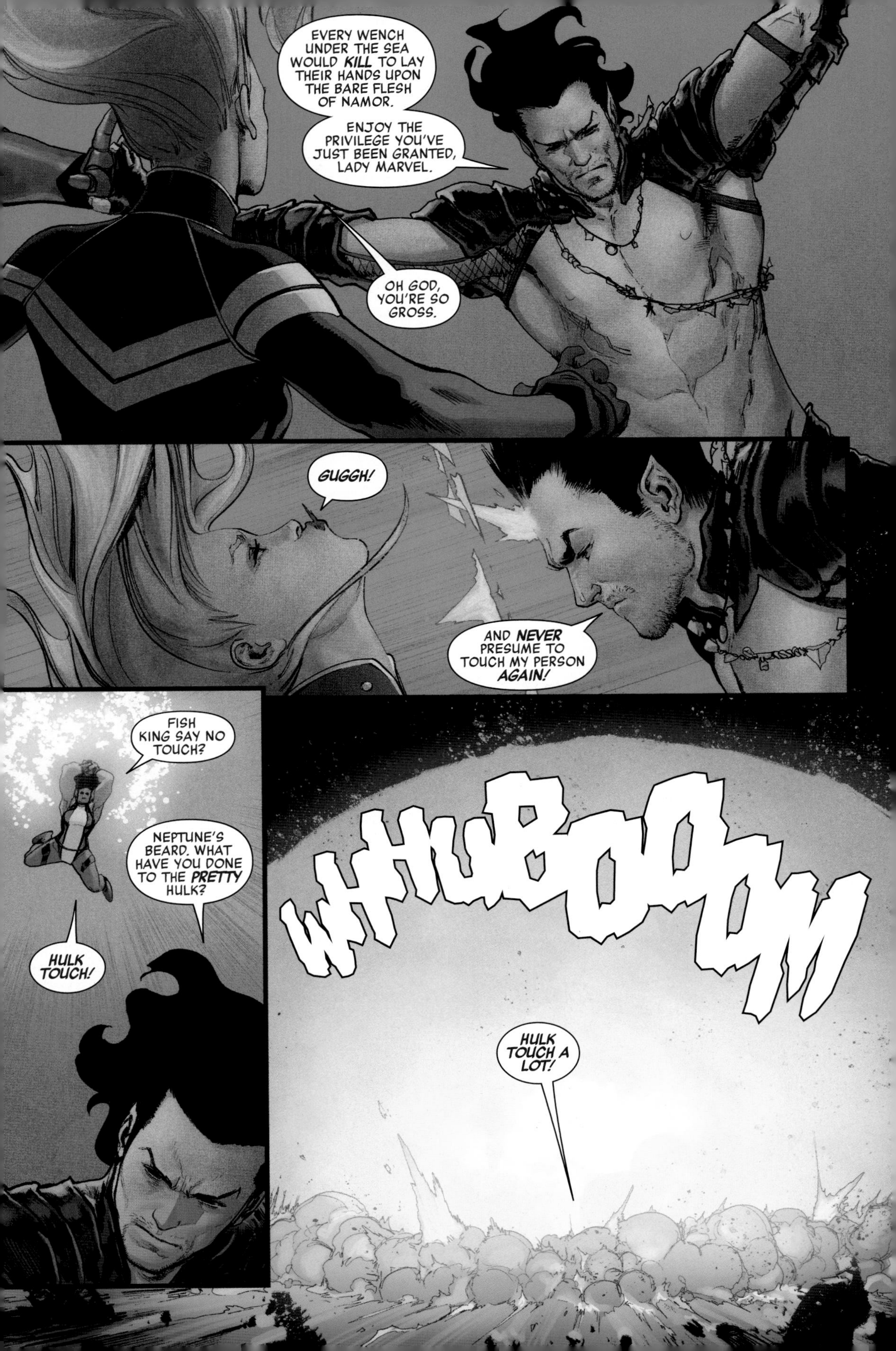

EVERY WENCH UNDER THE SEA WOULD KILL TO LAY THEIR HANDS UPON THE BARE FLESH OF NAMOR.
ENJOY THE PRIVILEGE YOU'VE JUST BEEN GRANTED, LADY MARVEL.
OH GOD, YOU'RE SO GROSS.
GUGGH!
AND NEVER PRESUME TO TOUCH MY PERSON AGAIN!
FISH KING SAY NO TOUCH?
NEPTUNE'S BEARD. WHAT HAVE YOU DONE TO THE PRETTY HULK?
HULK TOUCH!
WHUBOOOM
HULK TOUCH A LOT!

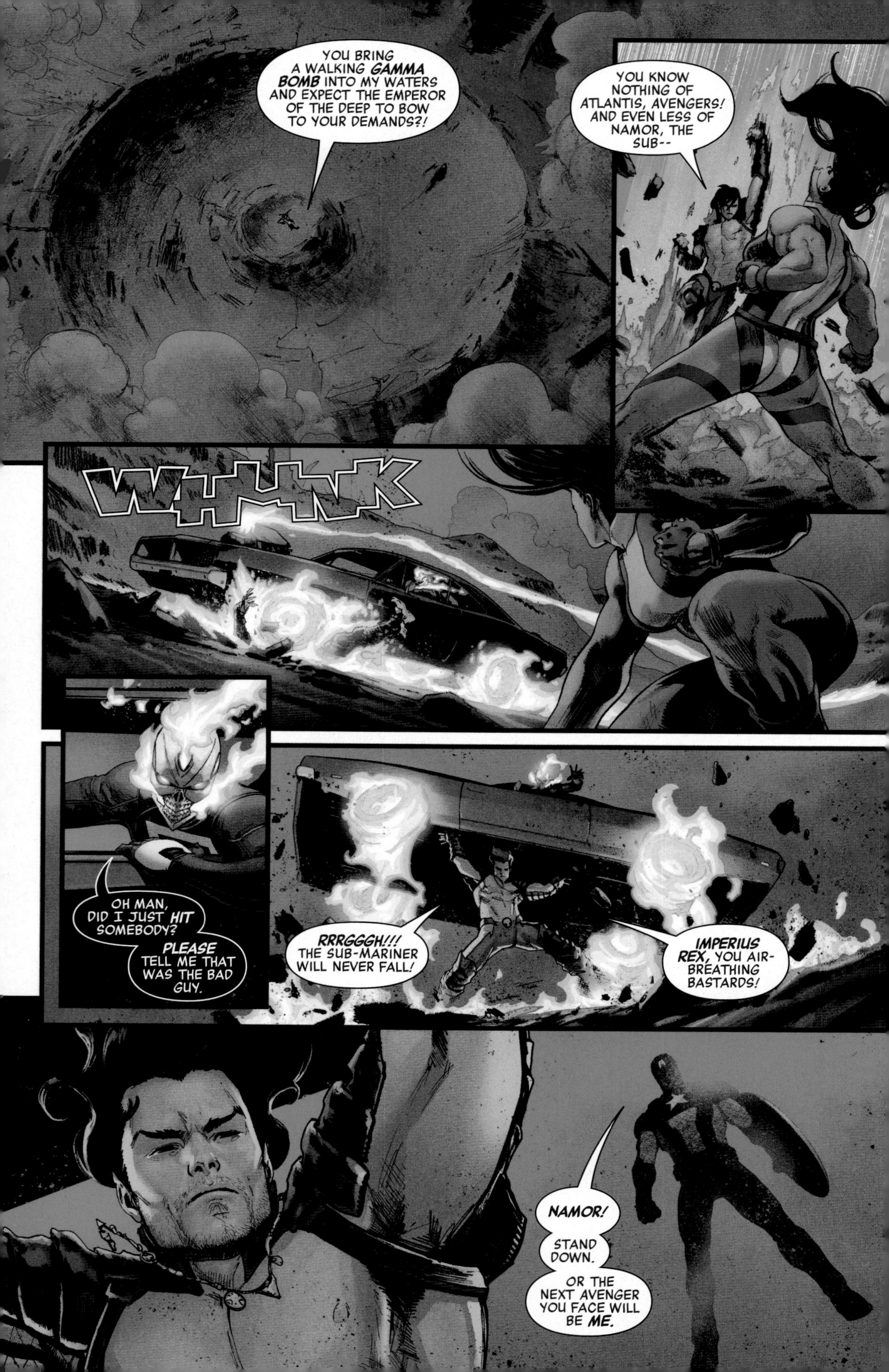
YOU BRING A WALKING GAMMA BOMB INTO MY WATERS AND EXPECT THE EMPEROR OF THE DEEP TO BOW TO YOUR DEMANDS?!
YOU KNOW NOTHING OF ATLANTIS, AVENGERS! AND EVEN LESS OF NAMOR, THE SUB--
WHHUNK
OH MAN, DID I JUST HIT SOMEBODY?
PLEASE TELL ME THAT WAS THE BAD GUY.
RRRGGGH!!! THE SUB-MARINER WILL NEVER FALL!
IMPERIUS REX, YOU AIR-BREATHING BASTARDS!
NAMOR!
STAND DOWN.
OR THE NEXT AVENGER YOU FACE WILL BE ME.

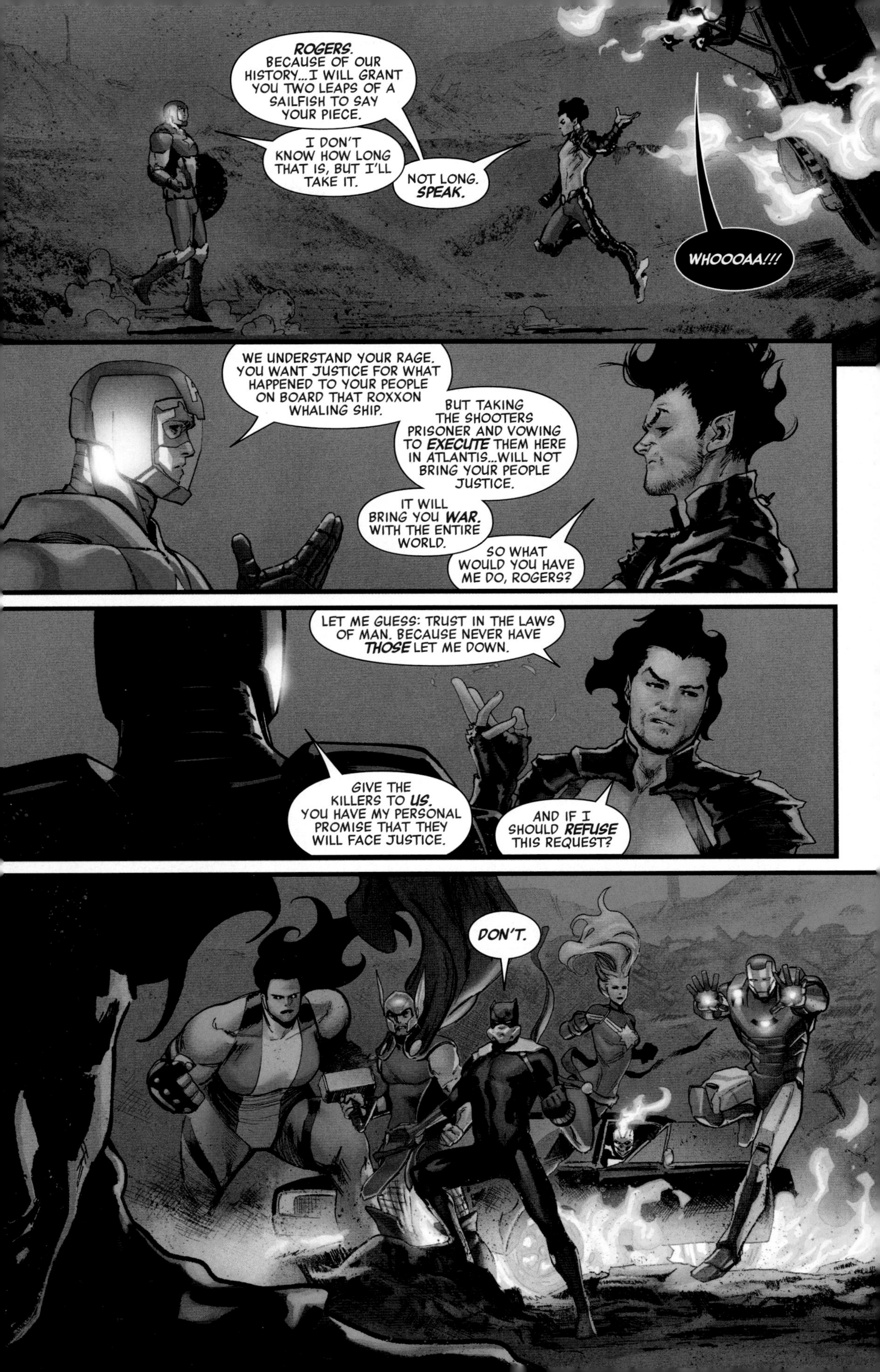
ROGERS. BECAUSE OF OUR HISTORY...I WILL GRANT YOU TWO LEAPS OF A SAILFISH TO SAY YOUR PIECE.
I DON'T KNOW HOW LONG THAT IS, BUT I'LL TAKE IT.
NOT LONG. SPEAK.
WHOOOAA!!!
WE UNDERSTAND YOUR RAGE. YOU WANT JUSTICE FOR WHAT HAPPENED TO YOUR PEOPLE ON BOARD THAT ROXXON WHALING SHIP.
BUT TAKING THE SHOOTERS PRISONER AND VOWING TO EXECUTE THEM HERE IN ATLANTIS...WILL NOT BRING YOUR PEOPLE JUSTICE.
IT WILL BRING YOU WAR. WITH THE ENTIRE WORLD.
SO WHAT WOULD YOU HAVE ME DO, ROGERS?
LET ME GUESS: TRUST IN THE LAWS OF MAN. BECAUSE NEVER HAVE THOSE LET ME DOWN.
GIVE THE KILLERS TO US. YOU HAVE MY PERSONAL PROMISE THAT THEY WILL FACE JUSTICE.
AND IF I SHOULD REFUSE THIS REQUEST?
DON'T.

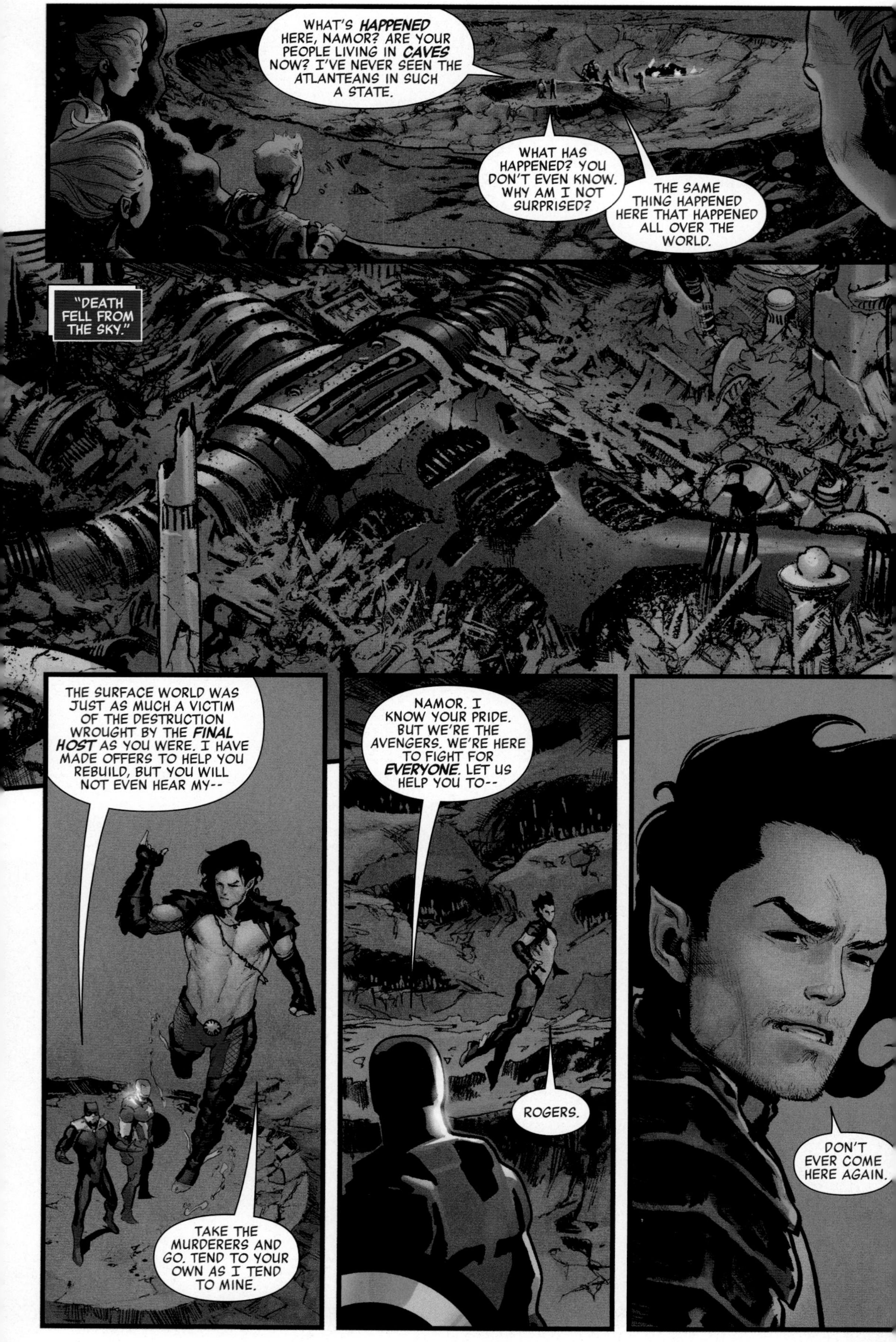
WHAT'S HAPPENED HERE, NAMOR? ARE YOUR PEOPLE LIVING IN CAVES NOW? I'VE NEVER SEEN THE ATLANTEANS IN SUCH A STATE.
WHAT HAS HAPPENED? YOU DON'T EVEN KNOW. WHY AM I NOT SURPRISED?
THE SAME THING HAPPENED HERE THAT HAPPENED ALL OVER THE WORLD.
"DEATH FELL FROM THE SKY."
THE SURFACE WORLD WAS JUST AS MUCH A VICTIM OF THE DESTRUCTION WROUGHT BY THE FINAL HOST AS YOU WERE. I HAVE MADE OFFERS TO HELP YOU REBUILD, BUT YOU WILL NOT EVEN HEAR MY--
TAKE THE MURDERERS AND GO. TEND TO YOUR OWN AS I TEND TO MINE.
NAMOR. I KNOW YOUR PRIDE. BUT WE'RE THE AVENGERS. WE'RE HERE TO FIGHT FOR EVERYONE. LET US HELP YOU TO--
ROGERS.
DON'T EVER COME HERE AGAIN.

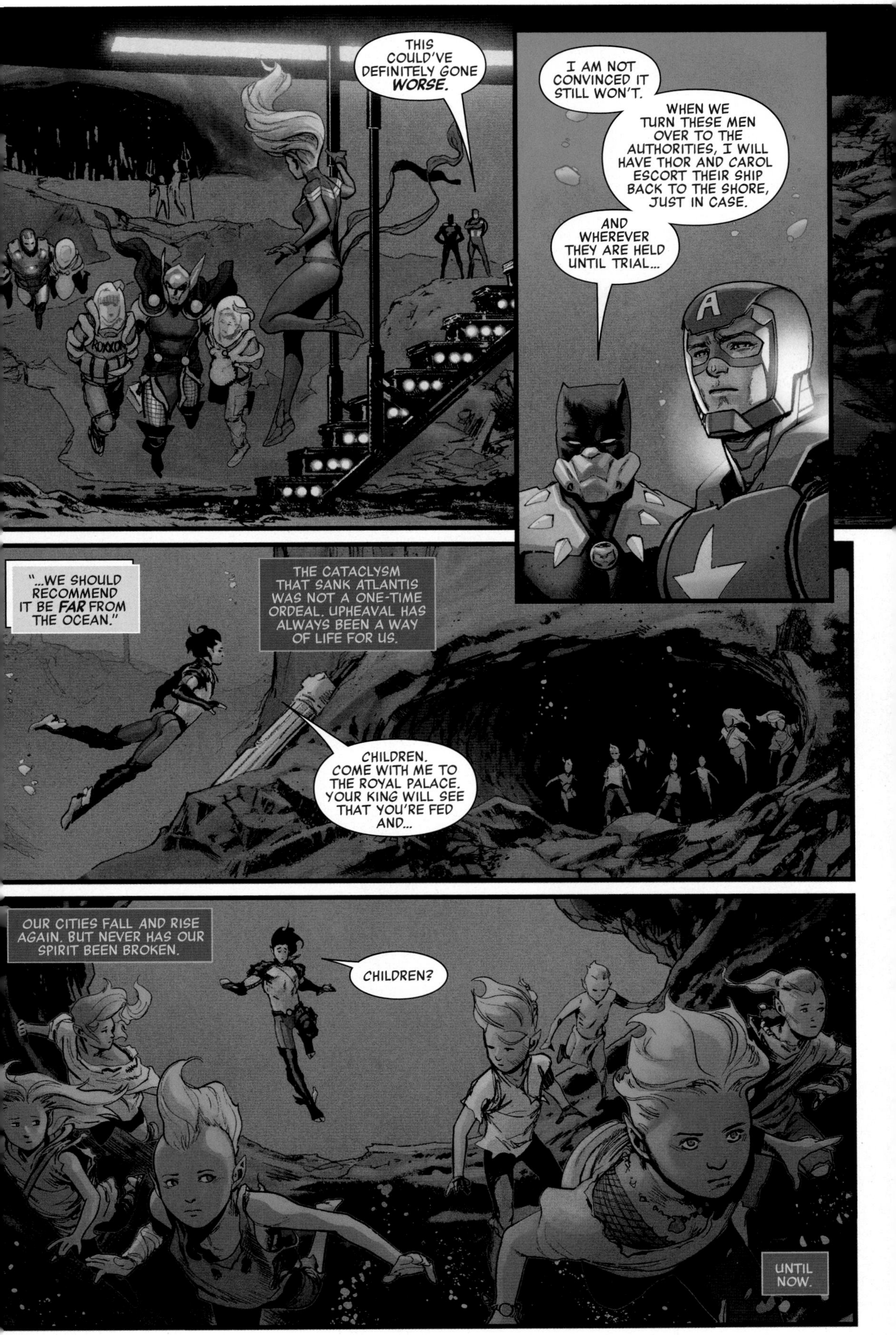

THIS COULD'VE DEFINITELY GONE WORSE.
I AM NOT CONVINCED IT STILL WON'T.
WHEN WE TURN THESE MEN OVER TO THE AUTHORITIES, I WILL HAVE THOR AND CAROL ESCORT THEIR SHIP BACK TO THE SHORE, JUST IN CASE.
AND WHEREVER THEY ARE HELD UNTIL TRIAL...
"...WE SHOULD RECOMMEND IT BE FAR FROM THE OCEAN."
THE CATACLYSM THAT SANK ATLANTIS WAS NOT A ONE-TIME ORDEAL. UPHEAVAL HAS ALWAYS BEEN A WAY OF LIFE FOR US.
CHILDREN. COME WITH ME TO THE ROYAL PALACE. YOUR KING WILL SEE THAT YOU'RE FED AND...
OUR CITIES FALL AND RISE AGAIN. BUT NEVER HAS OUR SPIRIT BEEN BROKEN.
CHILDREN?
UNTIL NOW.

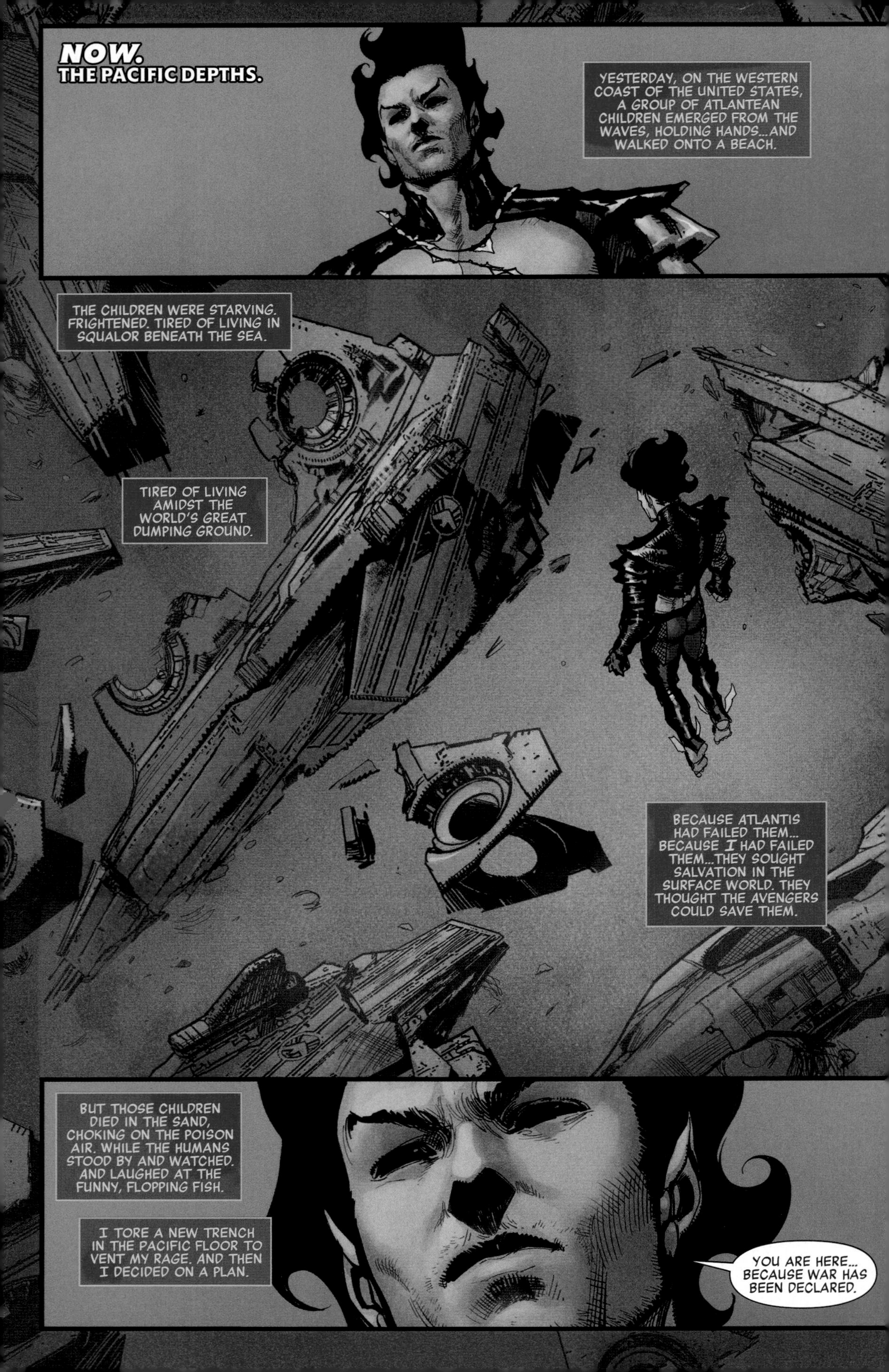
NOW.
THE PACIFIC DEPTHS.
YESTERDAY, ON THE WESTERN COAST OF THE UNITED STATES, A GROUP OF ATLANTEAN CHILDREN EMERGED FROM THE WAVES, HOLDING HANDS...AND WALKED ONTO A BEACH.
THE CHILDREN WERE STARVING. FRIGHTENED. TIRED OF LIVING IN SQUALOR BENEATH THE SEA.
TIRED OF LIVING AMIDST THE WORLD'S GREAT DUMPING GROUND.
BECAUSE ATLANTIS HAD FAILED THEM... BECAUSE I HAD FAILED THEM...THEY SOUGHT SALVATION IN THE SURFACE WORLD. THEY THOUGHT THE AVENGERS COULD SAVE THEM.
BUT THOSE CHILDREN DIED IN THE SAND, CHOKING ON THE POISON AIR. WHILE THE HUMANS STOOD BY AND WATCHED. AND LAUGHED AT THE FUNNY, FLOPPING FISH.
I TORE A NEW TRENCH IN THE PACIFIC FLOOR TO VENT MY RAGE. AND THEN I DECIDED ON A PLAN.
YOU ARE HERE... BECAUSE WAR HAS BEEN DECLARED.

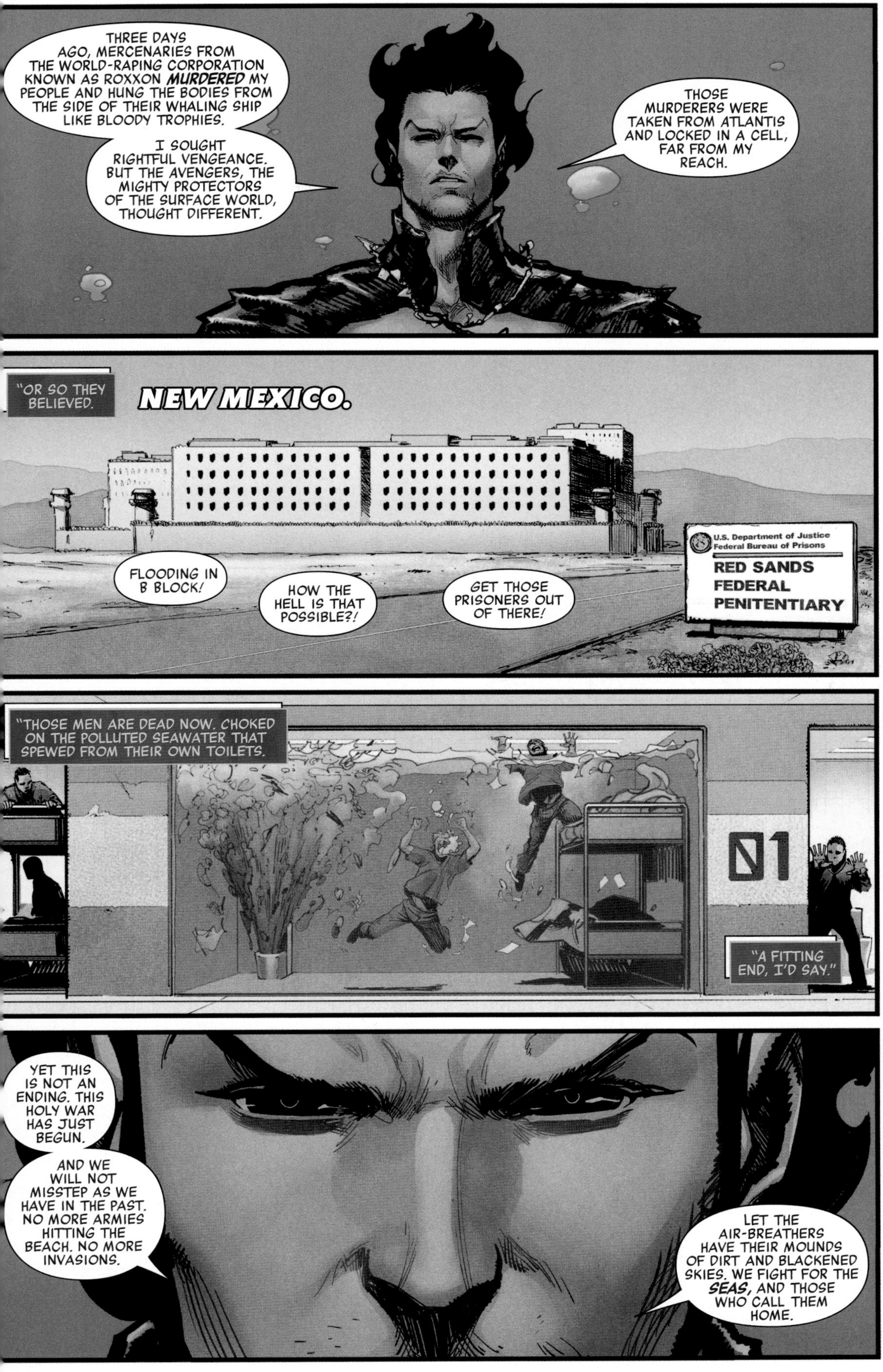
THREE DAYS AGO, MERCENARIES FROM THE WORLD-RAPING CORPORATION KNOWN AS ROXXON MURDERED MY PEOPLE AND HUNG THE BODIES FROM THE SIDE OF THEIR WHALING SHIP LIKE BLOODY TROPHIES.
I SOUGHT RIGHTFUL VENGEANCE. BUT THE AVENGERS, THE MIGHTY PROTECTORS OF THE SURFACE WORLD, THOUGHT DIFFERENT.
THOSE MURDERERS WERE TAKEN FROM ATLANTIS AND LOCKED IN A CELL, FAR FROM MY REACH.
"OR SO THEY BELIEVED.
NEW MEXICO.
U.S. Department of Justice
Federal Bureau of Prisons
RED SANDS FEDERAL PENITENTIARY
FLOODING IN B BLOCK!
HOW THE HELL IS THAT POSSIBLE?!
GET THOSE PRISONERS OUT OF THERE!
"THOSE MEN ARE DEAD NOW. CHOKED ON THE POLLUTED SEAWATER THAT SPEWED FROM THEIR OWN TOILETS.
01
"A FITTING END, I'D SAY."
YET THIS IS NOT AN ENDING. THIS HOLY WAR HAS JUST BEGUN.
AND WE WILL NOT MISSTEP AS WE HAVE IN THE PAST. NO MORE ARMIES HITTING THE BEACH. NO MORE INVASIONS.
LET THE AIR-BREATHERS HAVE THEIR MOUNDS OF DIRT AND BLACKENED SKIES. WE FIGHT FOR THE SEAS, AND THOSE WHO CALL THEM HOME.

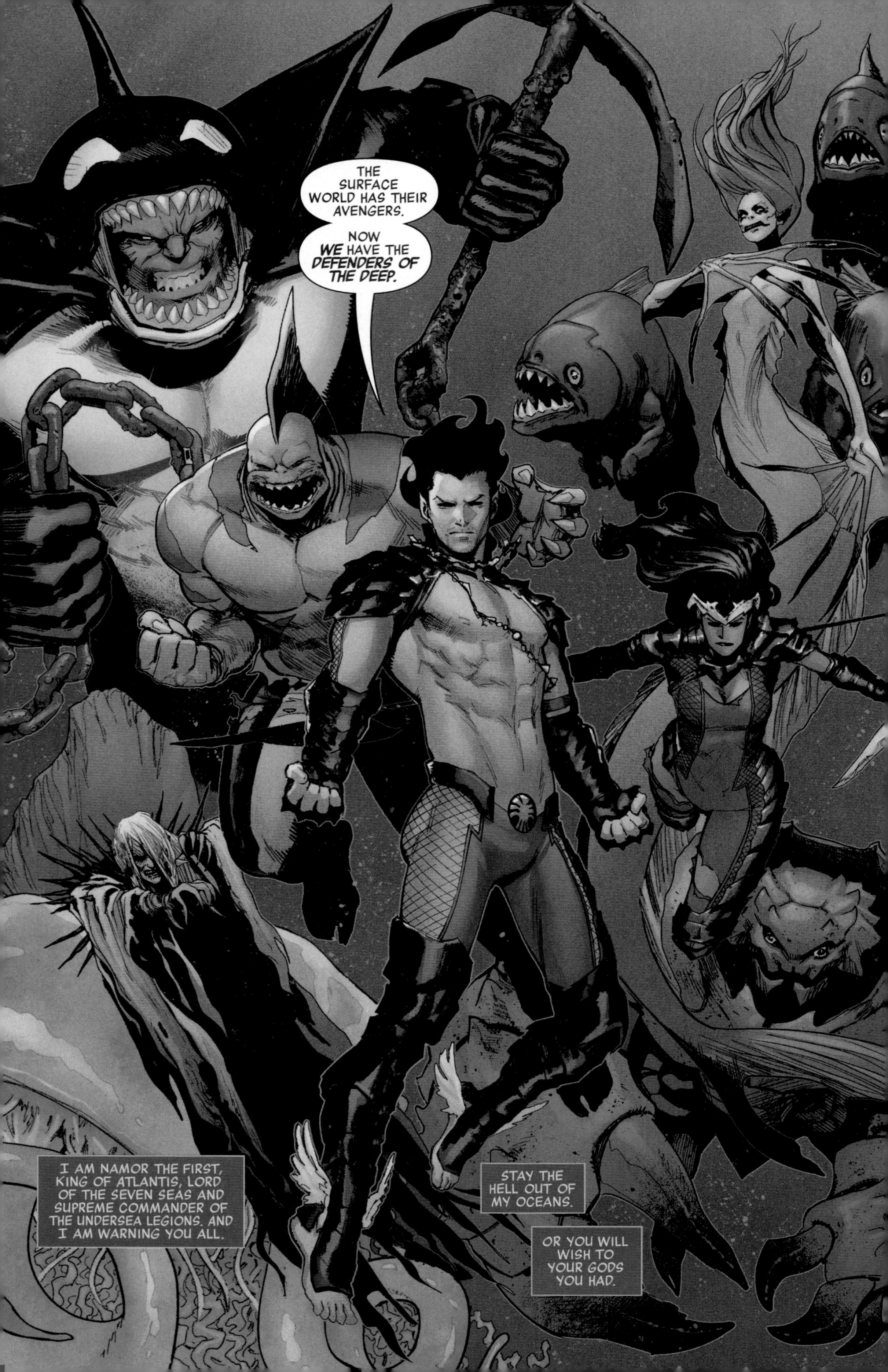
THE SURFACE WORLD HAS THEIR AVENGERS.
NOW WE HAVE THE DEFENDERS OF THE DEEP.
I AM NAMOR THE FIRST, KING OF ATLANTIS, LORD OF THE SEVEN SEAS AND SUPREME COMMANDER OF THE UNDERSEA LEGIONS. AND I AM WARNING YOU ALL.
STAY THE HELL OUT OF MY OCEANS.
OR YOU WILL WISH TO YOUR GODS YOU HAD.

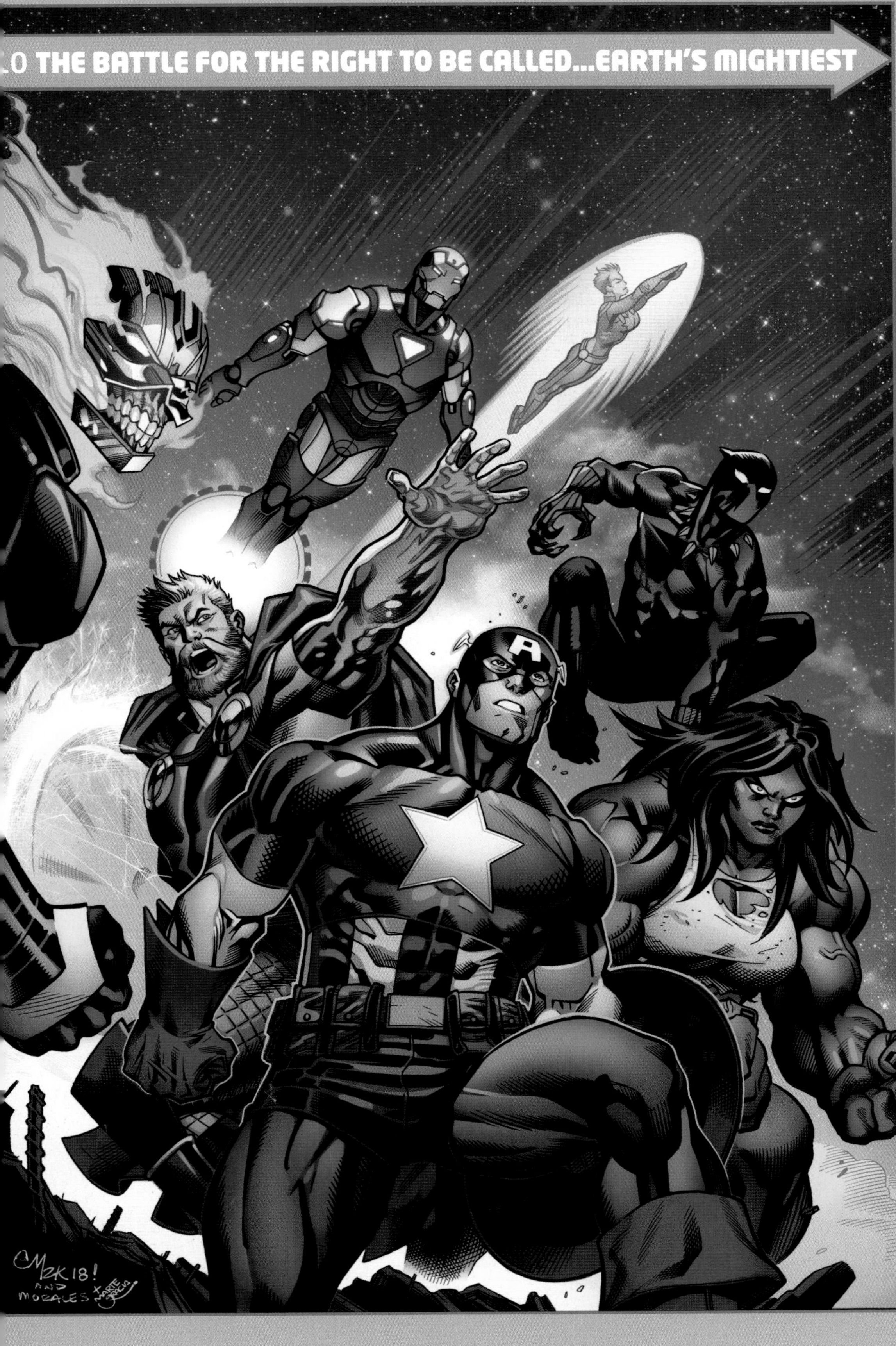
O THE BATTLE FOR THE RIGHT TO BE CALLED...EARTH'S MIGHTIEST

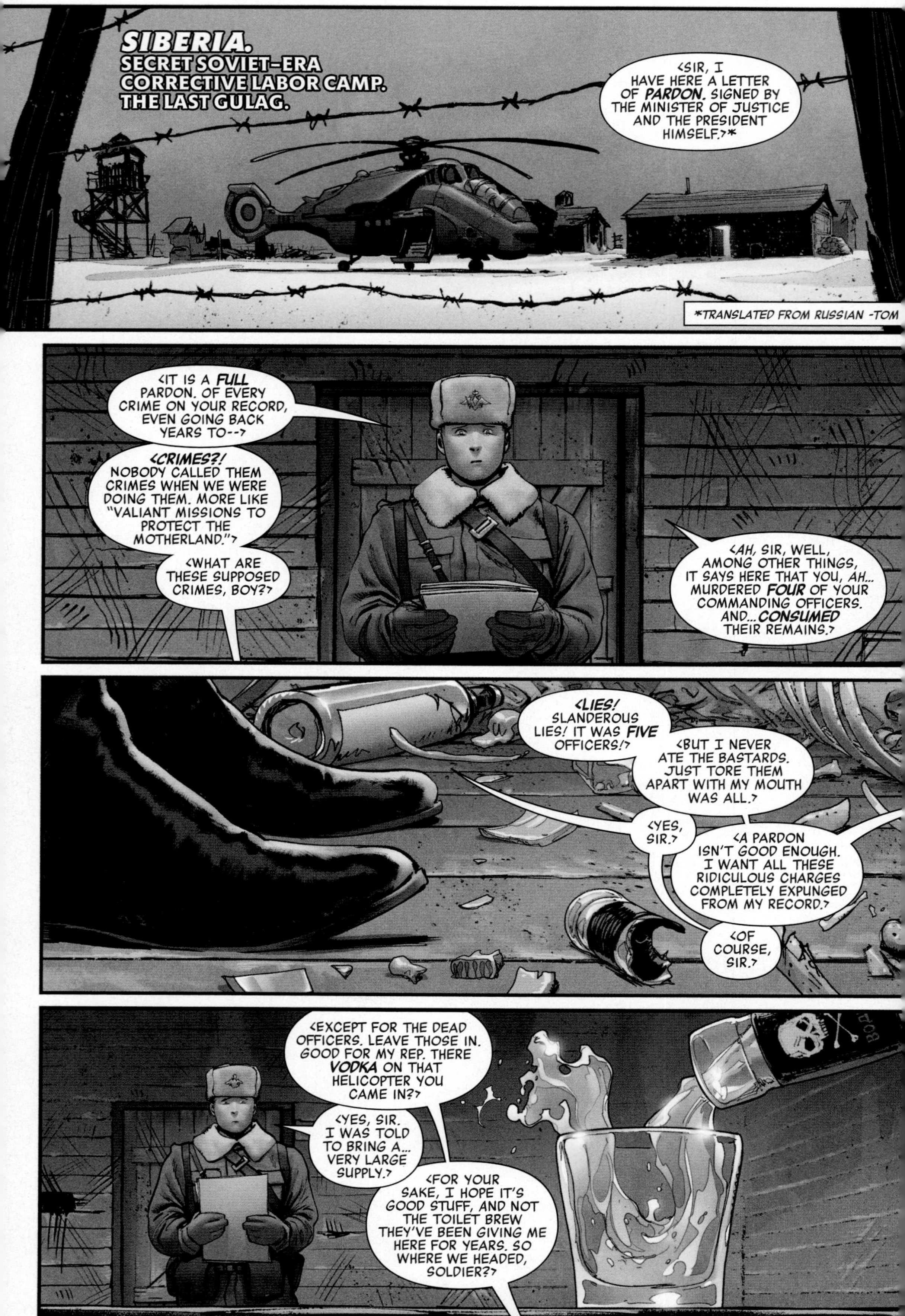
SIBERIA.
SECRET SOVIET-ERA CORRECTIVE LABOR CAMP. THE LAST GULAG.
<SIR, I HAVE HERE A LETTER OF PARDON. SIGNED BY THE MINISTER OF JUSTICE AND THE PRESIDENT HIMSELF.>*
*TRANSLATED FROM RUSSIAN -TOM
<IT IS A FULL PARDON. OF EVERY CRIME ON YOUR RECORD, EVEN GOING BACK YEARS TO-->
<CRIMES?! NOBODY CALLED THEM CRIMES WHEN WE WERE DOING THEM. MORE LIKE "VALIANT MISSIONS TO PROTECT THE MOTHERLAND.">
<WHAT ARE THESE SUPPOSED CRIMES, BOY?>
<AH, SIR, WELL, AMONG OTHER THINGS, IT SAYS HERE THAT YOU, AH... MURDERED FOUR OF YOUR COMMANDING OFFICERS. AND... CONSUMED THEIR REMAINS.>
<LIES! SLANDEROUS LIES! IT WAS FIVE OFFICERS!>
<BUT I NEVER ATE THE BASTARDS. JUST TORE THEM APART WITH MY MOUTH WAS ALL.>
<YES, SIR.>
<A PARDON ISN'T GOOD ENOUGH. I WANT ALL THESE RIDICULOUS CHARGES COMPLETELY EXPUNGED FROM MY RECORD.>
<OF COURSE, SIR.>
<EXCEPT FOR THE DEAD OFFICERS. LEAVE THOSE IN. GOOD FOR MY REP. THERE VODKA ON THAT HELICOPTER YOU CAME IN?>
<YES, SIR. I WAS TOLD TO BRING A... VERY LARGE SUPPLY.>
<FOR YOUR SAKE, I HOPE IT'S GOOD STUFF, AND NOT THE TOILET BREW THEY'VE BEEN GIVING ME HERE FOR YEARS. SO WHERE WE HEADED, SOLDIER?>

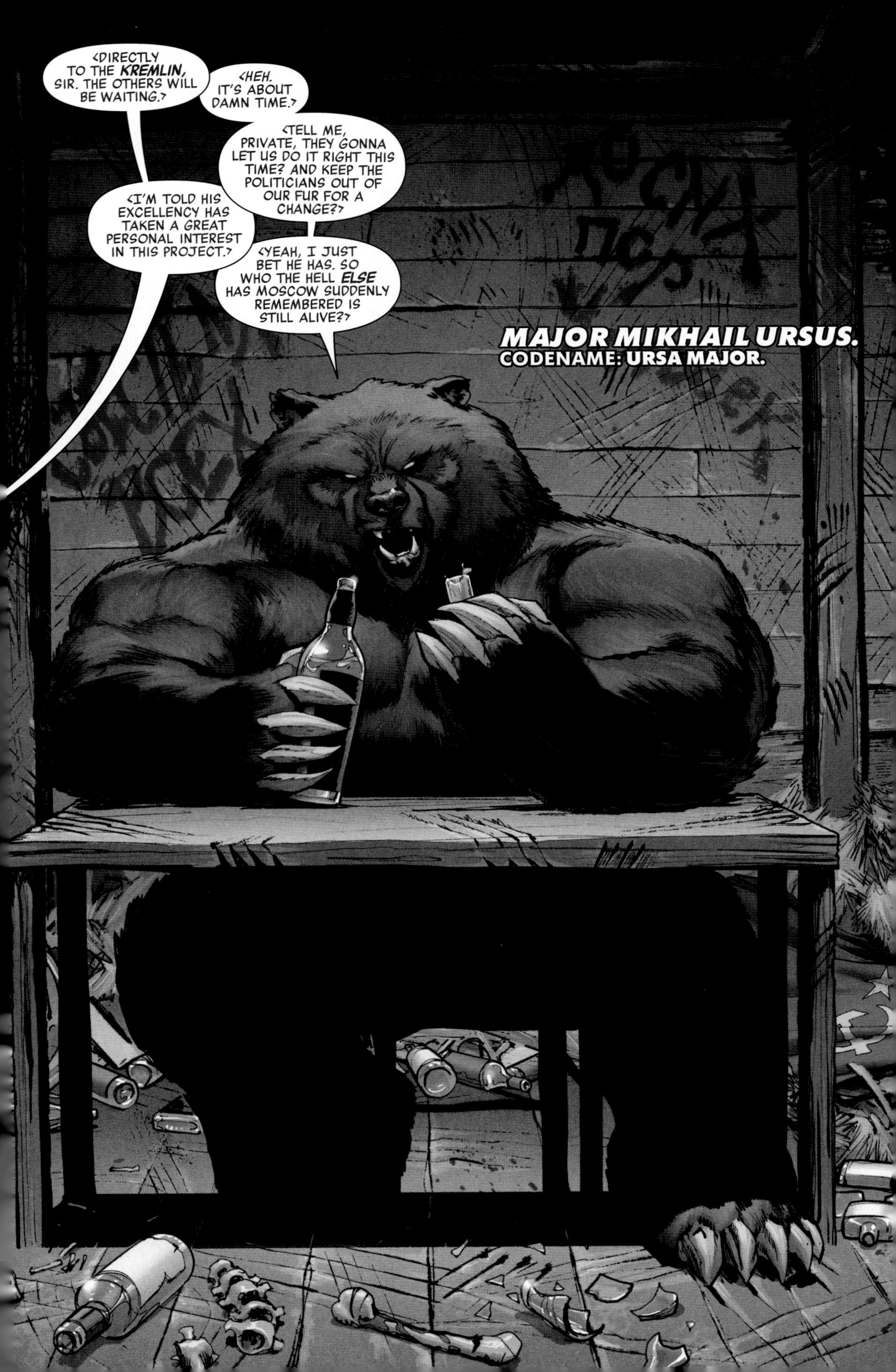
<DIRECTLY TO THE KREMLIN, SIR. THE OTHERS WILL BE WAITING.>
<HEH. IT'S ABOUT DAMN TIME.>
<TELL ME, PRIVATE, THEY GONNA LET US DO IT RIGHT THIS TIME? AND KEEP THE POLITICIANS OUT OF OUR FUR FOR A CHANGE?>
<I'M TOLD HIS EXCELLENCY HAS TAKEN A GREAT PERSONAL INTEREST IN THIS PROJECT.>
<YEAH, I JUST BET HE HAS. SO WHO THE HELL ELSE HAS MOSCOW SUDDENLY REMEMBERED IS STILL ALIVE?>
MAJOR MIKHAIL URSUS.
CODENAME: URSA MAJOR.

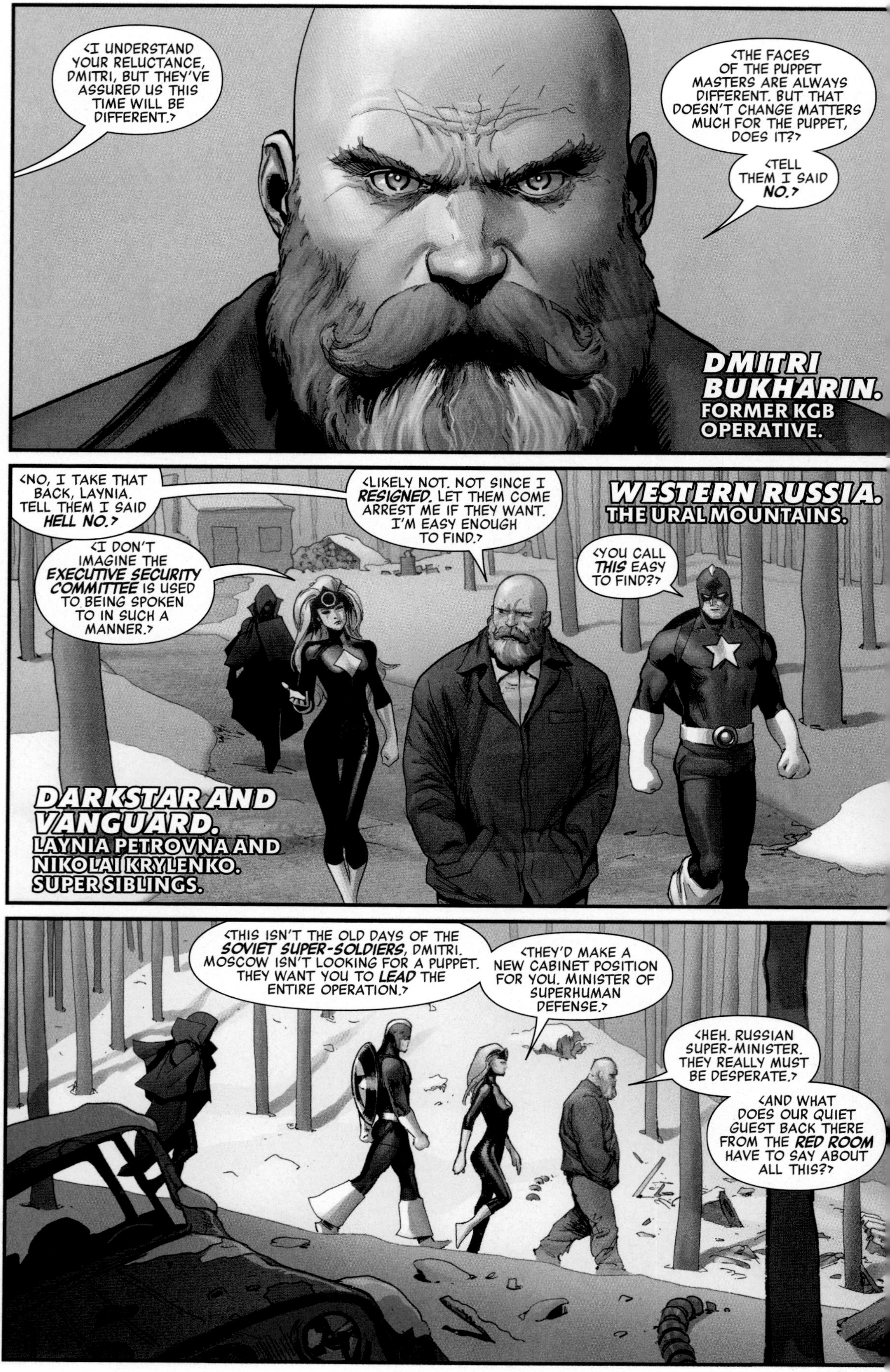
<I UNDERSTAND YOUR RELUCTANCE, DMITRI, BUT THEY'VE ASSURED US THIS TIME WILL BE DIFFERENT.>
<THE FACES OF THE PUPPET MASTERS ARE ALWAYS DIFFERENT. BUT THAT DOESN'T CHANGE MATTERS MUCH FOR THE PUPPET, DOES IT?>
<TELL THEM I SAID NO.>
DMITRI BUKHARIN. FORMER KGB OPERATIVE.
WESTERN RUSSIA. THE URAL MOUNTAINS.
<NO, I TAKE THAT BACK, LAYNIA. TELL THEM I SAID HELL NO.>
<I DON'T IMAGINE THE EXECUTIVE SECURITY COMMITTEE IS USED TO BEING SPOKEN TO IN SUCH A MANNER.>
<LIKELY NOT. NOT SINCE I RESIGNED. LET THEM COME ARREST ME IF THEY WANT. I'M EASY ENOUGH TO FIND.>
<YOU CALL THIS EASY TO FIND?>
DARKSTAR AND VANGUARD. LAYNIA PETROVNA AND NIKOLAI KRYLENKO. SUPER SIBLINGS.
<THIS ISN'T THE OLD DAYS OF THE SOVIET SUPER-SOLDIERS, DMITRI. MOSCOW ISN'T LOOKING FOR A PUPPET. THEY WANT YOU TO LEAD THE ENTIRE OPERATION.>
<THEY'D MAKE A NEW CABINET POSITION FOR YOU. MINISTER OF SUPERHUMAN DEFENSE.>
<HEH. RUSSIAN SUPER-MINISTER. THEY REALLY MUST BE DESPERATE.>
<AND WHAT DOES OUR QUIET GUEST BACK THERE FROM THE RED ROOM HAVE TO SAY ABOUT ALL THIS?>

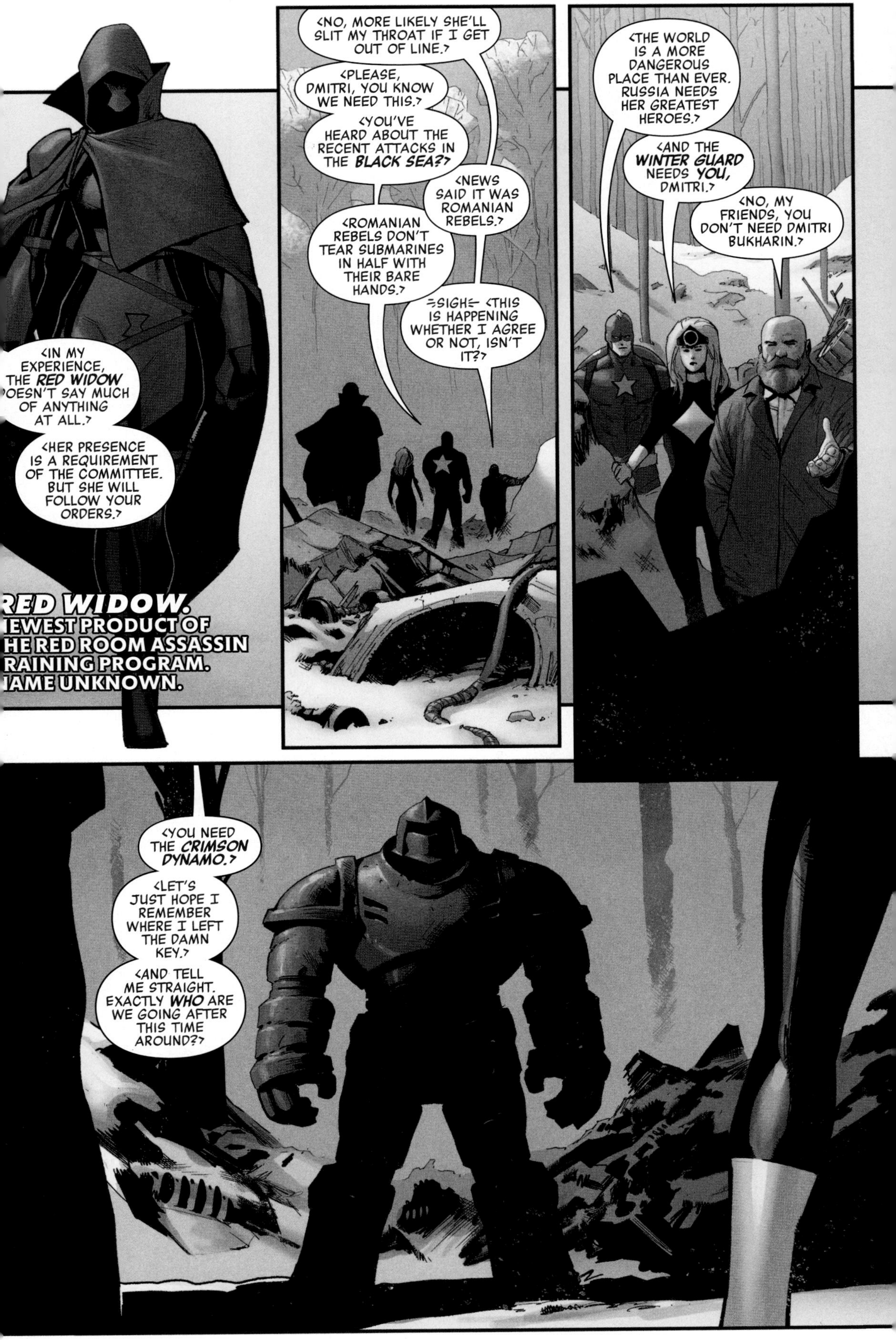

<IN MY EXPERIENCE, THE RED WIDOW OESN'T SAY MUCH OF ANYTHING AT ALL.>
<HER PRESENCE IS A REQUIREMENT OF THE COMMITTEE. BUT SHE WILL FOLLOW YOUR ORDERS.>
RED WIDOW. IEWEST PRODUCT OF HE RED ROOM ASSASSIN RAINING PROGRAM. IAME UNKNOWN.
<NO, MORE LIKELY SHE'LL SLIT MY THROAT IF I GET OUT OF LINE.>
<PLEASE, DMITRI, YOU KNOW WE NEED THIS.>
<YOU'VE HEARD ABOUT THE RECENT ATTACKS IN THE BLACK SEA?>
<NEWS SAID IT WAS ROMANIAN REBELS.>
<ROMANIAN REBELS DON'T TEAR SUBMARINES IN HALF WITH THEIR BARE HANDS.>
=SIGH= <THIS IS HAPPENING WHETHER I AGREE OR NOT, ISN'T IT?>
<THE WORLD IS A MORE DANGEROUS PLACE THAN EVER. RUSSIA NEEDS HER GREATEST HEROES.>
<AND THE WINTER GUARD NEEDS YOU, DMITRI.>
<NO, MY FRIENDS, YOU DON'T NEED DMITRI BUKHARIN.>
<YOU NEED THE CRIMSON DYNAMO.>
<LET'S JUST HOPE I REMEMBER WHERE I LEFT THE DAMN KEY.>
<AND TELL ME STRAIGHT. EXACTLY WHO ARE WE GOING AFTER THIS TIME AROUND?>

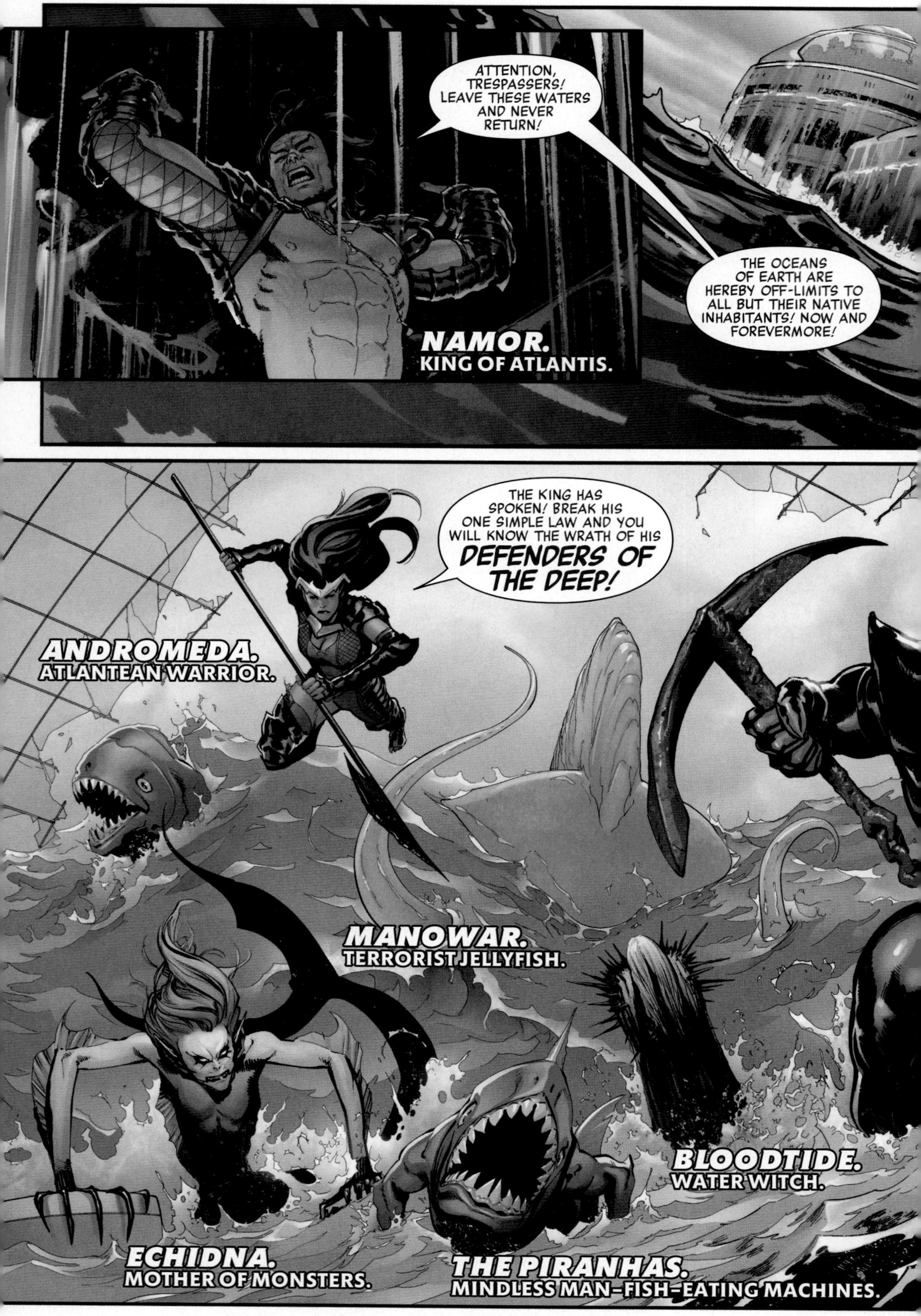
ATTENTION, TRESPASSERS! LEAVE THESE WATERS AND NEVER RETURN!
THE OCEANS OF EARTH ARE HEREBY OFF-LIMITS TO ALL BUT THEIR NATIVE INHABITANTS! NOW AND FOREVERMORE!
NAMOR. KING OF ATLANTIS.
THE KING HAS SPOKEN! BREAK HIS ONE SIMPLE LAW AND YOU WILL KNOW THE WRATH OF HIS DEFENDERS OF THE DEEP!
ANDROMEDA. ATLANTEAN WARRIOR.
MANOWAR. TERRORIST JELLYFISH.
BLOODTIDE. WATER WITCH.
ECHIDNA. MOTHER OF MONSTERS.
THE PIRANHAS. MINDLESS MAN-FISH-EATING MACHINES.

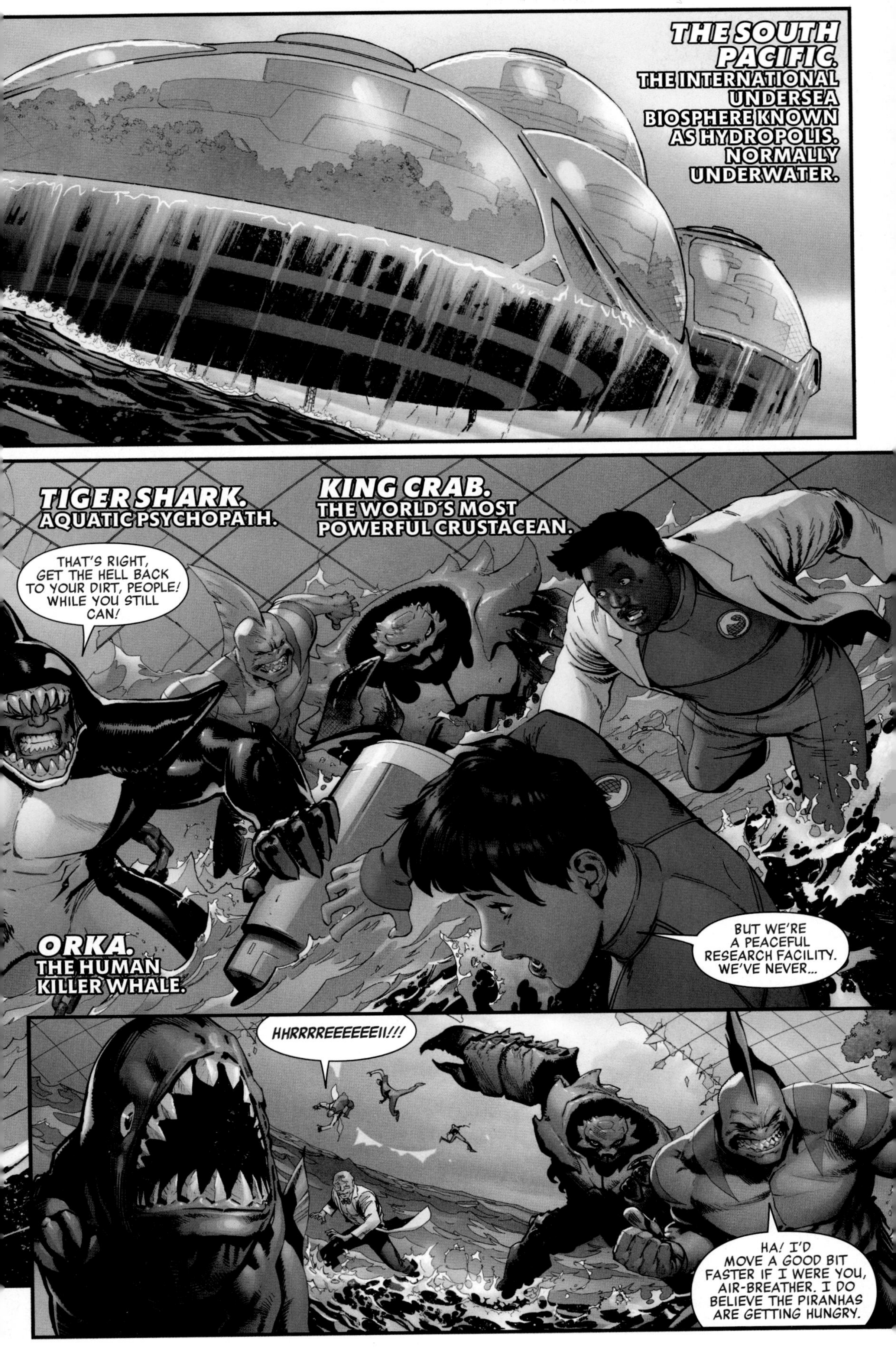
THE SOUTH PACIFIC.
THE INTERNATIONAL UNDERSEA BIOSPHERE KNOWN AS HYDROPOLIS. NORMALLY UNDERWATER.
TIGER SHARK. AQUATIC PSYCHOPATH.
KING CRAB. THE WORLD'S MOST POWERFUL CRUSTACEAN.
THAT'S RIGHT, GET THE HELL BACK TO YOUR DIRT, PEOPLE! WHILE YOU STILL CAN!
ORKA. THE HUMAN KILLER WHALE.
BUT WE'RE A PEACEFUL RESEARCH FACILITY. WE'VE NEVER...
HHRRRREEEEEEII!!!
HA! I'D MOVE A GOOD BIT FASTER IF I WERE YOU, AIR-BREATHER. I DO BELIEVE THE PIRANHAS ARE GETTING HUNGRY.

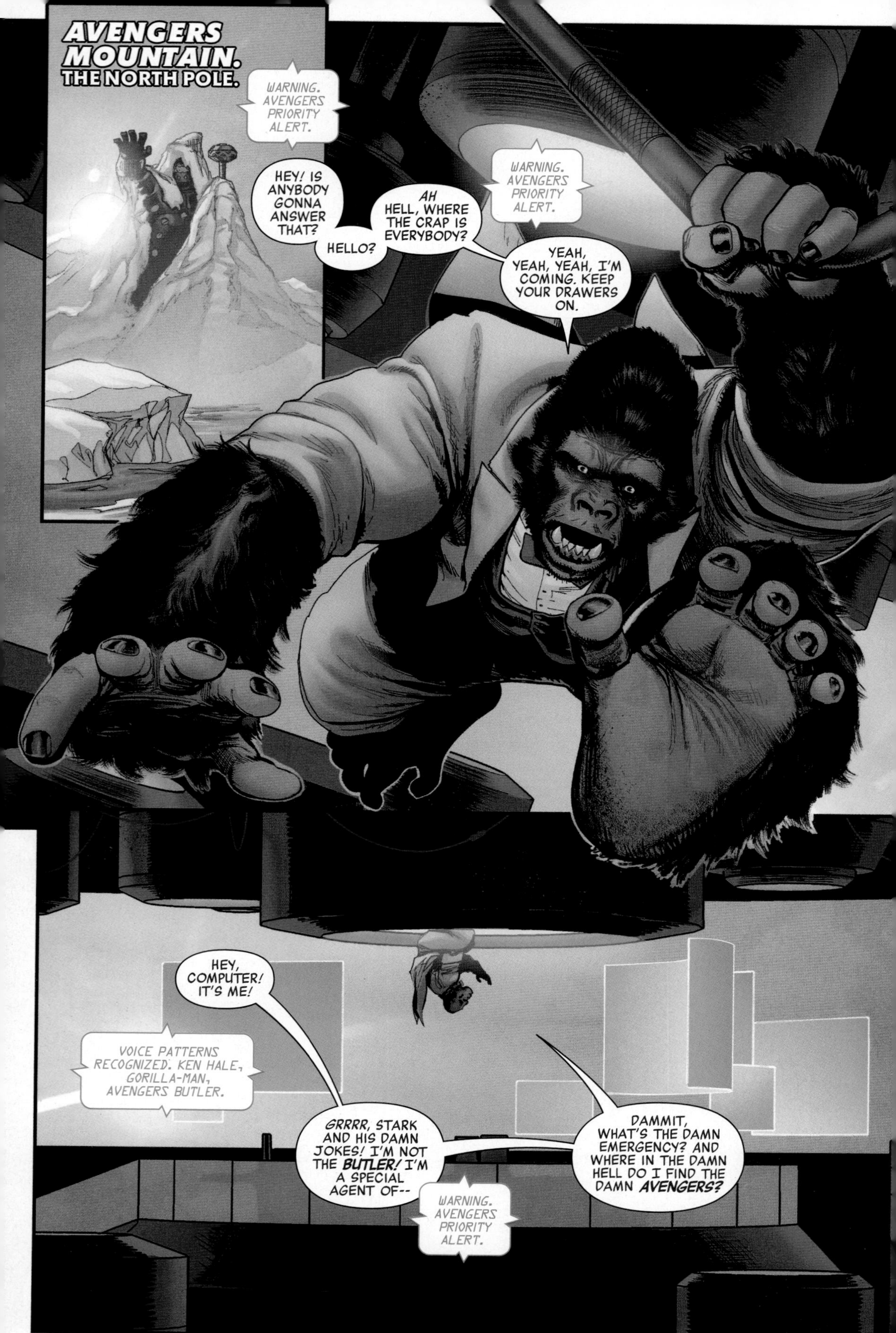
AVENGERS MOUNTAIN. THE NORTH POLE.
WARNING. AVENGERS PRIORITY ALERT.
HEY! IS ANYBODY GONNA ANSWER THAT?
HELLO?
AH HELL, WHERE THE CRAP IS EVERYBODY?
WARNING. AVENGERS PRIORITY ALERT.
YEAH, YEAH, YEAH, I'M COMING. KEEP YOUR DRAWERS ON.
HEY, COMPUTER! IT'S ME!
VOICE PATTERNS RECOGNIZED. KEN HALE, GORILLA-MAN, AVENGERS BUTLER.
GRRRR, STARK AND HIS DAMN JOKES! I'M NOT THE BUTLER! I'M A SPECIAL AGENT OF--
WARNING. AVENGERS PRIORITY ALERT.
DAMMIT, WHAT'S THE DAMN EMERGENCY? AND WHERE IN THE DAMN HELL DO I FIND THE DAMN AVENGERS?

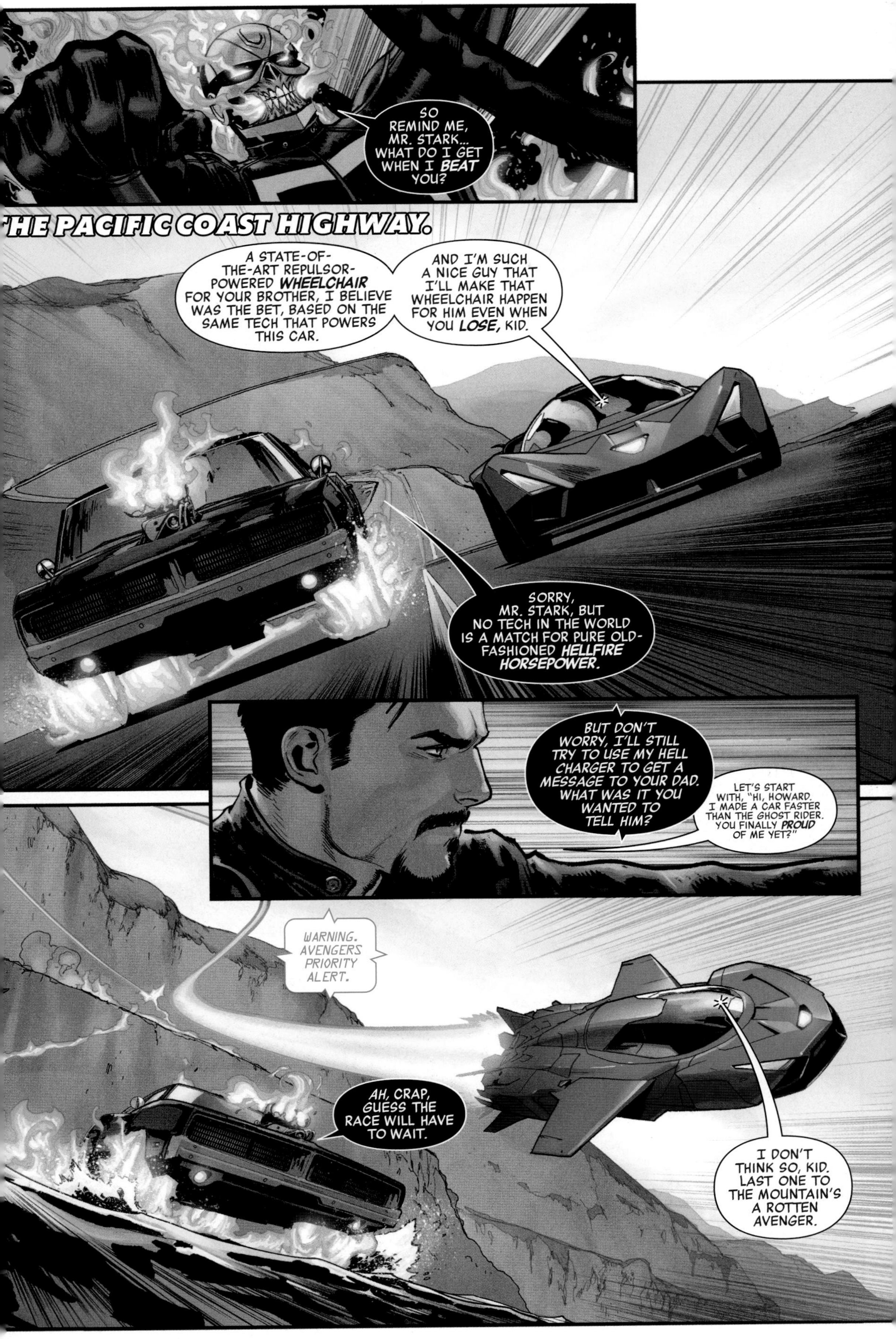
SO REMIND ME, MR. STARK... WHAT DO I GET WHEN I BEAT YOU?
THE PACIFIC COAST HIGHWAY.
A STATE-OF-THE-ART REPULSOR-POWERED WHEELCHAIR FOR YOUR BROTHER, I BELIEVE WAS THE BET, BASED ON THE SAME TECH THAT POWERS THIS CAR.
AND I'M SUCH A NICE GUY THAT I'LL MAKE THAT WHEELCHAIR HAPPEN FOR HIM EVEN WHEN YOU LOSE, KID.
SORRY, MR. STARK, BUT NO TECH IN THE WORLD IS A MATCH FOR PURE OLD-FASHIONED HELLFIRE HORSEPOWER.
BUT DON'T WORRY, I'LL STILL TRY TO USE MY HELL CHARGER TO GET A MESSAGE TO YOUR DAD. WHAT WAS IT YOU WANTED TO TELL HIM?
LET'S START WITH, "HI, HOWARD. I MADE A CAR FASTER THAN THE GHOST RIDER. YOU FINALLY PROUD OF ME YET?"
WARNING. AVENGERS PRIORITY ALERT.
AH, CRAP, GUESS THE RACE WILL HAVE TO WAIT.
I DON'T THINK SO, KID. LAST ONE TO THE MOUNTAIN'S A ROTTEN AVENGER.

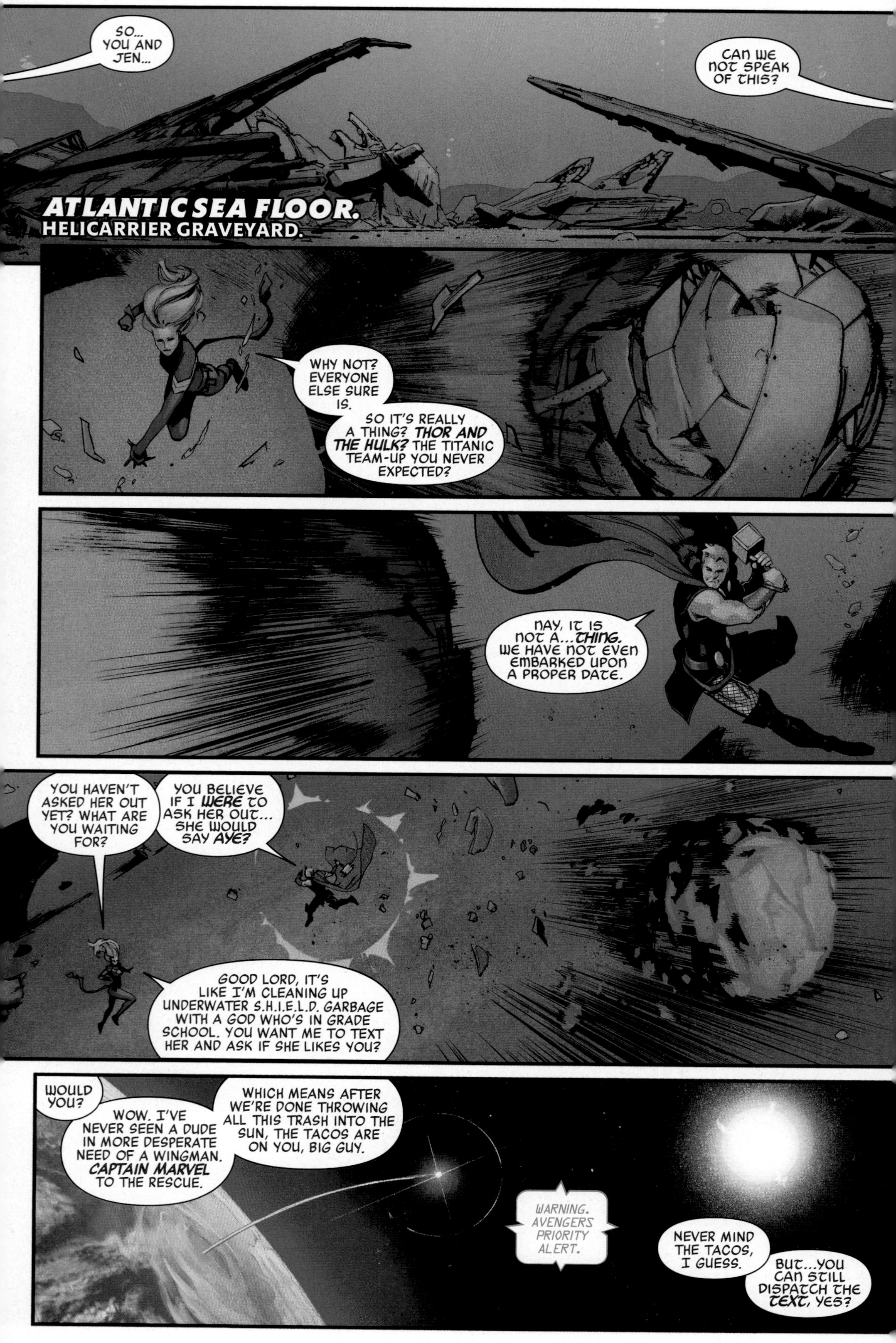

SO... YOU AND JEN...
CAN WE NOT SPEAK OF THIS?
ATLANTIC SEA FLOOR.
HELICARRIER GRAVEYARD.
WHY NOT? EVERYONE ELSE SURE IS.
SO IT'S REALLY A THING? THOR AND THE HULK? THE TITANIC TEAM-UP YOU NEVER EXPECTED?
NAY, IT IS NOT A...THING. WE HAVE NOT EVEN EMBARKED UPON A PROPER DATE.
YOU HAVEN'T ASKED HER OUT YET? WHAT ARE YOU WAITING FOR?
YOU BELIEVE IF I WERE TO ASK HER OUT... SHE WOULD SAY AYE?
GOOD LORD, IT'S LIKE I'M CLEANING UP UNDERWATER S.H.I.E.L.D. GARBAGE WITH A GOD WHO'S IN GRADE SCHOOL. YOU WANT ME TO TEXT HER AND ASK IF SHE LIKES YOU?
WOULD YOU?
WOW. I'VE NEVER SEEN A DUDE IN MORE DESPERATE NEED OF A WINGMAN. CAPTAIN MARVEL TO THE RESCUE.
WHICH MEANS AFTER WE'RE DONE THROWING ALL THIS TRASH INTO THE SUN, THE TACOS ARE ON YOU, BIG GUY.
WARNING. AVENGERS PRIORITY ALERT.
NEVER MIND THE TACOS, I GUESS.
BUT...YOU CAN STILL DISPATCH THE TEXT, YES?

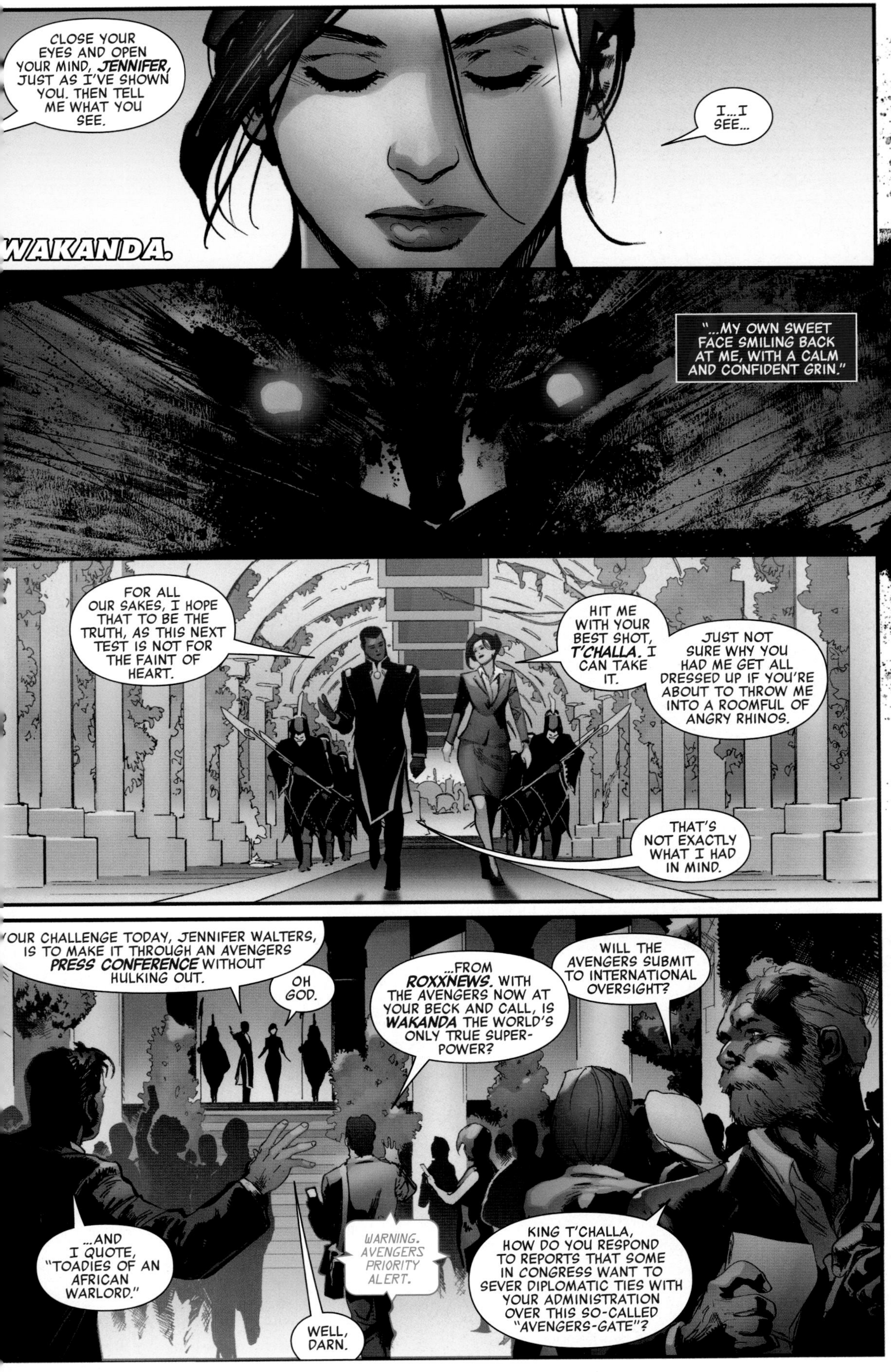
CLOSE YOUR EYES AND OPEN YOUR MIND, JENNIFER, JUST AS I'VE SHOWN YOU. THEN TELL ME WHAT YOU SEE.
I...I SEE...
WAKANDA.
"...MY OWN SWEET FACE SMILING BACK AT ME, WITH A CALM AND CONFIDENT GRIN."
FOR ALL OUR SAKES, I HOPE THAT TO BE THE TRUTH, AS THIS NEXT TEST IS NOT FOR THE FAINT OF HEART.
HIT ME WITH YOUR BEST SHOT, T'CHALLA. I CAN TAKE IT.
JUST NOT SURE WHY YOU HAD ME GET ALL DRESSED UP IF YOU'RE ABOUT TO THROW ME INTO A ROOMFUL OF ANGRY RHINOS.
THAT'S NOT EXACTLY WHAT I HAD IN MIND.
YOUR CHALLENGE TODAY, JENNIFER WALTERS, IS TO MAKE IT THROUGH AN AVENGERS PRESS CONFERENCE WITHOUT HULKING OUT.
OH GOD.
...FROM ROXXNEWS. WITH THE AVENGERS NOW AT YOUR BECK AND CALL, IS WAKANDA THE WORLD'S ONLY TRUE SUPER-POWER?
WILL THE AVENGERS SUBMIT TO INTERNATIONAL OVERSIGHT?
...AND I QUOTE, "TOADIES OF AN AFRICAN WARLORD."
WARNING. AVENGERS PRIORITY ALERT.
WELL, DARN.
KING T'CHALLA, HOW DO YOU RESPOND TO REPORTS THAT SOME IN CONGRESS WANT TO SEVER DIPLOMATIC TIES WITH YOUR ADMINISTRATION OVER THIS SO-CALLED "AVENGERS-GATE"?

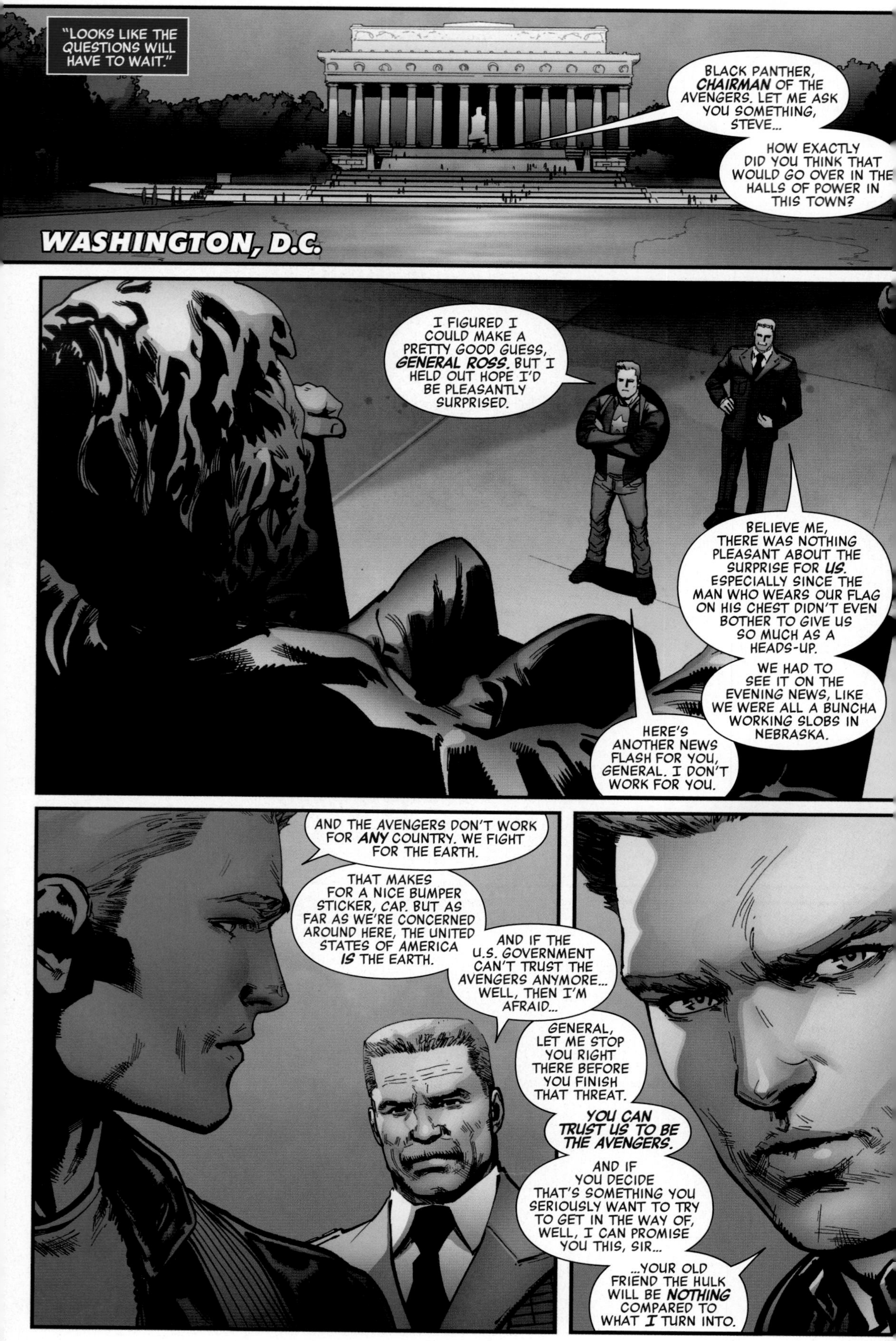
"LOOKS LIKE THE QUESTIONS WILL HAVE TO WAIT."
BLACK PANTHER, CHAIRMAN OF THE AVENGERS. LET ME ASK YOU SOMETHING, STEVE...
HOW EXACTLY DID YOU THINK THAT WOULD GO OVER IN THE HALLS OF POWER IN THIS TOWN?
WASHINGTON, D.C.
I FIGURED I COULD MAKE A PRETTY GOOD GUESS, GENERAL ROSS. BUT I HELD OUT HOPE I'D BE PLEASANTLY SURPRISED.
BELIEVE ME, THERE WAS NOTHING PLEASANT ABOUT THE SURPRISE FOR US. ESPECIALLY SINCE THE MAN WHO WEARS OUR FLAG ON HIS CHEST DIDN'T EVEN BOTHER TO GIVE US SO MUCH AS A HEADS-UP.
WE HAD TO SEE IT ON THE EVENING NEWS, LIKE WE WERE ALL A BUNCHA WORKING SLOBS IN NEBRASKA.
HERE'S ANOTHER NEWS FLASH FOR YOU, GENERAL. I DON'T WORK FOR YOU.
AND THE AVENGERS DON'T WORK FOR ANY COUNTRY. WE FIGHT FOR THE EARTH.
THAT MAKES FOR A NICE BUMPER STICKER, CAP. BUT AS FAR AS WE'RE CONCERNED AROUND HERE, THE UNITED STATES OF AMERICA IS THE EARTH.
AND IF THE U.S. GOVERNMENT CAN'T TRUST THE AVENGERS ANYMORE... WELL, THEN I'M AFRAID...
GENERAL, LET ME STOP YOU RIGHT THERE BEFORE YOU FINISH THAT THREAT.
YOU CAN TRUST US TO BE THE AVENGERS.
AND IF YOU DECIDE THAT'S SOMETHING YOU SERIOUSLY WANT TO TRY TO GET IN THE WAY OF, WELL, I CAN PROMISE YOU THIS, SIR...
...YOUR OLD FRIEND THE HULK WILL BE NOTHING COMPARED TO WHAT I TURN INTO.

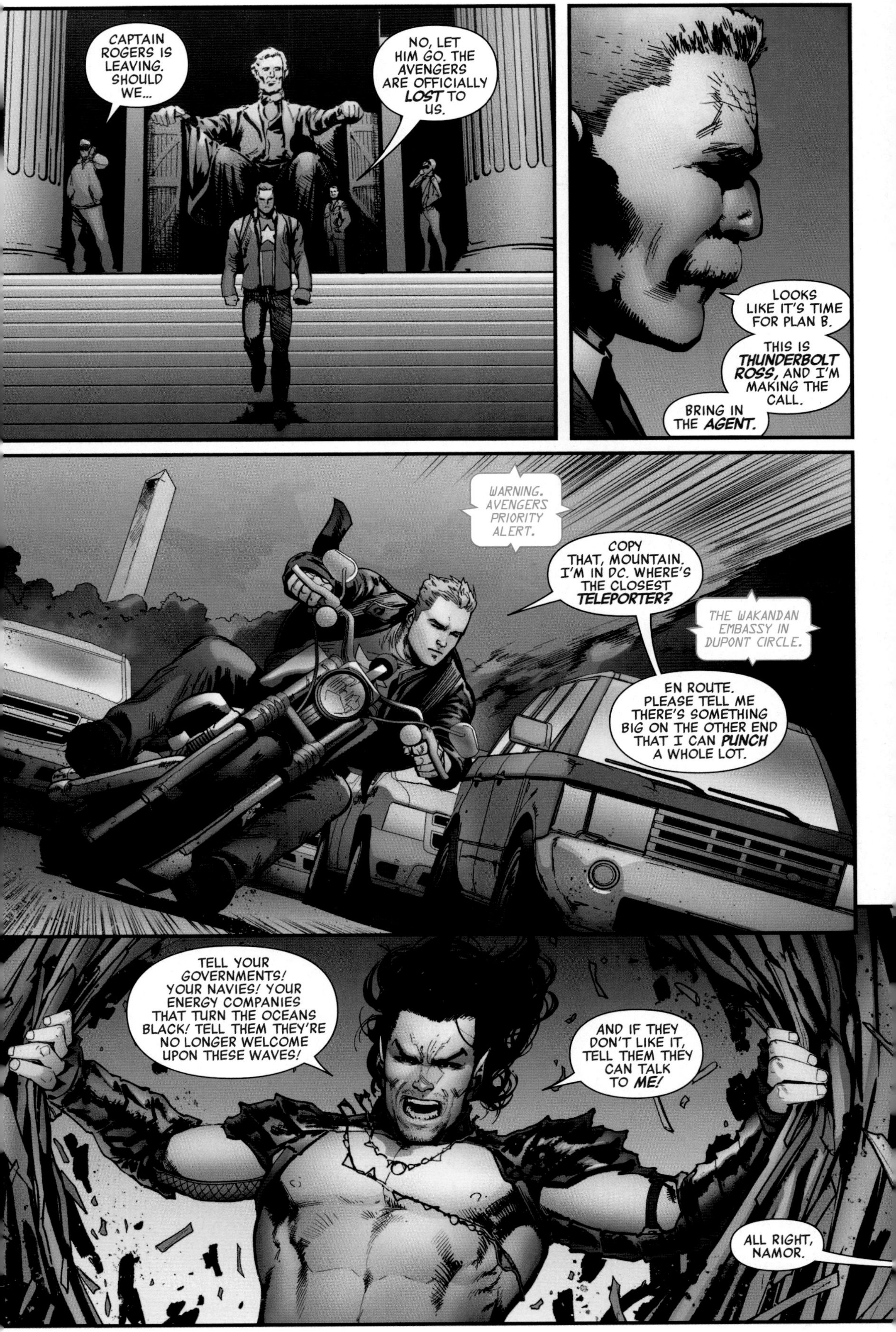
CAPTAIN ROGERS IS LEAVING. SHOULD WE...
NO, LET HIM GO. THE AVENGERS ARE OFFICIALLY LOST TO US.
LOOKS LIKE IT'S TIME FOR PLAN B.
THIS IS THUNDERBOLT ROSS, AND I'M MAKING THE CALL.
BRING IN THE AGENT.
WARNING. AVENGERS PRIORITY ALERT.
COPY THAT, MOUNTAIN. I'M IN DC. WHERE'S THE CLOSEST TELEPORTER?
THE WAKANDAN EMBASSY IN DUPONT CIRCLE.
EN ROUTE. PLEASE TELL ME THERE'S SOMETHING BIG ON THE OTHER END THAT I CAN PUNCH A WHOLE LOT.
TELL YOUR GOVERNMENTS! YOUR NAVIES! YOUR ENERGY COMPANIES THAT TURN THE OCEANS BLACK! TELL THEM THEY'RE NO LONGER WELCOME UPON THESE WAVES!
AND IF THEY DON'T LIKE IT, TELL THEM THEY CAN TALK TO ME!
ALL RIGHT, NAMOR.

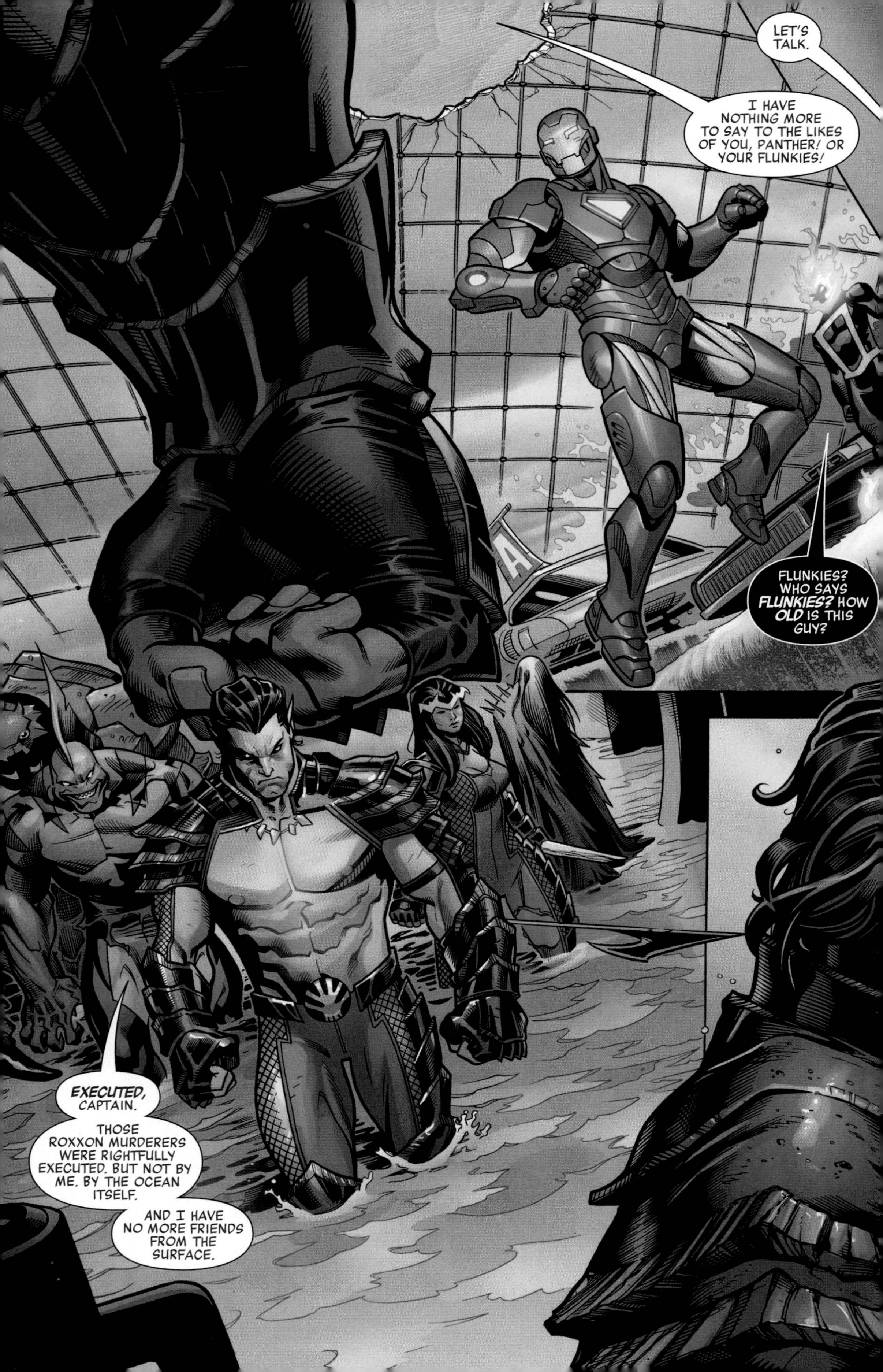
LET'S TALK.
I HAVE NOTHING MORE TO SAY TO THE LIKES OF YOU, PANTHER! OR YOUR FLUNKIES!
FLUNKIES? WHO SAYS FLUNKIES? HOW OLD IS THIS GUY?
EXECUTED, CAPTAIN.
THOSE ROXXON MURDERERS WERE RIGHTFULLY EXECUTED. BUT NOT BY ME. BY THE OCEAN ITSELF.
AND I HAVE NO MORE FRIENDS FROM THE SURFACE.

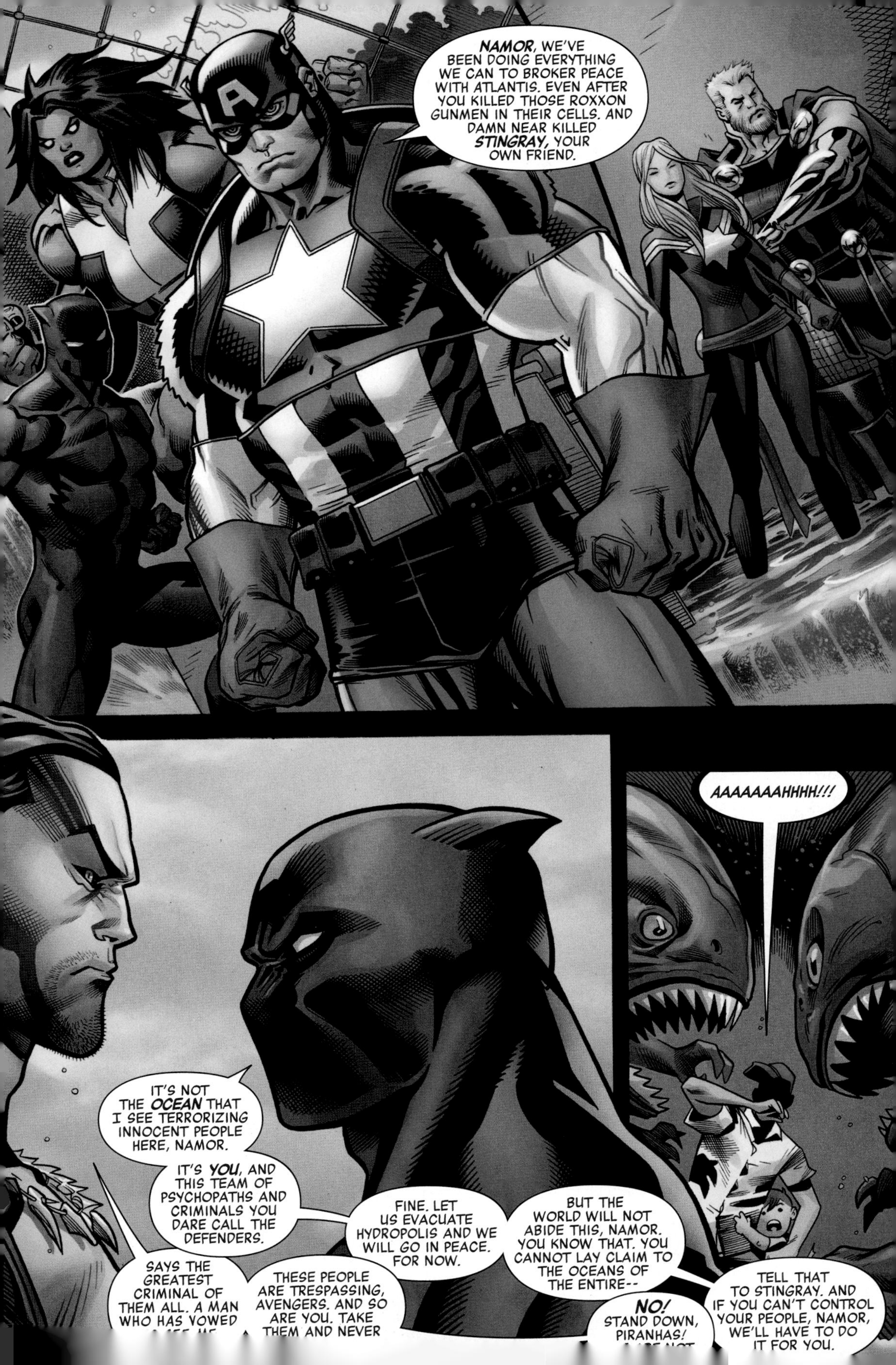
NAMOR, WE'VE BEEN DOING EVERYTHING WE CAN TO BROKER PEACE WITH ATLANTIS. EVEN AFTER YOU KILLED THOSE ROXXON GUNMEN IN THEIR CELLS. AND DAMN NEAR KILLED STINGRAY, YOUR OWN FRIEND.
IT'S NOT THE OCEAN THAT I SEE TERRORIZING INNOCENT PEOPLE HERE, NAMOR.
IT'S YOU, AND THIS TEAM OF PSYCHOPATHS AND CRIMINALS YOU DARE CALL THE DEFENDERS.
SAYS THE GREATEST CRIMINAL OF THEM ALL. A MAN WHO HAS VOWED
THESE PEOPLE ARE TRESPASSING, AVENGERS. AND SO ARE YOU. TAKE THEM AND NEVER
FINE. LET US EVACUATE HYDROPOLIS AND WE WILL GO IN PEACE. FOR NOW.
BUT THE WORLD WILL NOT ABIDE THIS, NAMOR. YOU KNOW THAT. YOU CANNOT LAY CLAIM TO THE OCEANS OF THE ENTIRE--
AAAAAAAHHHH!!!
NO! STAND DOWN, PIRANHAS!
TELL THAT TO STINGRAY. AND IF YOU CAN'T CONTROL YOUR PEOPLE, NAMOR, WE'LL HAVE TO DO IT FOR YOU.

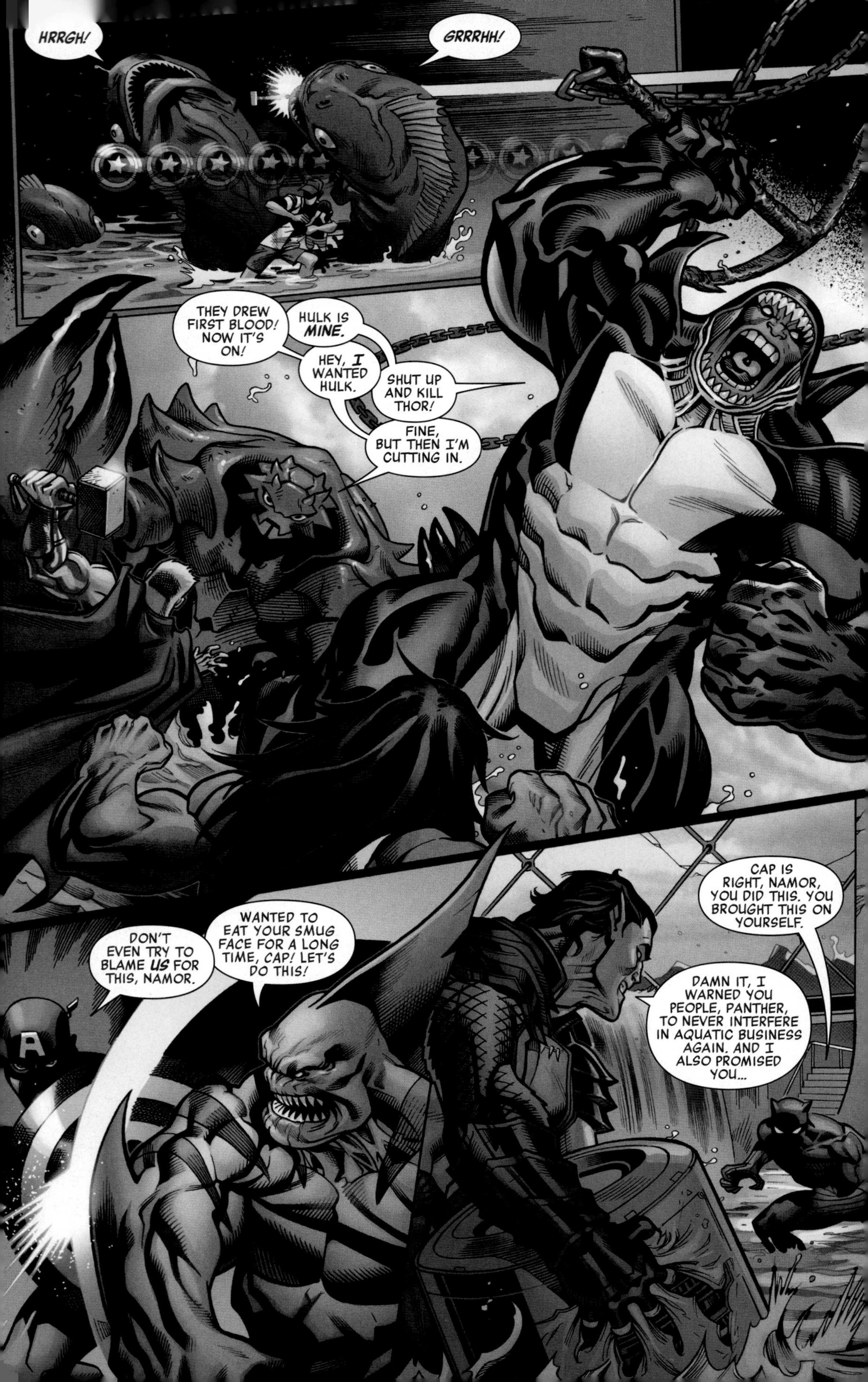
HRRGH!
GRRRHH!
THEY DREW FIRST BLOOD! NOW IT'S ON!
HULK IS MINE.
HEY, I WANTED HULK.
SHUT UP AND KILL THOR!
FINE, BUT THEN I'M CUTTING IN.
DON'T EVEN TRY TO BLAME US FOR THIS, NAMOR.
WANTED TO EAT YOUR SMUG FACE FOR A LONG TIME, CAP! LET'S DO THIS!
CAP IS RIGHT, NAMOR, YOU DID THIS. YOU BROUGHT THIS ON YOURSELF.
DAMN IT, I WARNED YOU PEOPLE, PANTHER, TO NEVER INTERFERE IN AQUATIC BUSINESS AGAIN. AND I ALSO PROMISED YOU...

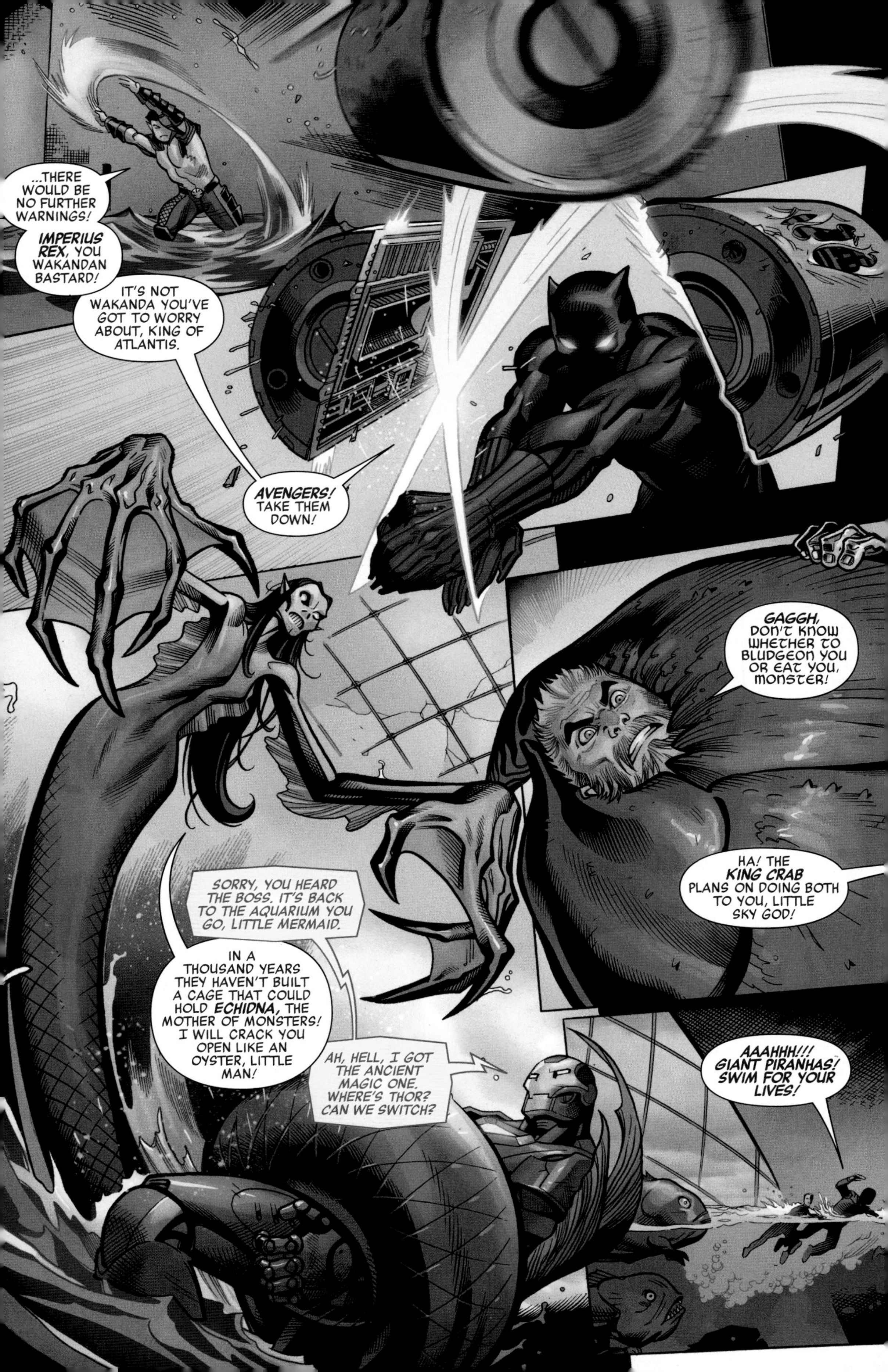

...THERE WOULD BE NO FURTHER WARNINGS!
IMPERIUS REX, YOU WAKANDAN BASTARD!
IT'S NOT WAKANDA YOU'VE GOT TO WORRY ABOUT, KING OF ATLANTIS.
AVENGERS! TAKE THEM DOWN!
GAGGH, DON'T KNOW WHETHER TO BLUDGEON YOU OR EAT YOU, MONSTER!
HA! THE KING CRAB PLANS ON DOING BOTH TO YOU, LITTLE SKY GOD!
SORRY, YOU HEARD THE BOSS. IT'S BACK TO THE AQUARIUM YOU GO, LITTLE MERMAID.
IN A THOUSAND YEARS THEY HAVEN'T BUILT A CAGE THAT COULD HOLD ECHIDNA, THE MOTHER OF MONSTERS! I WILL CRACK YOU OPEN LIKE AN OYSTER, LITTLE MAN!
AH, HELL, I GOT THE ANCIENT MAGIC ONE. WHERE'S THOR? CAN WE SWITCH?
AAAHHH!!! GIANT PIRANHAS! SWIM FOR YOUR LIVES!

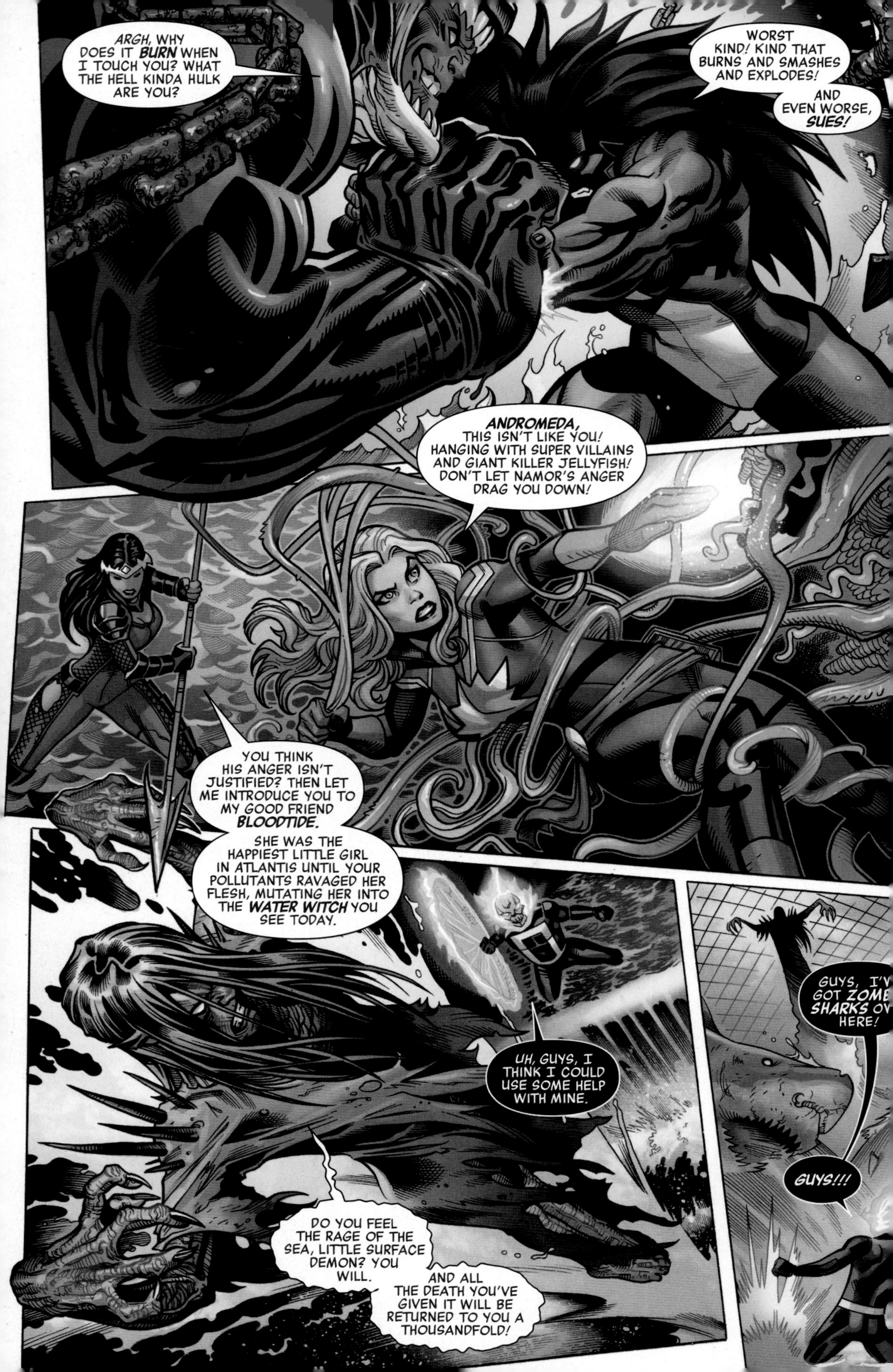
ARGH, WHY DOES IT BURN WHEN I TOUCH YOU? WHAT THE HELL KINDA HULK ARE YOU?
WORST KIND! KIND THAT BURNS AND SMASHES AND EXPLODES!
AND EVEN WORSE, SUES!
ANDROMEDA, THIS ISN'T LIKE YOU! HANGING WITH SUPER VILLAINS AND GIANT KILLER JELLYFISH! DON'T LET NAMOR'S ANGER DRAG YOU DOWN!
YOU THINK HIS ANGER ISN'T JUSTIFIED? THEN LET ME INTRODUCE YOU TO MY GOOD FRIEND BLOODTIDE.
SHE WAS THE HAPPIEST LITTLE GIRL IN ATLANTIS UNTIL YOUR POLLUTANTS RAVAGED HER FLESH, MUTATING HER INTO THE WATER WITCH YOU SEE TODAY.
UH, GUYS, I THINK I COULD USE SOME HELP WITH MINE.
GUYS!!!
DO YOU FEEL THE RAGE OF THE SEA, LITTLE SURFACE DEMON? YOU WILL.
AND ALL THE DEATH YOU'VE GIVEN IT WILL BE RETURNED TO YOU A THOUSANDFOLD!

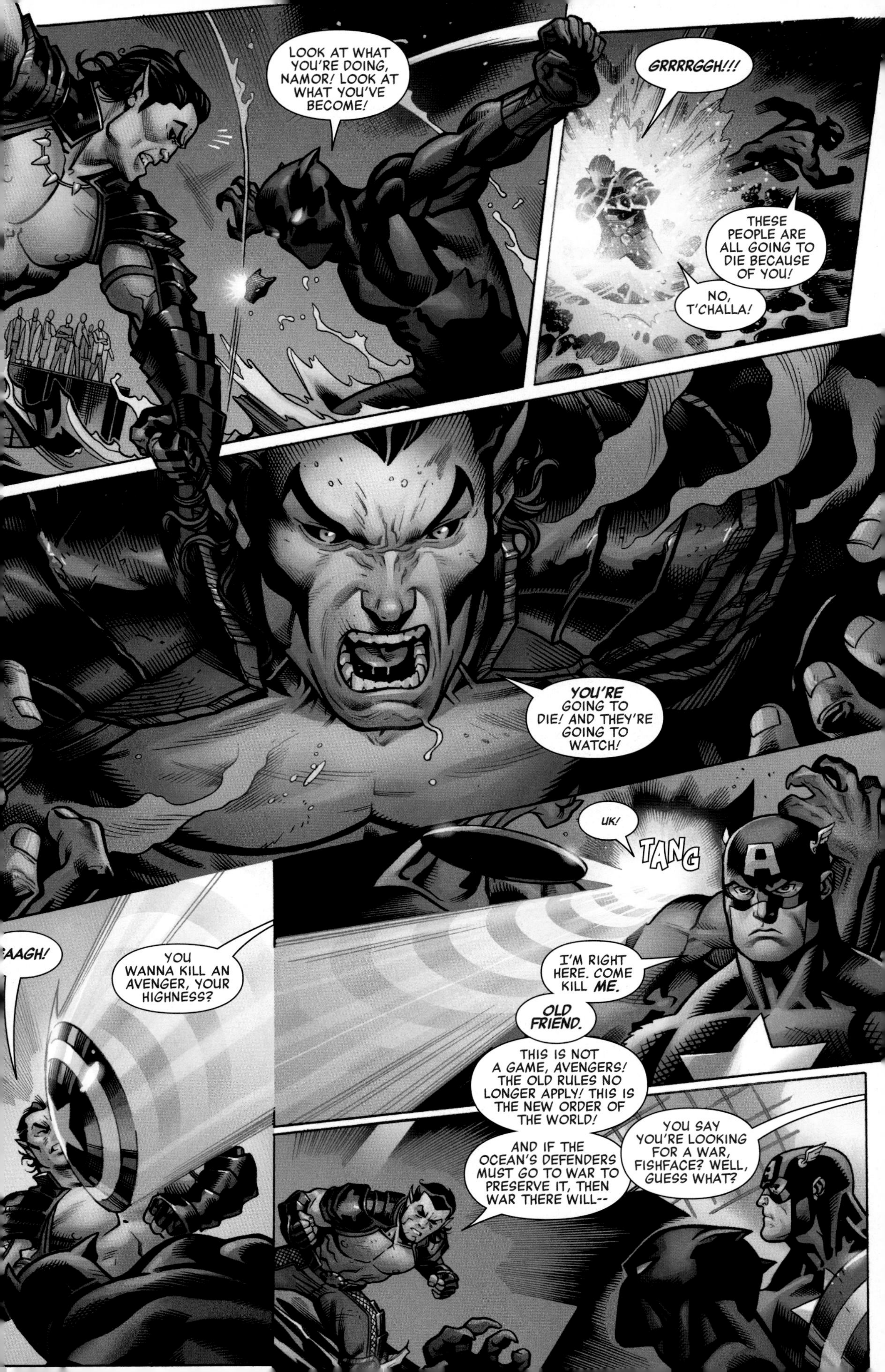
LOOK AT WHAT YOU'RE DOING, NAMOR! LOOK AT WHAT YOU'VE BECOME!
GRRRRGGH!!!
THESE PEOPLE ARE ALL GOING TO DIE BECAUSE OF YOU!
NO, T'CHALLA!
YOU'RE GOING TO DIE! AND THEY'RE GOING TO WATCH!
UK!
TANG
AAGH!
YOU WANNA KILL AN AVENGER, YOUR HIGHNESS?
I'M RIGHT HERE. COME KILL ME.
OLD FRIEND.
THIS IS NOT A GAME, AVENGERS! THE OLD RULES NO LONGER APPLY! THIS IS THE NEW ORDER OF THE WORLD!
AND IF THE OCEAN'S DEFENDERS MUST GO TO WAR TO PRESERVE IT, THEN WAR THERE WILL--
YOU SAY YOU'RE LOOKING FOR A WAR, FISHFACE? WELL, GUESS WHAT?

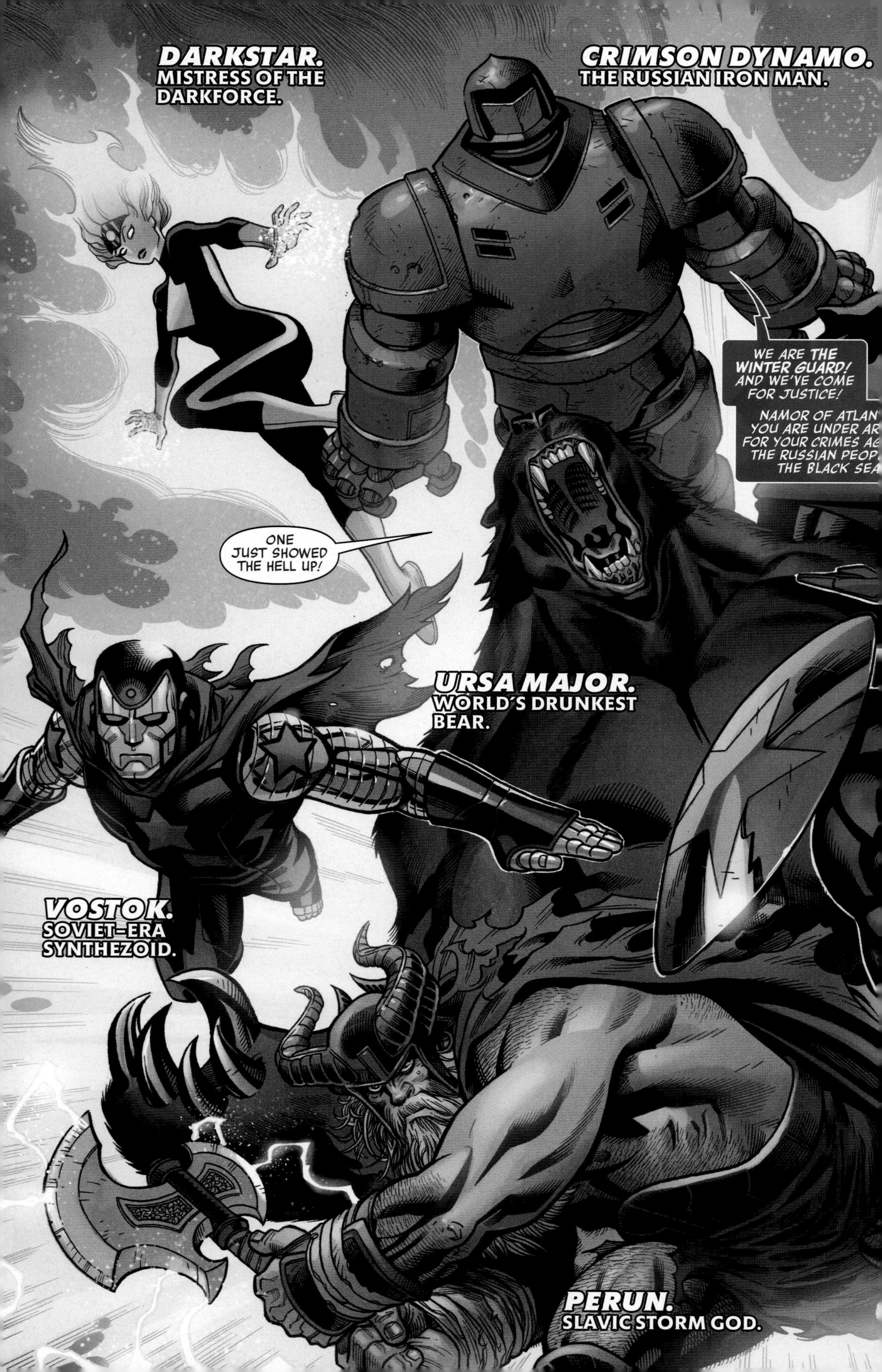
DARKSTAR.
MISTRESS OF THE DARKFORCE.
CRIMSON DYNAMO.
THE RUSSIAN IRON MAN.
WE ARE THE WINTER GUARD! AND WE'VE COME FOR JUSTICE!
NAMOR OF ATLAN
YOU ARE UNDER AR
FOR YOUR CRIMES AG
THE RUSSIAN PEOP
THE BLACK SEA
ONE JUST SHOWED THE HELL UP!
URSA MAJOR.
WORLD'S DRUNKEST BEAR.
VOSTOK.
SOVIET-ERA SYNTHEZOID.
PERUN.
SLAVIC STORM GOD.

CHERNOBOG.
SLAVIC GOD OF DARKNESS.

STAND ASIDE, LITTLE PUSSYCAT. LET A REAL ANIMAL TAKE IT FROM HERE.

PERUN! CHERNOBOG! YOU HEARD THE BOSS. TAKE NAMOR INTO CUSTODY. DON'T WORRY ABOUT BEING GENTLE.

AYE! WITH PLEASURE!

I DO HOPE HE RESISTS.

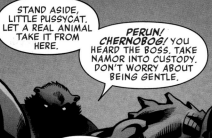

RED WIDOW.
ABILITIES UNKNOWN. PRESUMED MURDEROUS.

VANGUARD.
RUSSIAN SUPER-SOLDIER.

AVENGERS. RUSSIAN SUPER-SOLDIERS. LET THE SURFACE WORLD SEND ALL THE ARMIES IT WANTS! THEIR CARCASSES WILL LITTER THE DEPTHS!

YOU SHOULD SPEAK WITH MORE CARE WHEN YOU ADDRESS THE *GODS,* MAN OF ATLANTIS!

MAN OR HULK OR GOD, I CARE NOT! YOU ARE ALL JUST *AIR AND BONES* TO ME!

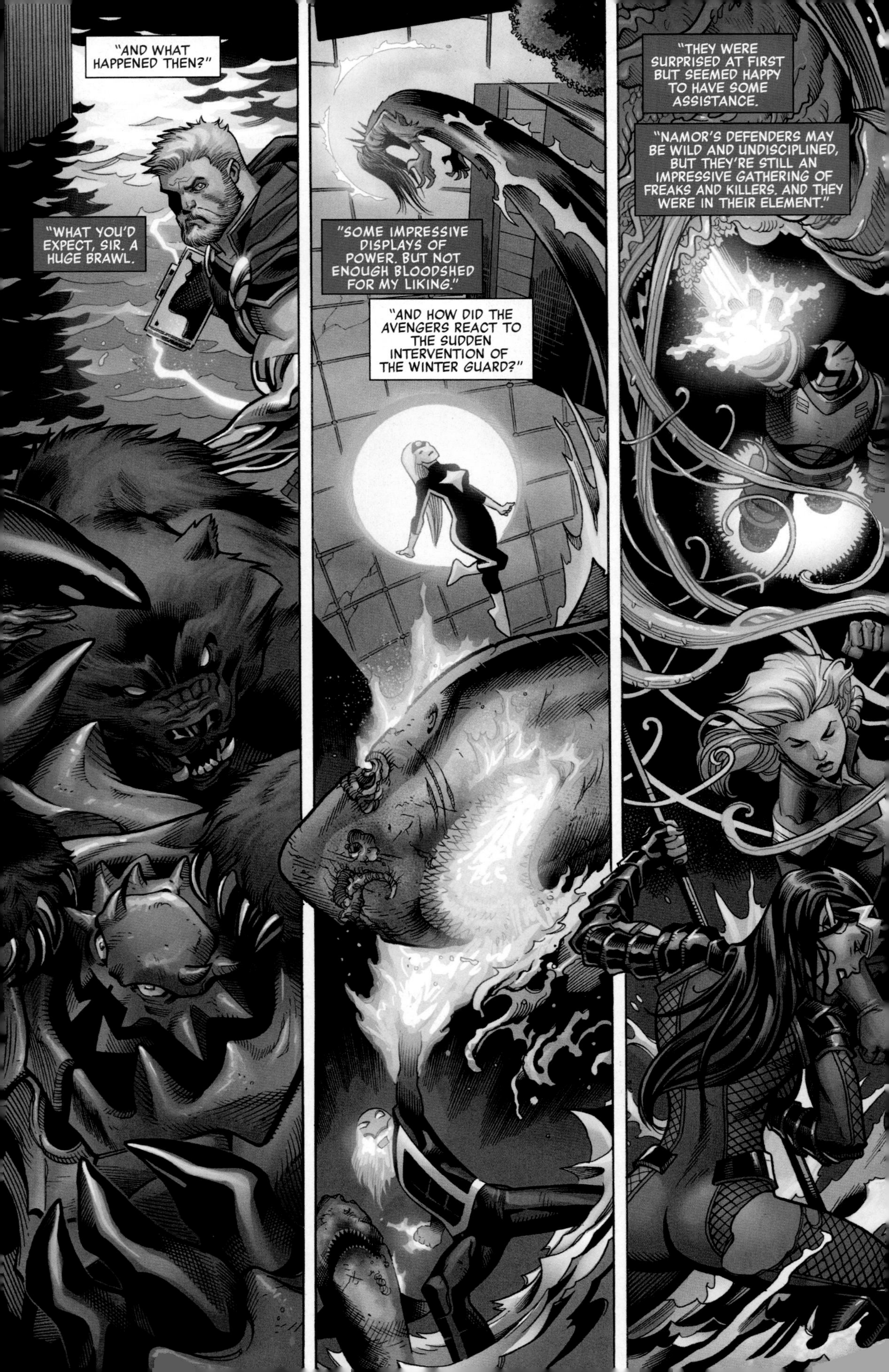
"AND WHAT HAPPENED THEN?"
"WHAT YOU'D EXPECT, SIR. A HUGE BRAWL.
"SOME IMPRESSIVE DISPLAYS OF POWER. BUT NOT ENOUGH BLOODSHED FOR MY LIKING."
"AND HOW DID THE AVENGERS REACT TO THE SUDDEN INTERVENTION OF THE WINTER GUARD?"
"THEY WERE SURPRISED AT FIRST BUT SEEMED HAPPY TO HAVE SOME ASSISTANCE.
"NAMOR'S DEFENDERS MAY BE WILD AND UNDISCIPLINED, BUT THEY'RE STILL AN IMPRESSIVE GATHERING OF FREAKS AND KILLERS. AND THEY WERE IN THEIR ELEMENT."

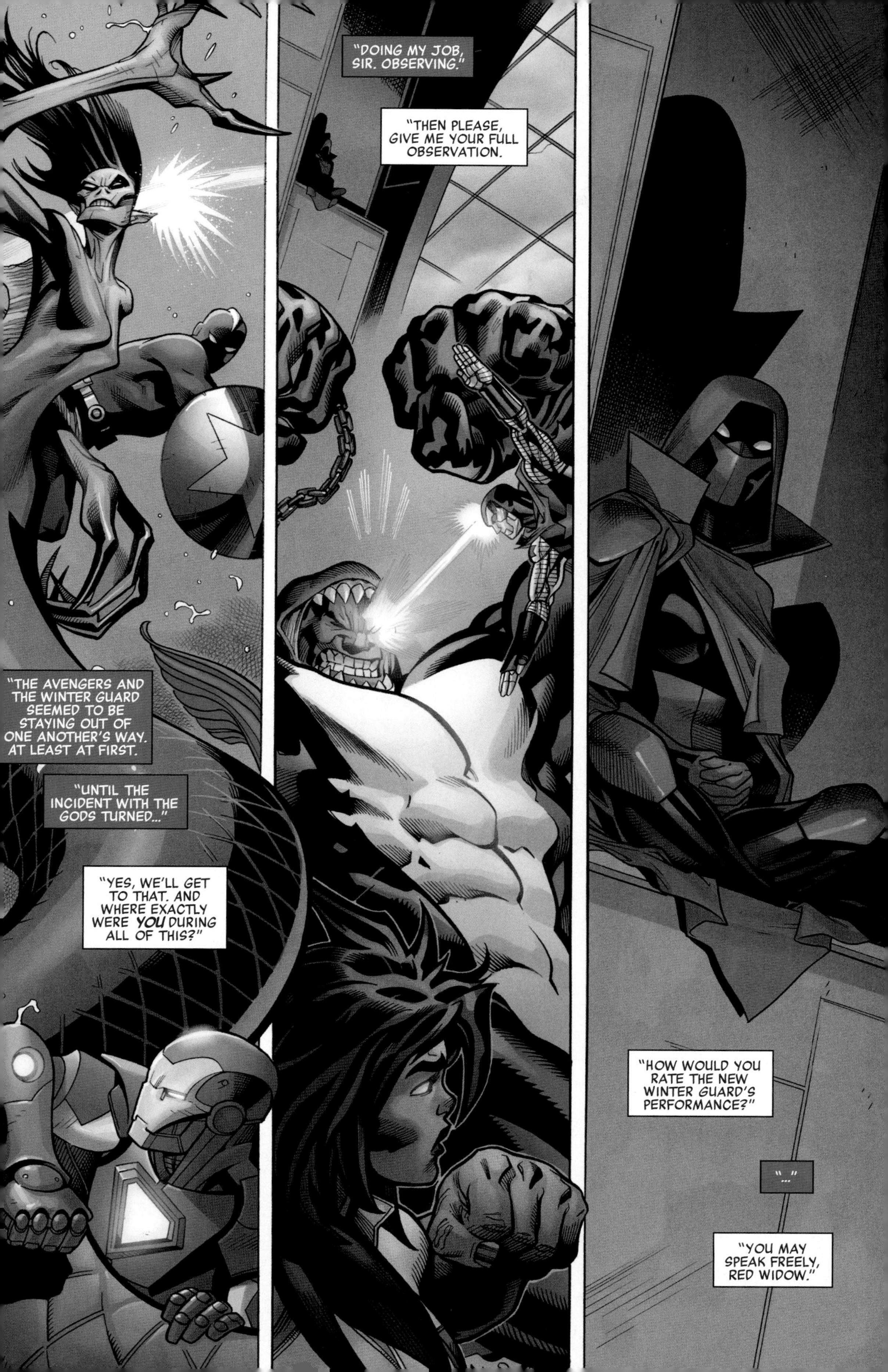
"DOING MY JOB, SIR. OBSERVING."
"THEN PLEASE, GIVE ME YOUR FULL OBSERVATION.
"THE AVENGERS AND THE WINTER GUARD SEEMED TO BE STAYING OUT OF ONE ANOTHER'S WAY. AT LEAST AT FIRST.
"UNTIL THE INCIDENT WITH THE GODS TURNED..."
"YES, WE'LL GET TO THAT. AND WHERE EXACTLY WERE *YOU* DURING ALL OF THIS?"
"HOW WOULD YOU RATE THE NEW WINTER GUARD'S PERFORMANCE?"
"..."
"YOU MAY SPEAK FREELY, RED WIDOW."

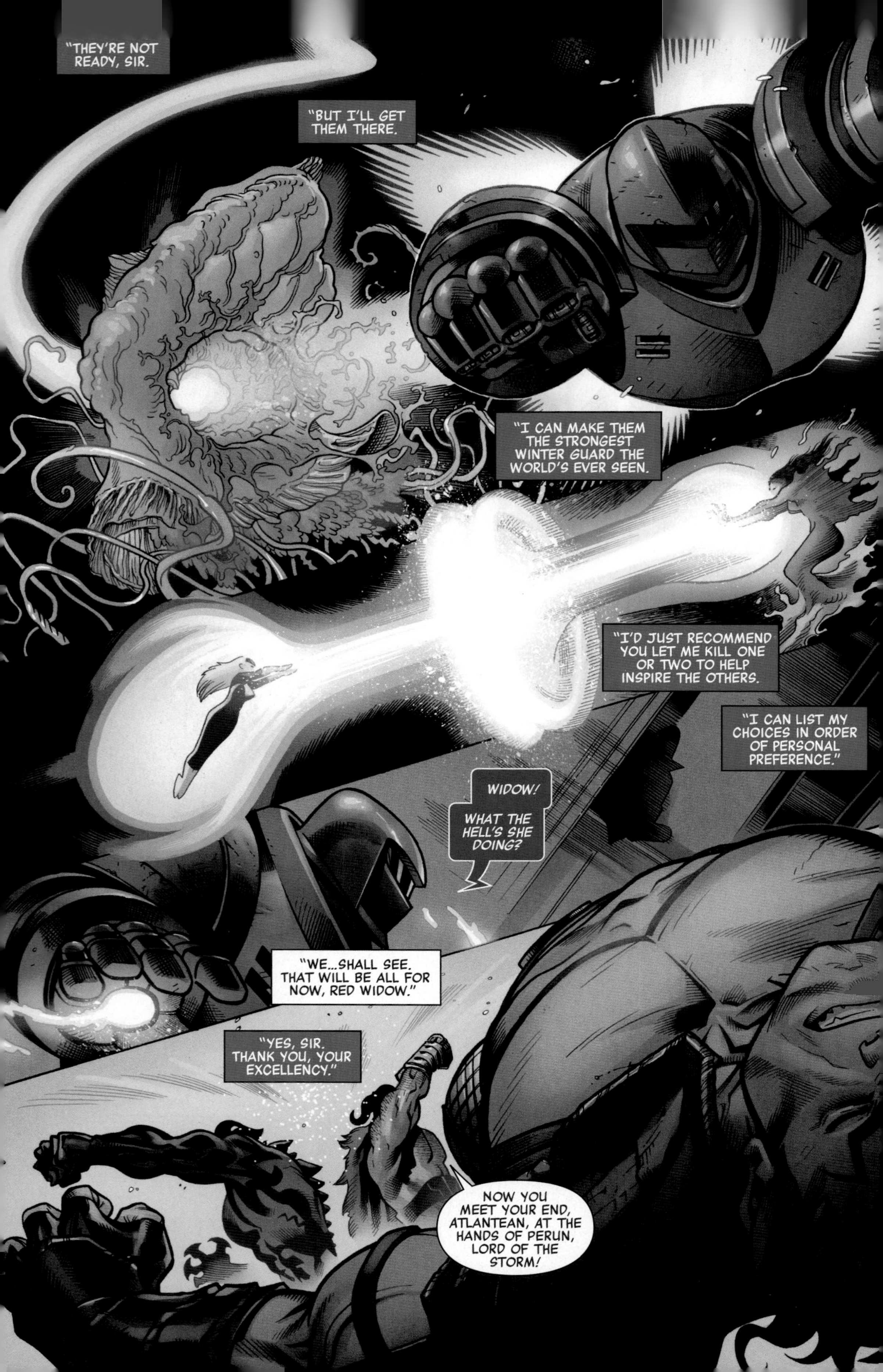
"THEY'RE NOT READY, SIR.
"BUT I'LL GET THEM THERE.
"I CAN MAKE THEM THE STRONGEST WINTER GUARD THE WORLD'S EVER SEEN.
"I'D JUST RECOMMEND YOU LET ME KILL ONE OR TWO TO HELP INSPIRE THE OTHERS.
"I CAN LIST MY CHOICES IN ORDER OF PERSONAL PREFERENCE."
WIDOW!
WHAT THE HELL'S SHE DOING?
"WE...SHALL SEE. THAT WILL BE ALL FOR NOW, RED WIDOW."
"YES, SIR. THANK YOU, YOUR EXCELLENCY."
NOW YOU MEET YOUR END, ATLANTEAN, AT THE HANDS OF PERUN, LORD OF THE STORM!

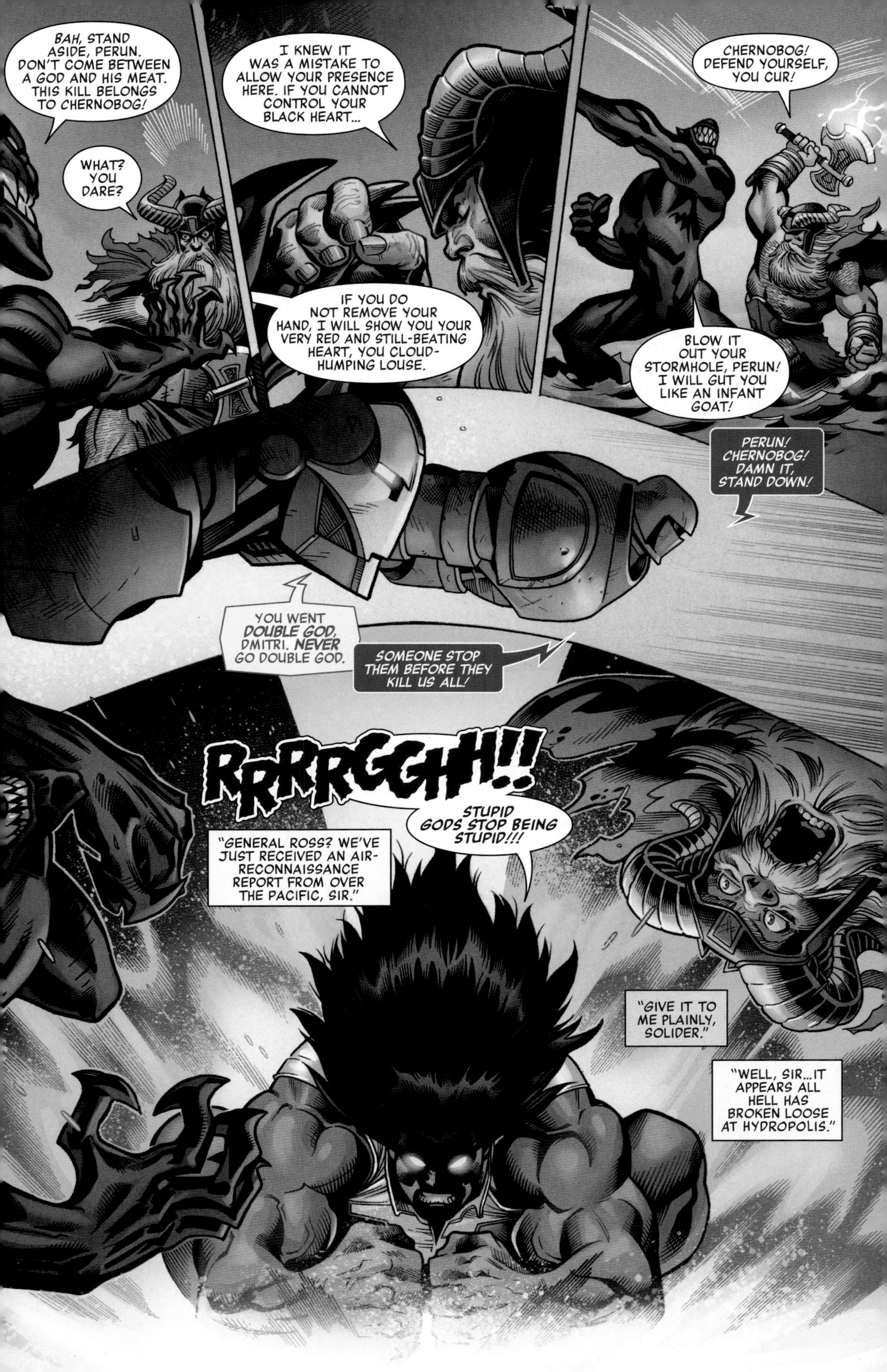
BAH, STAND ASIDE, PERUN. DON'T COME BETWEEN A GOD AND HIS MEAT. THIS KILL BELONGS TO CHERNOBOG!
WHAT? YOU DARE?
I KNEW IT WAS A MISTAKE TO ALLOW YOUR PRESENCE HERE. IF YOU CANNOT CONTROL YOUR BLACK HEART...
IF YOU DO NOT REMOVE YOUR HAND, I WILL SHOW YOU YOUR VERY RED AND STILL-BEATING HEART, YOU CLOUD-HUMPING LOUSE.
CHERNOBOG! DEFEND YOURSELF, YOU CUR!
BLOW IT OUT YOUR STORMHOLE, PERUN! I WILL GUT YOU LIKE AN INFANT GOAT!
PERUN! CHERNOBOG! DAMN IT, STAND DOWN!
YOU WENT DOUBLE GOD, DMITRI. NEVER GO DOUBLE GOD.
SOMEONE STOP THEM BEFORE THEY KILL US ALL!
RRRRGGHH!!
STUPID GODS STOP BEING STUPID!!!
"GENERAL ROSS? WE'VE JUST RECEIVED AN AIR-RECONNAISSANCE REPORT FROM OVER THE PACIFIC, SIR."
"GIVE IT TO ME PLAINLY, SOLIDER."
"WELL, SIR...IT APPEARS ALL HELL HAS BROKEN LOOSE AT HYDROPOLIS."

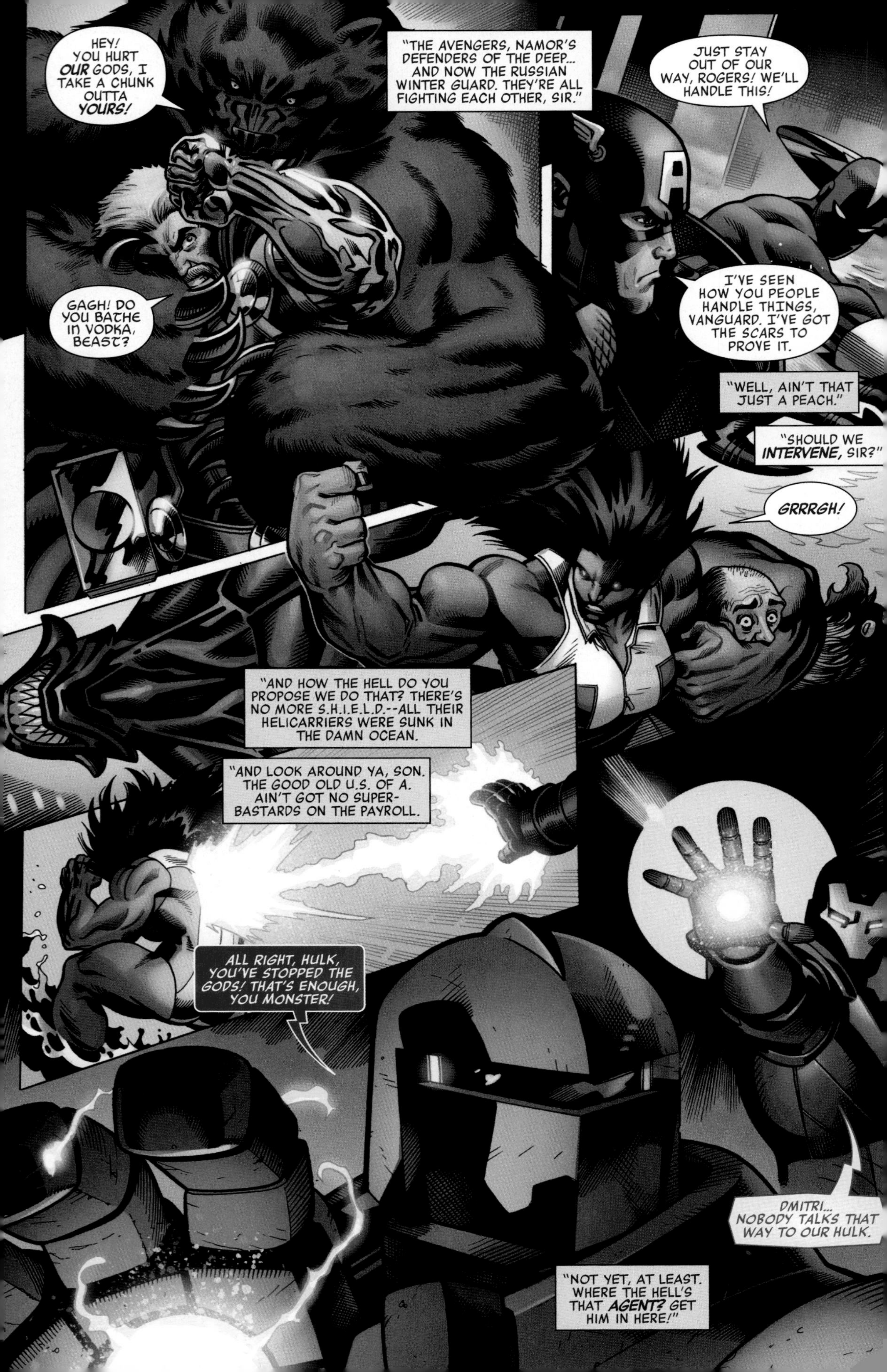
HEY! YOU HURT OUR GODS, I TAKE A CHUNK OUTTA YOURS!
"THE AVENGERS, NAMOR'S DEFENDERS OF THE DEEP... AND NOW THE RUSSIAN WINTER GUARD. THEY'RE ALL FIGHTING EACH OTHER, SIR."
JUST STAY OUT OF OUR WAY, ROGERS! WE'LL HANDLE THIS!
GAGH! DO YOU BATHE IN VODKA, BEAST?
I'VE SEEN HOW YOU PEOPLE HANDLE THINGS, VANGUARD. I'VE GOT THE SCARS TO PROVE IT.
"WELL, AIN'T THAT JUST A PEACH."
"SHOULD WE INTERVENE, SIR?"
GRRRGH!
"AND HOW THE HELL DO YOU PROPOSE WE DO THAT? THERE'S NO MORE S.H.I.E.L.D.--ALL THEIR HELICARRIERS WERE SUNK IN THE DAMN OCEAN.
"AND LOOK AROUND YA, SON. THE GOOD OLD U.S. OF A. AIN'T GOT NO SUPER-BASTARDS ON THE PAYROLL.
ALL RIGHT, HULK, YOU'VE STOPPED THE GODS! THAT'S ENOUGH, YOU MONSTER!
DMITRI... NOBODY TALKS THAT WAY TO OUR HULK.
"NOT YET, AT LEAST. WHERE THE HELL'S THAT AGENT? GET HIM IN HERE!"

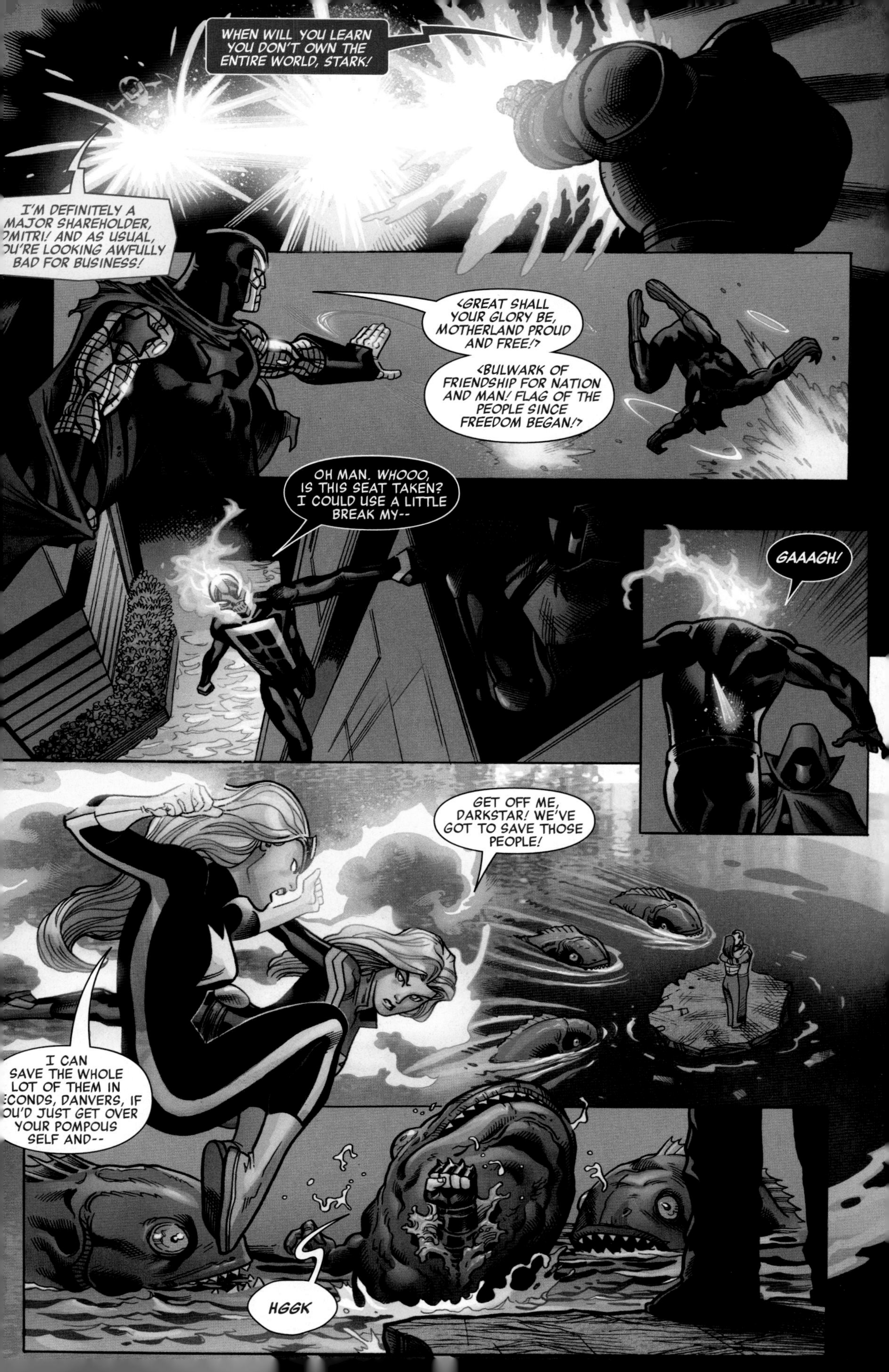
WHEN WILL YOU LEARN YOU DON'T OWN THE ENTIRE WORLD, STARK!
I'M DEFINITELY A MAJOR SHAREHOLDER, DMITRI! AND AS USUAL, OU'RE LOOKING AWFULLY BAD FOR BUSINESS!
<GREAT SHALL YOUR GLORY BE, MOTHERLAND PROUD AND FREE!>
<BULWARK OF FRIENDSHIP FOR NATION AND MAN! FLAG OF THE PEOPLE SINCE FREEDOM BEGAN!>
OH MAN. WHOOO, IS THIS SEAT TAKEN? I COULD USE A LITTLE BREAK MY--
GAAAGH!
GET OFF ME, DARKSTAR! WE'VE GOT TO SAVE THOSE PEOPLE!
I CAN SAVE THE WHOLE LOT OF THEM IN ECONDS, DANVERS, IF OU'D JUST GET OVER YOUR POMPOUS SELF AND--
HGGK

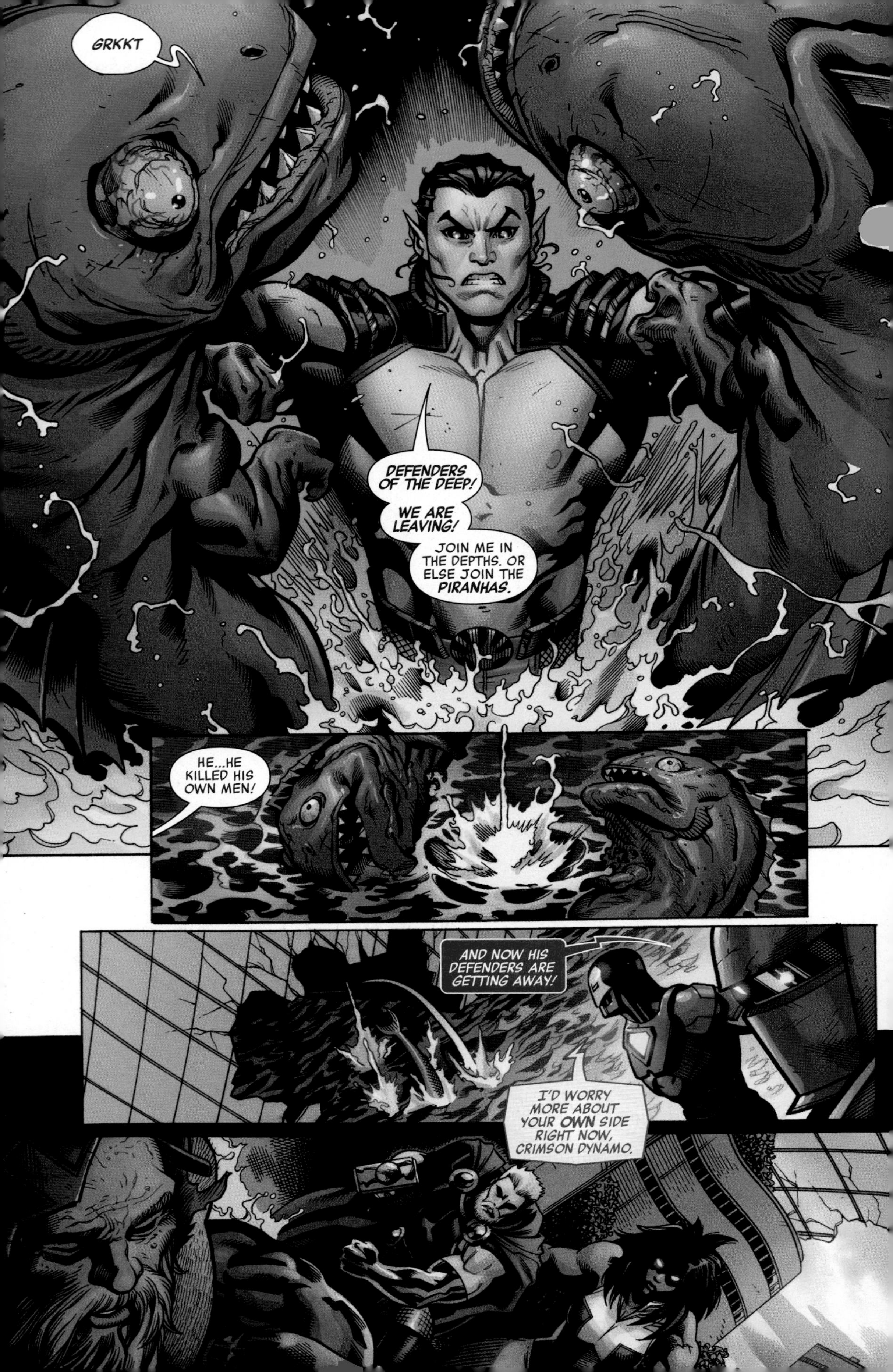
GRKKT
DEFENDERS OF THE DEEP!
WE ARE LEAVING!
JOIN ME IN THE DEPTHS. OR ELSE JOIN THE PIRANHAS.
HE...HE KILLED HIS OWN MEN!
AND NOW HIS DEFENDERS ARE GETTING AWAY!
I'D WORRY MORE ABOUT YOUR OWN SIDE RIGHT NOW, CRIMSON DYNAMO.

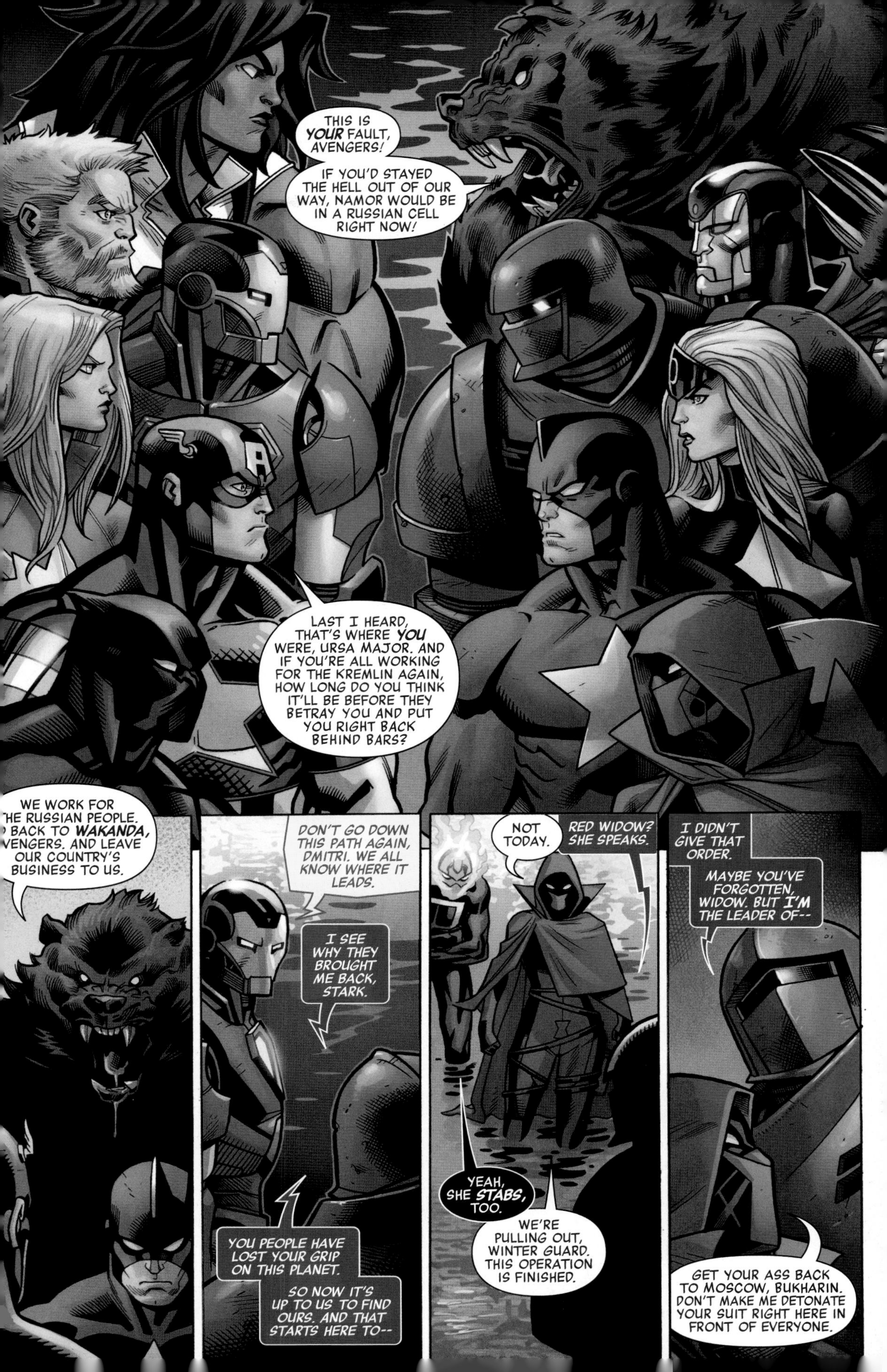
THIS IS *YOUR* FAULT, AVENGERS!
IF YOU'D STAYED THE HELL OUT OF OUR WAY, NAMOR WOULD BE IN A RUSSIAN CELL RIGHT NOW!
LAST I HEARD, THAT'S WHERE *YOU* WERE, URSA MAJOR. AND IF YOU'RE ALL WORKING FOR THE KREMLIN AGAIN, HOW LONG DO YOU THINK IT'LL BE BEFORE THEY BETRAY YOU AND PUT YOU RIGHT BACK BEHIND BARS?
WE WORK FOR THE RUSSIAN PEOPLE. BACK TO ***WAKANDA,*** VENGERS. AND LEAVE OUR COUNTRY'S BUSINESS TO US.
DON'T GO DOWN THIS PATH AGAIN, DMITRI. WE ALL KNOW WHERE IT LEADS.
I SEE WHY THEY BROUGHT ME BACK, STARK.
YOU PEOPLE HAVE LOST YOUR GRIP ON THIS PLANET.
SO NOW IT'S UP TO US TO FIND OURS. AND THAT STARTS HERE TO--
NOT TODAY.
RED WIDOW? SHE SPEAKS.
YEAH, SHE ***STABS,*** TOO.
WE'RE PULLING OUT, WINTER GUARD. THIS OPERATION IS FINISHED.
I DIDN'T GIVE THAT ORDER.
MAYBE YOU'VE FORGOTTEN, WIDOW. BUT ***I'M*** THE LEADER OF--
GET YOUR ASS BACK TO MOSCOW, BUKHARIN. DON'T MAKE ME DETONATE YOUR SUIT RIGHT HERE IN FRONT OF EVERYONE.

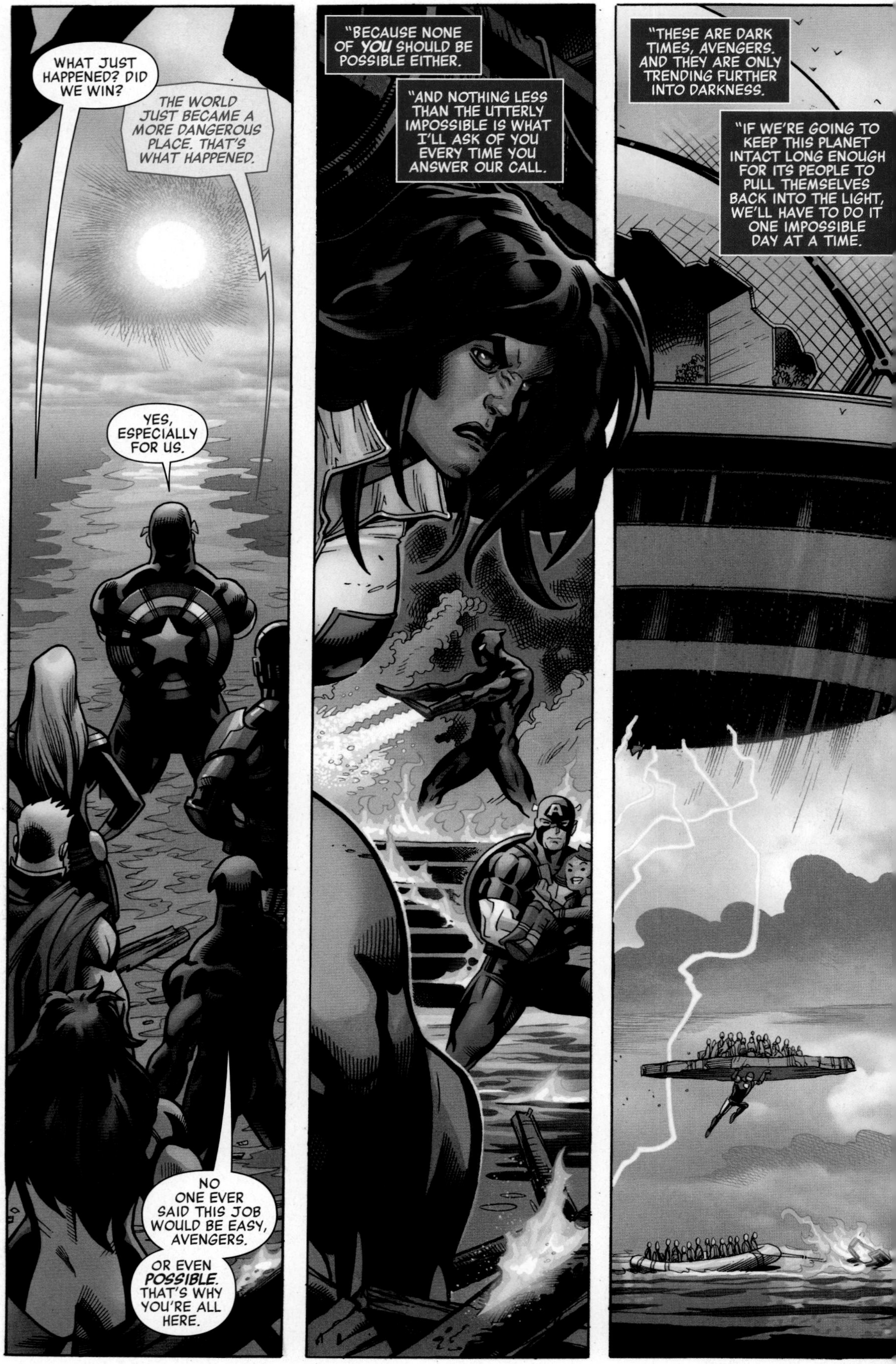
WHAT JUST HAPPENED? DID WE WIN?
THE WORLD JUST BECAME A MORE DANGEROUS PLACE. THAT'S WHAT HAPPENED.
YES, ESPECIALLY FOR US.
NO ONE EVER SAID THIS JOB WOULD BE EASY, AVENGERS.
OR EVEN POSSIBLE. THAT'S WHY YOU'RE ALL HERE.
"BECAUSE NONE OF YOU SHOULD BE POSSIBLE EITHER.
"AND NOTHING LESS THAN THE UTTERLY IMPOSSIBLE IS WHAT I'LL ASK OF YOU EVERY TIME YOU ANSWER OUR CALL.
"THESE ARE DARK TIMES, AVENGERS. AND THEY ARE ONLY TRENDING FURTHER INTO DARKNESS.
"IF WE'RE GOING TO KEEP THIS PLANET INTACT LONG ENOUGH FOR ITS PEOPLE TO PULL THEMSELVES BACK INTO THE LIGHT, WE'LL HAVE TO DO IT ONE IMPOSSIBLE DAY AT A TIME.

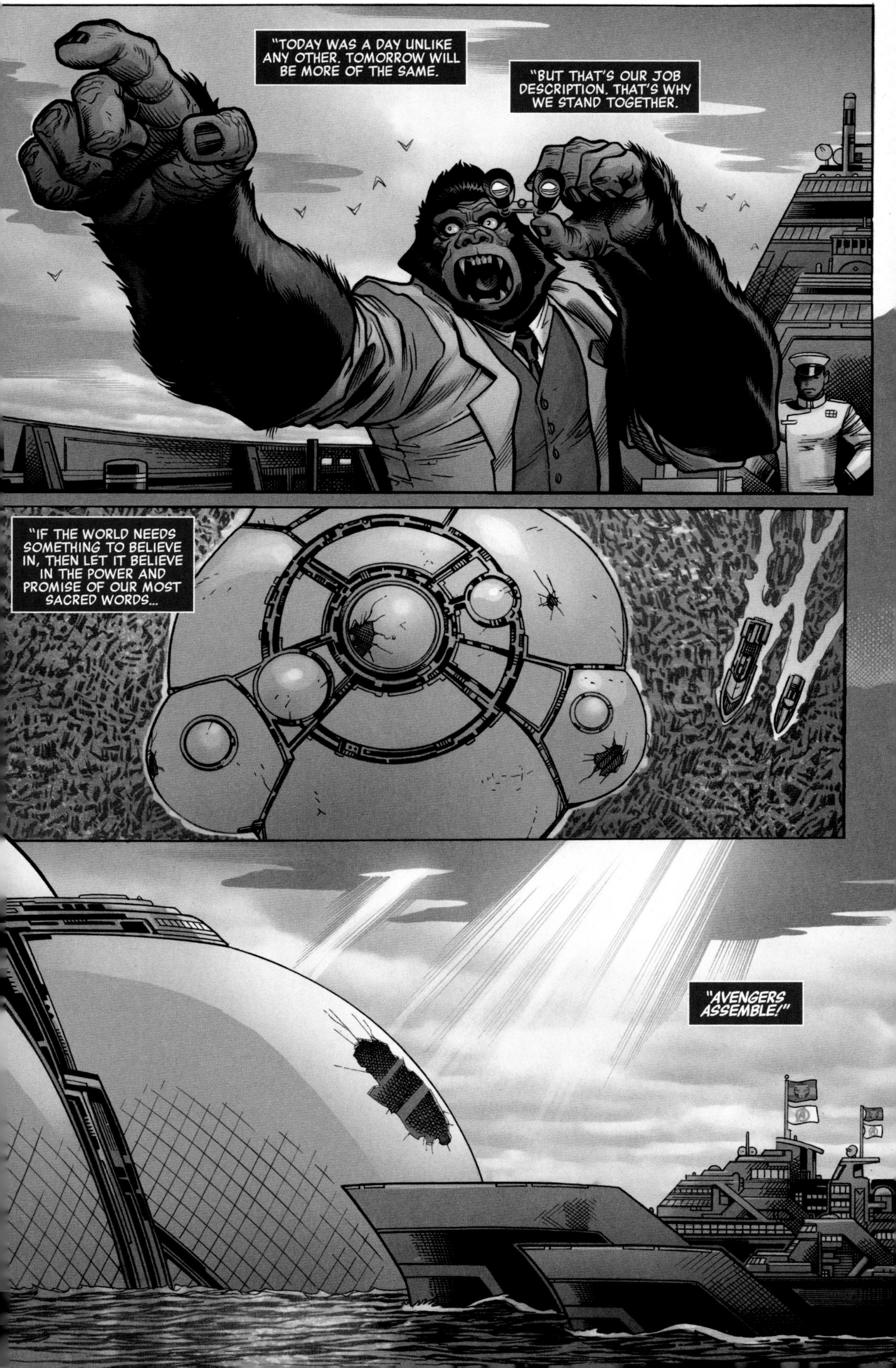
"TODAY WAS A DAY UNLIKE ANY OTHER. TOMORROW WILL BE MORE OF THE SAME.
"BUT THAT'S OUR JOB DESCRIPTION. THAT'S WHY WE STAND TOGETHER.
"IF THE WORLD NEEDS SOMETHING TO BELIEVE IN, THEN LET IT BELIEVE IN THE POWER AND PROMISE OF OUR MOST SACRED WORDS...
"AVENGERS ASSEMBLE!"

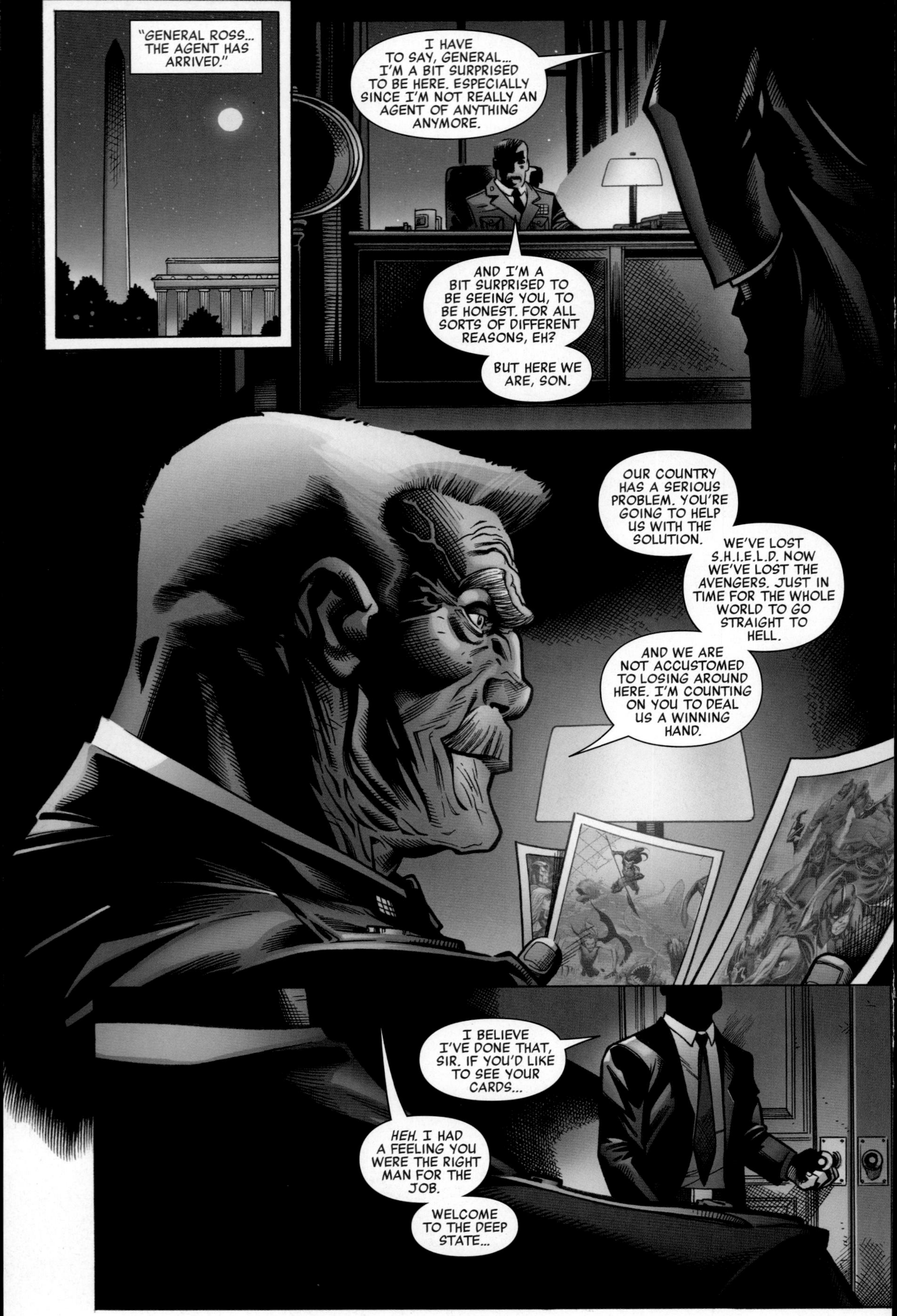

"GENERAL ROSS... THE AGENT HAS ARRIVED."
I HAVE TO SAY, GENERAL... I'M A BIT SURPRISED TO BE HERE. ESPECIALLY SINCE I'M NOT REALLY AN AGENT OF ANYTHING ANYMORE.
AND I'M A BIT SURPRISED TO BE SEEING YOU, TO BE HONEST. FOR ALL SORTS OF DIFFERENT REASONS, EH?
BUT HERE WE ARE, SON.
OUR COUNTRY HAS A SERIOUS PROBLEM. YOU'RE GOING TO HELP US WITH THE SOLUTION.
WE'VE LOST S.H.I.E.L.D. NOW WE'VE LOST THE AVENGERS. JUST IN TIME FOR THE WHOLE WORLD TO GO STRAIGHT TO HELL.
AND WE ARE NOT ACCUSTOMED TO LOSING AROUND HERE. I'M COUNTING ON YOU TO DEAL US A WINNING HAND.
I BELIEVE I'VE DONE THAT, SIR. IF YOU'D LIKE TO SEE YOUR CARDS...
HEH. I HAD A FEELING YOU WERE THE RIGHT MAN FOR THE JOB.
WELCOME TO THE DEEP STATE...

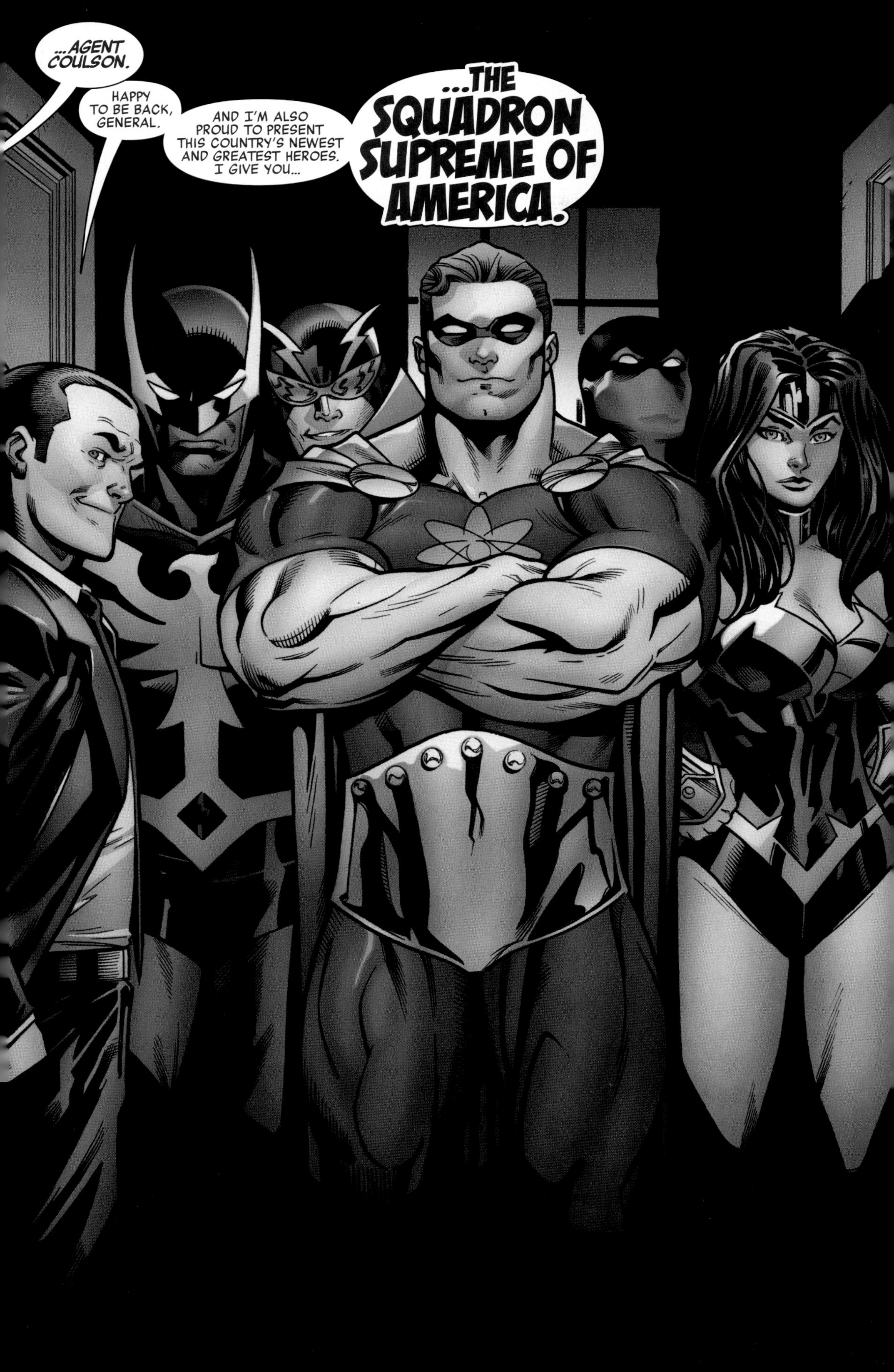
...AGENT COULSON.
HAPPY TO BE BACK, GENERAL.
AND I'M ALSO PROUD TO PRESENT THIS COUNTRY'S NEWEST AND GREATEST HEROES. I GIVE YOU...
...THE SQUADRON SUPREME OF AMERICA.

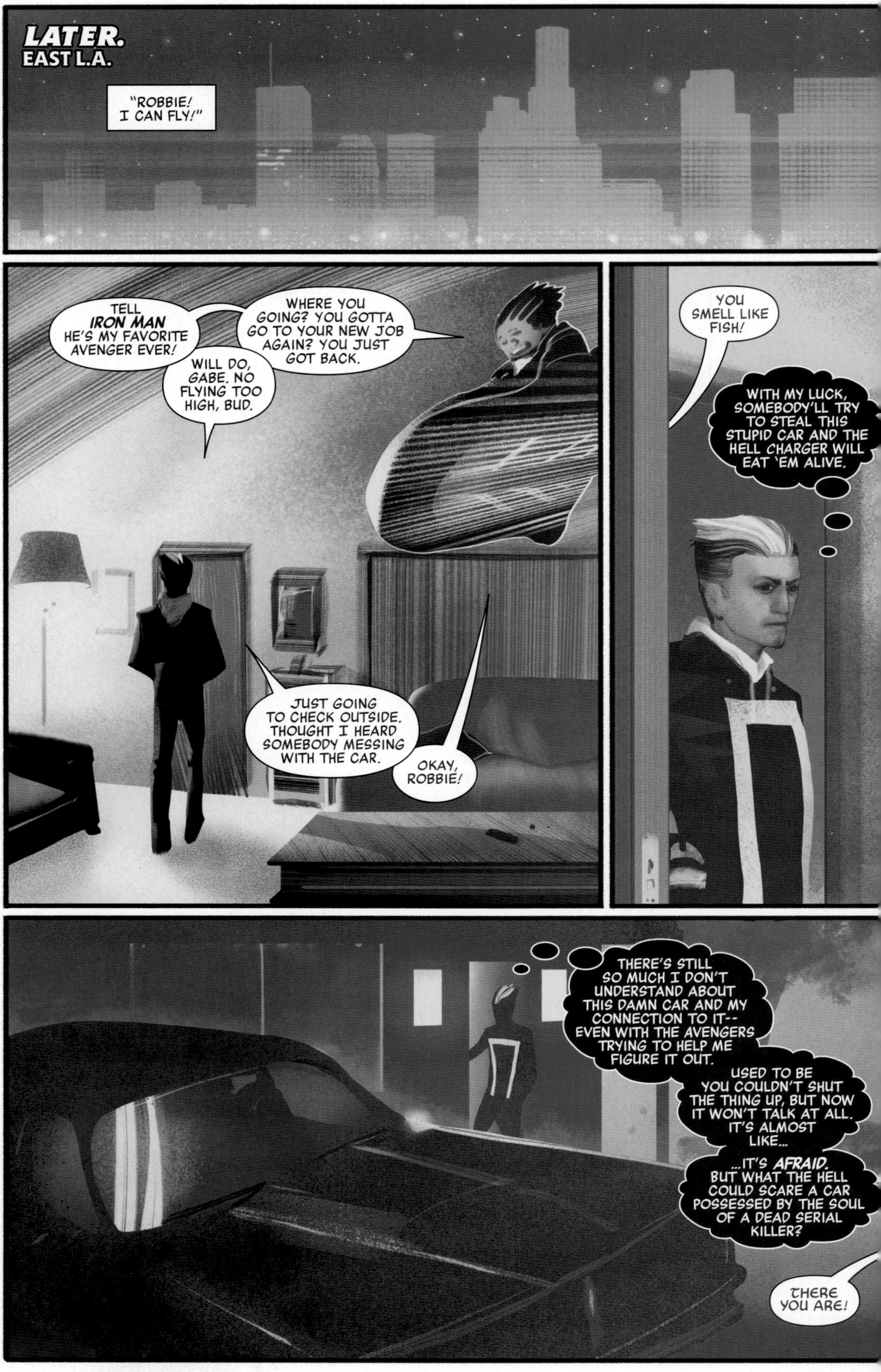
LATER. EAST L.A.
"ROBBIE! I CAN FLY!"
WHERE YOU GOING? YOU GOTTA GO TO YOUR NEW JOB AGAIN? YOU JUST GOT BACK.
TELL IRON MAN HE'S MY FAVORITE AVENGER EVER!
WILL DO, GABE. NO FLYING TOO HIGH, BUD.
JUST GOING TO CHECK OUTSIDE. THOUGHT I HEARD SOMEBODY MESSING WITH THE CAR.
OKAY, ROBBIE!
YOU SMELL LIKE FISH!
WITH MY LUCK, SOMEBODY'LL TRY TO STEAL THIS STUPID CAR AND THE HELL CHARGER WILL EAT 'EM ALIVE.
THERE'S STILL SO MUCH I DON'T UNDERSTAND ABOUT THIS DAMN CAR AND MY CONNECTION TO IT-- EVEN WITH THE AVENGERS TRYING TO HELP ME FIGURE IT OUT.
USED TO BE YOU COULDN'T SHUT THE THING UP, BUT NOW IT WON'T TALK AT ALL. IT'S ALMOST LIKE...
...IT'S AFRAID. BUT WHAT THE HELL COULD SCARE A CAR POSSESSED BY THE SOUL OF A DEAD SERIAL KILLER?
THERE YOU ARE!

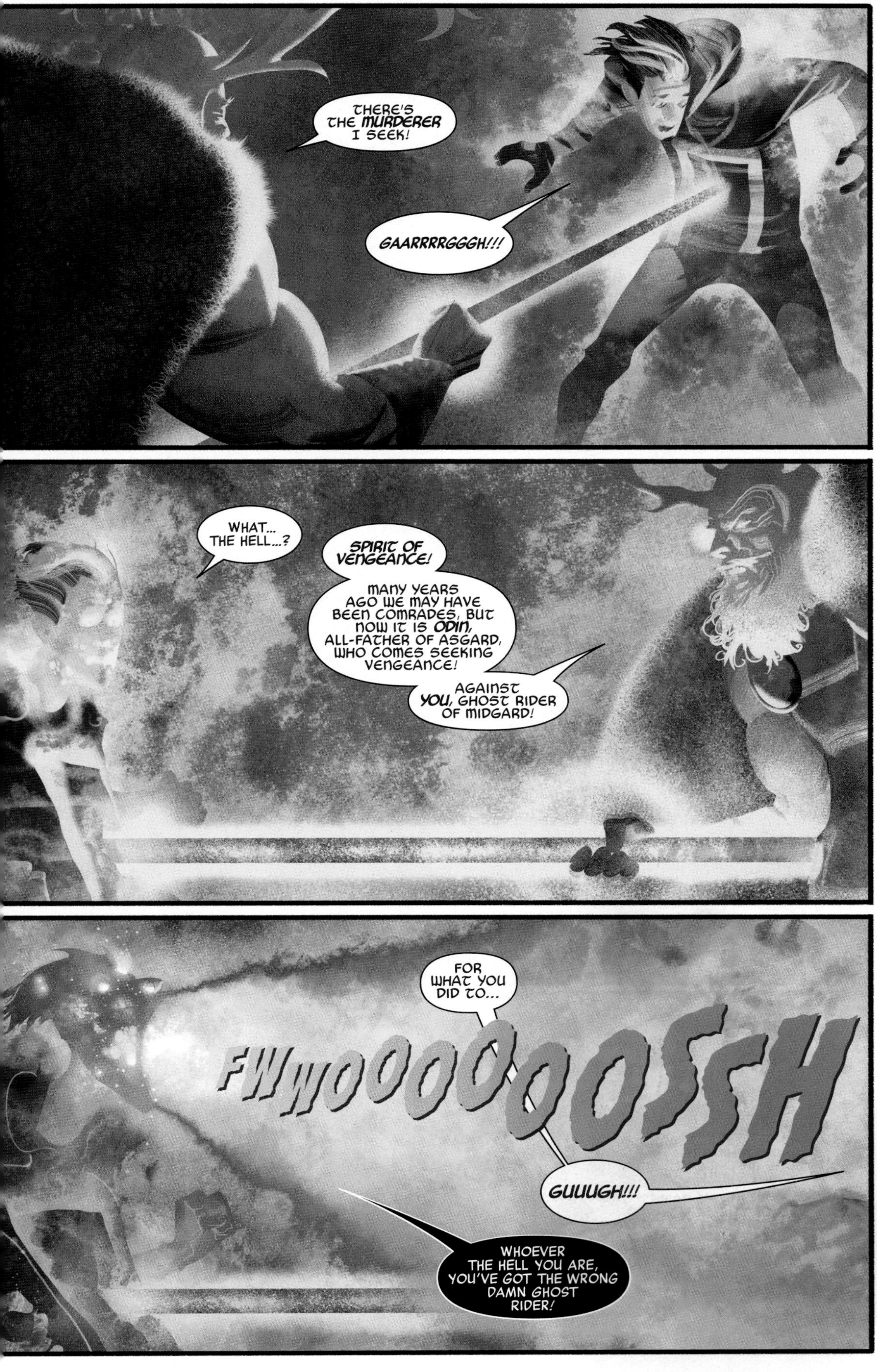
THERE'S THE MURDERER I SEEK!
GAARRRRGGGH!!!
WHAT... THE HELL...?
SPIRIT OF VENGEANCE!
MANY YEARS AGO WE MAY HAVE BEEN COMRADES, BUT NOW IT IS ODIN, ALL-FATHER OF ASGARD, WHO COMES SEEKING VENGEANCE!
AGAINST YOU, GHOST RIDER OF MIDGARD!
FOR WHAT YOU DID TO...
FWWOOOOOOOSSH
GUUUGH!!!
WHOEVER THE HELL YOU ARE, YOU'VE GOT THE WRONG DAMN GHOST RIDER!

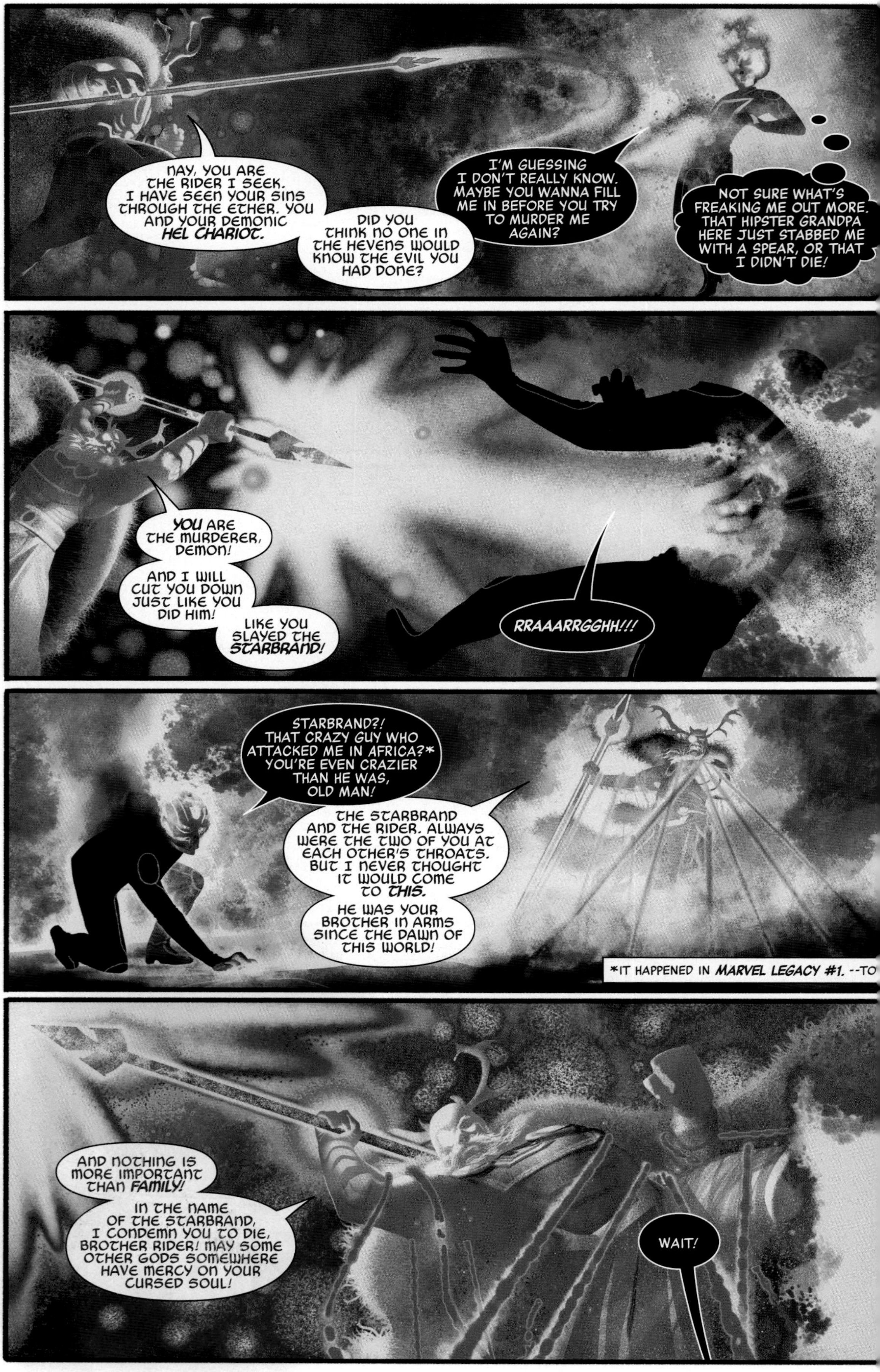
NAY, YOU ARE THE RIDER I SEEK. I HAVE SEEN YOUR SINS THROUGH THE ETHER. YOU AND YOUR DEMONIC HEL CHARIOT.
DID YOU THINK NO ONE IN THE HEVENS WOULD KNOW THE EVIL YOU HAD DONE?
I'M GUESSING I DON'T REALLY KNOW. MAYBE YOU WANNA FILL ME IN BEFORE YOU TRY TO MURDER ME AGAIN?
NOT SURE WHAT'S FREAKING ME OUT MORE. THAT HIPSTER GRANDPA HERE JUST STABBED ME WITH A SPEAR, OR THAT I DIDN'T DIE!
YOU ARE THE MURDERER, DEMON!
AND I WILL CUT YOU DOWN JUST LIKE YOU DID HIM!
LIKE YOU SLAYED THE STARBRAND!
RRAAARRGGHH!!!
STARBRAND?! THAT CRAZY GUY WHO ATTACKED ME IN AFRICA?* YOU'RE EVEN CRAZIER THAN HE WAS, OLD MAN!
THE STARBRAND AND THE RIDER. ALWAYS WERE THE TWO OF YOU AT EACH OTHER'S THROATS. BUT I NEVER THOUGHT IT WOULD COME TO THIS.
HE WAS YOUR BROTHER IN ARMS SINCE THE DAWN OF THIS WORLD!
*IT HAPPENED IN MARVEL LEGACY #1. --TO
AND NOTHING IS MORE IMPORTANT THAN FAMILY!
IN THE NAME OF THE STARBRAND, I CONDEMN YOU TO DIE, BROTHER RIDER! MAY SOME OTHER GODS SOMEWHERE HAVE MERCY ON YOUR CURSED SOUL!
WAIT!

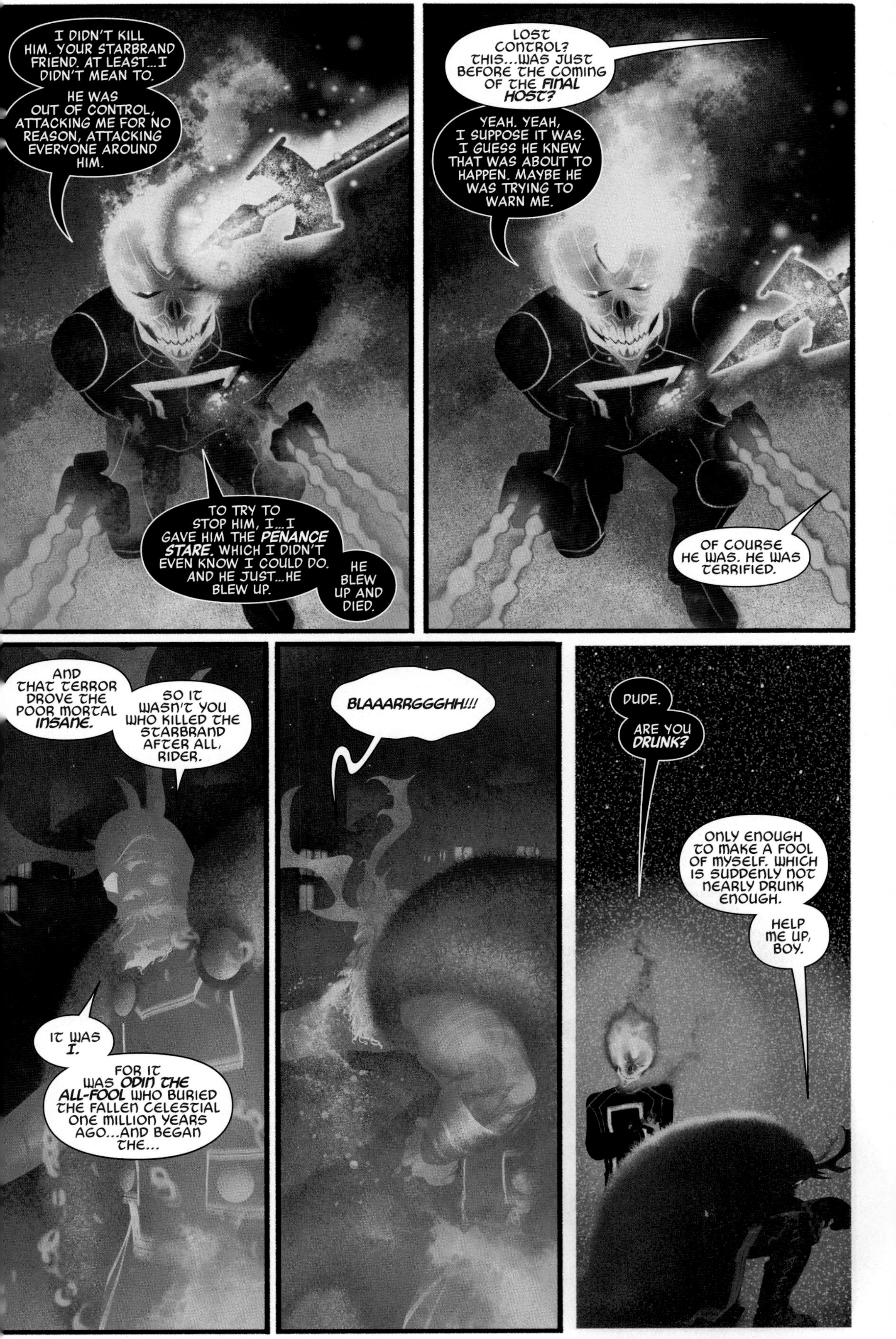
I DIDN'T KILL HIM. YOUR STARBRAND FRIEND. AT LEAST...I DIDN'T MEAN TO.
HE WAS OUT OF CONTROL, ATTACKING ME FOR NO REASON, ATTACKING EVERYONE AROUND HIM.
TO TRY TO STOP HIM, I...I GAVE HIM THE PENANCE STARE. WHICH I DIDN'T EVEN KNOW I COULD DO. AND HE JUST...HE BLEW UP.
HE BLEW UP AND DIED.
LOST CONTROL? THIS...WAS JUST BEFORE THE COMING OF THE FINAL HOST?
YEAH. YEAH, I SUPPOSE IT WAS. I GUESS HE KNEW THAT WAS ABOUT TO HAPPEN. MAYBE HE WAS TRYING TO WARN ME.
OF COURSE HE WAS. HE WAS TERRIFIED.
AND THAT TERROR DROVE THE POOR MORTAL INSANE.
SO IT WASN'T YOU WHO KILLED THE STARBRAND AFTER ALL, RIDER.
IT WAS I.
FOR IT WAS ODIN THE ALL-FOOL WHO BURIED THE FALLEN CELESTIAL ONE MILLION YEARS AGO...AND BEGAN THE...
BLAAARRGGGHH!!!
DUDE.
ARE YOU DRUNK?
ONLY ENOUGH TO MAKE A FOOL OF MYSELF. WHICH IS SUDDENLY NOT NEARLY DRUNK ENOUGH.
HELP ME UP, BOY.

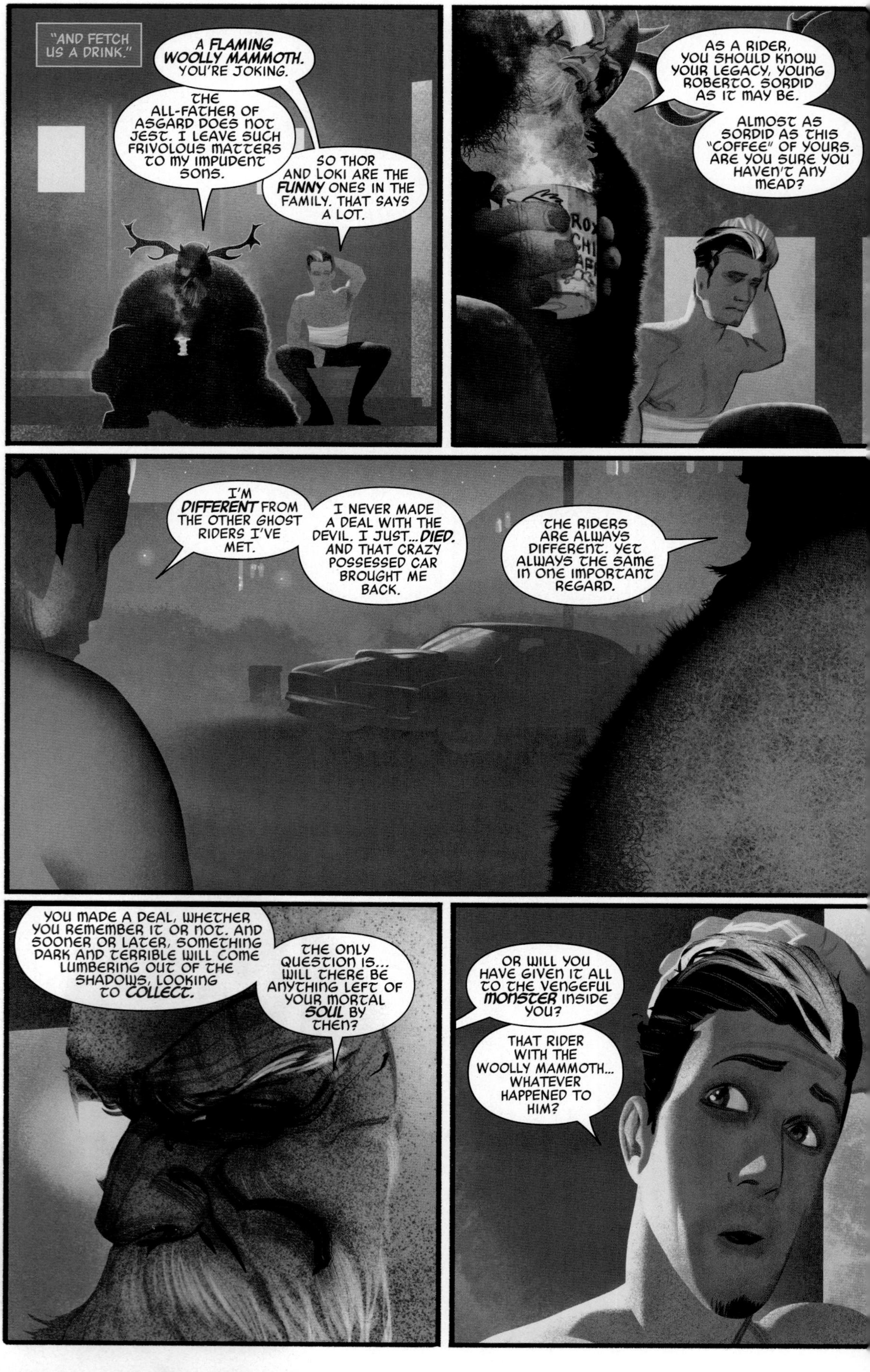
"AND FETCH US A DRINK."
A FLAMING WOOLLY MAMMOTH. YOU'RE JOKING.
THE ALL-FATHER OF ASGARD DOES NOT JEST. I LEAVE SUCH FRIVOLOUS MATTERS TO MY IMPUDENT SONS.
SO THOR AND LOKI ARE THE FUNNY ONES IN THE FAMILY. THAT SAYS A LOT.
AS A RIDER, YOU SHOULD KNOW YOUR LEGACY, YOUNG ROBERTO. SORDID AS IT MAY BE.
ALMOST AS SORDID AS THIS "COFFEE" OF YOURS. ARE YOU SURE YOU HAVEN'T ANY MEAD?
I'M DIFFERENT FROM THE OTHER GHOST RIDERS I'VE MET.
I NEVER MADE A DEAL WITH THE DEVIL. I JUST...DIED. AND THAT CRAZY POSSESSED CAR BROUGHT ME BACK.
THE RIDERS ARE ALWAYS DIFFERENT. YET ALWAYS THE SAME IN ONE IMPORTANT REGARD.
YOU MADE A DEAL, WHETHER YOU REMEMBER IT OR NOT. AND SOONER OR LATER, SOMETHING DARK AND TERRIBLE WILL COME LUMBERING OUT OF THE SHADOWS, LOOKING TO COLLECT.
THE ONLY QUESTION IS... WILL THERE BE ANYTHING LEFT OF YOUR MORTAL SOUL BY THEN?
OR WILL YOU HAVE GIVEN IT ALL TO THE VENGEFUL MONSTER INSIDE YOU?
THAT RIDER WITH THE WOOLLY MAMMOTH... WHATEVER HAPPENED TO HIM?

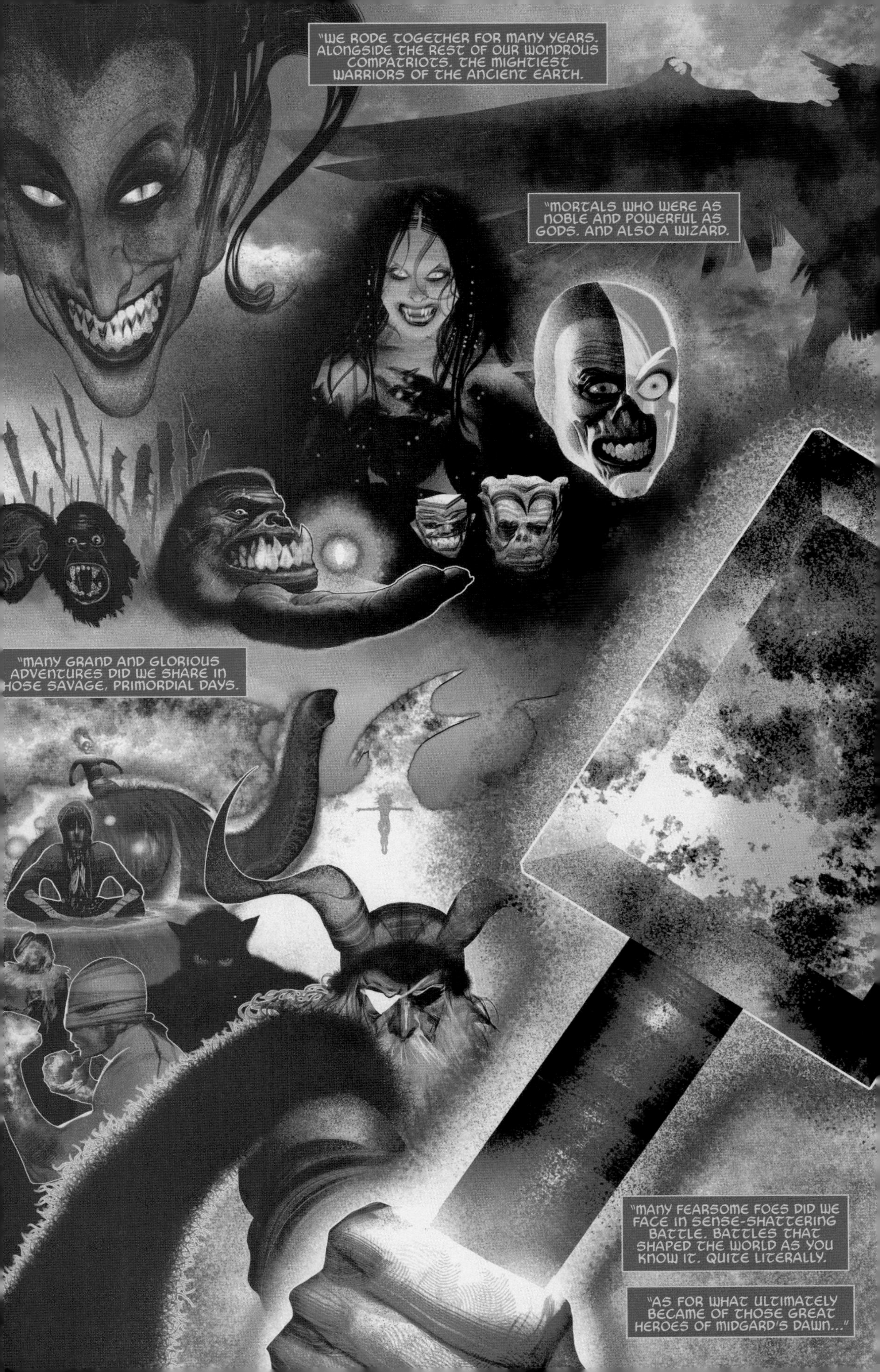
"WE RODE TOGETHER FOR MANY YEARS. ALONGSIDE THE REST OF OUR WONDROUS COMPATRIOTS. THE MIGHTIEST WARRIORS OF THE ANCIENT EARTH.
"MORTALS WHO WERE AS NOBLE AND POWERFUL AS GODS. AND ALSO A WIZARD.
"MANY GRAND AND GLORIOUS ADVENTURES DID WE SHARE IN HOSE SAVAGE, PRIMORDIAL DAYS.
"MANY FEARSOME FOES DID WE FACE IN SENSE-SHATTERING BATTLE. BATTLES THAT SHAPED THE WORLD AS YOU KNOW IT. QUITE LITERALLY.
"AS FOR WHAT ULTIMATELY BECAME OF THOSE GREAT HEROES OF MIDGARD'S DAWN..."

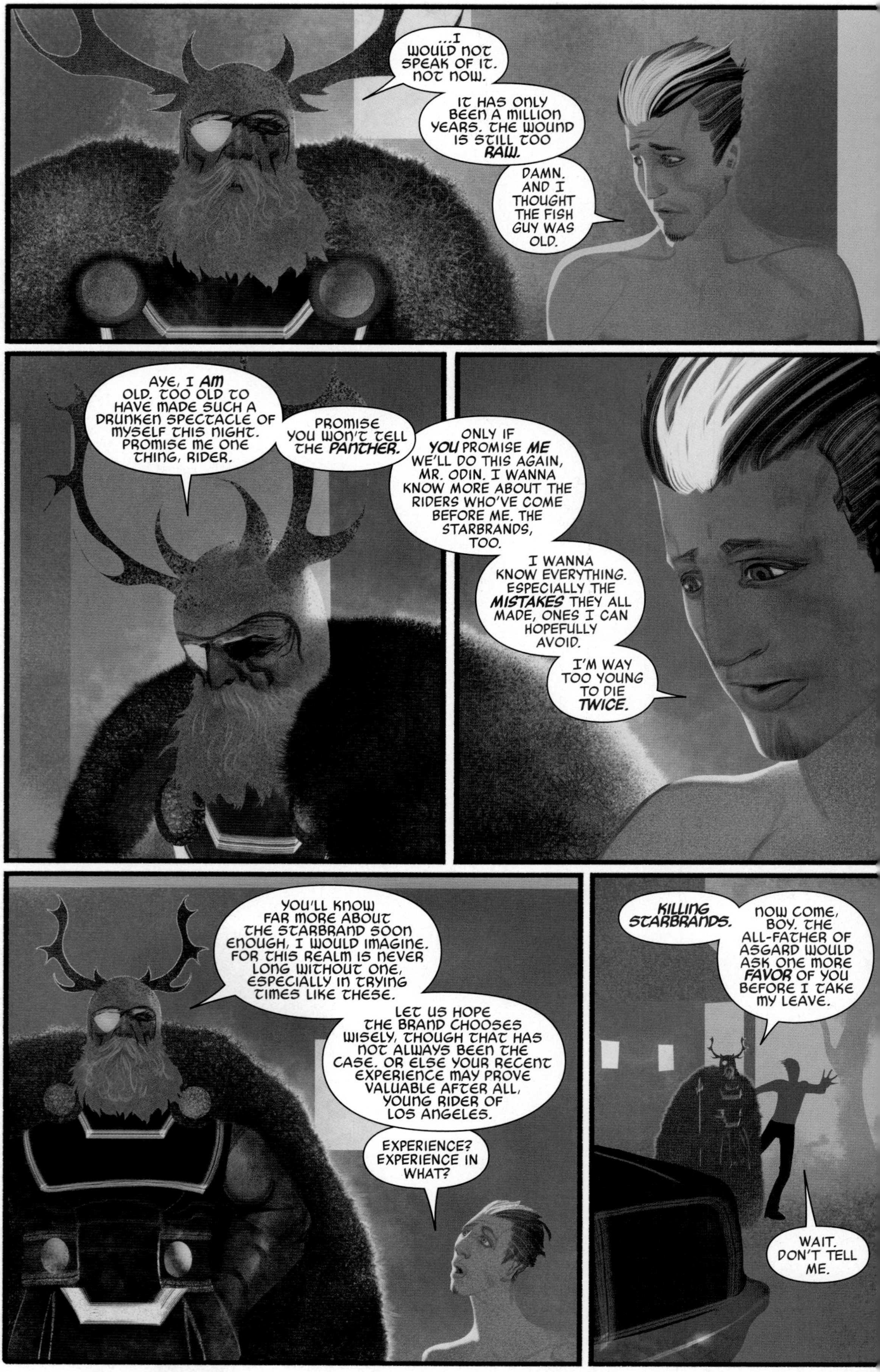
...I WOULD NOT SPEAK OF IT. NOT NOW.
IT HAS ONLY BEEN A MILLION YEARS. THE WOUND IS STILL TOO RAW.
DAMN. AND I THOUGHT THE FISH GUY WAS OLD.
AYE, I AM OLD. TOO OLD TO HAVE MADE SUCH A DRUNKEN SPECTACLE OF MYSELF THIS NIGHT. PROMISE ME ONE THING, RIDER.
PROMISE YOU WON'T TELL THE PANTHER.
ONLY IF YOU PROMISE ME WE'LL DO THIS AGAIN, MR. ODIN. I WANNA KNOW MORE ABOUT THE RIDERS WHO'VE COME BEFORE ME. THE STARBRANDS, TOO.
I WANNA KNOW EVERYTHING. ESPECIALLY THE MISTAKES THEY ALL MADE, ONES I CAN HOPEFULLY AVOID.
I'M WAY TOO YOUNG TO DIE TWICE.
YOU'LL KNOW FAR MORE ABOUT THE STARBRAND SOON ENOUGH, I WOULD IMAGINE. FOR THIS REALM IS NEVER LONG WITHOUT ONE, ESPECIALLY IN TRYING TIMES LIKE THESE.
LET US HOPE THE BRAND CHOOSES WISELY, THOUGH THAT HAS NOT ALWAYS BEEN THE CASE. OR ELSE YOUR RECENT EXPERIENCE MAY PROVE VALUABLE AFTER ALL, YOUNG RIDER OF LOS ANGELES.
EXPERIENCE? EXPERIENCE IN WHAT?
KILLING STARBRANDS.
NOW COME, BOY. THE ALL-FATHER OF ASGARD WOULD ASK ONE MORE FAVOR OF YOU BEFORE I TAKE MY LEAVE.
WAIT. DON'T TELL ME.

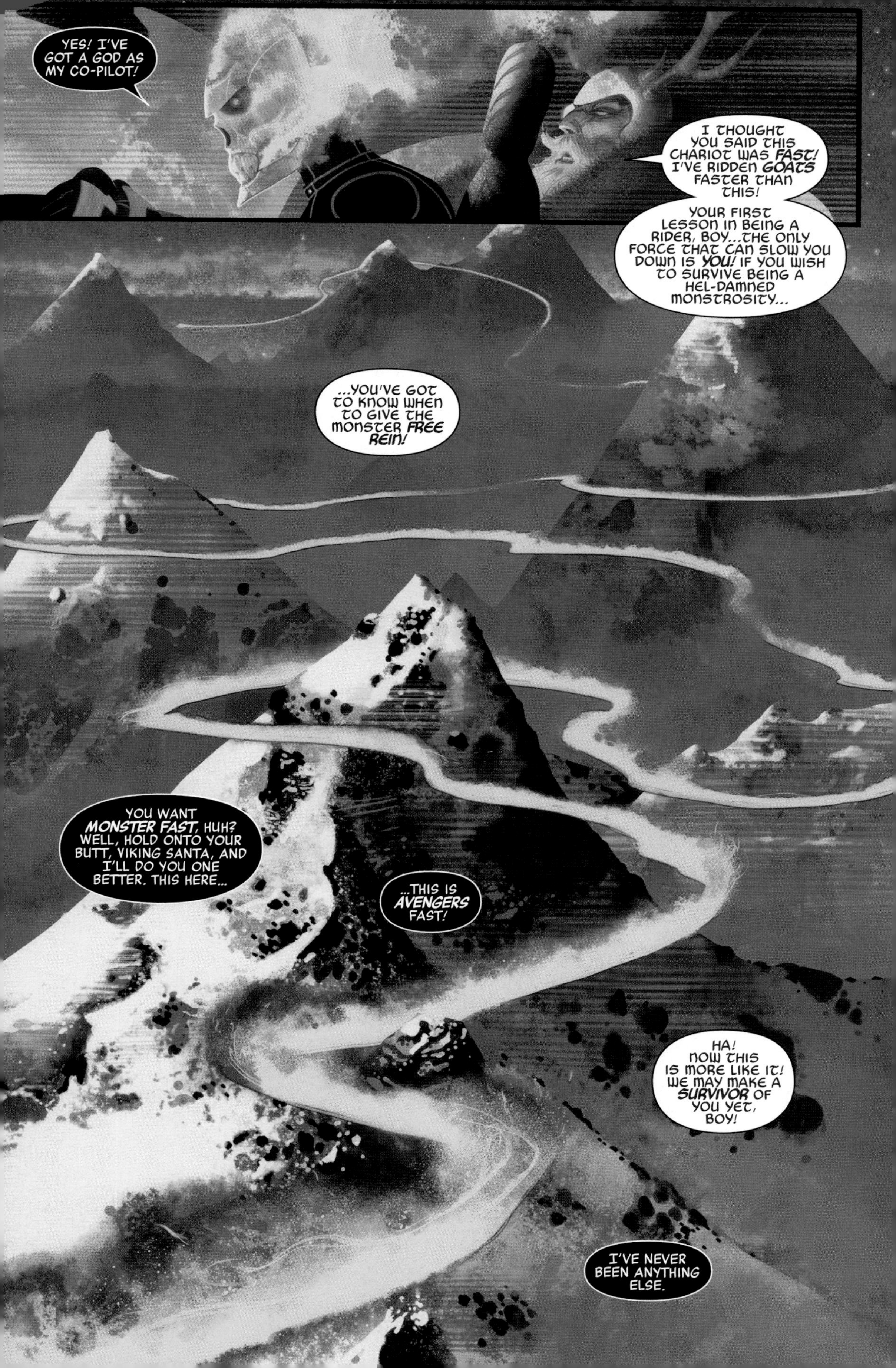
YES! I'VE GOT A GOD AS MY CO-PILOT!
I THOUGHT YOU SAID THIS CHARIOT WAS FAST! I'VE RIDDEN GOATS FASTER THAN THIS!
YOUR FIRST LESSON IN BEING A RIDER, BOY...THE ONLY FORCE THAT CAN SLOW YOU DOWN IS YOU! IF YOU WISH TO SURVIVE BEING A HEL-DAMNED MONSTROSITY...
...YOU'VE GOT TO KNOW WHEN TO GIVE THE MONSTER FREE REIN!
YOU WANT MONSTER FAST, HUH? WELL, HOLD ONTO YOUR BUTT, VIKING SANTA, AND I'LL DO YOU ONE BETTER. THIS HERE...
...THIS IS AVENGERS FAST!
HA! NOW THIS IS MORE LIKE IT! WE MAY MAKE A SURVIVOR OF YOU YET, BOY!
I'VE NEVER BEEN ANYTHING ELSE.

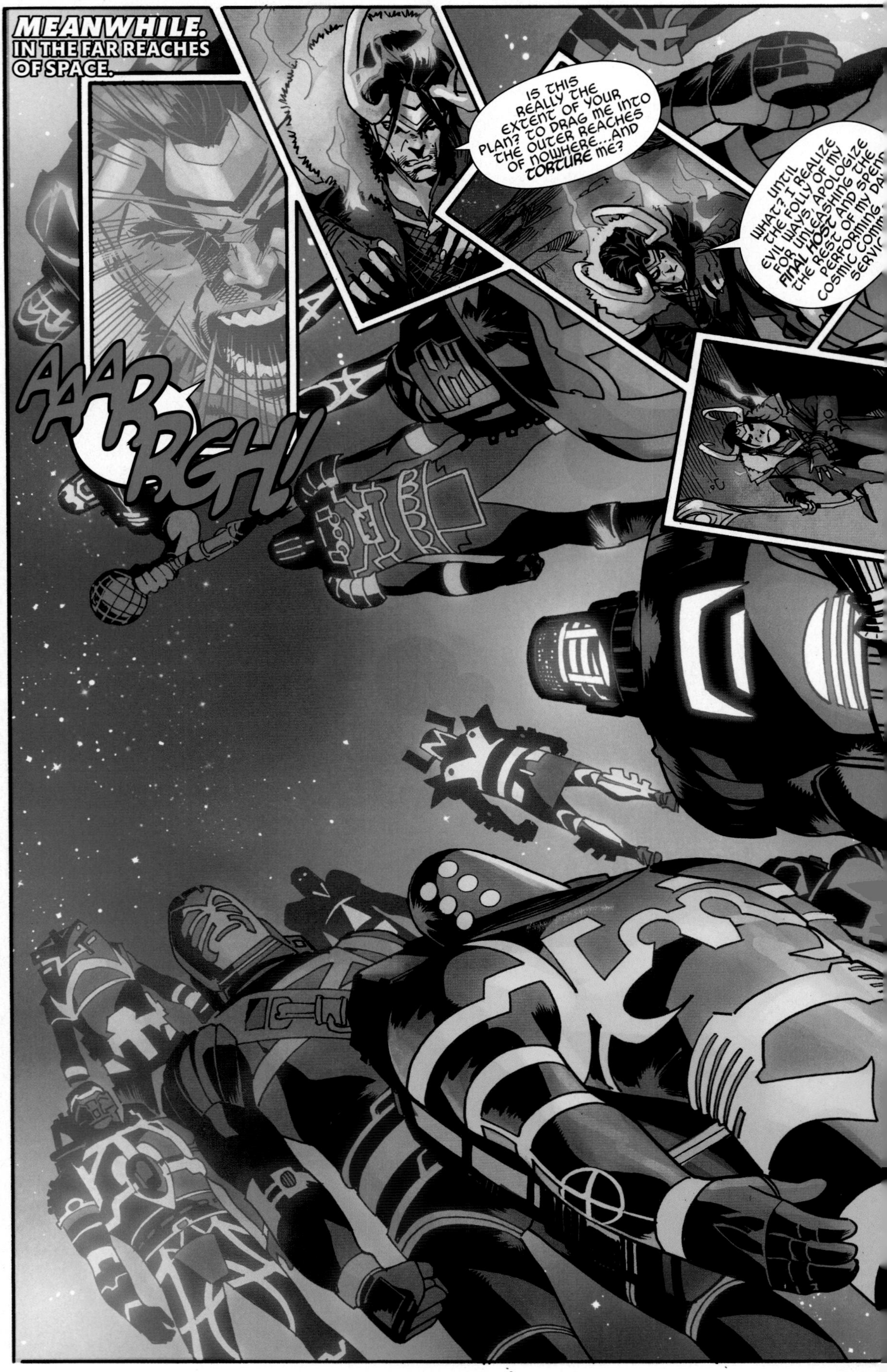
MEANWHILE.
IN THE FAR REACHES OF SPACE.
AAARRGH!
IS THIS REALLY THE EXTENT OF YOUR PLAN? TO DRAG ME INTO THE OUTER REACHES OF NOWHERE...AND TORTURE ME?
UNTIL WHAT? I REALIZE THE FOLLY OF MY EVIL WAYS, APOLOGIZE FOR UNLEASHING THE FINAL HOST AND SPEN THE REST OF MY DA PERFORMING COSMIC COMM SERVIC

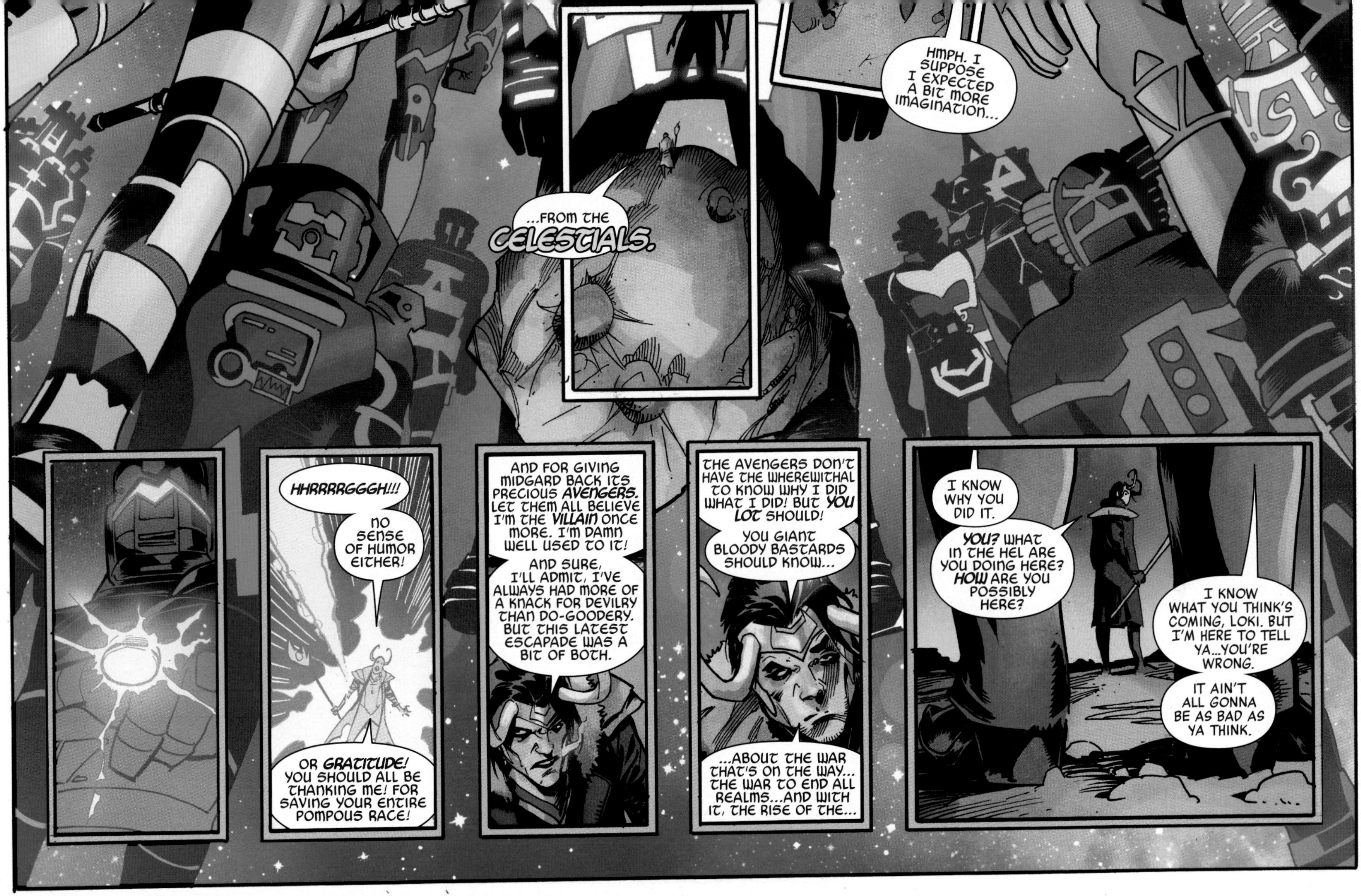
...FROM THE CELESTIALS.
HMPH. I SUPPOSE I EXPECTED A BIT MORE IMAGINATION...
HHRRRRGGGH!!!
NO SENSE OF HUMOR EITHER!
OR GRATITUDE! YOU SHOULD ALL BE THANKING ME! FOR SAVING YOUR ENTIRE POMPOUS RACE!
AND FOR GIVING MIDGARD BACK ITS PRECIOUS AVENGERS. LET THEM ALL BELIEVE I'M THE VILLAIN ONCE MORE. I'M DAMN WELL USED TO IT!
AND SURE, I'LL ADMIT, I'VE ALWAYS HAD MORE OF A KNACK FOR DEVILRY THAN DO-GOODERY. BUT THIS LATEST ESCAPADE WAS A BIT OF BOTH.
THE AVENGERS DON'T HAVE THE WHEREWITHAL TO KNOW WHY I DID WHAT I DID! BUT YOU LOT SHOULD!
YOU GIANT BLOODY BASTARDS SHOULD KNOW...
...ABOUT THE WAR THAT'S ON THE WAY... THE WAR TO END ALL REALMS...AND WITH IT, THE RISE OF THE...
I KNOW WHY YOU DID IT.
YOU? WHAT IN THE HEL ARE YOU DOING HERE? HOW ARE YOU POSSIBLY HERE?
I KNOW WHAT YOU THINK'S COMING, LOKI. BUT I'M HERE TO TELL YA...YOU'RE WRONG.
IT AIN'T ALL GONNA BE AS BAD AS YA THINK.

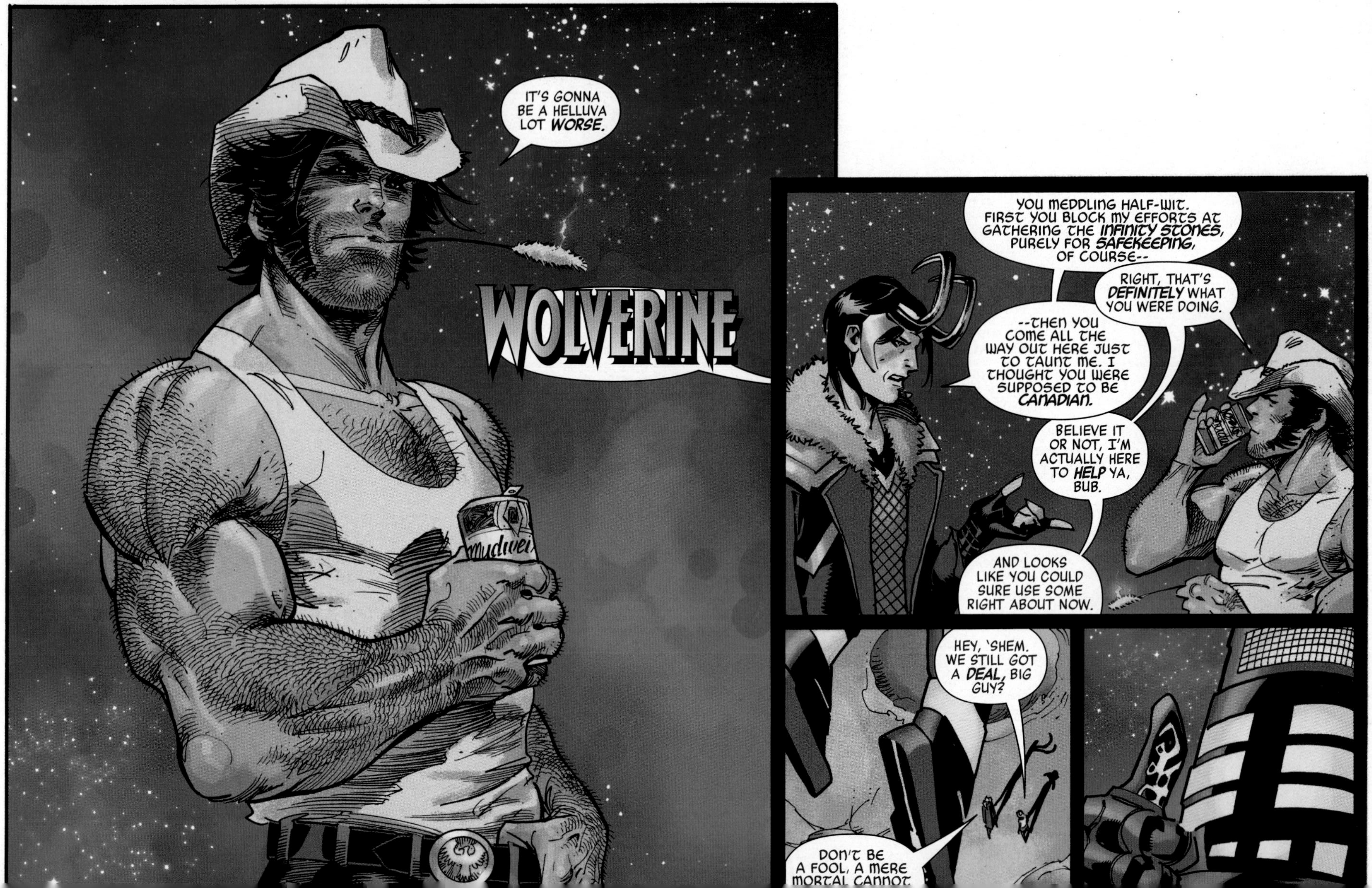

IT'S GONNA BE A HELLUVA LOT WORSE.
WOLVERINE
YOU MEDDLING HALF-WIT. FIRST YOU BLOCK MY EFFORTS AT GATHERING THE INFINITY STONES, PURELY FOR SAFEKEEPING, OF COURSE--
RIGHT, THAT'S DEFINITELY WHAT YOU WERE DOING.
--THEN YOU COME ALL THE WAY OUT HERE JUST TO TAUNT ME. I THOUGHT YOU WERE SUPPOSED TO BE CANADIAN.
BELIEVE IT OR NOT, I'M ACTUALLY HERE TO HELP YA, BUB.
AND LOOKS LIKE YOU COULD SURE USE SOME RIGHT ABOUT NOW.
HEY, 'SHEM. WE STILL GOT A DEAL, BIG GUY?
DON'T BE A FOOL, A MERE MORTAL CANNOT

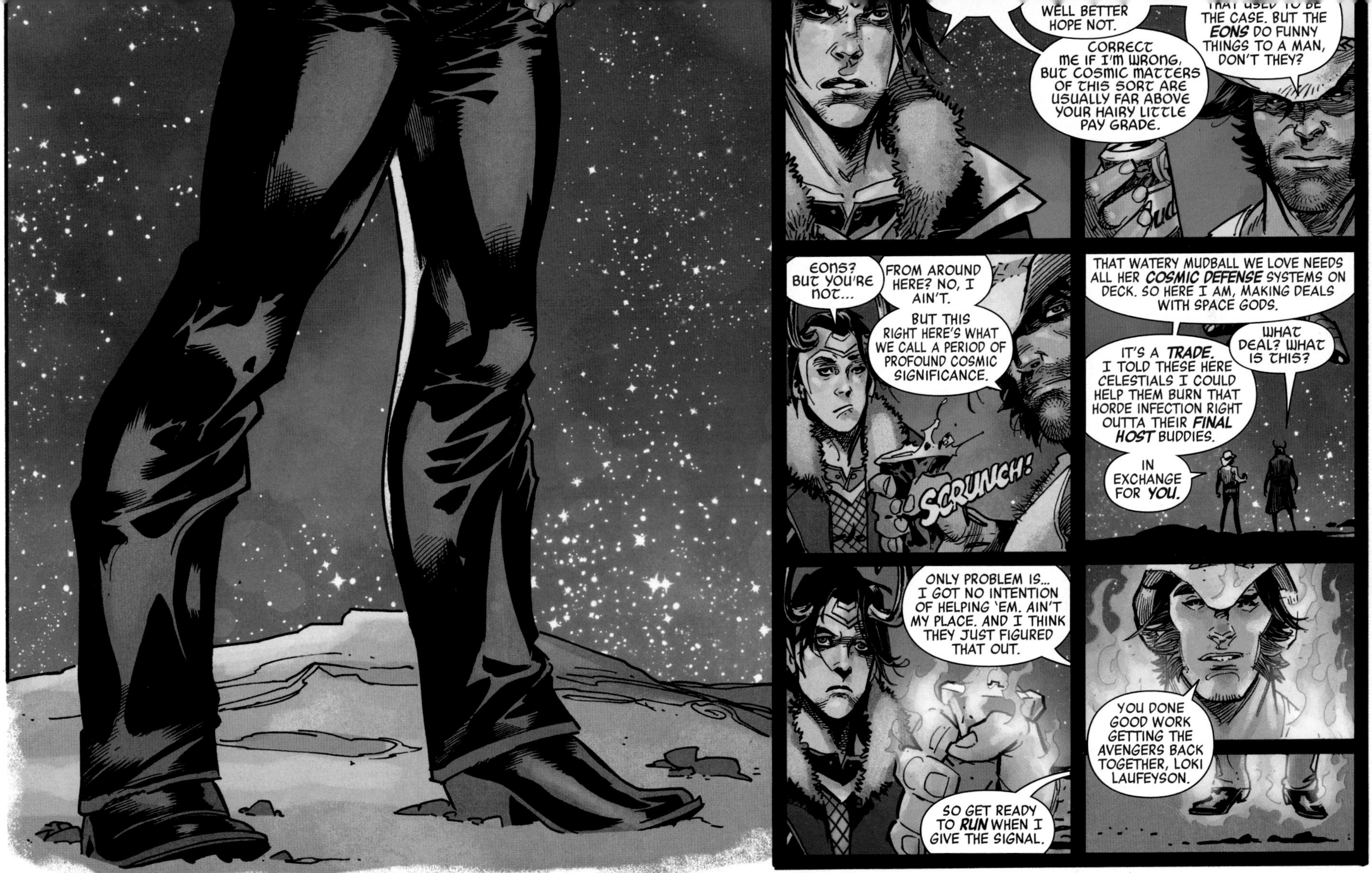
WELL BETTER HOPE NOT.
CORRECT ME IF I'M WRONG, BUT COSMIC MATTERS OF THIS SORT ARE USUALLY FAR ABOVE YOUR HAIRY LITTLE PAY GRADE.
THE CASE. BUT THE EONS DO FUNNY THINGS TO A MAN, DON'T THEY?
EONS? BUT YOU'RE NOT...
FROM AROUND HERE? NO, I AIN'T.
BUT THIS RIGHT HERE'S WHAT WE CALL A PERIOD OF PROFOUND COSMIC SIGNIFICANCE.
SCRUNCH!
THAT WATERY MUDBALL WE LOVE NEEDS ALL HER COSMIC DEFENSE SYSTEMS ON DECK. SO HERE I AM, MAKING DEALS WITH SPACE GODS.
WHAT DEAL? WHAT IS THIS?
IT'S A TRADE. I TOLD THESE HERE CELESTIALS I COULD HELP THEM BURN THAT HORDE INFECTION RIGHT OUTTA THEIR FINAL HOST BUDDIES.
IN EXCHANGE FOR YOU.
ONLY PROBLEM IS... I GOT NO INTENTION OF HELPING 'EM. AIN'T MY PLACE. AND I THINK THEY JUST FIGURED THAT OUT.
SO GET READY TO RUN WHEN I GIVE THE SIGNAL.
YOU DONE GOOD WORK GETTING THE AVENGERS BACK TOGETHER, LOKI LAUFEYSON.

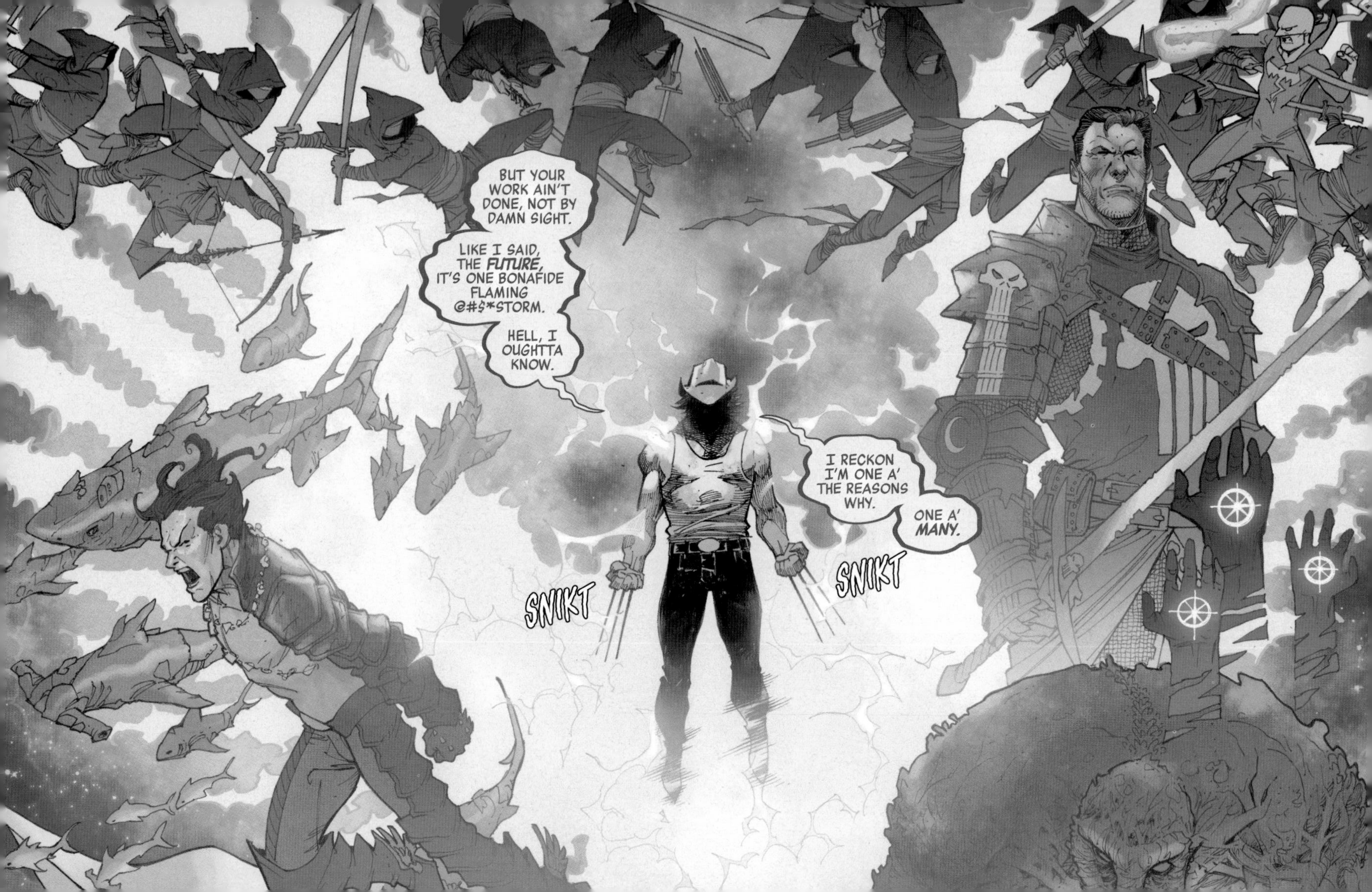
BUT YOUR WORK AIN'T DONE, NOT BY DAMN SIGHT.
LIKE I SAID, THE *FUTURE,* IT'S ONE BONAFIDE FLAMING @#$*STORM.
HELL, I OUGHTTA KNOW.
I RECKON I'M ONE A' THE REASONS WHY.
ONE A' *MANY.*
SNIKT
SNIKT

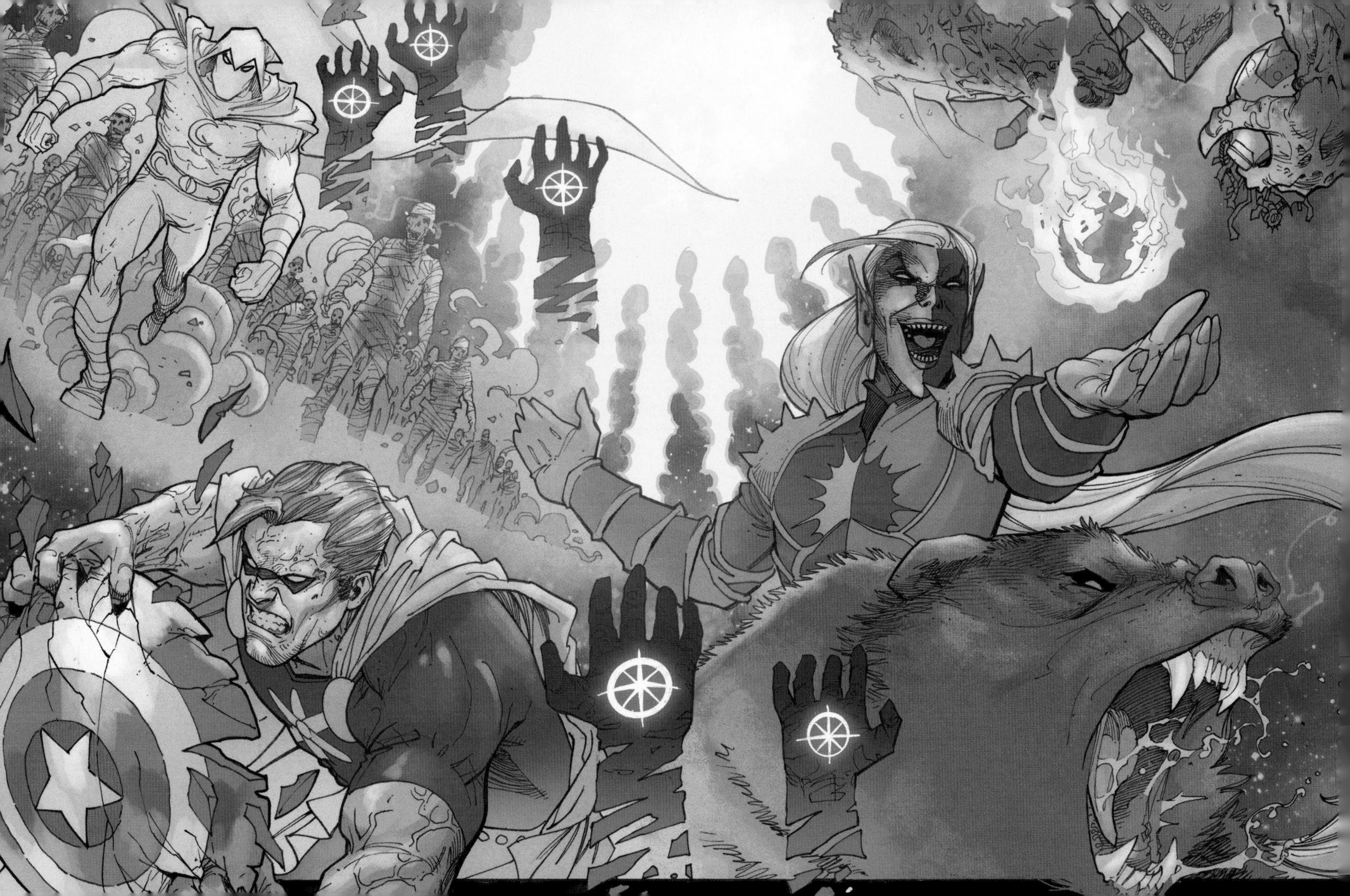

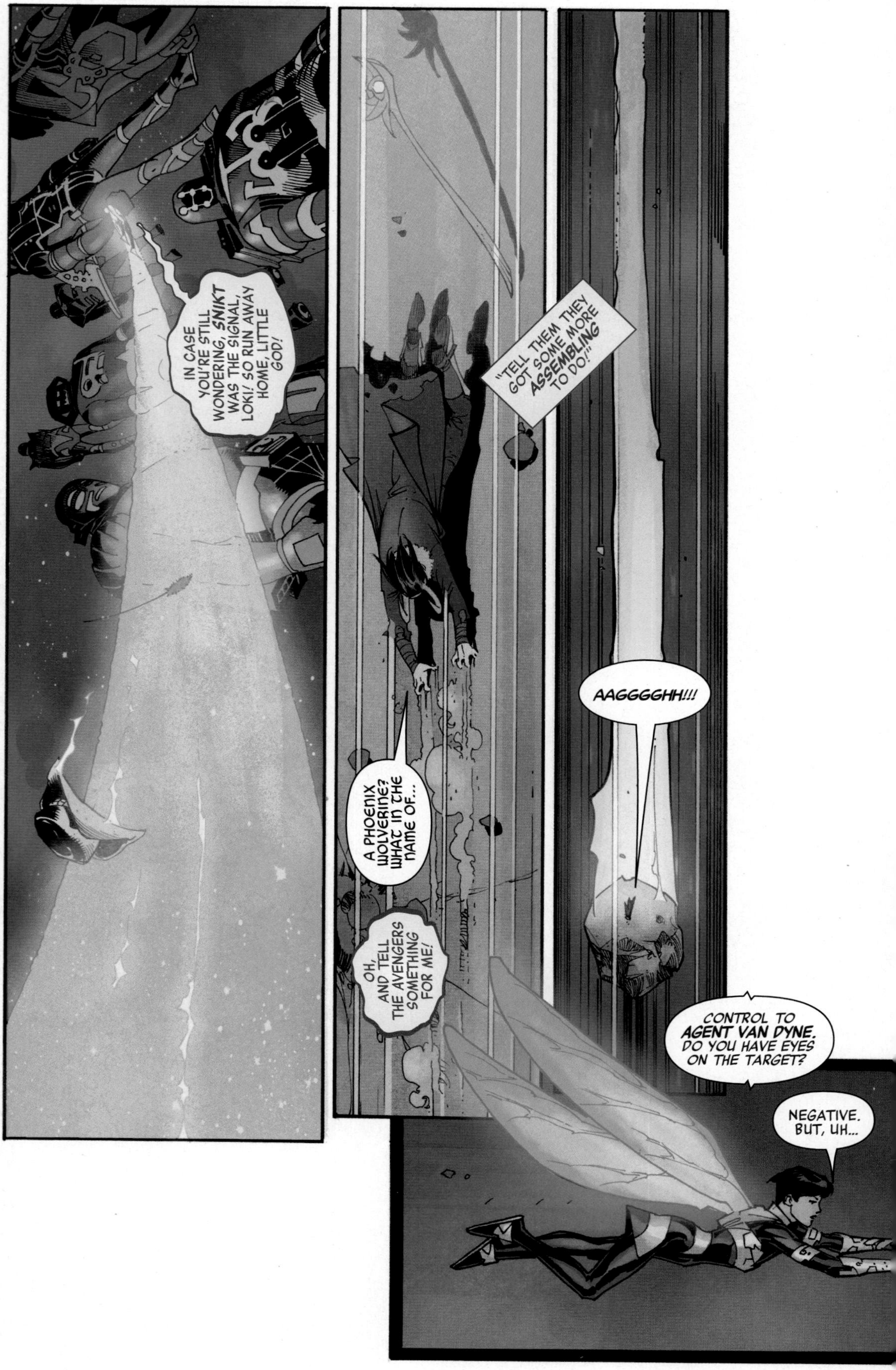
IN CASE YOU'RE STILL WONDERING, SNIKT WAS THE SIGNAL, LOKI! SO RUN AWAY HOME, LITTLE GOD!
OH, AND TELL THE AVENGERS SOMETHING FOR ME!
A PHOENIX WOLVERINE? WHAT IN THE NAME OF...
"TELL THEM THEY GOT SOME MORE ASSEMBLING TO DO!"
AAGGGGHH!!!
CONTROL TO AGENT VAN DYNE. DO YOU HAVE EYES ON THE TARGET?
NEGATIVE. BUT, UH...

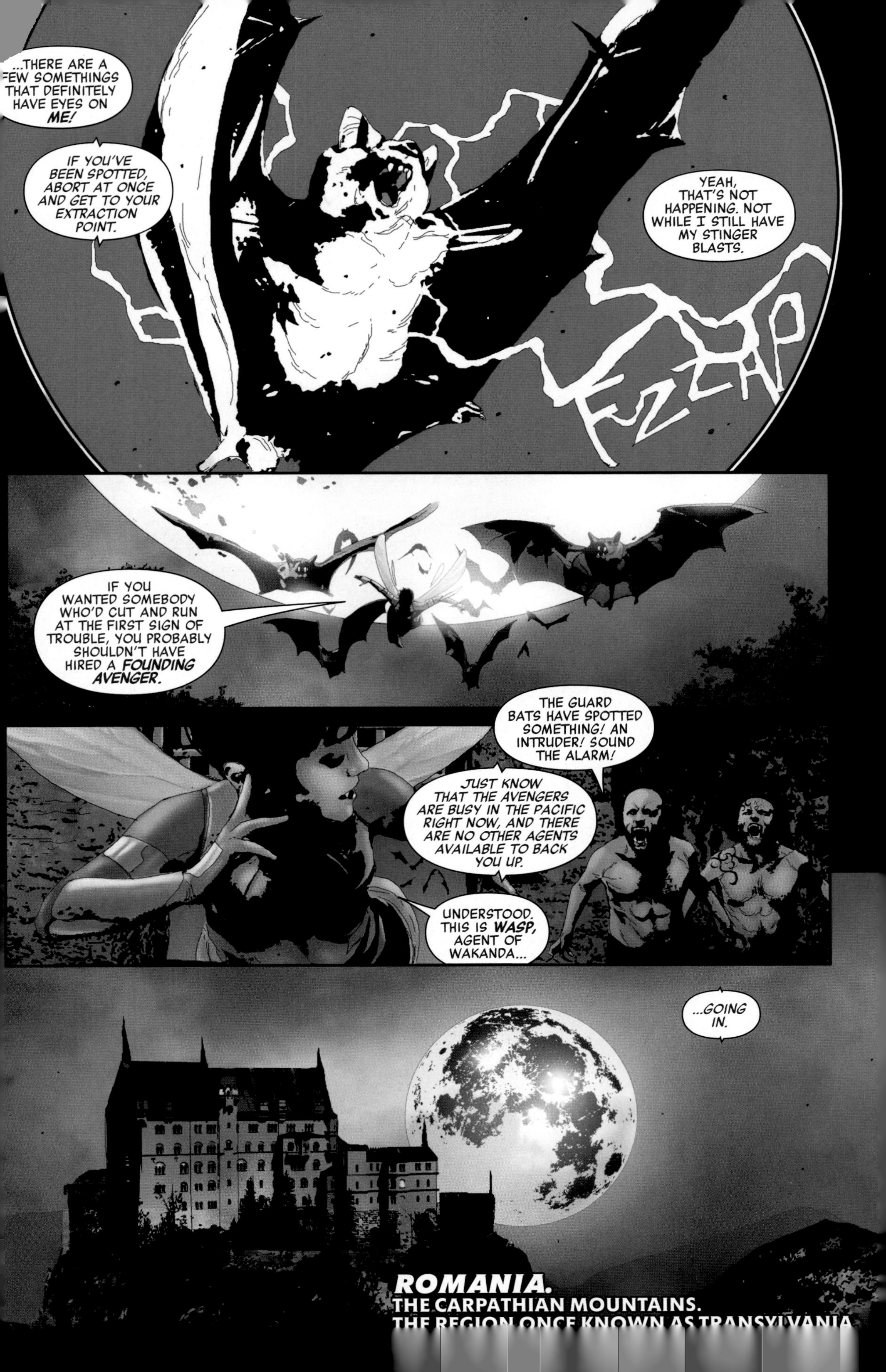
...THERE ARE A FEW SOMETHINGS THAT DEFINITELY HAVE EYES ON ME!
IF YOU'VE BEEN SPOTTED, ABORT AT ONCE AND GET TO YOUR EXTRACTION POINT.
YEAH, THAT'S NOT HAPPENING. NOT WHILE I STILL HAVE MY STINGER BLASTS.
FZZZAP
IF YOU WANTED SOMEBODY WHO'D CUT AND RUN AT THE FIRST SIGN OF TROUBLE, YOU PROBABLY SHOULDN'T HAVE HIRED A FOUNDING AVENGER.
THE GUARD BATS HAVE SPOTTED SOMETHING! AN INTRUDER! SOUND THE ALARM!
JUST KNOW THAT THE AVENGERS ARE BUSY IN THE PACIFIC RIGHT NOW, AND THERE ARE NO OTHER AGENTS AVAILABLE TO BACK YOU UP.
UNDERSTOOD. THIS IS WASP, AGENT OF WAKANDA...
...GOING IN.
ROMANIA.
THE CARPATHIAN MOUNTAINS.
THE REGION ONCE KNOWN AS TRANSYLVANIA

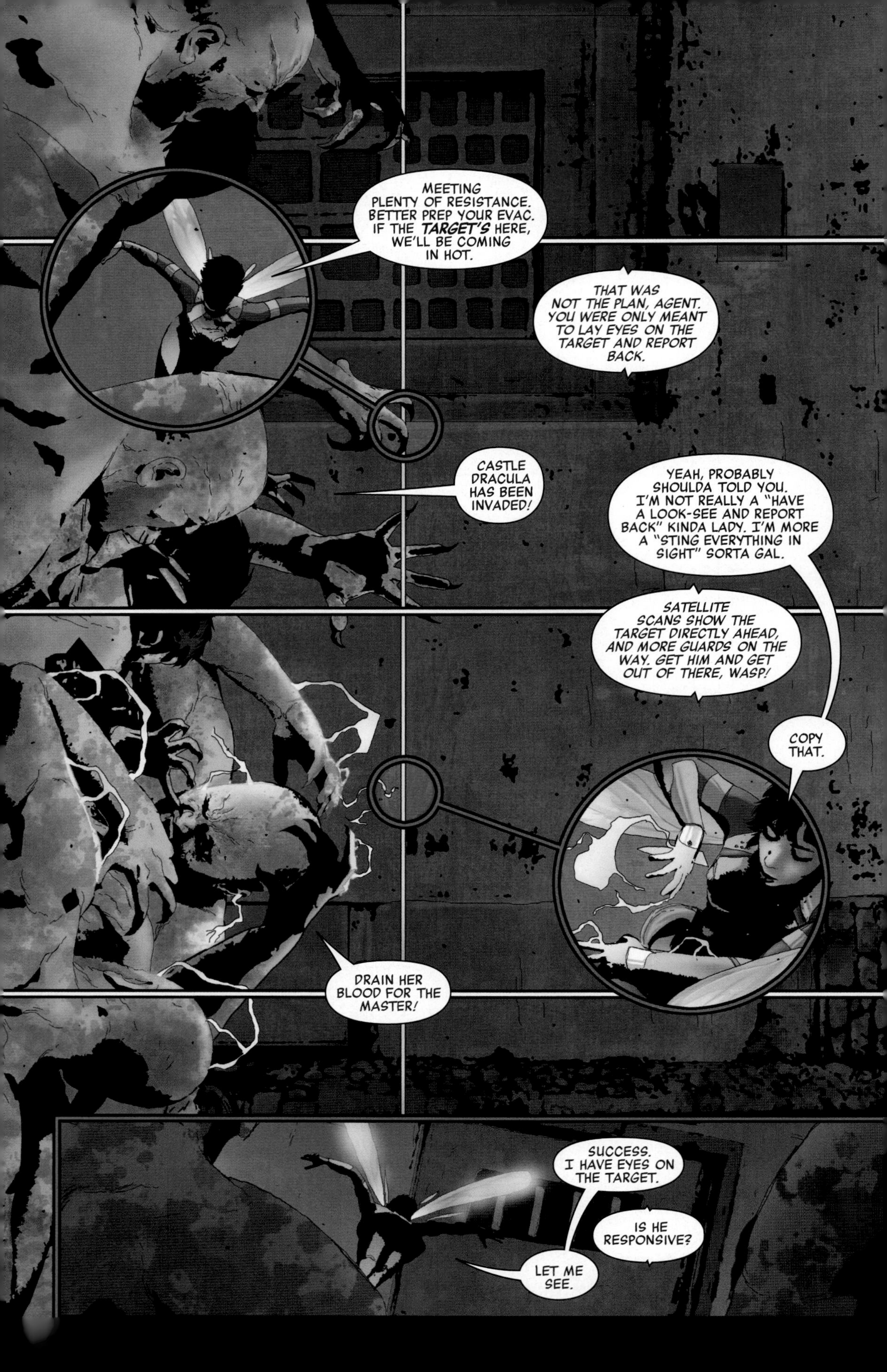
MEETING PLENTY OF RESISTANCE. BETTER PREP YOUR EVAC. IF THE *TARGET'S* HERE, WE'LL BE COMING IN HOT.
THAT WAS NOT THE PLAN, AGENT. YOU WERE ONLY MEANT TO LAY EYES ON THE TARGET AND REPORT BACK.
CASTLE DRACULA HAS BEEN INVADED!
YEAH, PROBABLY SHOULDA TOLD YOU. I'M NOT REALLY A "HAVE A LOOK-SEE AND REPORT BACK" KINDA LADY. I'M MORE A "STING EVERYTHING IN SIGHT" SORTA GAL.
SATELLITE SCANS SHOW THE TARGET DIRECTLY AHEAD, AND MORE GUARDS ON THE WAY. GET HIM AND GET OUT OF THERE, WASP!
COPY THAT.
DRAIN HER BLOOD FOR THE MASTER!
SUCCESS. I HAVE EYES ON THE TARGET.
IS HE RESPONSIVE?
LET ME SEE.

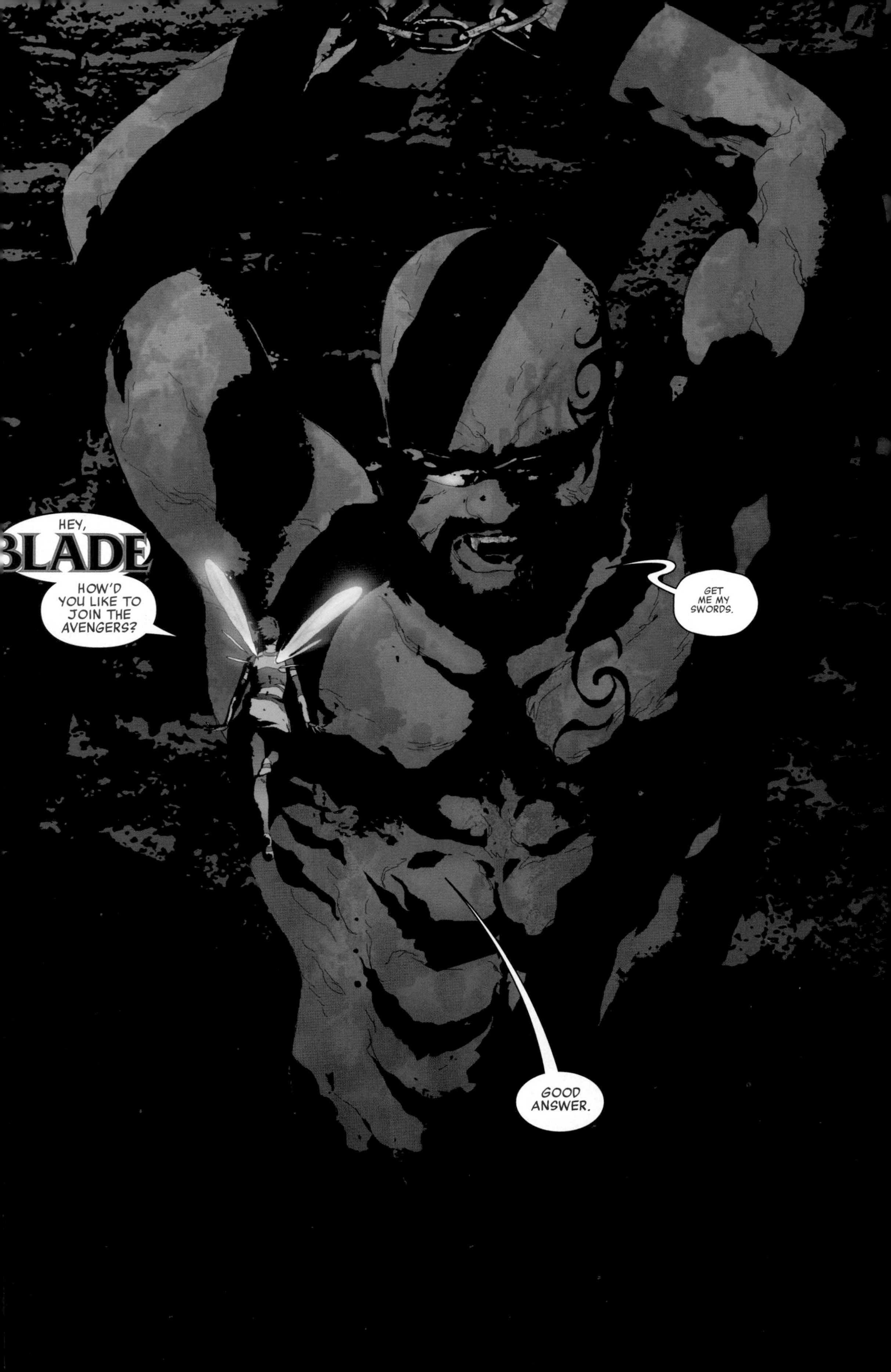
HEY,
BLADE
HOW'D YOU LIKE TO JOIN THE AVENGERS?
GET ME MY SWORDS.
GOOD ANSWER.

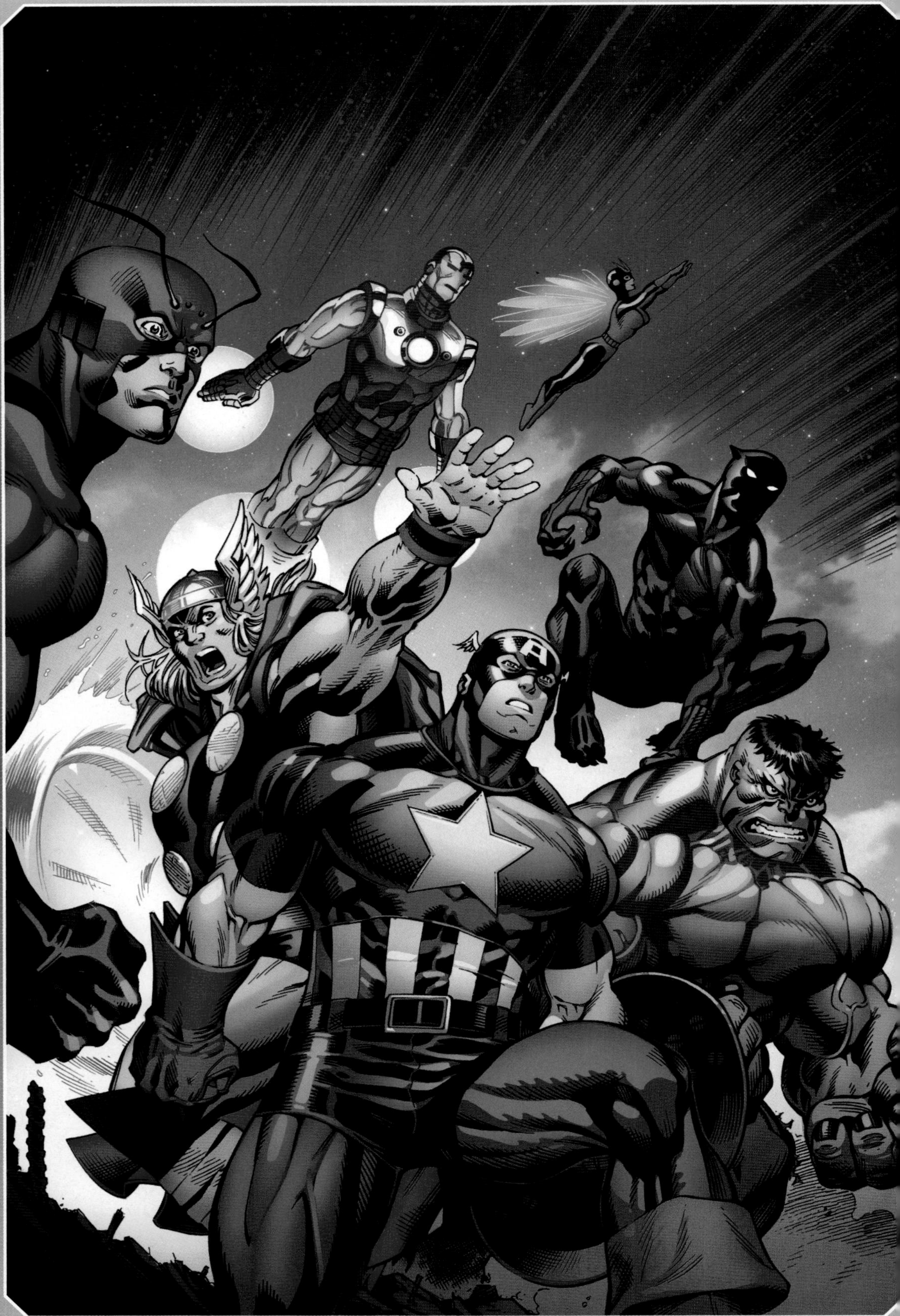

ED McGUINNESS & MARTE GRACIA
10 CLASSIC AVENGERS VARIANT

11 THE STRENGTH AND CONVICTION OF PHILLIP COULSON

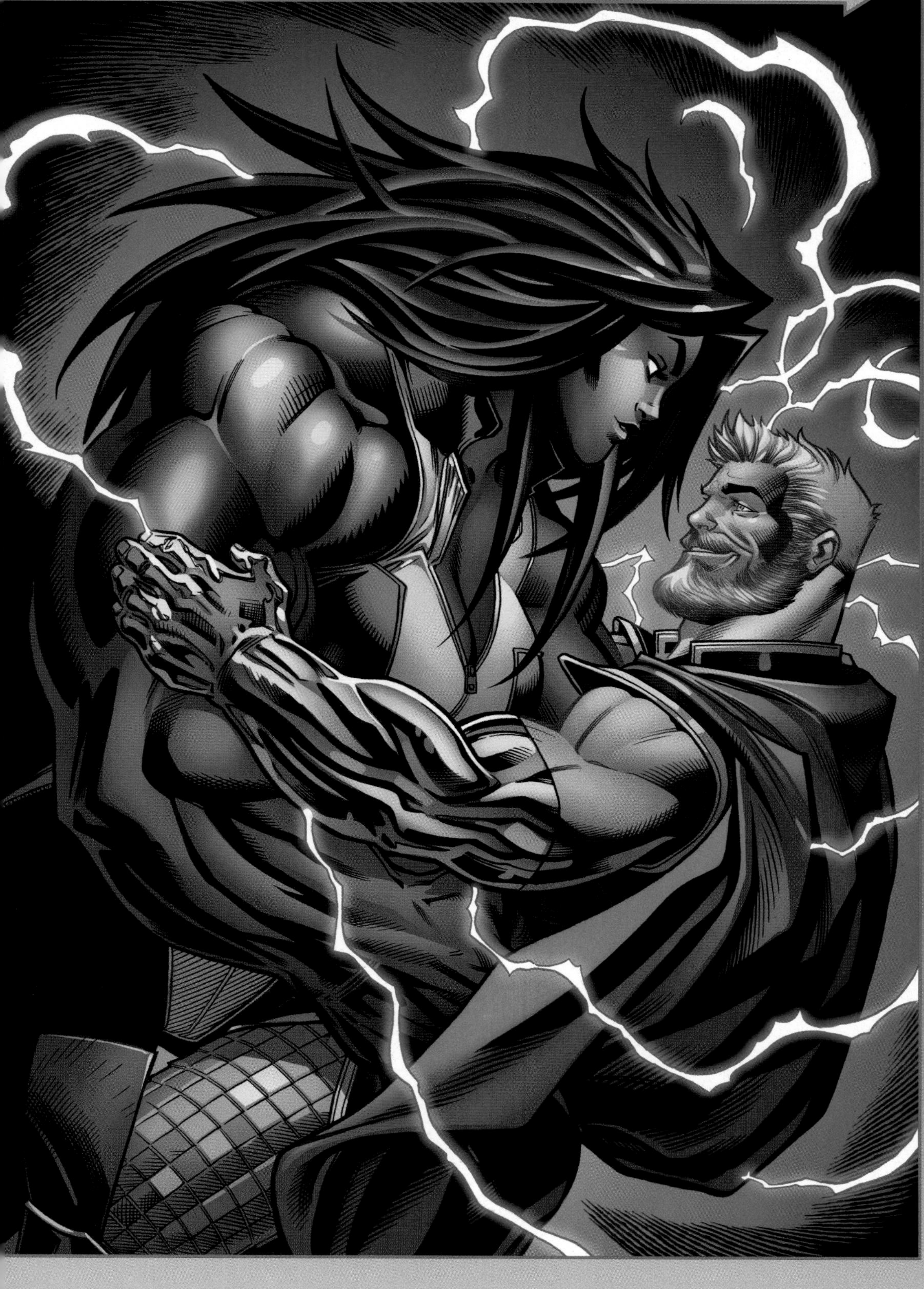

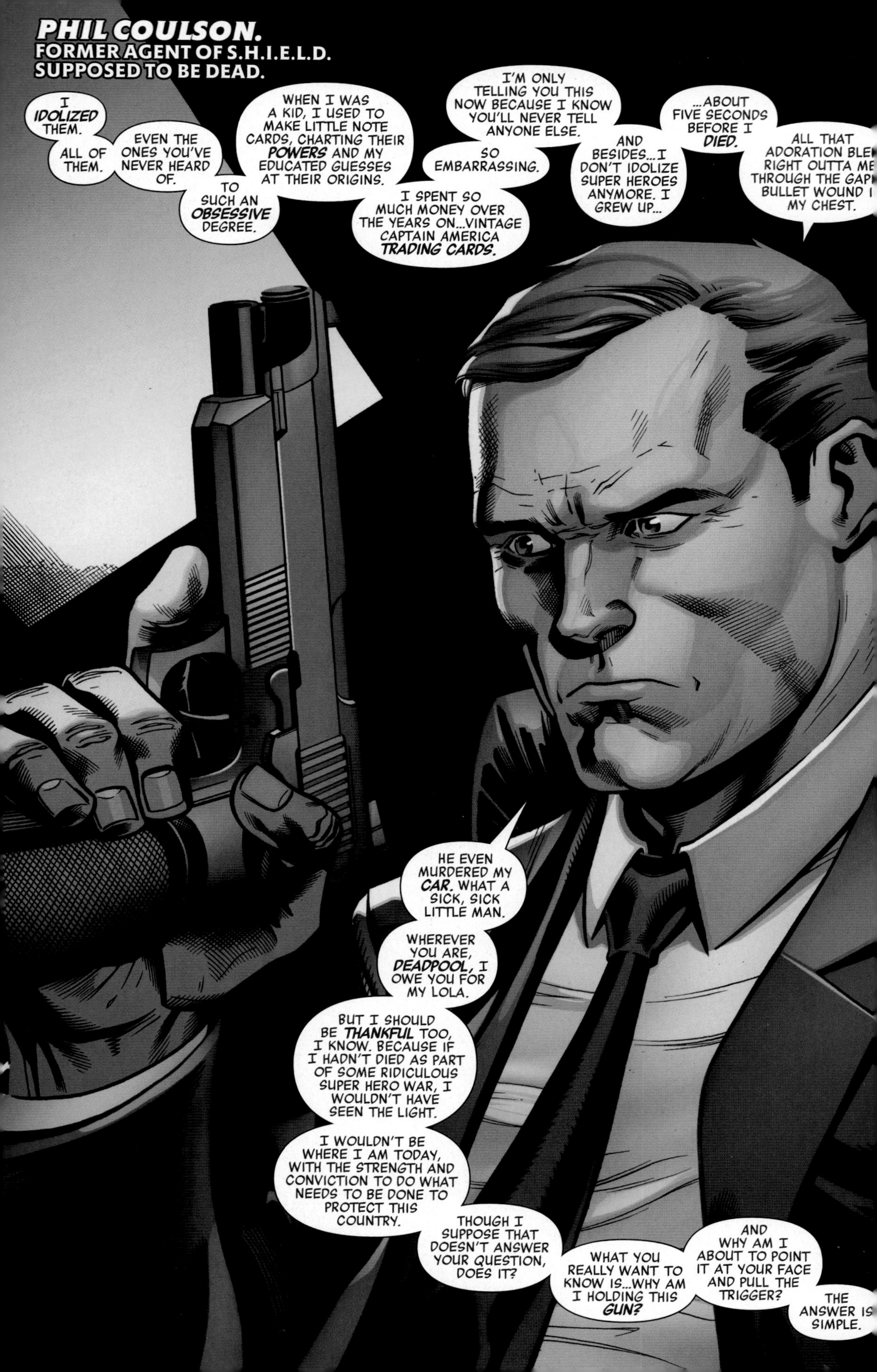
PHIL COULSON.
FORMER AGENT OF S.H.I.E.L.D.
SUPPOSED TO BE DEAD.
I IDOLIZED THEM.
ALL OF THEM.
EVEN THE ONES YOU'VE NEVER HEARD OF.
TO SUCH AN OBSESSIVE DEGREE.
WHEN I WAS A KID, I USED TO MAKE LITTLE NOTE CARDS, CHARTING THEIR POWERS AND MY EDUCATED GUESSES AT THEIR ORIGINS.
I SPENT SO MUCH MONEY OVER THE YEARS ON...VINTAGE CAPTAIN AMERICA TRADING CARDS.
I'M ONLY TELLING YOU THIS NOW BECAUSE I KNOW YOU'LL NEVER TELL ANYONE ELSE.
SO EMBARRASSING.
AND BESIDES...I DON'T IDOLIZE SUPER HEROES ANYMORE. I GREW UP...
...ABOUT FIVE SECONDS BEFORE I DIED.
HE EVEN MURDERED MY CAR. WHAT A SICK, SICK LITTLE MAN.
WHEREVER YOU ARE, DEADPOOL, I OWE YOU FOR MY LOLA.
BUT I SHOULD BE THANKFUL TOO, I KNOW. BECAUSE IF I HADN'T DIED AS PART OF SOME RIDICULOUS SUPER HERO WAR, I WOULDN'T HAVE SEEN THE LIGHT.
I WOULDN'T BE WHERE I AM TODAY, WITH THE STRENGTH AND CONVICTION TO DO WHAT NEEDS TO BE DONE TO PROTECT THIS COUNTRY.
THOUGH I SUPPOSE THAT DOESN'T ANSWER YOUR QUESTION, DOES IT?
WHAT YOU REALLY WANT TO KNOW IS...WHY AM I HOLDING THIS GUN?
AND WHY AM I ABOUT TO POINT IT AT YOUR FACE AND PULL THE TRIGGER?
THE ANSWER IS SIMPLE.

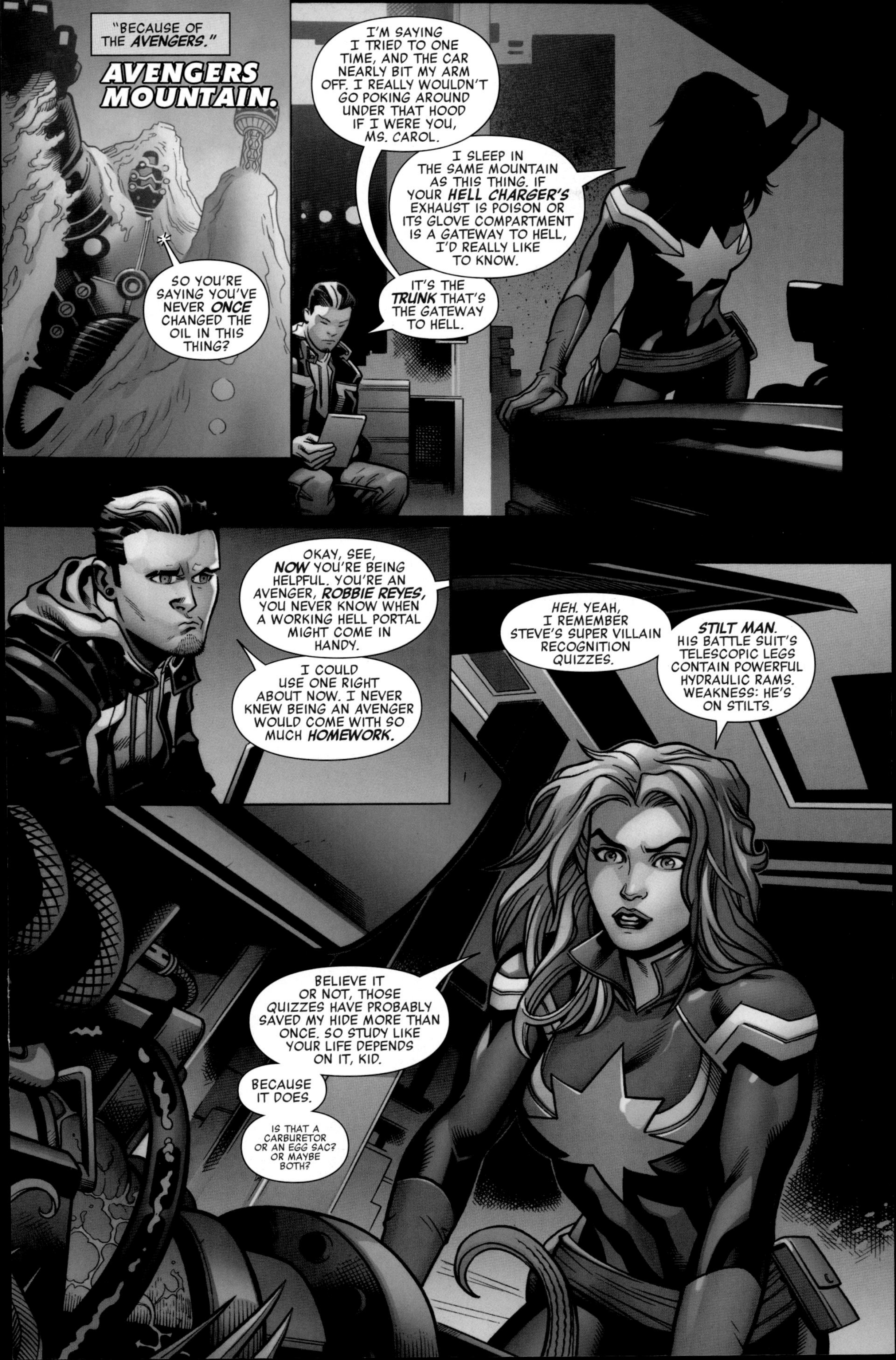
"BECAUSE OF THE AVENGERS."
AVENGERS MOUNTAIN.
SO YOU'RE SAYING YOU'VE NEVER ONCE CHANGED THE OIL IN THIS THING?
I'M SAYING I TRIED TO ONE TIME, AND THE CAR NEARLY BIT MY ARM OFF. I REALLY WOULDN'T GO POKING AROUND UNDER THAT HOOD IF I WERE YOU, MS. CAROL.
I SLEEP IN THE SAME MOUNTAIN AS THIS THING. IF YOUR HELL CHARGER'S EXHAUST IS POISON OR ITS GLOVE COMPARTMENT IS A GATEWAY TO HELL, I'D REALLY LIKE TO KNOW.
IT'S THE TRUNK THAT'S THE GATEWAY TO HELL.
OKAY, SEE, NOW YOU'RE BEING HELPFUL. YOU'RE AN AVENGER, ROBBIE REYES, YOU NEVER KNOW WHEN A WORKING HELL PORTAL MIGHT COME IN HANDY.
I COULD USE ONE RIGHT ABOUT NOW. I NEVER KNEW BEING AN AVENGER WOULD COME WITH SO MUCH HOMEWORK.
HEH. YEAH, I REMEMBER STEVE'S SUPER VILLAIN RECOGNITION QUIZZES.
STILT MAN. HIS BATTLE SUIT'S TELESCOPIC LEGS CONTAIN POWERFUL HYDRAULIC RAMS. WEAKNESS: HE'S ON STILTS.
BELIEVE IT OR NOT, THOSE QUIZZES HAVE PROBABLY SAVED MY HIDE MORE THAN ONCE. SO STUDY LIKE YOUR LIFE DEPENDS ON IT, KID.
BECAUSE IT DOES.
IS THAT A CARBURETOR OR AN EGG SAC? OR MAYBE BOTH?

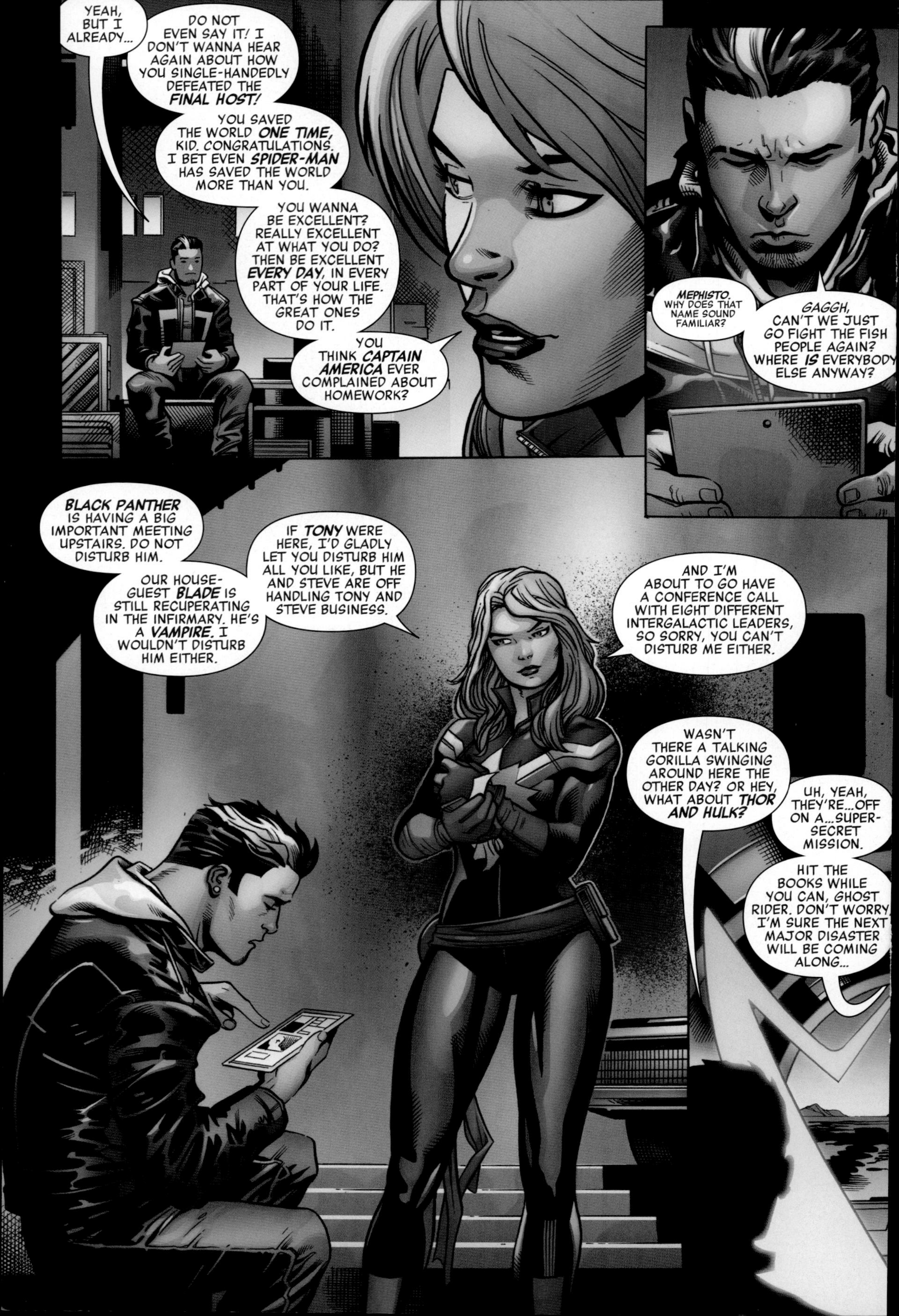
YEAH, BUT I ALREADY...
DO NOT EVEN SAY IT! I DON'T WANNA HEAR AGAIN ABOUT HOW YOU SINGLE-HANDEDLY DEFEATED THE FINAL HOST!
YOU SAVED THE WORLD ONE TIME, KID. CONGRATULATIONS. I BET EVEN SPIDER-MAN HAS SAVED THE WORLD MORE THAN YOU.
YOU WANNA BE EXCELLENT? REALLY EXCELLENT AT WHAT YOU DO? THEN BE EXCELLENT EVERY DAY, IN EVERY PART OF YOUR LIFE. THAT'S HOW THE GREAT ONES DO IT.
YOU THINK CAPTAIN AMERICA EVER COMPLAINED ABOUT HOMEWORK?
MEPHISTO. WHY DOES THAT NAME SOUND FAMILIAR?
GAGGH, CAN'T WE JUST GO FIGHT THE FISH PEOPLE AGAIN? WHERE IS EVERYBODY ELSE ANYWAY?
BLACK PANTHER IS HAVING A BIG IMPORTANT MEETING UPSTAIRS. DO NOT DISTURB HIM.
OUR HOUSE-GUEST BLADE IS STILL RECUPERATING IN THE INFIRMARY. HE'S A VAMPIRE. I WOULDN'T DISTURB HIM EITHER.
IF TONY WERE HERE, I'D GLADLY LET YOU DISTURB HIM ALL YOU LIKE, BUT HE AND STEVE ARE OFF HANDLING TONY AND STEVE BUSINESS.
AND I'M ABOUT TO GO HAVE A CONFERENCE CALL WITH EIGHT DIFFERENT INTERGALACTIC LEADERS, SO SORRY, YOU CAN'T DISTURB ME EITHER.
WASN'T THERE A TALKING GORILLA SWINGING AROUND HERE THE OTHER DAY? OR HEY, WHAT ABOUT THOR AND HULK?
UH, YEAH, THEY'RE...OFF ON A...SUPER-SECRET MISSION.
HIT THE BOOKS WHILE YOU CAN, GHOST RIDER. DON'T WORRY. I'M SURE THE NEXT MAJOR DISASTER WILL BE COMING ALONG...

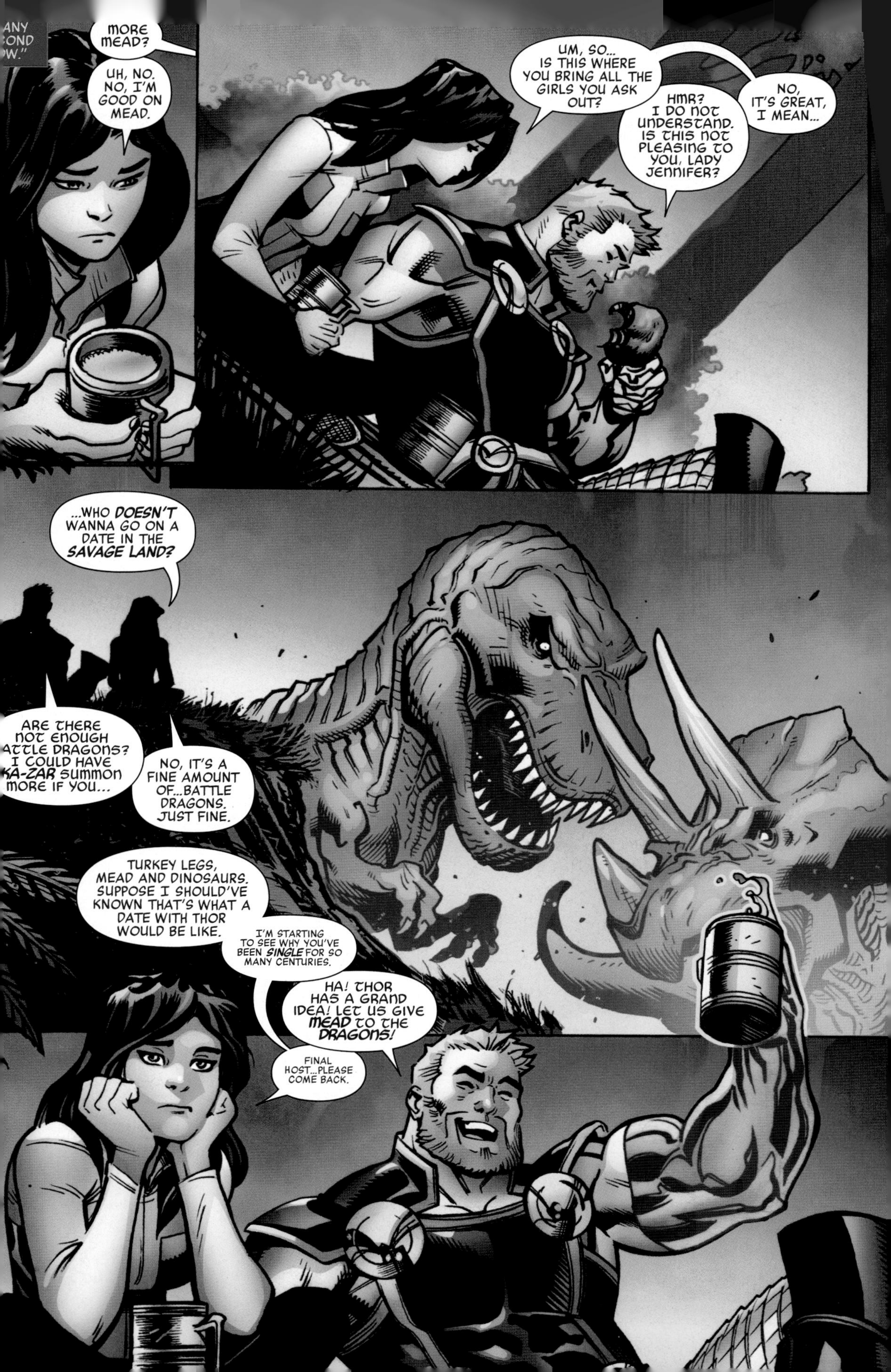
MORE MEAD?
UH, NO. NO, I'M GOOD ON MEAD.
UM, SO... IS THIS WHERE YOU BRING ALL THE GIRLS YOU ASK OUT?
HMR? I DO NOT UNDERSTAND. IS THIS NOT PLEASING TO YOU, LADY JENNIFER?
NO, IT'S GREAT, I MEAN...
...WHO DOESN'T WANNA GO ON A DATE IN THE SAVAGE LAND?
ARE THERE NOT ENOUGH ATTLE DRAGONS? I COULD HAVE KA-ZAR SUMMON MORE IF YOU...
NO, IT'S A FINE AMOUNT OF...BATTLE DRAGONS. JUST FINE.
TURKEY LEGS, MEAD AND DINOSAURS. SUPPOSE I SHOULD'VE KNOWN THAT'S WHAT A DATE WITH THOR WOULD BE LIKE.
I'M STARTING TO SEE WHY YOU'VE BEEN SINGLE FOR SO MANY CENTURIES.
HA! THOR HAS A GRAND IDEA! LET US GIVE MEAD TO THE DRAGONS!
FINAL HOST...PLEASE COME BACK.

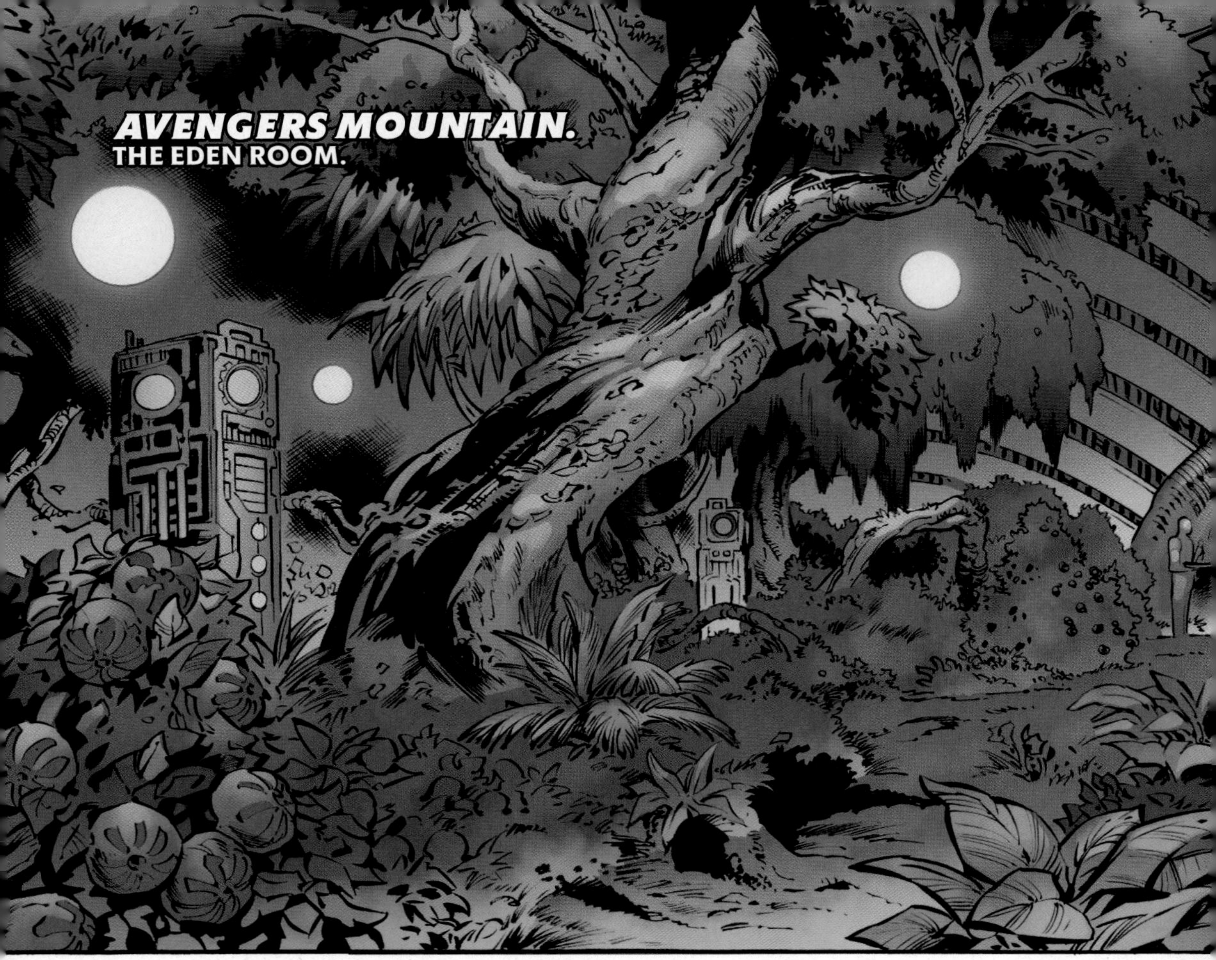
AVENGERS MOUNTAIN.
THE EDEN ROOM.

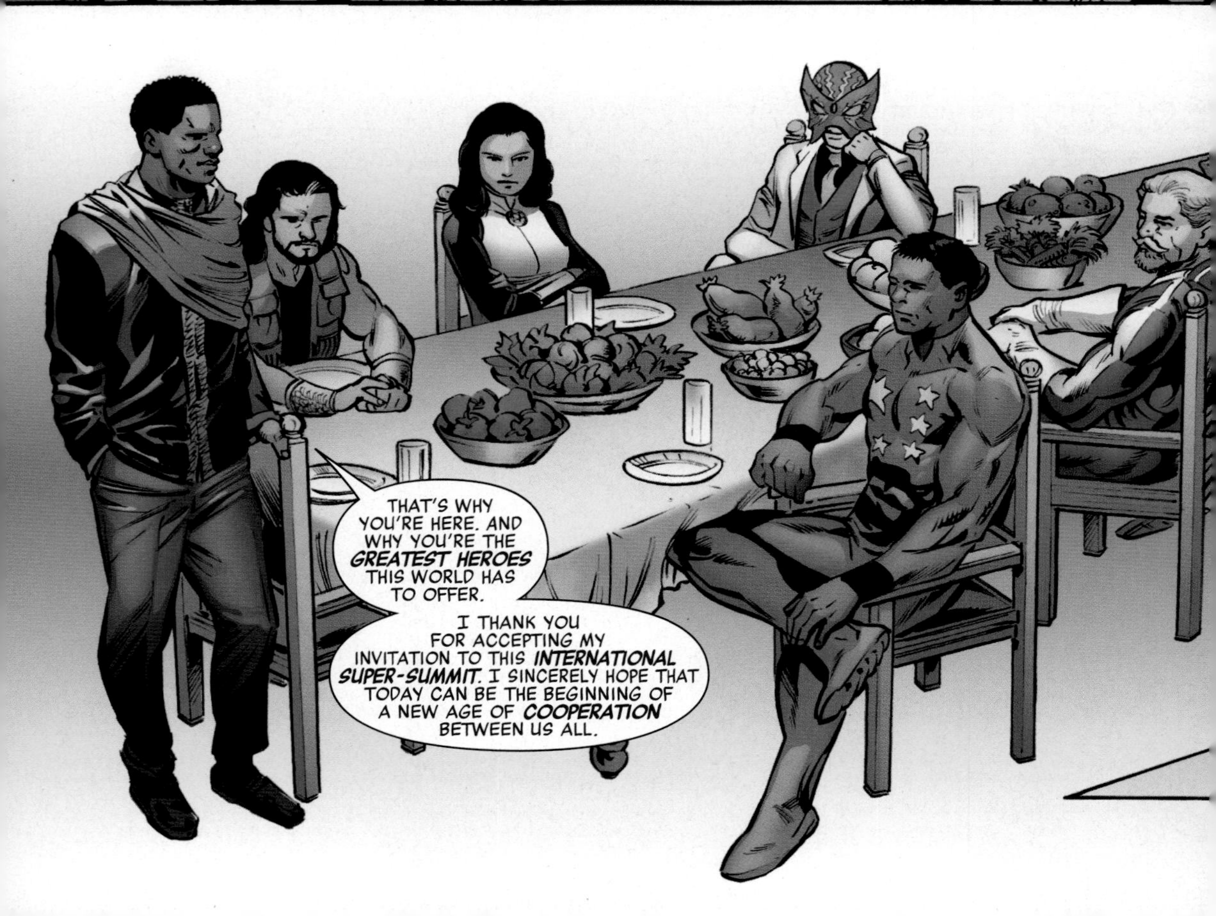
THAT'S WHY YOU'RE HERE. AND WHY YOU'RE THE GREATEST HEROES THIS WORLD HAS TO OFFER.
I THANK YOU FOR ACCEPTING MY INVITATION TO THIS INTERNATIONAL SUPER-SUMMIT. I SINCERELY HOPE THAT TODAY CAN BE THE BEGINNING OF A NEW AGE OF COOPERATION BETWEEN US ALL.

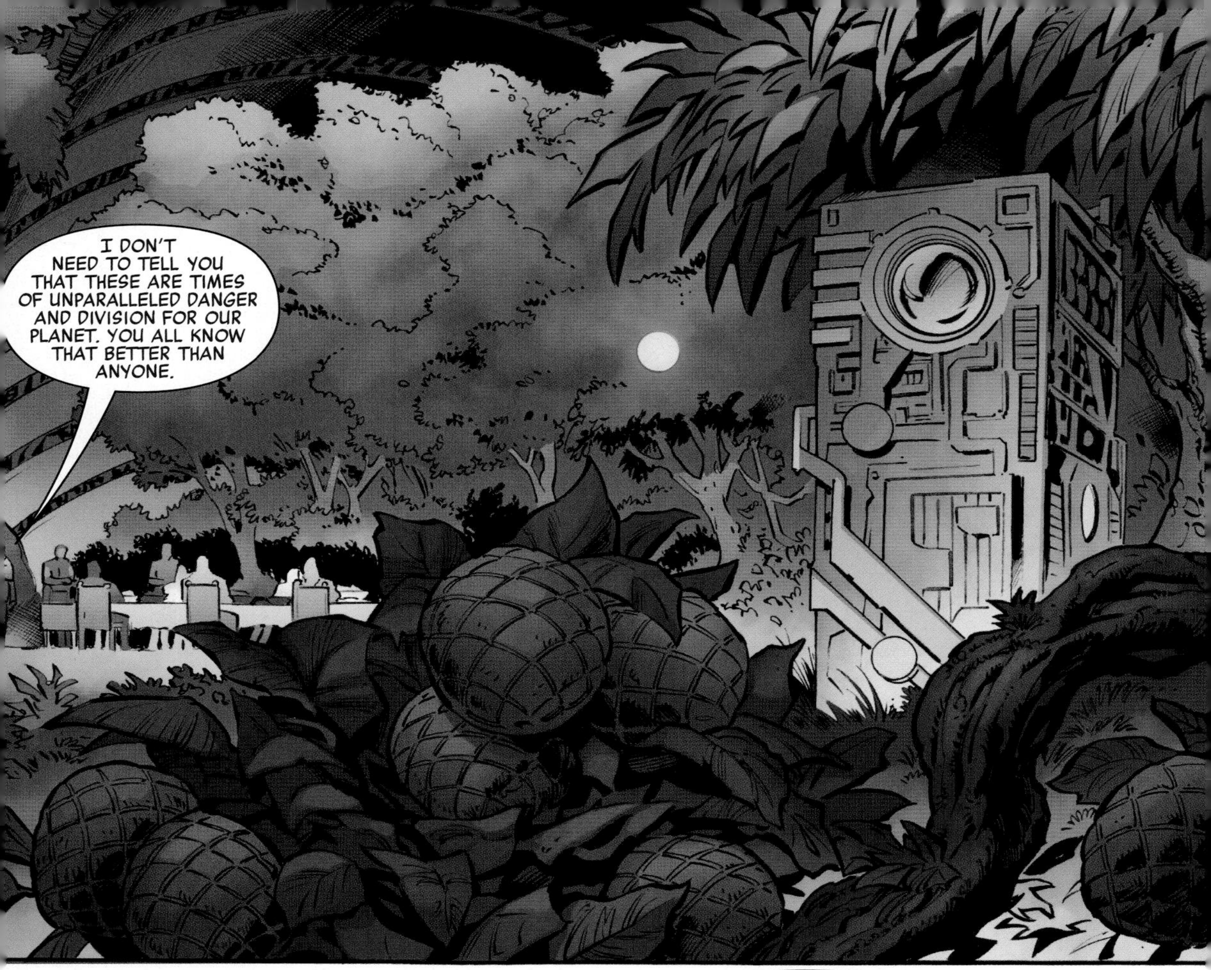
I DON'T NEED TO TELL YOU THAT THESE ARE TIMES OF UNPARALLELED DANGER AND DIVISION FOR OUR PLANET. YOU ALL KNOW THAT BETTER THAN ANYONE.

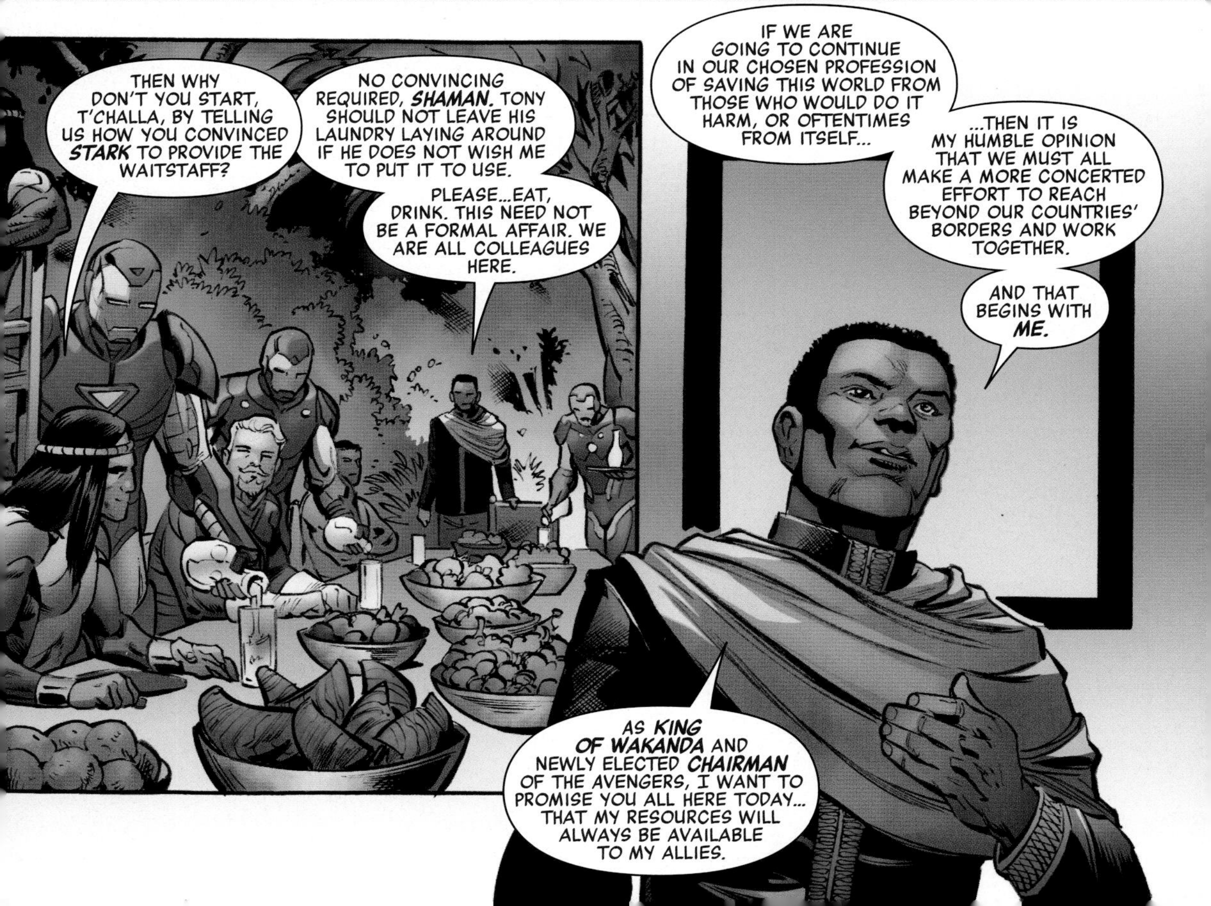
THEN WHY DON'T YOU START, T'CHALLA, BY TELLING US HOW YOU CONVINCED STARK TO PROVIDE THE WAITSTAFF?
NO CONVINCING REQUIRED, SHAMAN. TONY SHOULD NOT LEAVE HIS LAUNDRY LAYING AROUND IF HE DOES NOT WISH ME TO PUT IT TO USE.
PLEASE...EAT, DRINK. THIS NEED NOT BE A FORMAL AFFAIR. WE ARE ALL COLLEAGUES HERE.
IF WE ARE GOING TO CONTINUE IN OUR CHOSEN PROFESSION OF SAVING THIS WORLD FROM THOSE WHO WOULD DO IT HARM, OR OFTENTIMES FROM ITSELF...
...THEN IT IS MY HUMBLE OPINION THAT WE MUST ALL MAKE A MORE CONCERTED EFFORT TO REACH BEYOND OUR COUNTRIES' BORDERS AND WORK TOGETHER.
AND THAT BEGINS WITH ME.
AS KING OF WAKANDA AND NEWLY ELECTED CHAIRMAN OF THE AVENGERS, I WANT TO PROMISE YOU ALL HERE TODAY... THAT MY RESOURCES WILL ALWAYS BE AVAILABLE TO MY ALLIES.

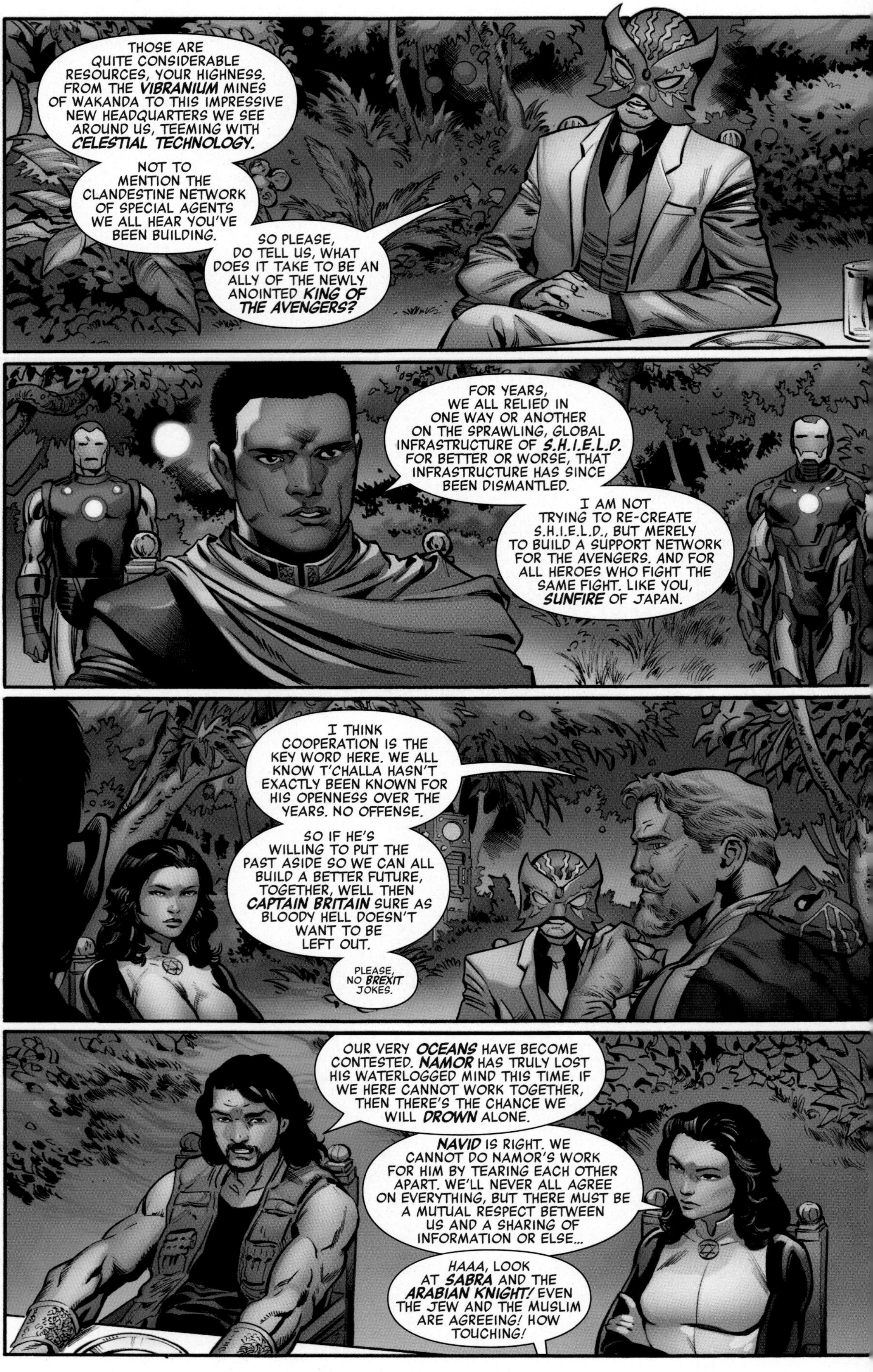
THOSE ARE QUITE CONSIDERABLE RESOURCES, YOUR HIGHNESS. FROM THE VIBRANIUM MINES OF WAKANDA TO THIS IMPRESSIVE NEW HEADQUARTERS WE SEE AROUND US, TEEMING WITH CELESTIAL TECHNOLOGY.
NOT TO MENTION THE CLANDESTINE NETWORK OF SPECIAL AGENTS WE ALL HEAR YOU'VE BEEN BUILDING.
SO PLEASE, DO TELL US, WHAT DOES IT TAKE TO BE AN ALLY OF THE NEWLY ANOINTED KING OF THE AVENGERS?
FOR YEARS, WE ALL RELIED IN ONE WAY OR ANOTHER ON THE SPRAWLING, GLOBAL INFRASTRUCTURE OF S.H.I.E.L.D. FOR BETTER OR WORSE, THAT INFRASTRUCTURE HAS SINCE BEEN DISMANTLED.
I AM NOT TRYING TO RE-CREATE S.H.I.E.L.D., BUT MERELY TO BUILD A SUPPORT NETWORK FOR THE AVENGERS. AND FOR ALL HEROES WHO FIGHT THE SAME FIGHT. LIKE YOU, SUNFIRE OF JAPAN.
I THINK COOPERATION IS THE KEY WORD HERE. WE ALL KNOW T'CHALLA HASN'T EXACTLY BEEN KNOWN FOR HIS OPENNESS OVER THE YEARS. NO OFFENSE.
SO IF HE'S WILLING TO PUT THE PAST ASIDE SO WE CAN ALL BUILD A BETTER FUTURE, TOGETHER, WELL THEN CAPTAIN BRITAIN SURE AS BLOODY HELL DOESN'T WANT TO BE LEFT OUT.
PLEASE, NO BREXIT JOKES.
OUR VERY OCEANS HAVE BECOME CONTESTED. NAMOR HAS TRULY LOST HIS WATERLOGGED MIND THIS TIME. IF WE HERE CANNOT WORK TOGETHER, THEN THERE'S THE CHANCE WE WILL DROWN ALONE.
NAVID IS RIGHT. WE CANNOT DO NAMOR'S WORK FOR HIM BY TEARING EACH OTHER APART. WE'LL NEVER ALL AGREE ON EVERYTHING, BUT THERE MUST BE A MUTUAL RESPECT BETWEEN US AND A SHARING OF INFORMATION OR ELSE...
HAAA, LOOK AT SABRA AND THE ARABIAN KNIGHT! EVEN THE JEW AND THE MUSLIM ARE AGREEING! HOW TOUCHING!

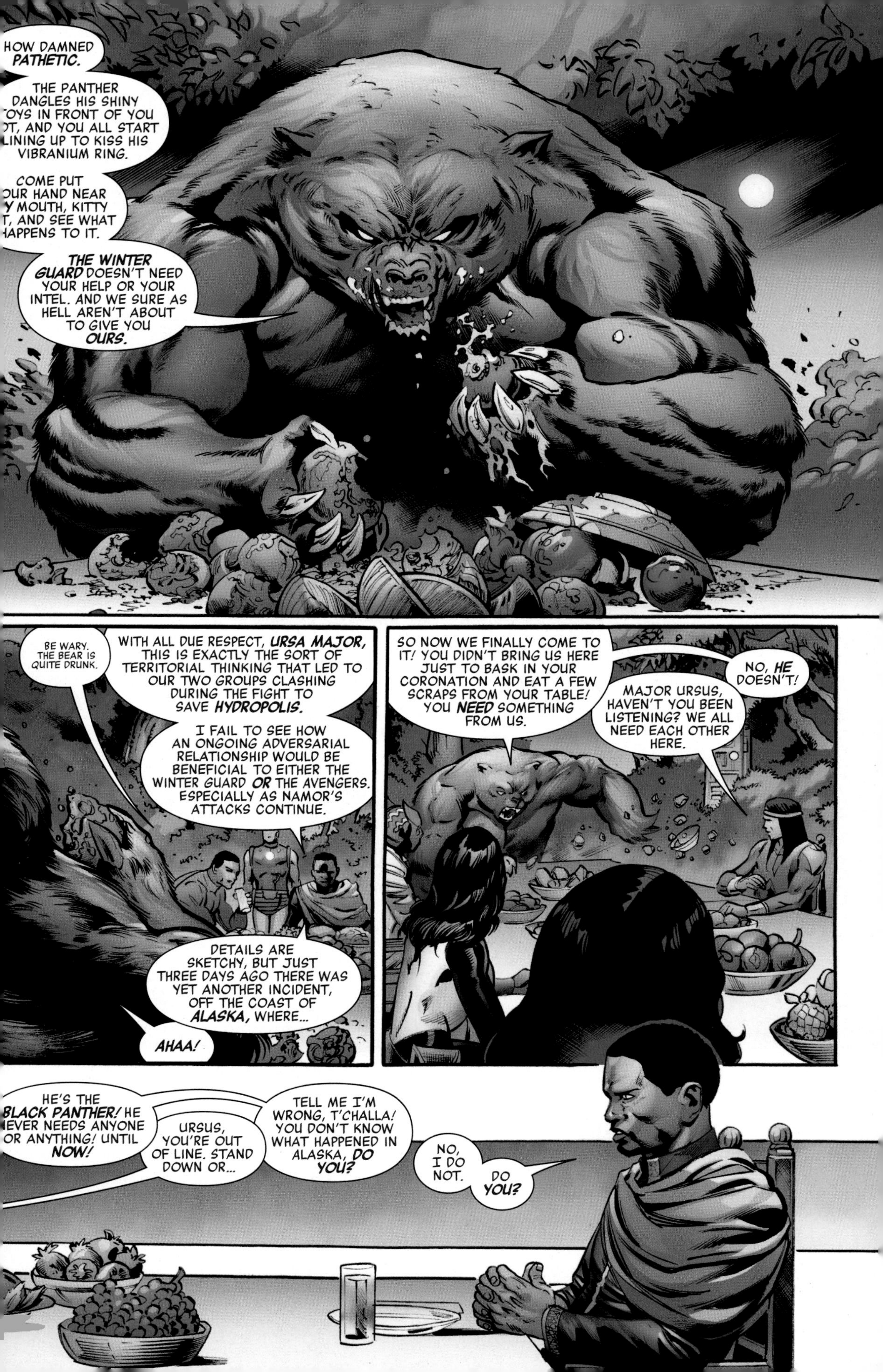
HOW DAMNED PATHETIC.
THE PANTHER DANGLES HIS SHINY TOYS IN FRONT OF YOU OT, AND YOU ALL START LINING UP TO KISS HIS VIBRANIUM RING.
COME PUT OUR HAND NEAR Y MOUTH, KITTY T, AND SEE WHAT APPENS TO IT.
THE WINTER GUARD DOESN'T NEED YOUR HELP OR YOUR INTEL. AND WE SURE AS HELL AREN'T ABOUT TO GIVE YOU OURS.
BE WARY. THE BEAR IS QUITE DRUNK.
WITH ALL DUE RESPECT, URSA MAJOR, THIS IS EXACTLY THE SORT OF TERRITORIAL THINKING THAT LED TO OUR TWO GROUPS CLASHING DURING THE FIGHT TO SAVE HYDROPOLIS.
I FAIL TO SEE HOW AN ONGOING ADVERSARIAL RELATIONSHIP WOULD BE BENEFICIAL TO EITHER THE WINTER GUARD OR THE AVENGERS. ESPECIALLY AS NAMOR'S ATTACKS CONTINUE.
DETAILS ARE SKETCHY, BUT JUST THREE DAYS AGO THERE WAS YET ANOTHER INCIDENT, OFF THE COAST OF ALASKA, WHERE...
AHAA!
SO NOW WE FINALLY COME TO IT! YOU DIDN'T BRING US HERE JUST TO BASK IN YOUR CORONATION AND EAT A FEW SCRAPS FROM YOUR TABLE! YOU NEED SOMETHING FROM US.
NO, HE DOESN'T!
MAJOR URSUS, HAVEN'T YOU BEEN LISTENING? WE ALL NEED EACH OTHER HERE.
HE'S THE BLACK PANTHER! HE NEVER NEEDS ANYONE OR ANYTHING! UNTIL NOW!
URSUS, YOU'RE OUT OF LINE. STAND DOWN OR...
TELL ME I'M WRONG, T'CHALLA! YOU DON'T KNOW WHAT HAPPENED IN ALASKA, DO YOU?
NO, I DO NOT.
DO YOU?

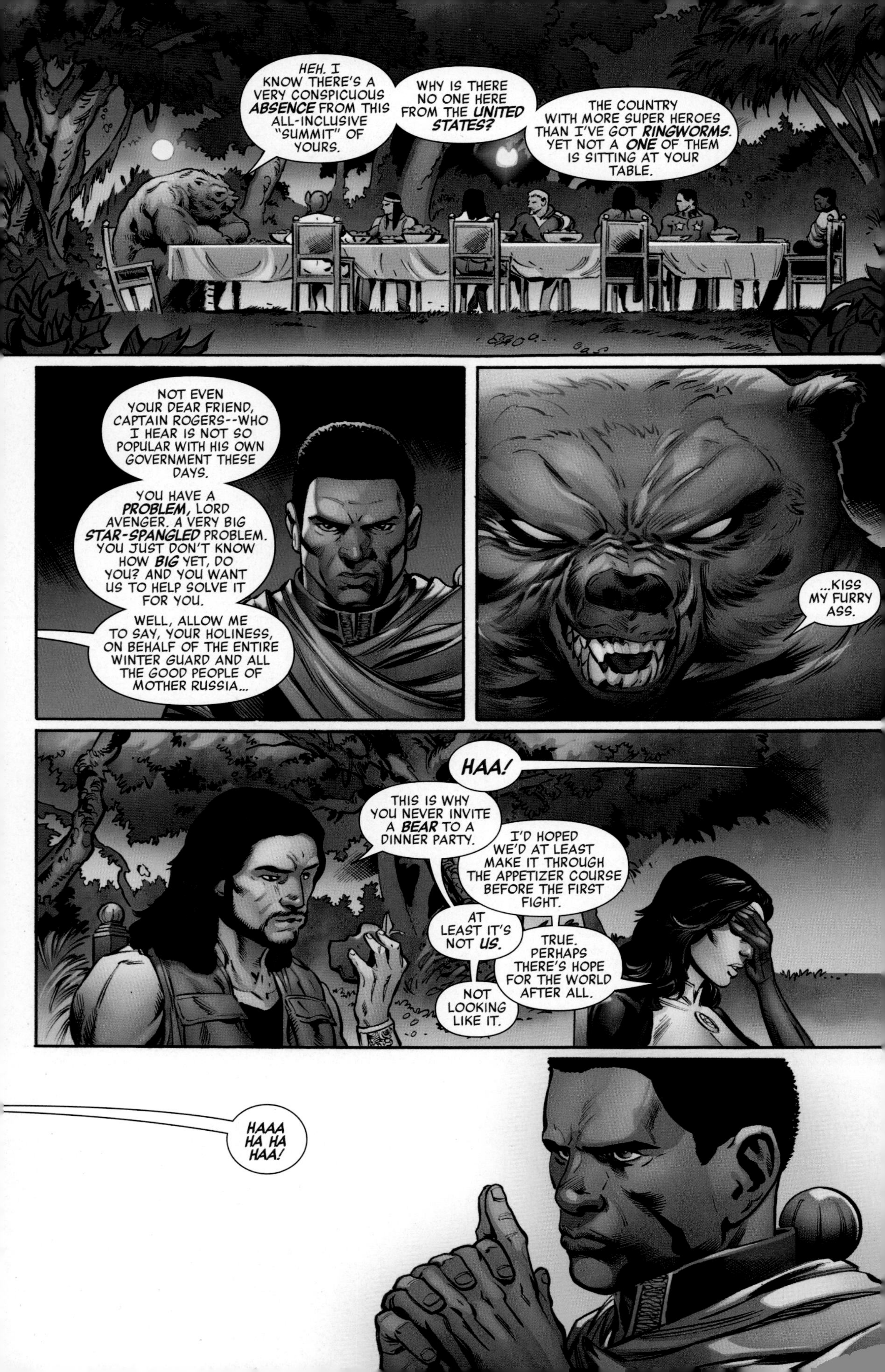
HEH. I KNOW THERE'S A VERY CONSPICUOUS ABSENCE FROM THIS ALL-INCLUSIVE "SUMMIT" OF YOURS.
WHY IS THERE NO ONE HERE FROM THE UNITED STATES?
THE COUNTRY WITH MORE SUPER HEROES THAN I'VE GOT RINGWORMS. YET NOT A ONE OF THEM IS SITTING AT YOUR TABLE.
NOT EVEN YOUR DEAR FRIEND, CAPTAIN ROGERS--WHO I HEAR IS NOT SO POPULAR WITH HIS OWN GOVERNMENT THESE DAYS.
YOU HAVE A PROBLEM, LORD AVENGER. A VERY BIG STAR-SPANGLED PROBLEM. YOU JUST DON'T KNOW HOW BIG YET, DO YOU? AND YOU WANT US TO HELP SOLVE IT FOR YOU.
WELL, ALLOW ME TO SAY, YOUR HOLINESS, ON BEHALF OF THE ENTIRE WINTER GUARD AND ALL THE GOOD PEOPLE OF MOTHER RUSSIA...
...KISS MY FURRY ASS.
HAA!
THIS IS WHY YOU NEVER INVITE A BEAR TO A DINNER PARTY.
I'D HOPED WE'D AT LEAST MAKE IT THROUGH THE APPETIZER COURSE BEFORE THE FIRST FIGHT.
AT LEAST IT'S NOT US.
TRUE. PERHAPS THERE'S HOPE FOR THE WORLD AFTER ALL.
NOT LOOKING LIKE IT.
HAAA HA HA HAA!

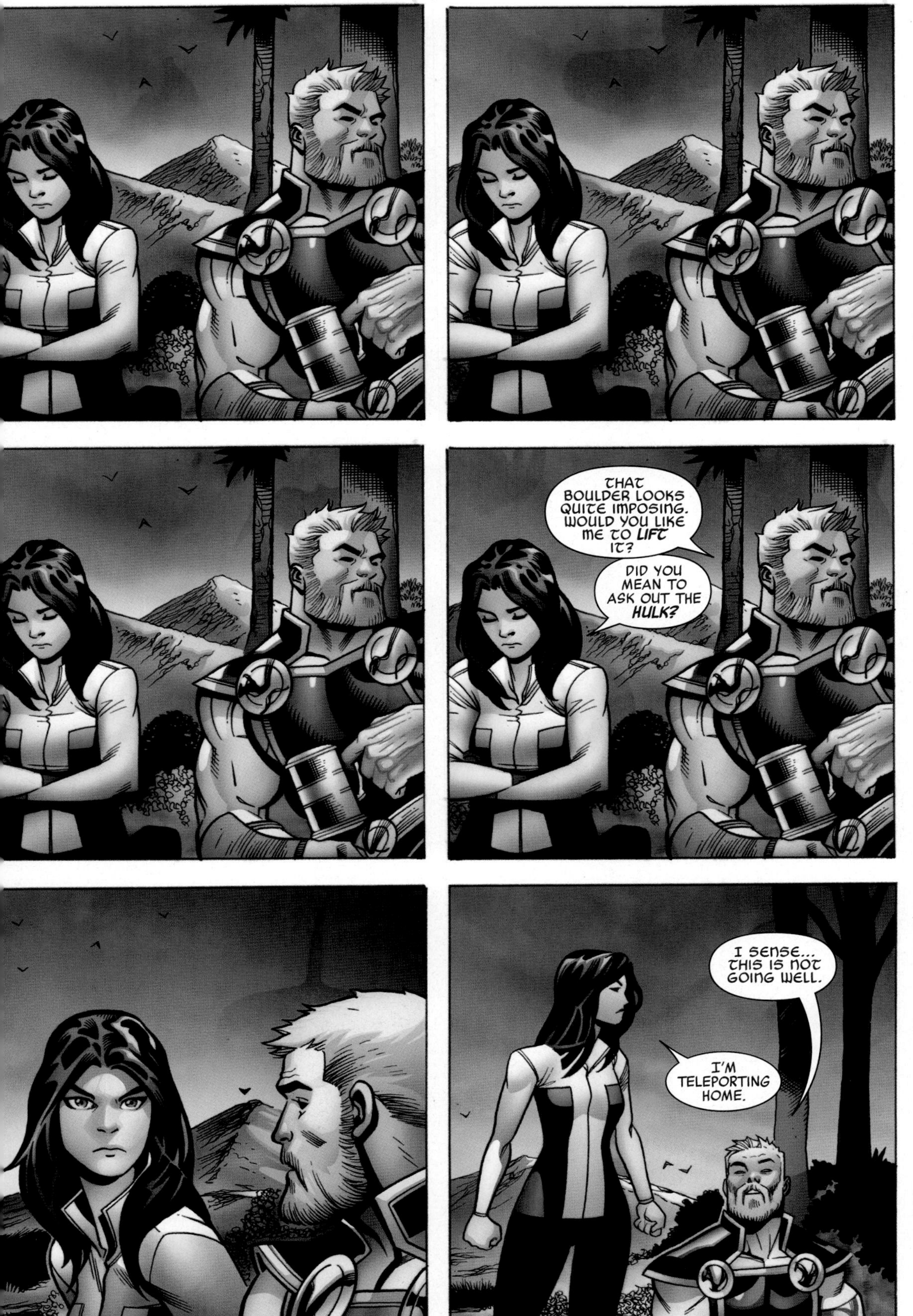
THAT BOULDER LOOKS QUITE IMPOSING. WOULD YOU LIKE ME TO LIFT IT?
DID YOU MEAN TO ASK OUT THE HULK?
I SENSE... THIS IS NOT GOING WELL.
I'M TELEPORTING HOME.

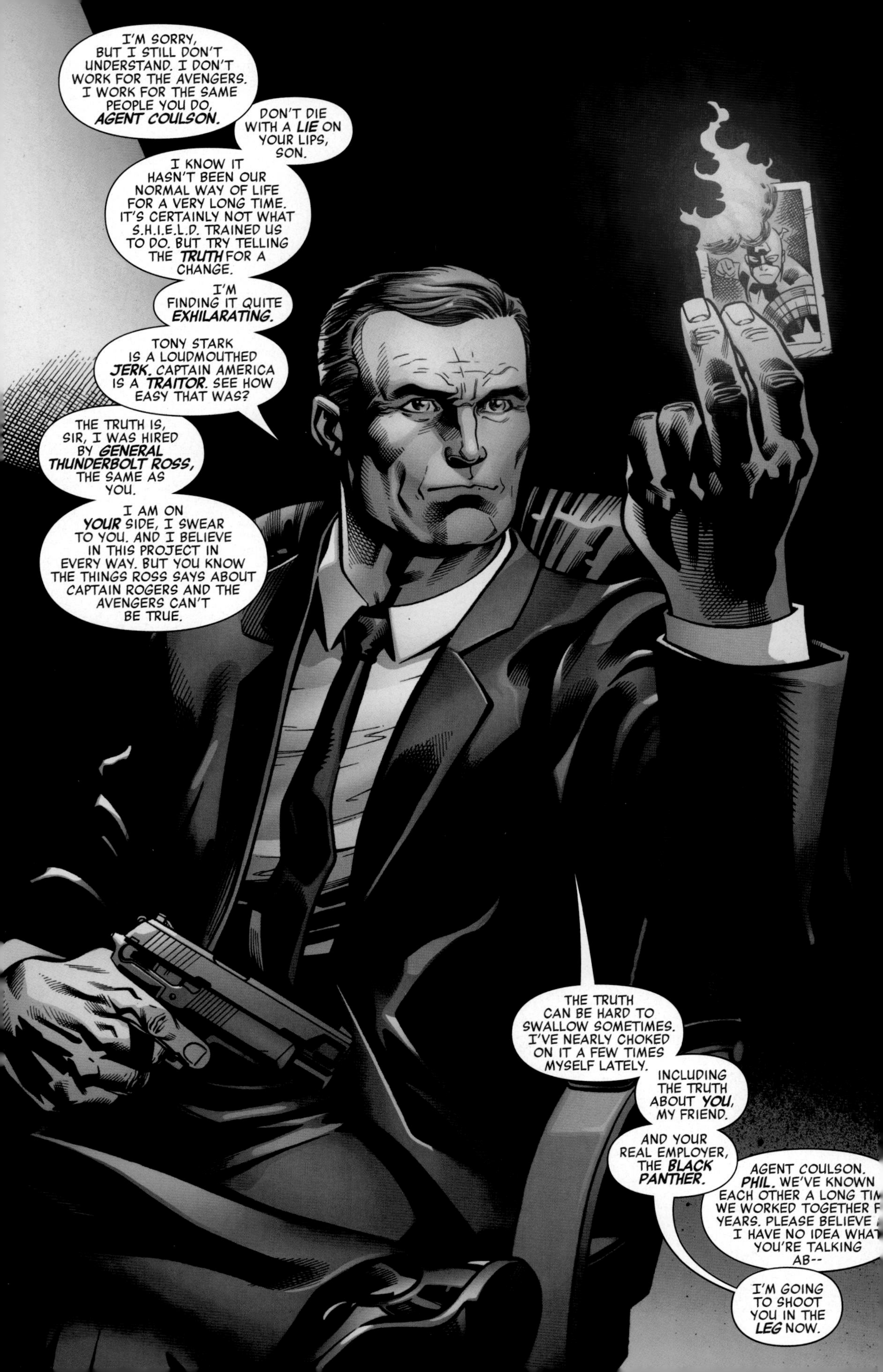
I'M SORRY, BUT I STILL DON'T UNDERSTAND. I DON'T WORK FOR THE AVENGERS. I WORK FOR THE SAME PEOPLE YOU DO, AGENT COULSON.
DON'T DIE WITH A LIE ON YOUR LIPS, SON.
I KNOW IT HASN'T BEEN OUR NORMAL WAY OF LIFE FOR A VERY LONG TIME. IT'S CERTAINLY NOT WHAT S.H.I.E.L.D. TRAINED US TO DO. BUT TRY TELLING THE TRUTH FOR A CHANGE.
I'M FINDING IT QUITE EXHILARATING.
TONY STARK IS A LOUDMOUTHED JERK. CAPTAIN AMERICA IS A TRAITOR. SEE HOW EASY THAT WAS?
THE TRUTH IS, SIR, I WAS HIRED BY GENERAL THUNDERBOLT ROSS, THE SAME AS YOU.
I AM ON YOUR SIDE, I SWEAR TO YOU. AND I BELIEVE IN THIS PROJECT IN EVERY WAY. BUT YOU KNOW THE THINGS ROSS SAYS ABOUT CAPTAIN ROGERS AND THE AVENGERS CAN'T BE TRUE.
THE TRUTH CAN BE HARD TO SWALLOW SOMETIMES. I'VE NEARLY CHOKED ON IT A FEW TIMES MYSELF LATELY.
INCLUDING THE TRUTH ABOUT YOU, MY FRIEND.
AND YOUR REAL EMPLOYER, THE BLACK PANTHER.
AGENT COULSON. PHIL. WE'VE KNOWN EACH OTHER A LONG TIM WE WORKED TOGETHER F YEARS. PLEASE BELIEVE I HAVE NO IDEA WHAT YOU'RE TALKING AB--
I'M GOING TO SHOOT YOU IN THE LEG NOW.

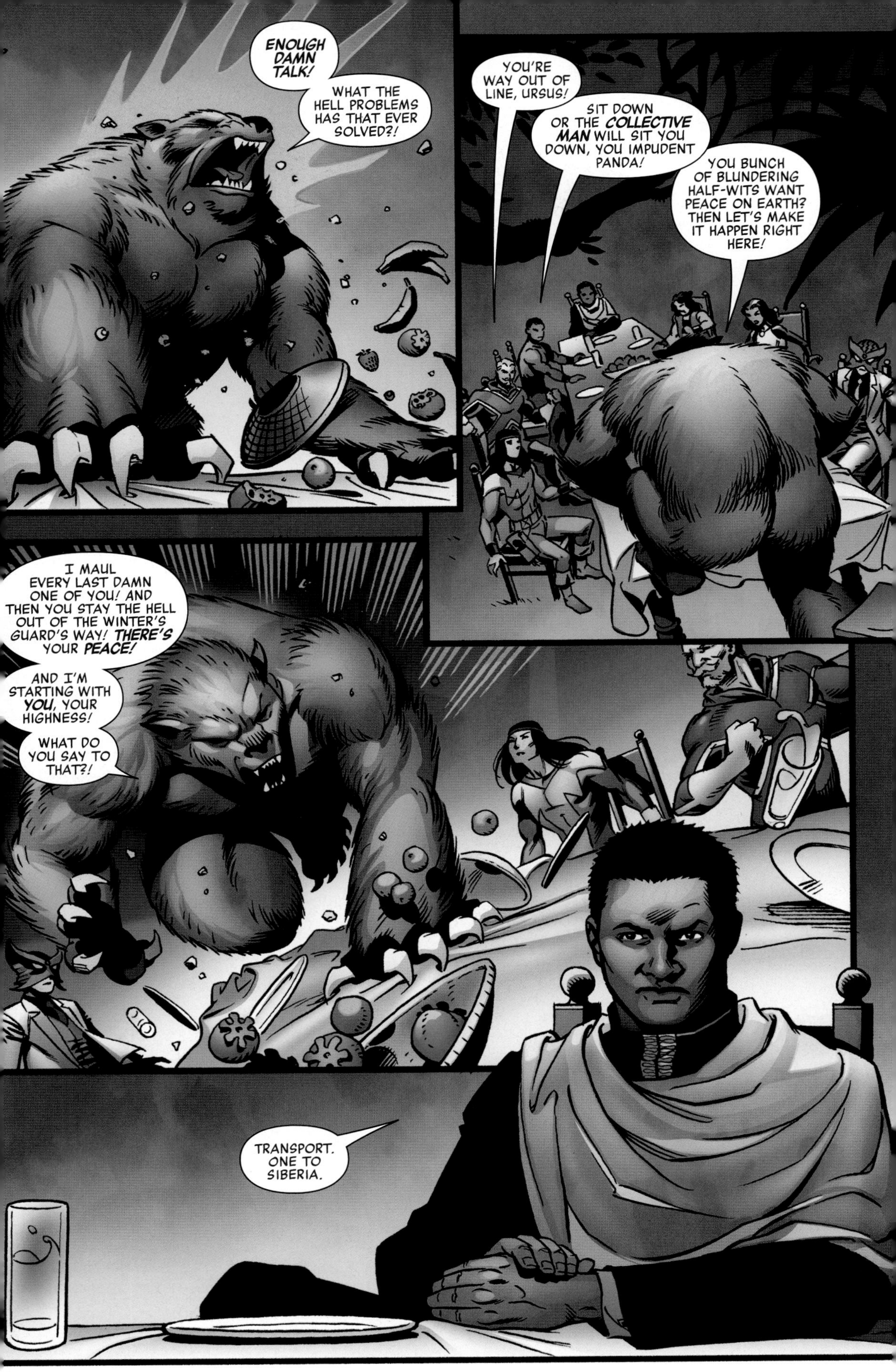
ENOUGH DAMN TALK!
WHAT THE HELL PROBLEMS HAS THAT EVER SOLVED?!
YOU'RE WAY OUT OF LINE, URSUS!
SIT DOWN OR THE COLLECTIVE MAN WILL SIT YOU DOWN, YOU IMPUDENT PANDA!
YOU BUNCH OF BLUNDERING HALF-WITS WANT PEACE ON EARTH? THEN LET'S MAKE IT HAPPEN RIGHT HERE!
I MAUL EVERY LAST DAMN ONE OF YOU! AND THEN YOU STAY THE HELL OUT OF THE WINTER'S GUARD'S WAY! THERE'S YOUR PEACE!
AND I'M STARTING WITH YOU, YOUR HIGHNESS!
WHAT DO YOU SAY TO THAT?!
TRANSPORT. ONE TO SIBERIA.

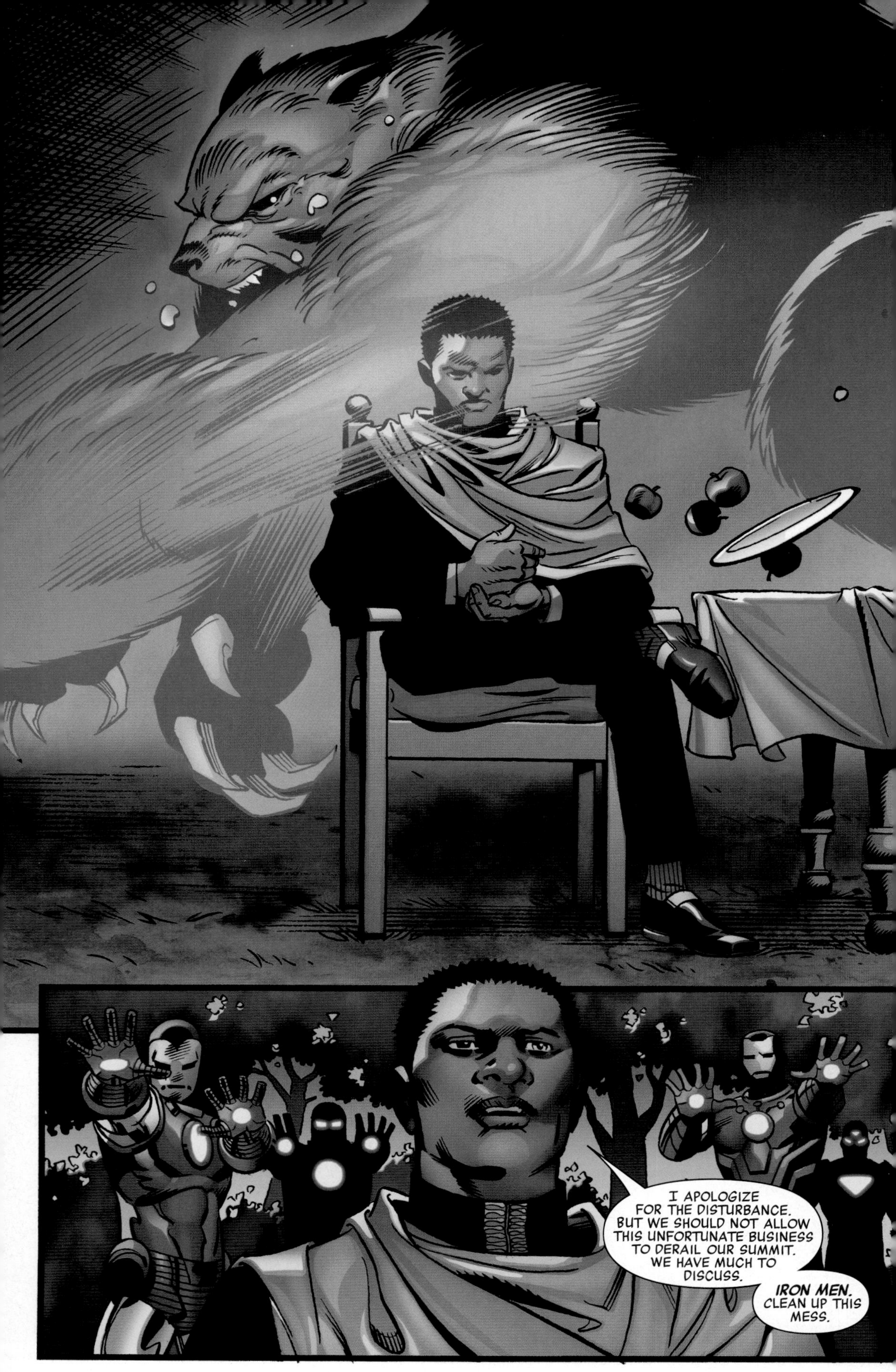
I APOLOGIZE FOR THE DISTURBANCE. BUT WE SHOULD NOT ALLOW THIS UNFORTUNATE BUSINESS TO DERAIL OUR SUMMIT. WE HAVE MUCH TO DISCUSS.
IRON MEN. CLEAN UP THIS MESS.

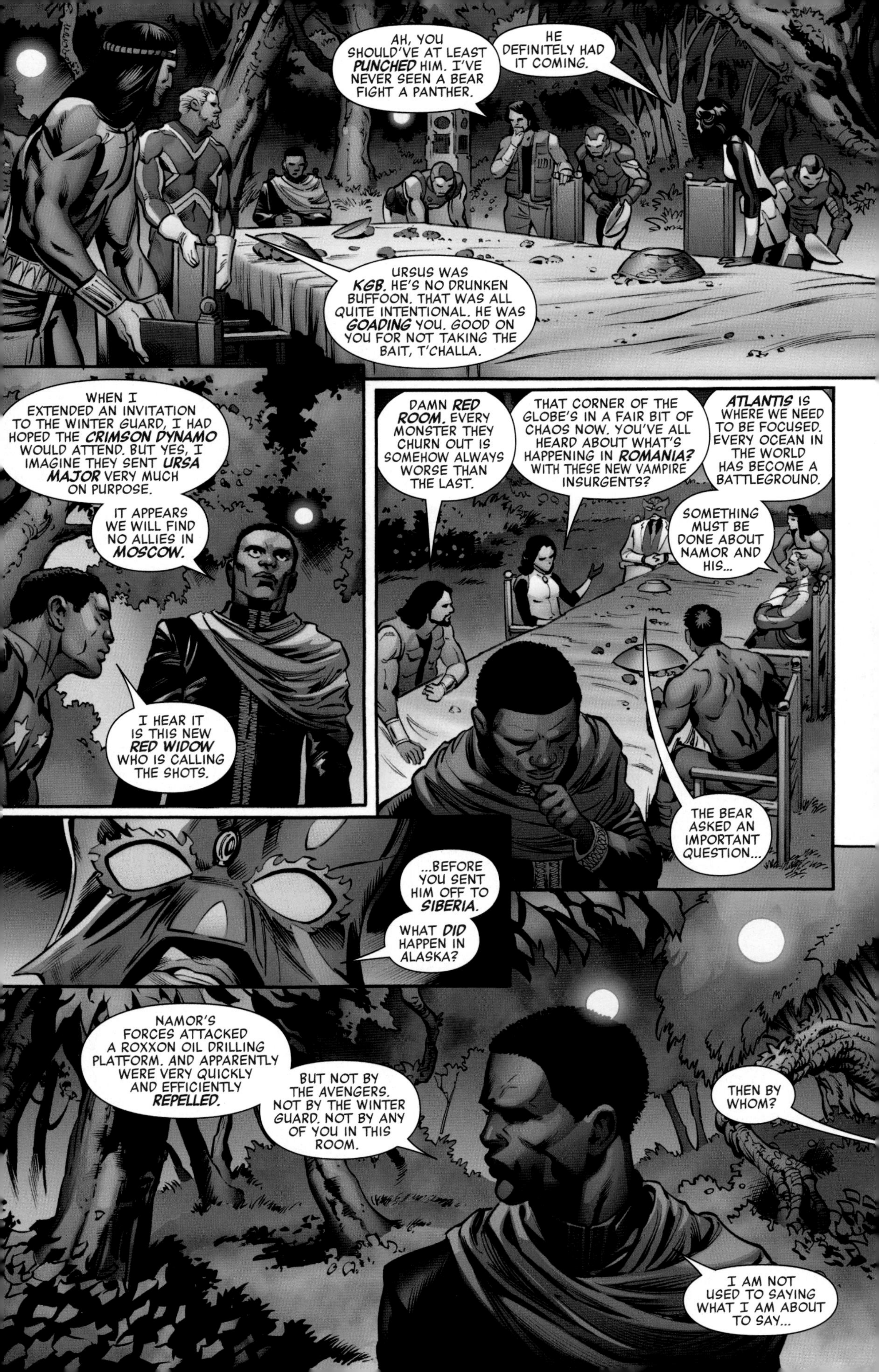
AH, YOU SHOULD'VE AT LEAST PUNCHED HIM. I'VE NEVER SEEN A BEAR FIGHT A PANTHER.
HE DEFINITELY HAD IT COMING.
URSUS WAS KGB. HE'S NO DRUNKEN BUFFOON. THAT WAS ALL QUITE INTENTIONAL. HE WAS GOADING YOU. GOOD ON YOU FOR NOT TAKING THE BAIT, T'CHALLA.
WHEN I EXTENDED AN INVITATION TO THE WINTER GUARD, I HAD HOPED THE CRIMSON DYNAMO WOULD ATTEND. BUT YES, I IMAGINE THEY SENT URSA MAJOR VERY MUCH ON PURPOSE.
IT APPEARS WE WILL FIND NO ALLIES IN MOSCOW.
I HEAR IT IS THIS NEW RED WIDOW WHO IS CALLING THE SHOTS.
DAMN RED ROOM. EVERY MONSTER THEY CHURN OUT IS SOMEHOW ALWAYS WORSE THAN THE LAST.
THAT CORNER OF THE GLOBE'S IN A FAIR BIT OF CHAOS NOW. YOU'VE ALL HEARD ABOUT WHAT'S HAPPENING IN ROMANIA? WITH THESE NEW VAMPIRE INSURGENTS?
ATLANTIS IS WHERE WE NEED TO BE FOCUSED. EVERY OCEAN IN THE WORLD HAS BECOME A BATTLEGROUND.
SOMETHING MUST BE DONE ABOUT NAMOR AND HIS...
THE BEAR ASKED AN IMPORTANT QUESTION...
...BEFORE YOU SENT HIM OFF TO SIBERIA.
WHAT DID HAPPEN IN ALASKA?
NAMOR'S FORCES ATTACKED A ROXXON OIL DRILLING PLATFORM. AND APPARENTLY WERE VERY QUICKLY AND EFFICIENTLY REPELLED.
BUT NOT BY THE AVENGERS. NOT BY THE WINTER GUARD. NOT BY ANY OF YOU IN THIS ROOM.
THEN BY WHOM?
I AM NOT USED TO SAYING WHAT I AM ABOUT TO SAY...

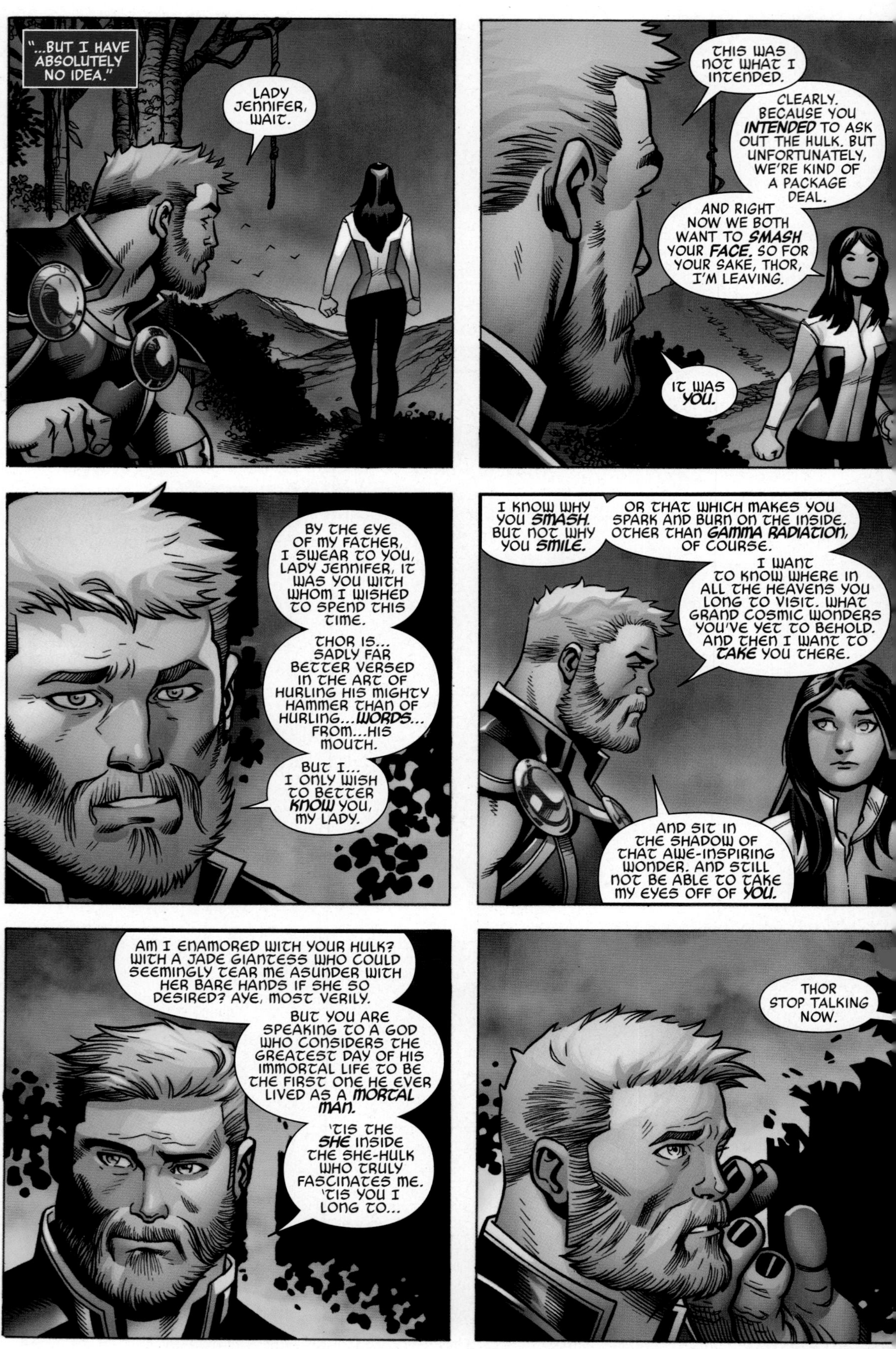
"...BUT I HAVE ABSOLUTELY NO IDEA."
LADY JENNIFER, WAIT.
THIS WAS NOT WHAT I INTENDED.
CLEARLY. BECAUSE YOU INTENDED TO ASK OUT THE HULK. BUT UNFORTUNATELY, WE'RE KIND OF A PACKAGE DEAL.
AND RIGHT NOW WE BOTH WANT TO SMASH YOUR FACE. SO FOR YOUR SAKE, THOR, I'M LEAVING.
IT WAS YOU.
BY THE EYE OF MY FATHER, I SWEAR TO YOU, LADY JENNIFER, IT WAS YOU WITH WHOM I WISHED TO SPEND THIS TIME.
THOR IS... SADLY FAR BETTER VERSED IN THE ART OF HURLING HIS MIGHTY HAMMER THAN OF HURLING...WORDS... FROM...HIS MOUTH.
BUT I... I ONLY WISH TO BETTER KNOW YOU, MY LADY.
I KNOW WHY YOU SMASH. BUT NOT WHY YOU SMILE.
OR THAT WHICH MAKES YOU SPARK AND BURN ON THE INSIDE. OTHER THAN GAMMA RADIATION, OF COURSE.
I WANT TO KNOW WHERE IN ALL THE HEAVENS YOU LONG TO VISIT. WHAT GRAND COSMIC WONDERS YOU'VE YET TO BEHOLD. AND THEN I WANT TO TAKE YOU THERE.
AND SIT IN THE SHADOW OF THAT AWE-INSPIRING WONDER. AND STILL NOT BE ABLE TO TAKE MY EYES OFF OF YOU.
AM I ENAMORED WITH YOUR HULK? WITH A JADE GIANTESS WHO COULD SEEMINGLY TEAR ME ASUNDER WITH HER BARE HANDS IF SHE SO DESIRED? AYE, MOST VERILY.
BUT YOU ARE SPEAKING TO A GOD WHO CONSIDERS THE GREATEST DAY OF HIS IMMORTAL LIFE TO BE THE FIRST ONE HE EVER LIVED AS A MORTAL MAN.
'TIS THE SHE INSIDE THE SHE-HULK WHO TRULY FASCINATES ME. 'TIS YOU I LONG TO...
THOR STOP TALKING NOW.

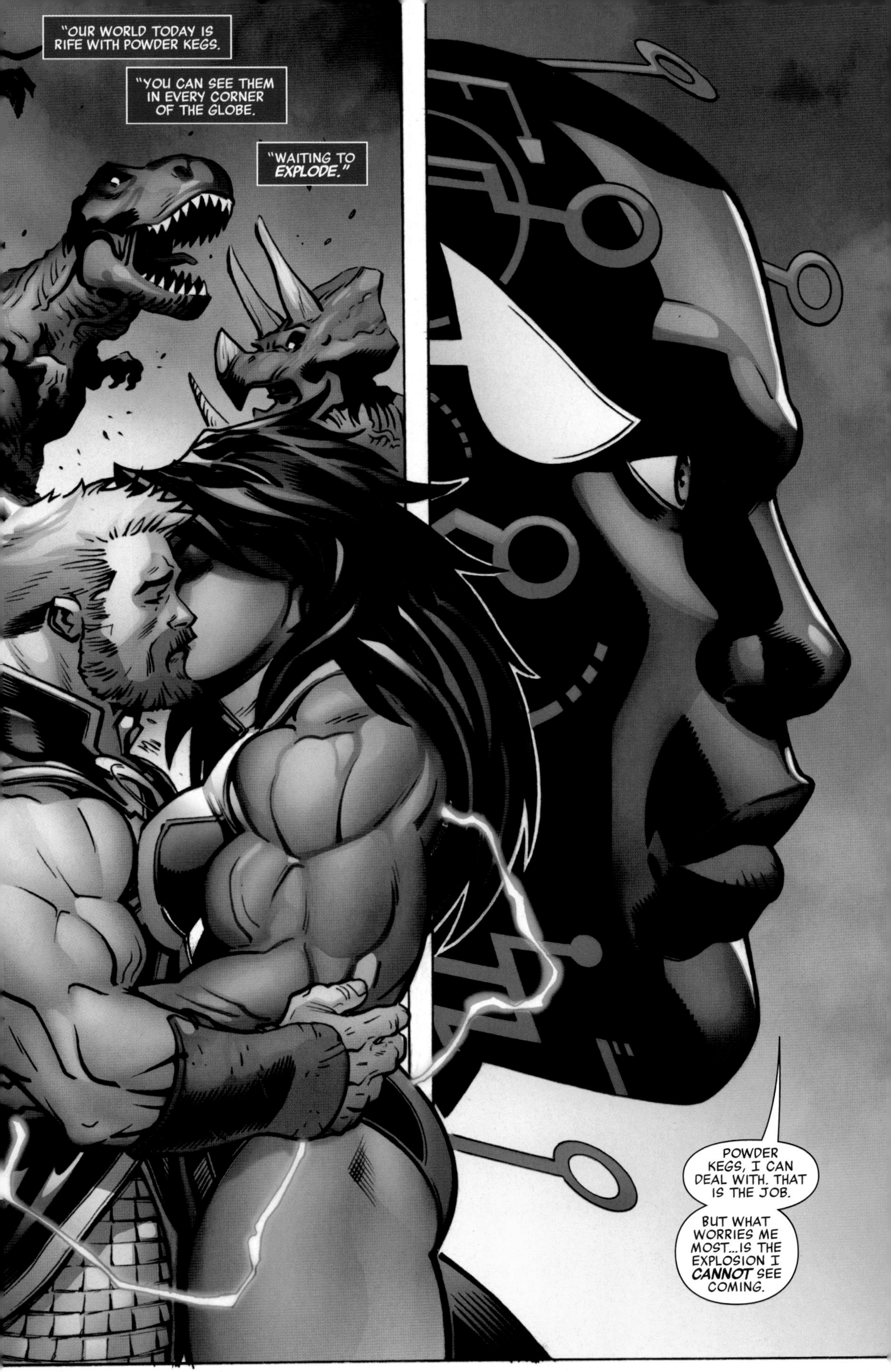
"OUR WORLD TODAY IS RIFE WITH POWDER KEGS.
"YOU CAN SEE THEM IN EVERY CORNER OF THE GLOBE.
"WAITING TO *EXPLODE*."
POWDER KEGS, I CAN DEAL WITH. THAT IS THE JOB.
BUT WHAT WORRIES ME MOST...IS THE EXPLOSION I ***CANNOT*** SEE COMING.

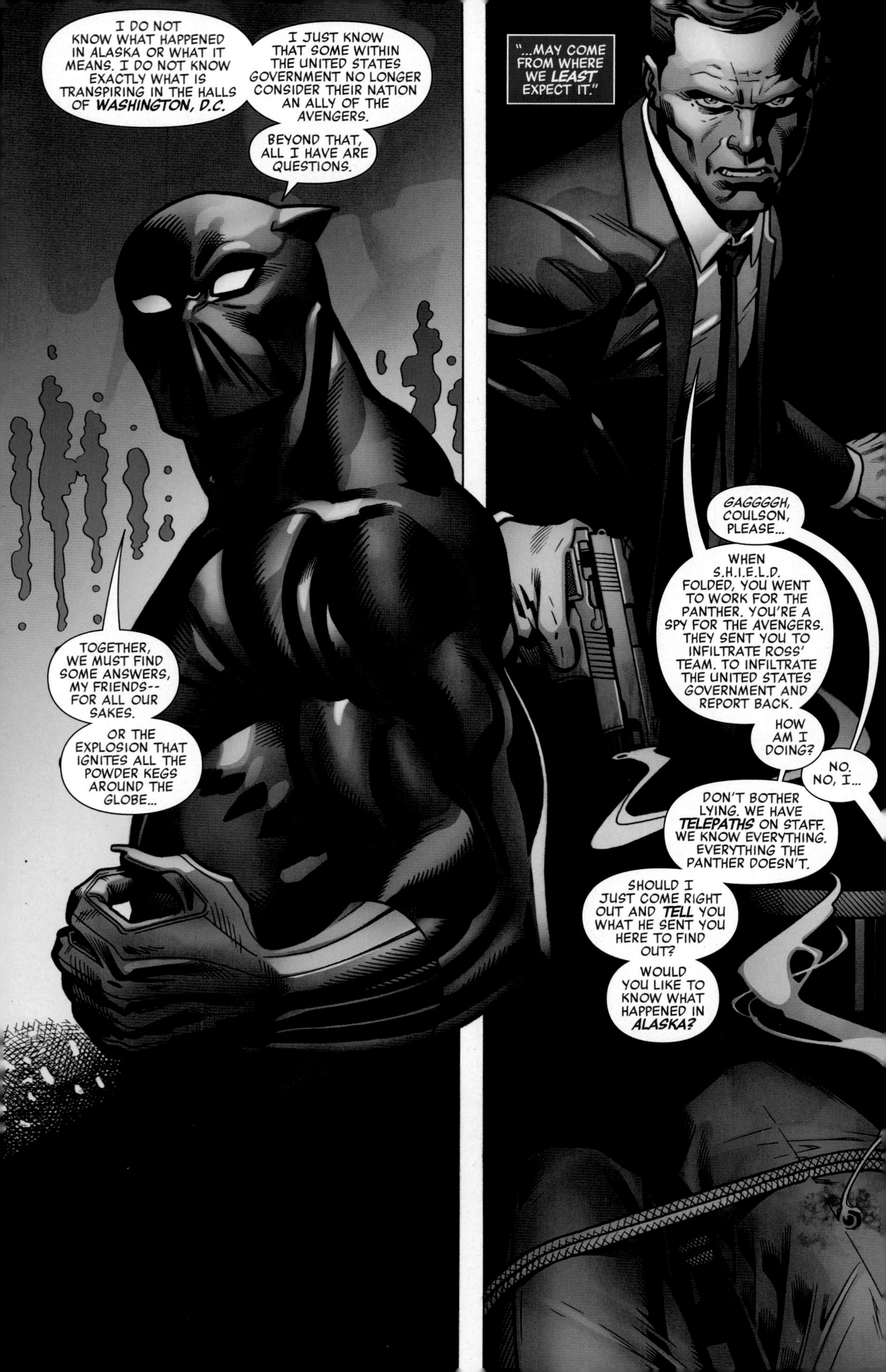
I DO NOT KNOW WHAT HAPPENED IN ALASKA OR WHAT IT MEANS. I DO NOT KNOW EXACTLY WHAT IS TRANSPIRING IN THE HALLS OF WASHINGTON, D.C.
I JUST KNOW THAT SOME WITHIN THE UNITED STATES GOVERNMENT NO LONGER CONSIDER THEIR NATION AN ALLY OF THE AVENGERS.
BEYOND THAT, ALL I HAVE ARE QUESTIONS.
TOGETHER, WE MUST FIND SOME ANSWERS, MY FRIENDS-- FOR ALL OUR SAKES.
OR THE EXPLOSION THAT IGNITES ALL THE POWDER KEGS AROUND THE GLOBE...
"...MAY COME FROM WHERE WE LEAST EXPECT IT."
GAGGGGH, COULSON, PLEASE...
WHEN S.H.I.E.L.D. FOLDED, YOU WENT TO WORK FOR THE PANTHER. YOU'RE A SPY FOR THE AVENGERS. THEY SENT YOU TO INFILTRATE ROSS' TEAM. TO INFILTRATE THE UNITED STATES GOVERNMENT AND REPORT BACK.
HOW AM I DOING?
NO. NO, I...
DON'T BOTHER LYING. WE HAVE TELEPATHS ON STAFF. WE KNOW EVERYTHING. EVERYTHING THE PANTHER DOESN'T.
SHOULD I JUST COME RIGHT OUT AND TELL YOU WHAT HE SENT YOU HERE TO FIND OUT?
WOULD YOU LIKE TO KNOW WHAT HAPPENED IN ALASKA?

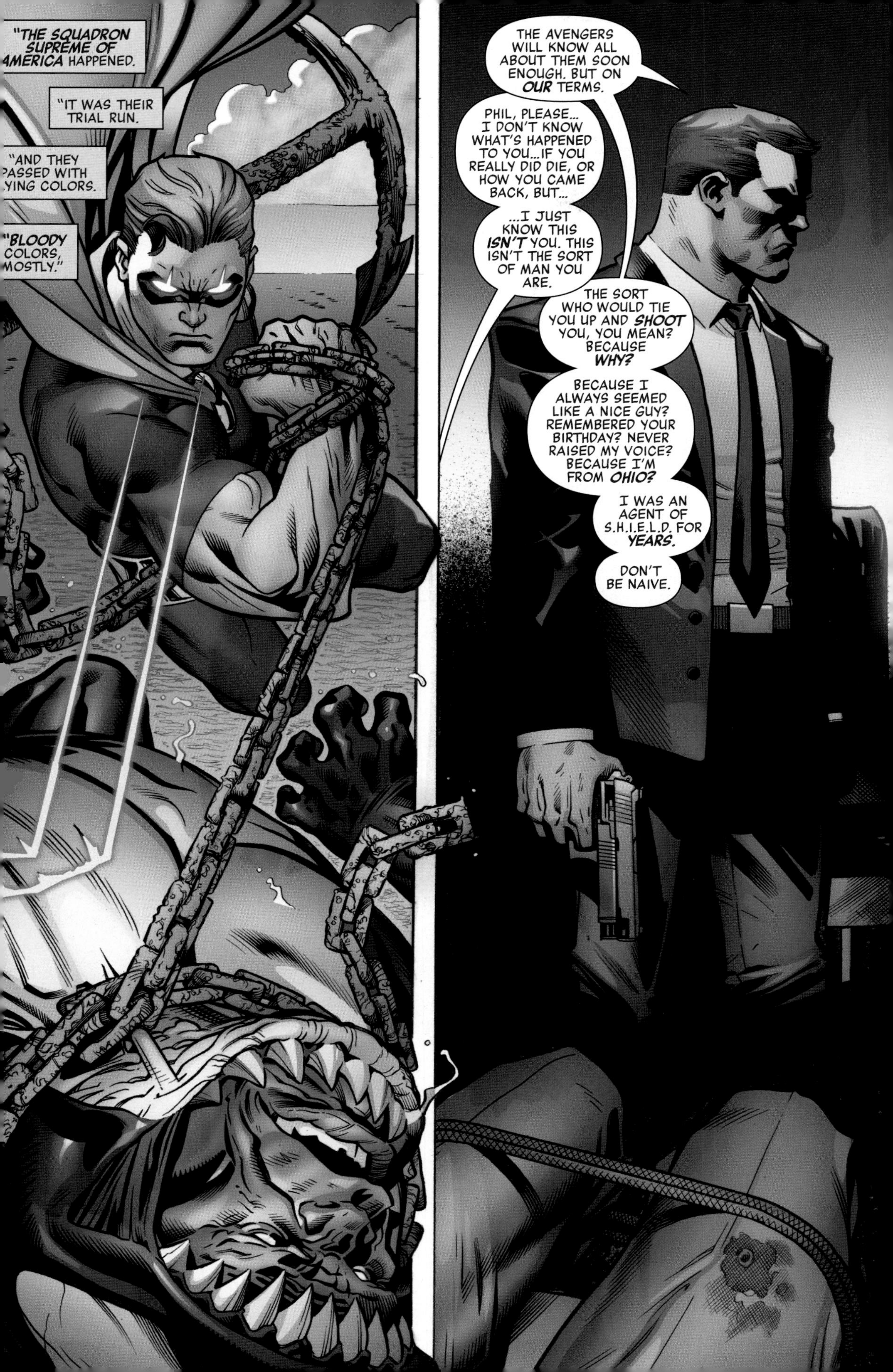
"THE SQUADRON SUPREME OF AMERICA HAPPENED.
"IT WAS THEIR TRIAL RUN.
"AND THEY PASSED WITH YING COLORS.
"BLOODY COLORS, MOSTLY."
THE AVENGERS WILL KNOW ALL ABOUT THEM SOON ENOUGH. BUT ON OUR TERMS.
PHIL, PLEASE... I DON'T KNOW WHAT'S HAPPENED TO YOU...IF YOU REALLY DID DIE, OR HOW YOU CAME BACK, BUT...
...I JUST KNOW THIS ISN'T YOU. THIS ISN'T THE SORT OF MAN YOU ARE.
THE SORT WHO WOULD TIE YOU UP AND SHOOT YOU, YOU MEAN? BECAUSE WHY?
BECAUSE I ALWAYS SEEMED LIKE A NICE GUY? REMEMBERED YOUR BIRTHDAY? NEVER RAISED MY VOICE? BECAUSE I'M FROM OHIO?
I WAS AN AGENT OF S.H.I.E.L.D. FOR YEARS.
DON'T BE NAIVE.

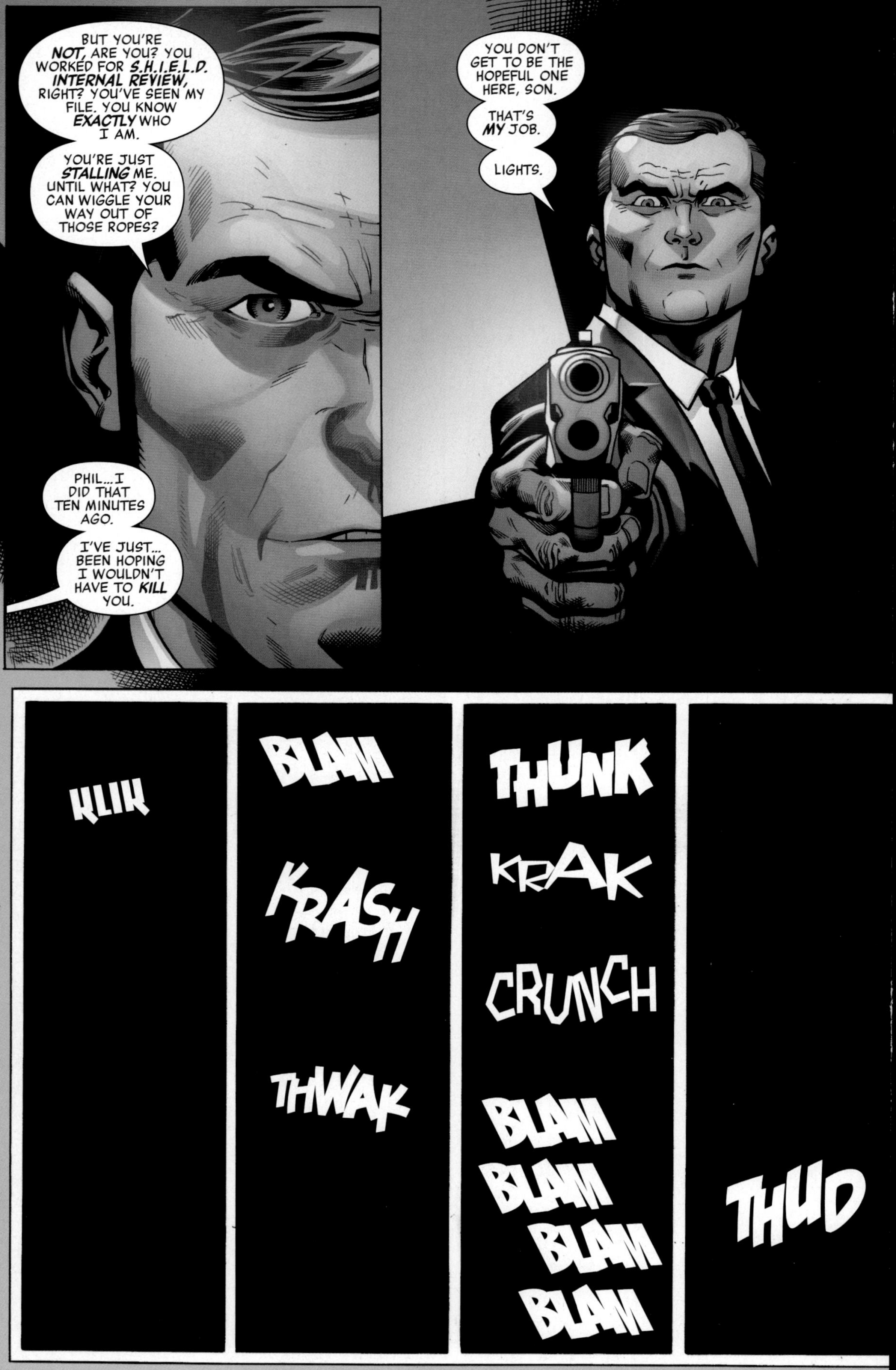

BUT YOU'RE NOT, ARE YOU? YOU WORKED FOR S.H.I.E.L.D. INTERNAL REVIEW, RIGHT? YOU'VE SEEN MY FILE. YOU KNOW EXACTLY WHO I AM.
YOU'RE JUST STALLING ME. UNTIL WHAT? YOU CAN WIGGLE YOUR WAY OUT OF THOSE ROPES?
YOU DON'T GET TO BE THE HOPEFUL ONE HERE, SON.
THAT'S MY JOB.
LIGHTS.
PHIL...I DID THAT TEN MINUTES AGO.
I'VE JUST... BEEN HOPING I WOULDN'T HAVE TO KILL YOU.
KLIK
BLAM
KRASH
THWAK
THUNK
KRAK
CRUNCH
BLAM
BLAM
BLAM
BLAM
THUD

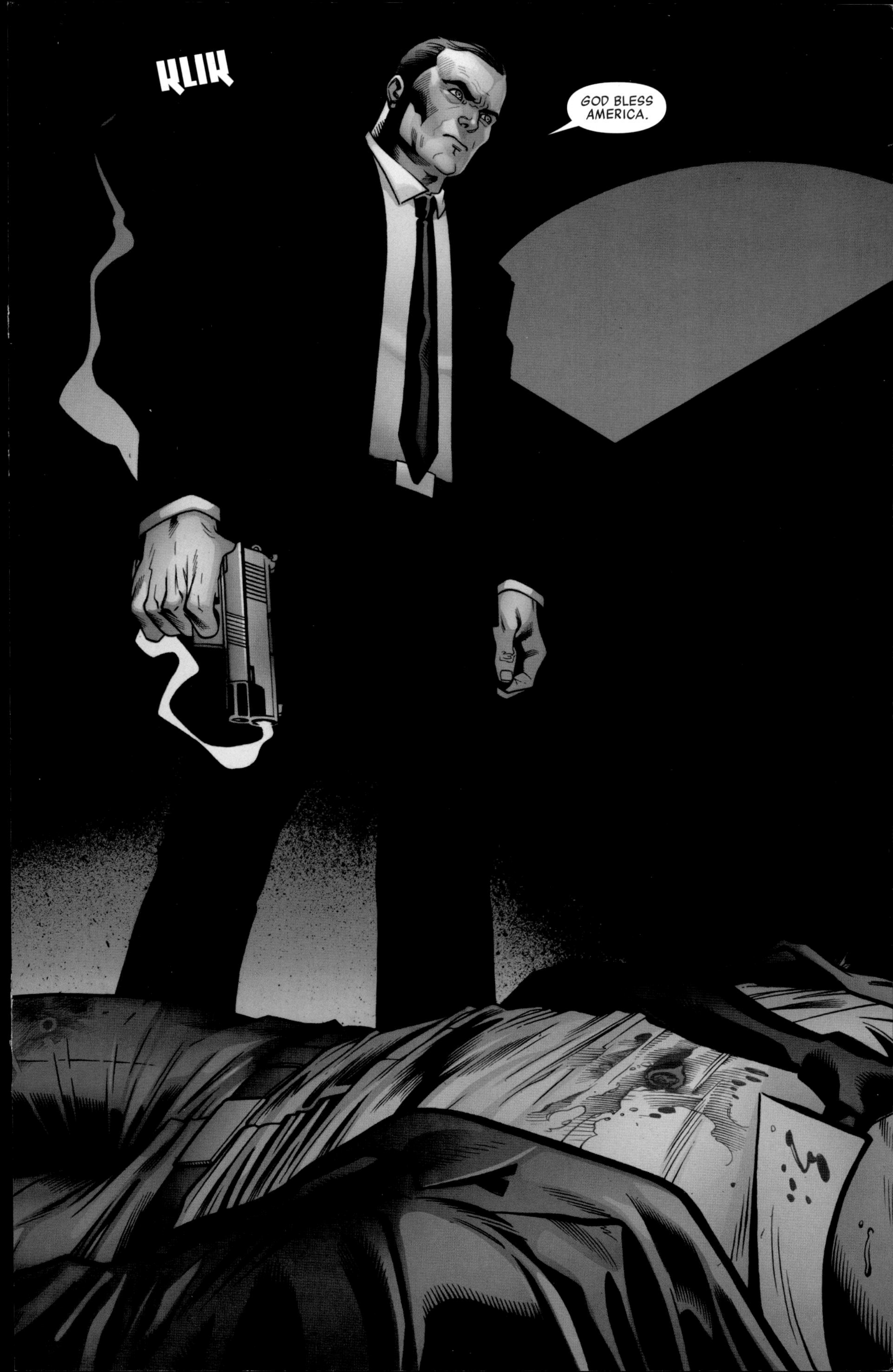
KLIK
GOD BLESS AMERICA.

12 THE AGENTS OF WAKANDA

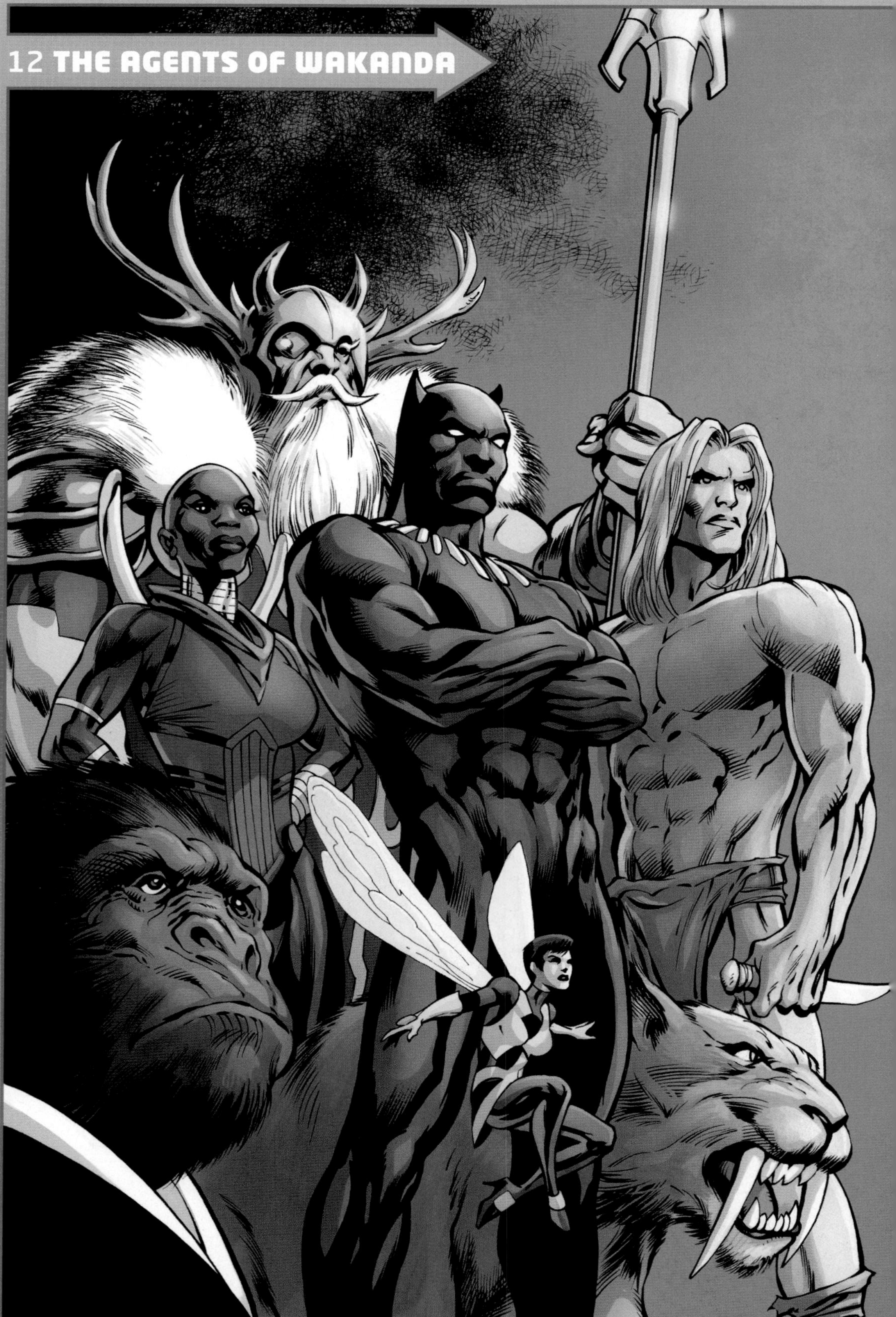

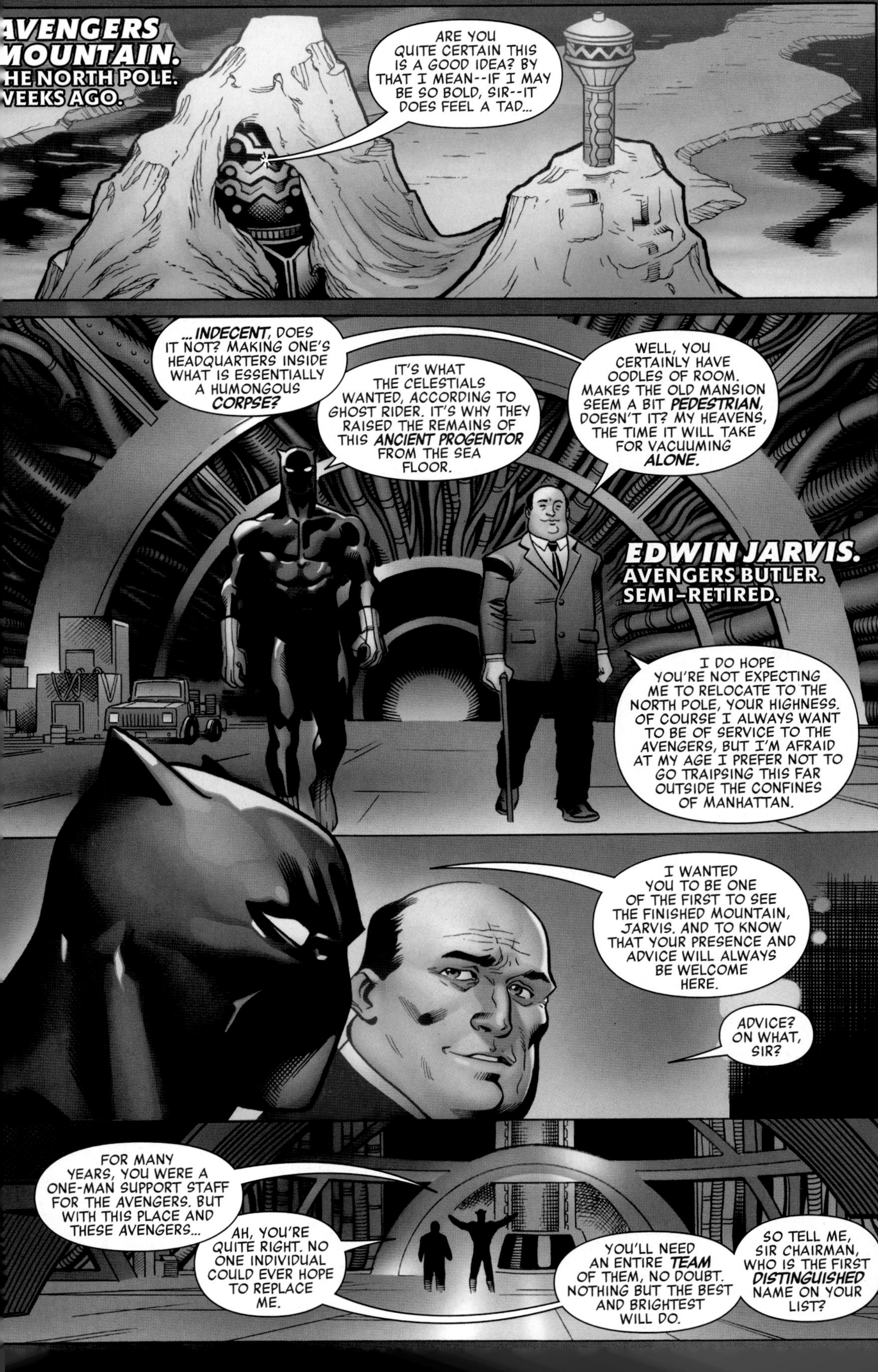

AVENGERS MOUNTAIN.
HE NORTH POLE.
VEEKS AGO.
ARE YOU QUITE CERTAIN THIS IS A GOOD IDEA? BY THAT I MEAN--IF I MAY BE SO BOLD, SIR--IT DOES FEEL A TAD...
...INDECENT, DOES IT NOT? MAKING ONE'S HEADQUARTERS INSIDE WHAT IS ESSENTIALLY A HUMONGOUS CORPSE?
IT'S WHAT THE CELESTIALS WANTED, ACCORDING TO GHOST RIDER. IT'S WHY THEY RAISED THE REMAINS OF THIS ANCIENT PROGENITOR FROM THE SEA FLOOR.
WELL, YOU CERTAINLY HAVE OODLES OF ROOM. MAKES THE OLD MANSION SEEM A BIT PEDESTRIAN, DOESN'T IT? MY HEAVENS, THE TIME IT WILL TAKE FOR VACUUMING ALONE.
EDWIN JARVIS.
AVENGERS BUTLER.
SEMI-RETIRED.
I DO HOPE YOU'RE NOT EXPECTING ME TO RELOCATE TO THE NORTH POLE, YOUR HIGHNESS. OF COURSE I ALWAYS WANT TO BE OF SERVICE TO THE AVENGERS, BUT I'M AFRAID AT MY AGE I PREFER NOT TO GO TRAIPSING THIS FAR OUTSIDE THE CONFINES OF MANHATTAN.
I WANTED YOU TO BE ONE OF THE FIRST TO SEE THE FINISHED MOUNTAIN, JARVIS, AND TO KNOW THAT YOUR PRESENCE AND ADVICE WILL ALWAYS BE WELCOME HERE.
ADVICE? ON WHAT, SIR?
FOR MANY YEARS, YOU WERE A ONE-MAN SUPPORT STAFF FOR THE AVENGERS. BUT WITH THIS PLACE AND THESE AVENGERS...
AH, YOU'RE QUITE RIGHT. NO ONE INDIVIDUAL COULD EVER HOPE TO REPLACE ME.
YOU'LL NEED AN ENTIRE TEAM OF THEM, NO DOUBT. NOTHING BUT THE BEST AND BRIGHTEST WILL DO.
SO TELL ME, SIR CHAIRMAN, WHO IS THE FIRST DISTINGUISHED NAME ON YOUR LIST?

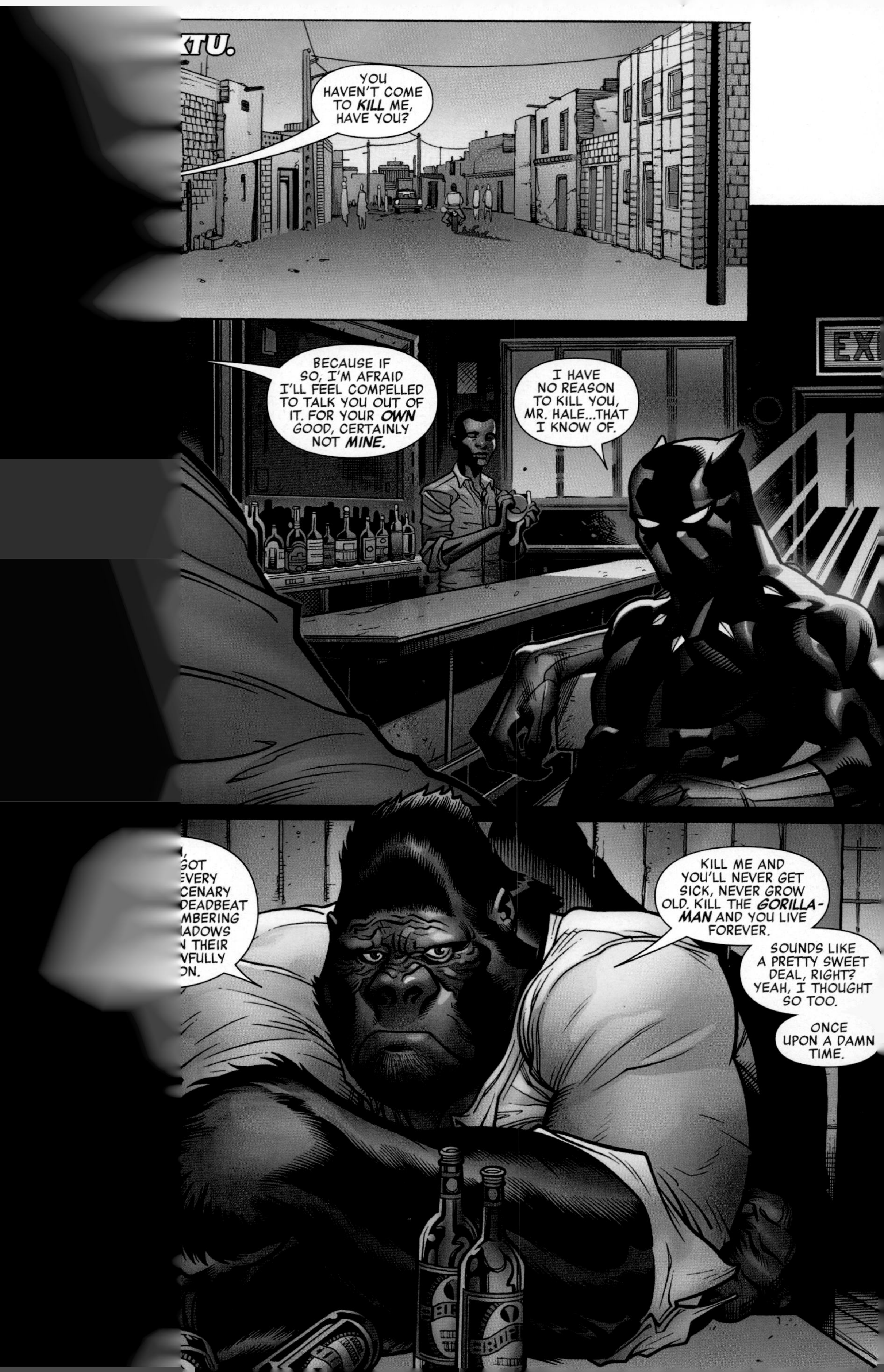
YOU HAVEN'T COME TO KILL ME, HAVE YOU?
BECAUSE IF SO, I'M AFRAID I'LL FEEL COMPELLED TO TALK YOU OUT OF IT. FOR YOUR OWN GOOD, CERTAINLY NOT MINE.
I HAVE NO REASON TO KILL YOU, MR. HALE...THAT I KNOW OF.
KILL ME AND YOU'LL NEVER GET SICK, NEVER GROW OLD. KILL THE GORILLA-MAN AND YOU LIVE FOREVER.
SOUNDS LIKE A PRETTY SWEET DEAL, RIGHT? YEAH, I THOUGHT SO TOO.
ONCE UPON A DAMN TIME.

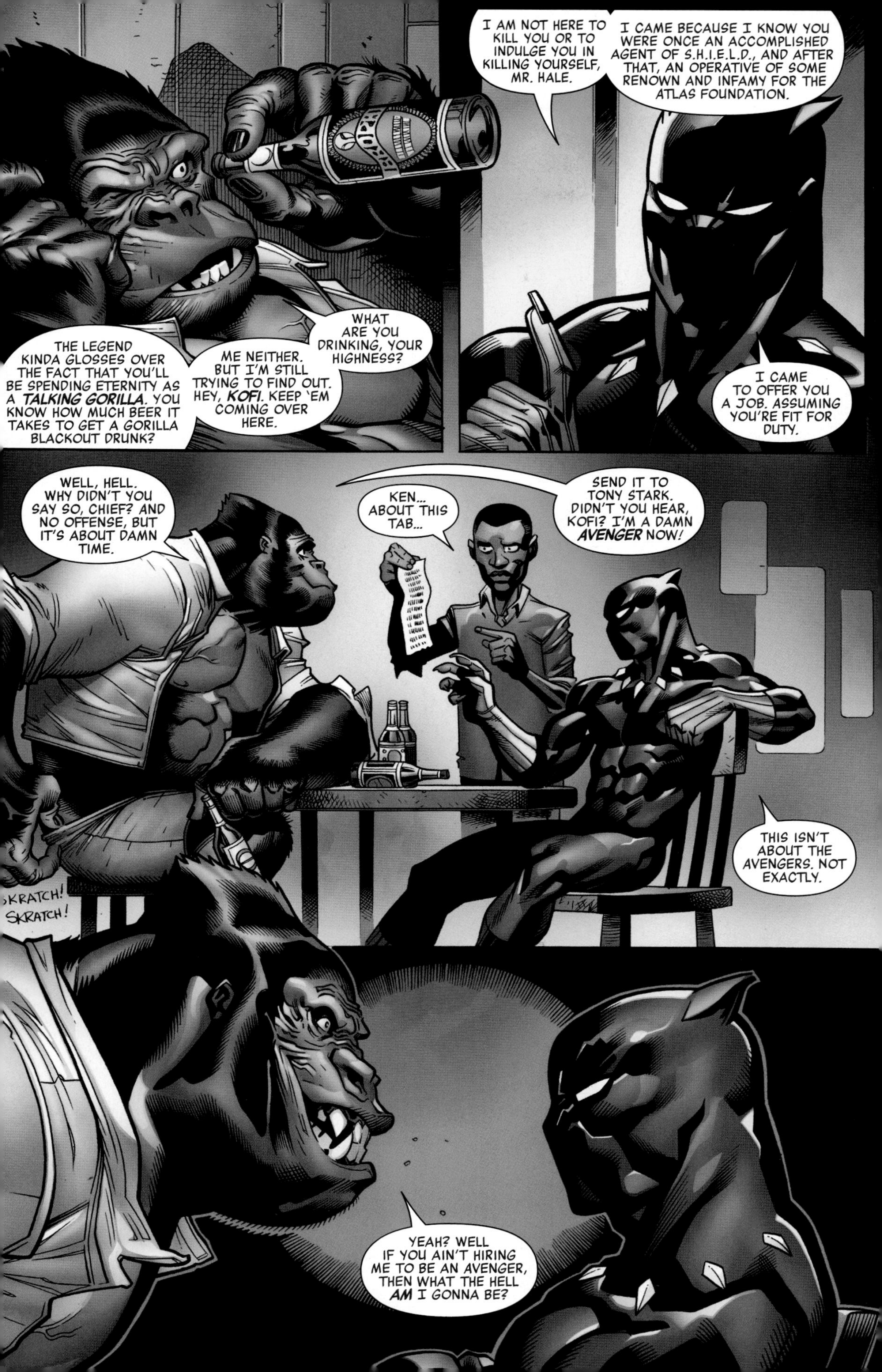
I AM NOT HERE TO KILL YOU OR TO INDULGE YOU IN KILLING YOURSELF, MR. HALE.
I CAME BECAUSE I KNOW YOU WERE ONCE AN ACCOMPLISHED AGENT OF S.H.I.E.L.D., AND AFTER THAT, AN OPERATIVE OF SOME RENOWN AND INFAMY FOR THE ATLAS FOUNDATION.
THE LEGEND KINDA GLOSSES OVER THE FACT THAT YOU'LL BE SPENDING ETERNITY AS A *TALKING GORILLA*. YOU KNOW HOW MUCH BEER IT TAKES TO GET A GORILLA BLACKOUT DRUNK?
WHAT ARE YOU DRINKING, YOUR HIGHNESS?
ME NEITHER. BUT I'M STILL TRYING TO FIND OUT. HEY, *KOFI*. KEEP 'EM COMING OVER HERE.
I CAME TO OFFER YOU A JOB. ASSUMING YOU'RE FIT FOR DUTY.
WELL, HELL. WHY DIDN'T YOU SAY SO, CHIEF? AND NO OFFENSE, BUT IT'S ABOUT DAMN TIME.
KEN... ABOUT THIS TAB...
SEND IT TO TONY STARK. DIDN'T YOU HEAR, KOFI? I'M A DAMN *AVENGER* NOW!
THIS ISN'T ABOUT THE AVENGERS. NOT EXACTLY.
SKRATCH! SKRATCH!
YEAH? WELL IF YOU AIN'T HIRING ME TO BE AN AVENGER, THEN WHAT THE HELL *AM* I GONNA BE?

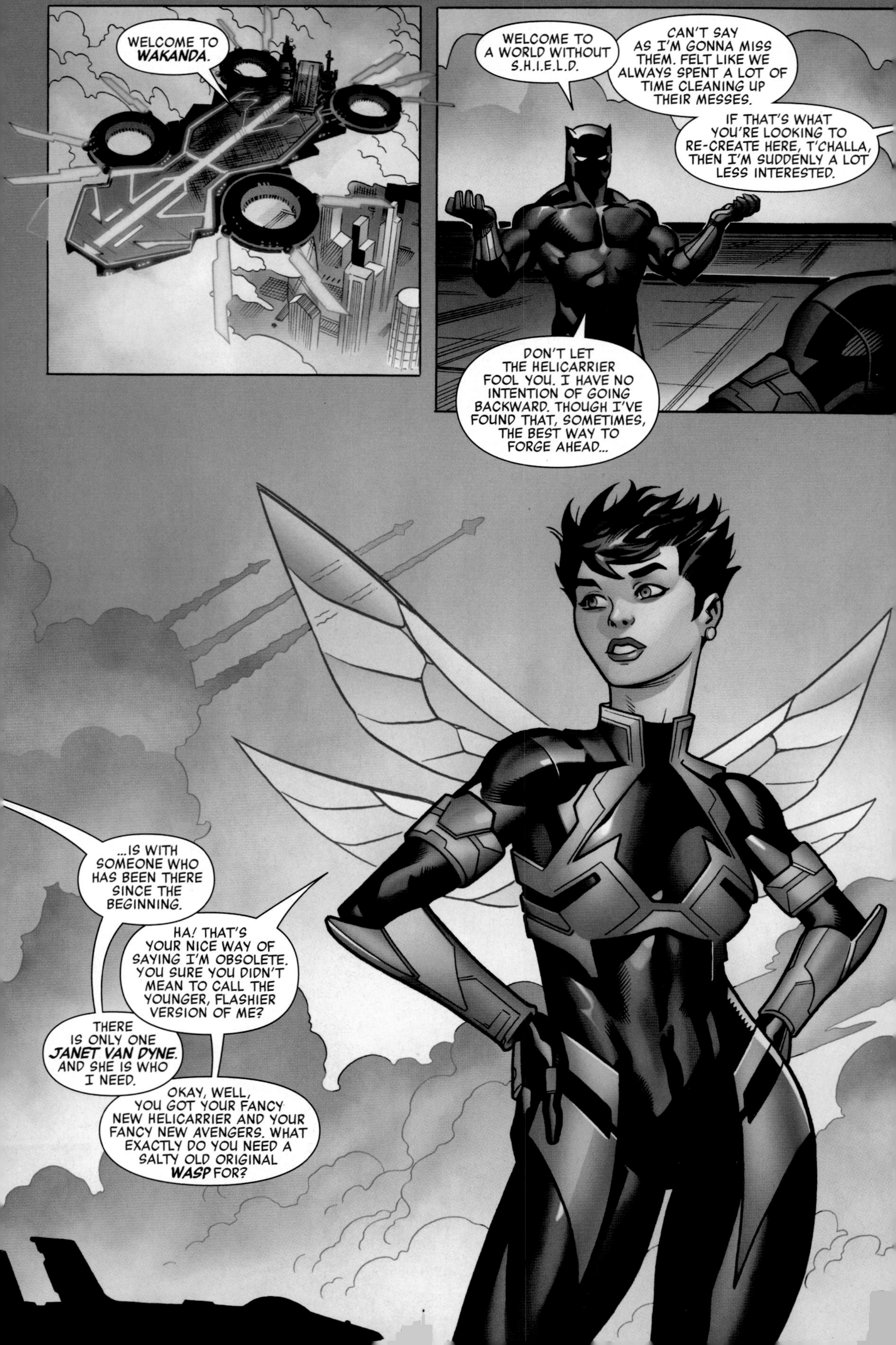
WELCOME TO WAKANDA.
WELCOME TO A WORLD WITHOUT S.H.I.E.L.D.
CAN'T SAY AS I'M GONNA MISS THEM. FELT LIKE WE ALWAYS SPENT A LOT OF TIME CLEANING UP THEIR MESSES.
IF THAT'S WHAT YOU'RE LOOKING TO RE-CREATE HERE, T'CHALLA, THEN I'M SUDDENLY A LOT LESS INTERESTED.
DON'T LET THE HELICARRIER FOOL YOU. I HAVE NO INTENTION OF GOING BACKWARD. THOUGH I'VE FOUND THAT, SOMETIMES, THE BEST WAY TO FORGE AHEAD...
...IS WITH SOMEONE WHO HAS BEEN THERE SINCE THE BEGINNING.
HA! THAT'S YOUR NICE WAY OF SAYING I'M OBSOLETE. YOU SURE YOU DIDN'T MEAN TO CALL THE YOUNGER, FLASHIER VERSION OF ME?
THERE IS ONLY ONE JANET VAN DYNE. AND SHE IS WHO I NEED.
OKAY, WELL, YOU GOT YOUR FANCY NEW HELICARRIER AND YOUR FANCY NEW AVENGERS. WHAT EXACTLY DO YOU NEED A SALTY OLD ORIGINAL WASP FOR?

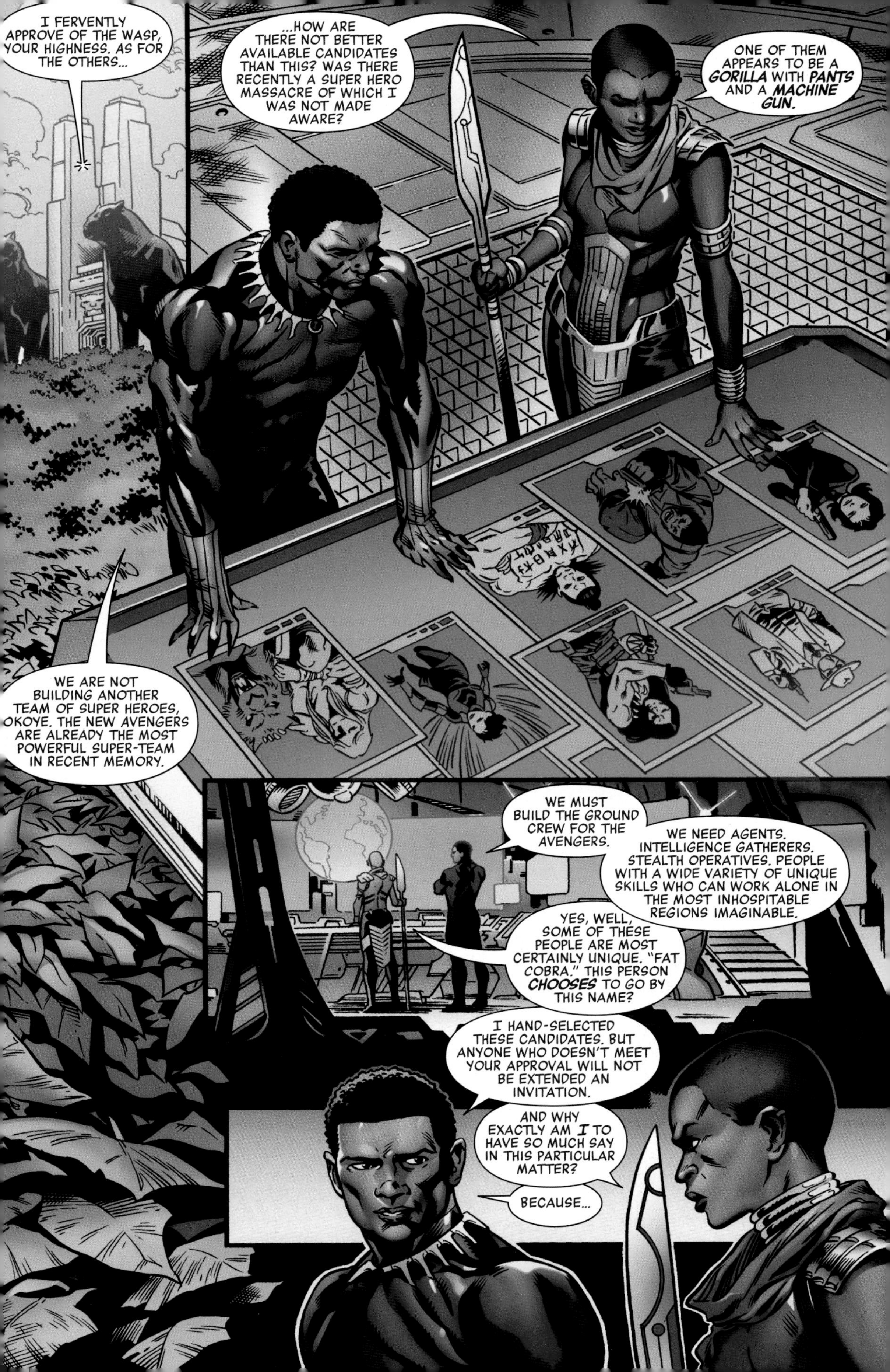
I FERVENTLY APPROVE OF THE WASP, YOUR HIGHNESS. AS FOR THE OTHERS...
...HOW ARE THERE NOT BETTER AVAILABLE CANDIDATES THAN THIS? WAS THERE RECENTLY A SUPER HERO MASSACRE OF WHICH I WAS NOT MADE AWARE?
ONE OF THEM APPEARS TO BE A GORILLA WITH PANTS AND A MACHINE GUN.
WE ARE NOT BUILDING ANOTHER TEAM OF SUPER HEROES, OKOYE. THE NEW AVENGERS ARE ALREADY THE MOST POWERFUL SUPER-TEAM IN RECENT MEMORY.
WE MUST BUILD THE GROUND CREW FOR THE AVENGERS.
WE NEED AGENTS. INTELLIGENCE GATHERERS. STEALTH OPERATIVES. PEOPLE WITH A WIDE VARIETY OF UNIQUE SKILLS WHO CAN WORK ALONE IN THE MOST INHOSPITABLE REGIONS IMAGINABLE.
YES, WELL, SOME OF THESE PEOPLE ARE MOST CERTAINLY UNIQUE. "FAT COBRA." THIS PERSON CHOOSES TO GO BY THIS NAME?
I HAND-SELECTED THESE CANDIDATES. BUT ANYONE WHO DOESN'T MEET YOUR APPROVAL WILL NOT BE EXTENDED AN INVITATION.
AND WHY EXACTLY AM I TO HAVE SO MUCH SAY IN THIS PARTICULAR MATTER?
BECAUSE...

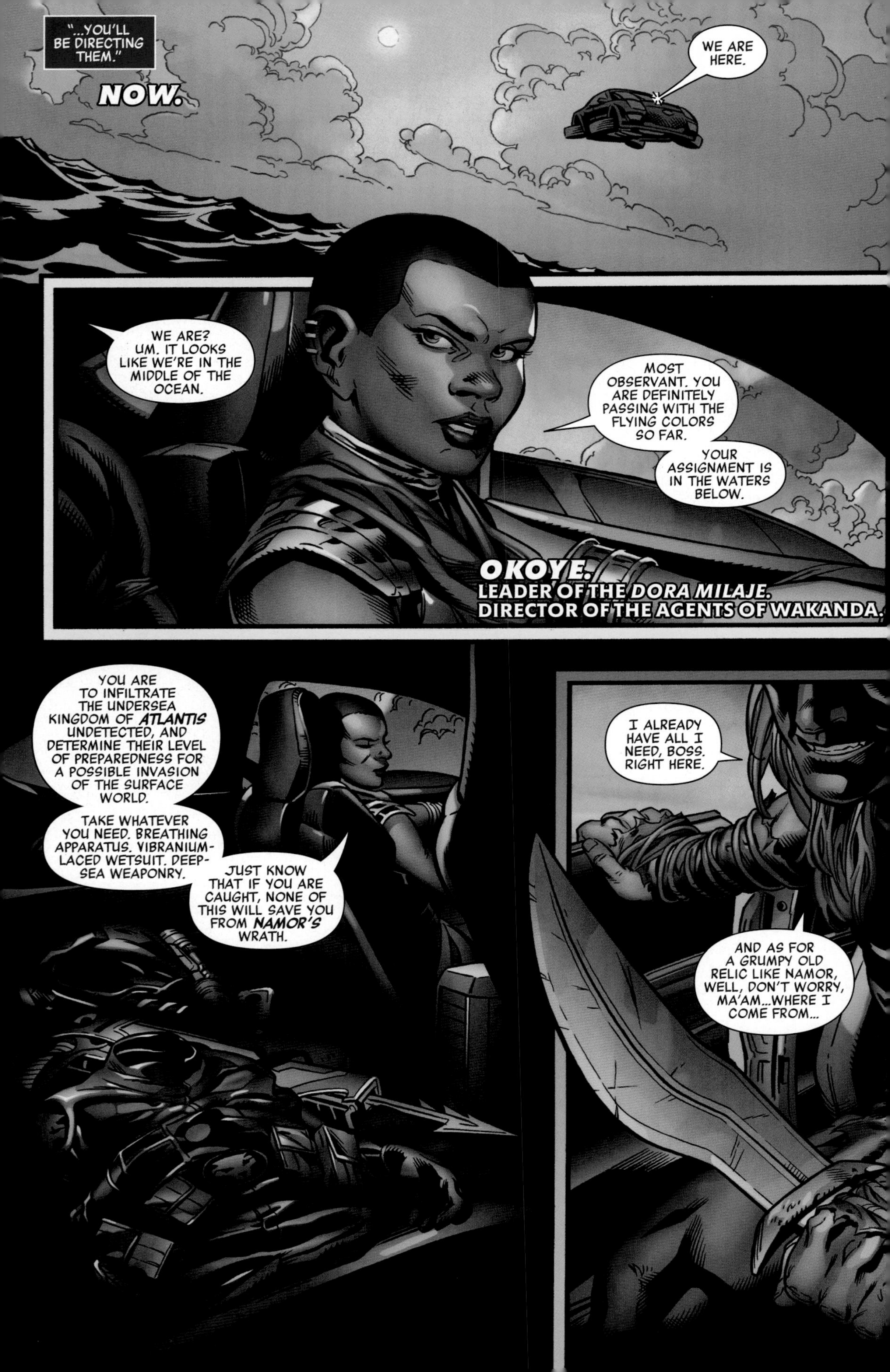

"...YOU'LL BE DIRECTING THEM."
NOW.
WE ARE HERE.
WE ARE? UM. IT LOOKS LIKE WE'RE IN THE MIDDLE OF THE OCEAN.
MOST OBSERVANT. YOU ARE DEFINITELY PASSING WITH THE FLYING COLORS SO FAR.
YOUR ASSIGNMENT IS IN THE WATERS BELOW.
OKOYE.
LEADER OF THE DORA MILAJE.
DIRECTOR OF THE AGENTS OF WAKANDA.
YOU ARE TO INFILTRATE THE UNDERSEA KINGDOM OF ATLANTIS UNDETECTED, AND DETERMINE THEIR LEVEL OF PREPAREDNESS FOR A POSSIBLE INVASION OF THE SURFACE WORLD.
TAKE WHATEVER YOU NEED. BREATHING APPARATUS. VIBRANIUM-LACED WETSUIT. DEEP-SEA WEAPONRY.
JUST KNOW THAT IF YOU ARE CAUGHT, NONE OF THIS WILL SAVE YOU FROM NAMOR'S WRATH.
I ALREADY HAVE ALL I NEED, BOSS. RIGHT HERE.
AND AS FOR A GRUMPY OLD RELIC LIKE NAMOR, WELL, DON'T WORRY, MA'AM...WHERE I COME FROM...

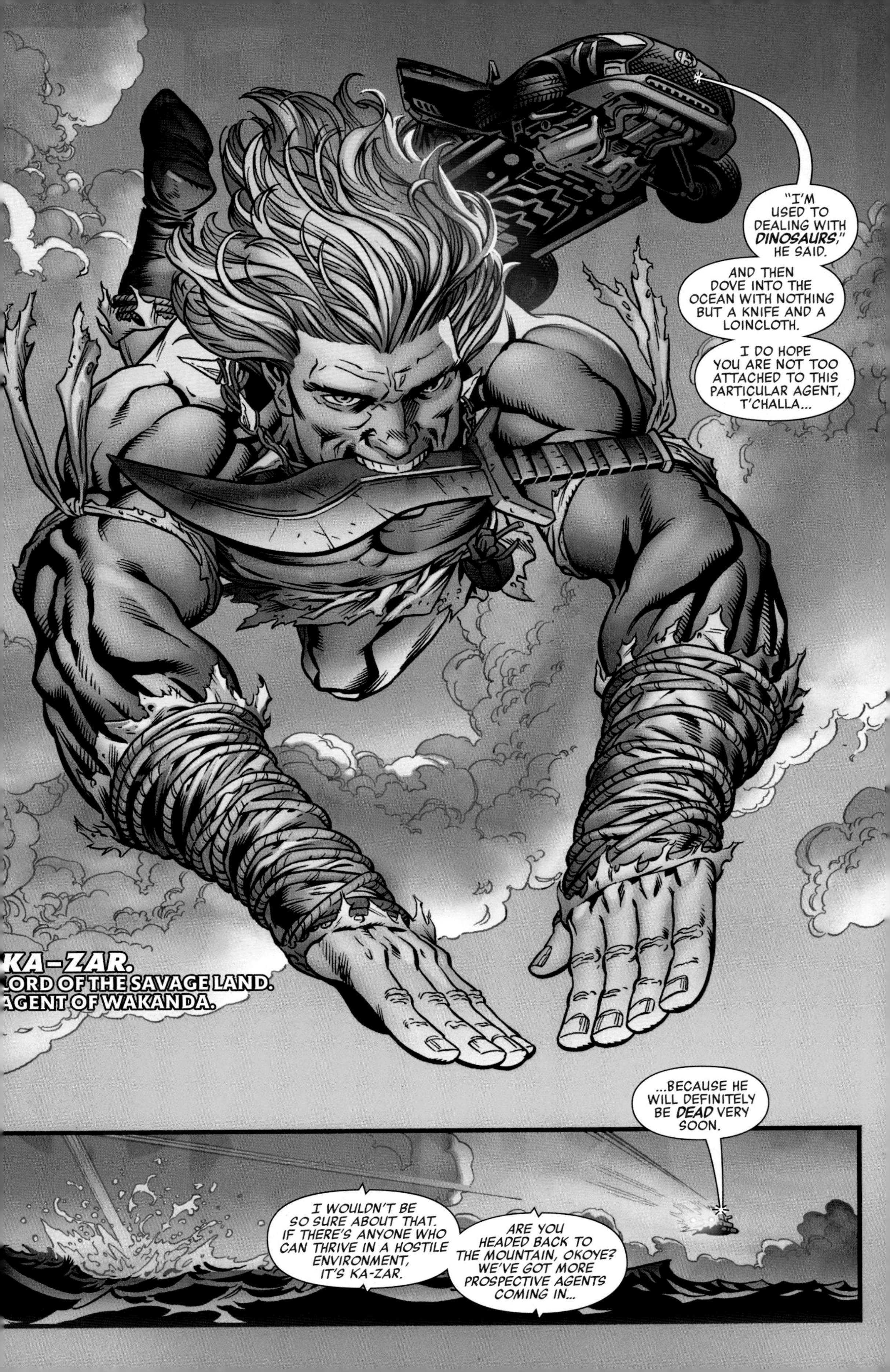
"I'M USED TO DEALING WITH DINOSAURS," HE SAID.
AND THEN DOVE INTO THE OCEAN WITH NOTHING BUT A KNIFE AND A LOINCLOTH.
I DO HOPE YOU ARE NOT TOO ATTACHED TO THIS PARTICULAR AGENT, T'CHALLA...
KA-ZAR.
LORD OF THE SAVAGE LAND.
AGENT OF WAKANDA.
...BECAUSE HE WILL DEFINITELY BE DEAD VERY SOON.
I WOULDN'T BE SO SURE ABOUT THAT. IF THERE'S ANYONE WHO CAN THRIVE IN A HOSTILE ENVIRONMENT, IT'S KA-ZAR.
ARE YOU HEADED BACK TO THE MOUNTAIN, OKOYE? WE'VE GOT MORE PROSPECTIVE AGENTS COMING IN...

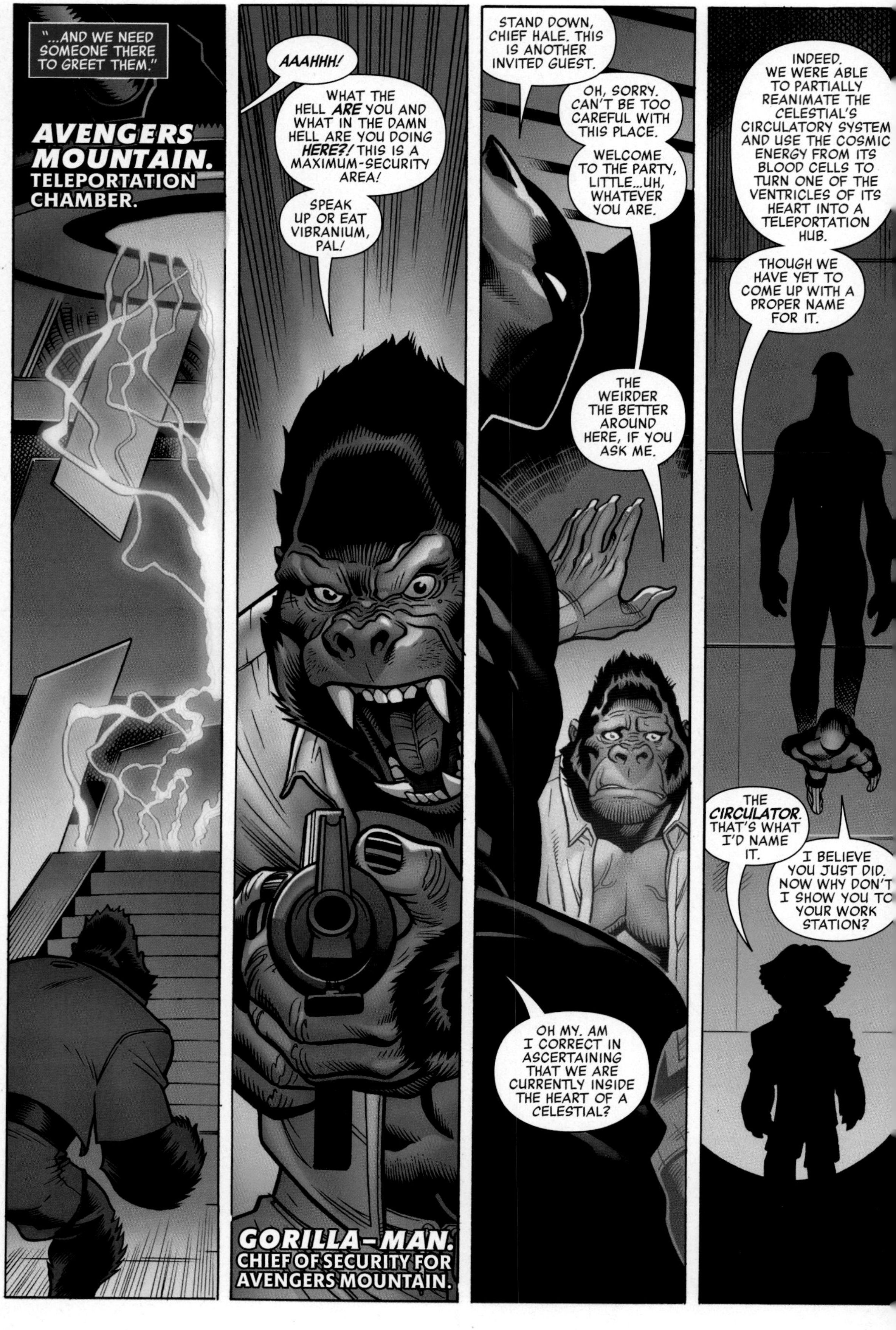
"...AND WE NEED SOMEONE THERE TO GREET THEM."
AVENGERS MOUNTAIN. TELEPORTATION CHAMBER.
AAAHHH!
WHAT THE HELL ARE YOU AND WHAT IN THE DAMN HELL ARE YOU DOING HERE?! THIS IS A MAXIMUM-SECURITY AREA!
SPEAK UP OR EAT VIBRANIUM, PAL!
GORILLA-MAN. CHIEF OF SECURITY FOR AVENGERS MOUNTAIN.
STAND DOWN, CHIEF HALE. THIS IS ANOTHER INVITED GUEST.
OH, SORRY. CAN'T BE TOO CAREFUL WITH THIS PLACE.
WELCOME TO THE PARTY, LITTLE...UH, WHATEVER YOU ARE.
THE WEIRDER THE BETTER AROUND HERE, IF YOU ASK ME.
OH MY. AM I CORRECT IN ASCERTAINING THAT WE ARE CURRENTLY INSIDE THE HEART OF A CELESTIAL?
INDEED. WE WERE ABLE TO PARTIALLY REANIMATE THE CELESTIAL'S CIRCULATORY SYSTEM AND USE THE COSMIC ENERGY FROM ITS BLOOD CELLS TO TURN ONE OF THE VENTRICLES OF ITS HEART INTO A TELEPORTATION HUB.
THOUGH WE HAVE YET TO COME UP WITH A PROPER NAME FOR IT.
THE CIRCULATOR. THAT'S WHAT I'D NAME IT.
I BELIEVE YOU JUST DID. NOW WHY DON'T I SHOW YOU TO YOUR WORK STATION?

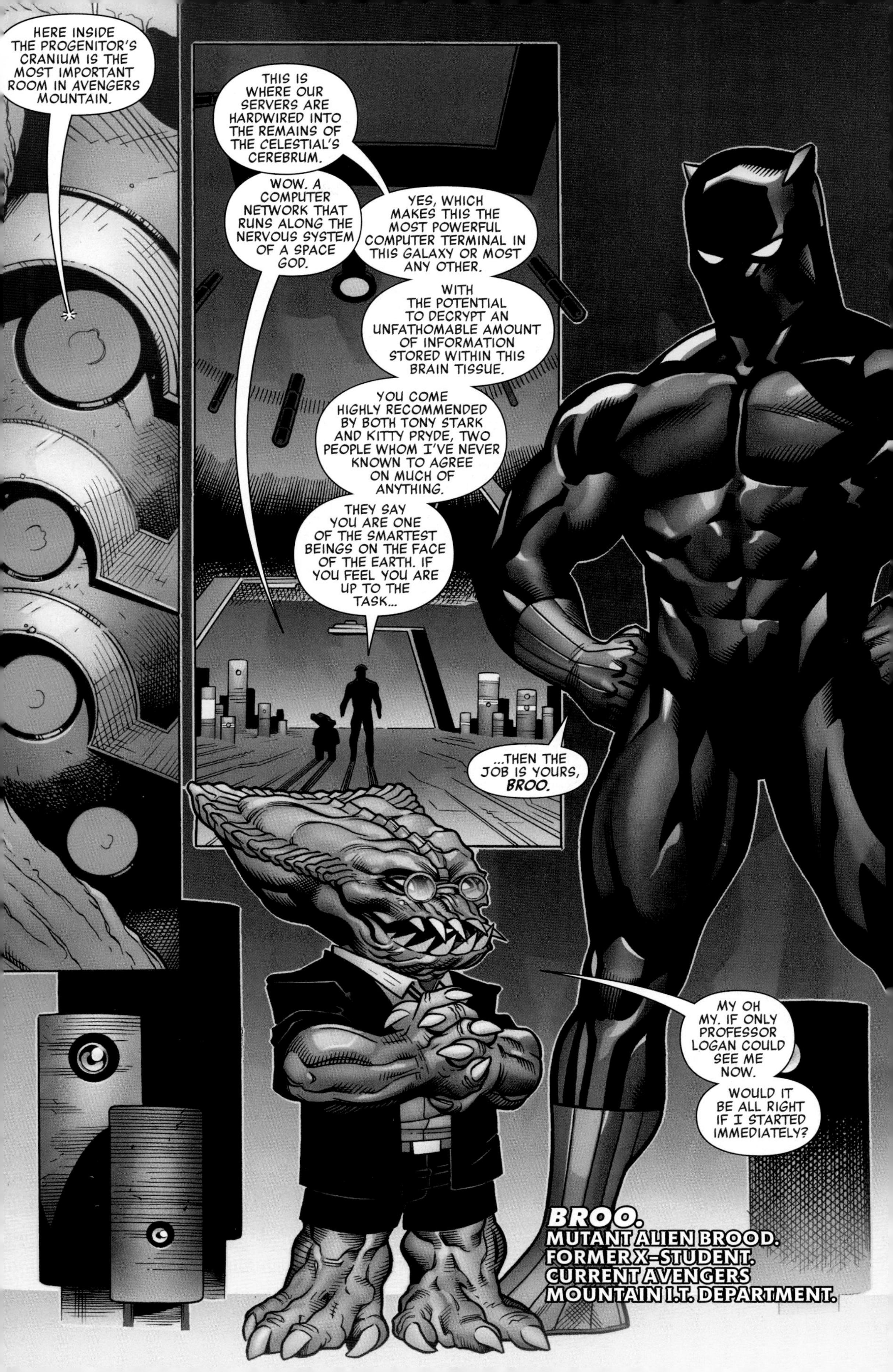
HERE INSIDE THE PROGENITOR'S CRANIUM IS THE MOST IMPORTANT ROOM IN AVENGERS MOUNTAIN.
THIS IS WHERE OUR SERVERS ARE HARDWIRED INTO THE REMAINS OF THE CELESTIAL'S CEREBRUM.
WOW. A COMPUTER NETWORK THAT RUNS ALONG THE NERVOUS SYSTEM OF A SPACE GOD.
YES, WHICH MAKES THIS THE MOST POWERFUL COMPUTER TERMINAL IN THIS GALAXY OR MOST ANY OTHER.
WITH THE POTENTIAL TO DECRYPT AN UNFATHOMABLE AMOUNT OF INFORMATION STORED WITHIN THIS BRAIN TISSUE.
YOU COME HIGHLY RECOMMENDED BY BOTH TONY STARK AND KITTY PRYDE, TWO PEOPLE WHOM I'VE NEVER KNOWN TO AGREE ON MUCH OF ANYTHING.
THEY SAY YOU ARE ONE OF THE SMARTEST BEINGS ON THE FACE OF THE EARTH. IF YOU FEEL YOU ARE UP TO THE TASK...
...THEN THE JOB IS YOURS, BROO.
MY OH MY. IF ONLY PROFESSOR LOGAN COULD SEE ME NOW.
WOULD IT BE ALL RIGHT IF I STARTED IMMEDIATELY?
BROO.
MUTANT ALIEN BROOD.
FORMER X-STUDENT.
CURRENT AVENGERS MOUNTAIN I.T. DEPARTMENT.

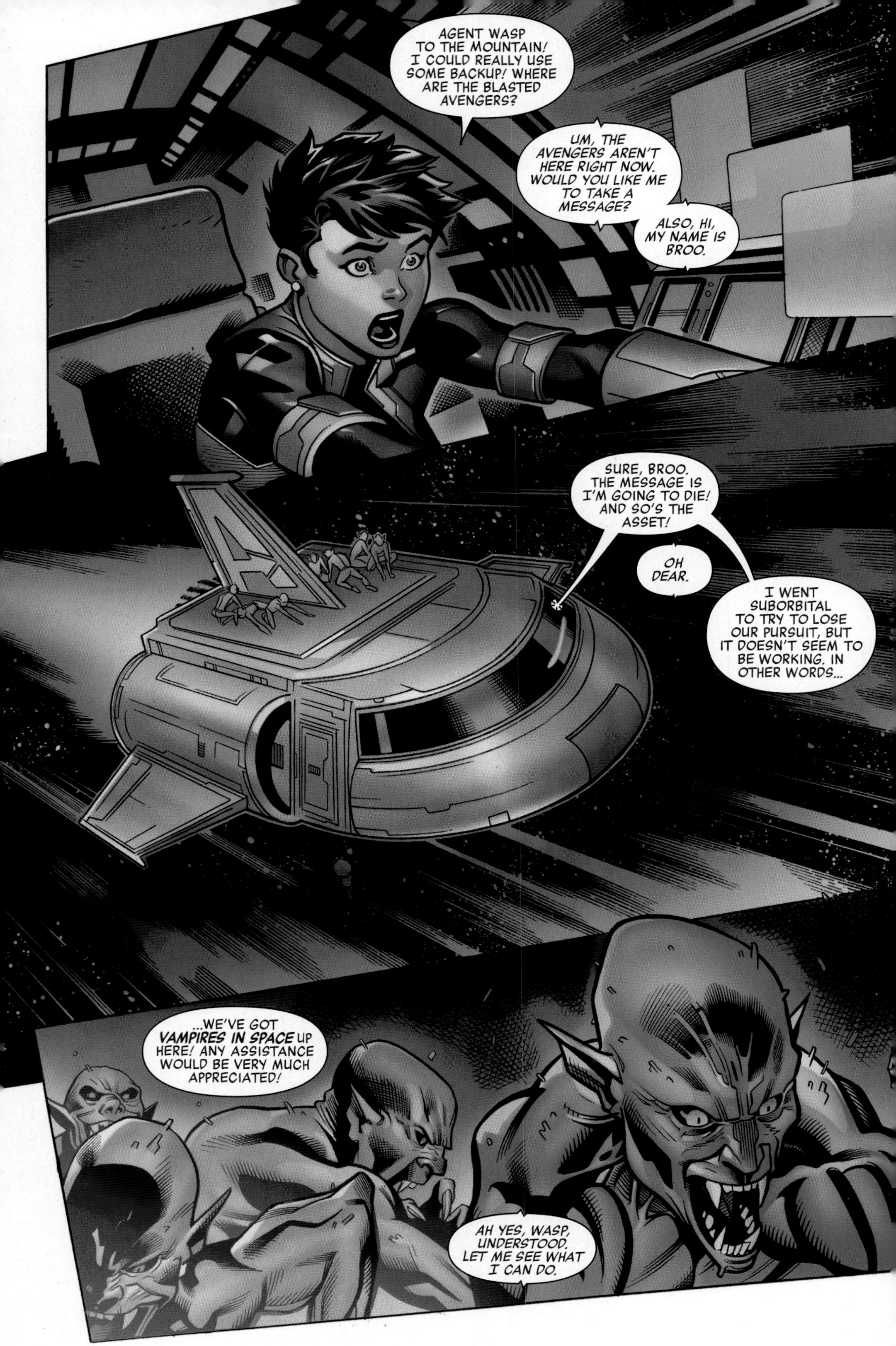
AGENT WASP TO THE MOUNTAIN! I COULD REALLY USE SOME BACKUP! WHERE ARE THE BLASTED AVENGERS?
UM, THE AVENGERS AREN'T HERE RIGHT NOW. WOULD YOU LIKE ME TO TAKE A MESSAGE?
ALSO, HI, MY NAME IS BROO.
SURE, BROO. THE MESSAGE IS I'M GOING TO DIE! AND SO'S THE ASSET!
OH DEAR.
I WENT SUBORBITAL TO TRY TO LOSE OUR PURSUIT, BUT IT DOESN'T SEEM TO BE WORKING. IN OTHER WORDS...
...WE'VE GOT VAMPIRES IN SPACE UP HERE! ANY ASSISTANCE WOULD BE VERY MUCH APPRECIATED!
AH YES, WASP, UNDERSTOOD. LET ME SEE WHAT I CAN DO.

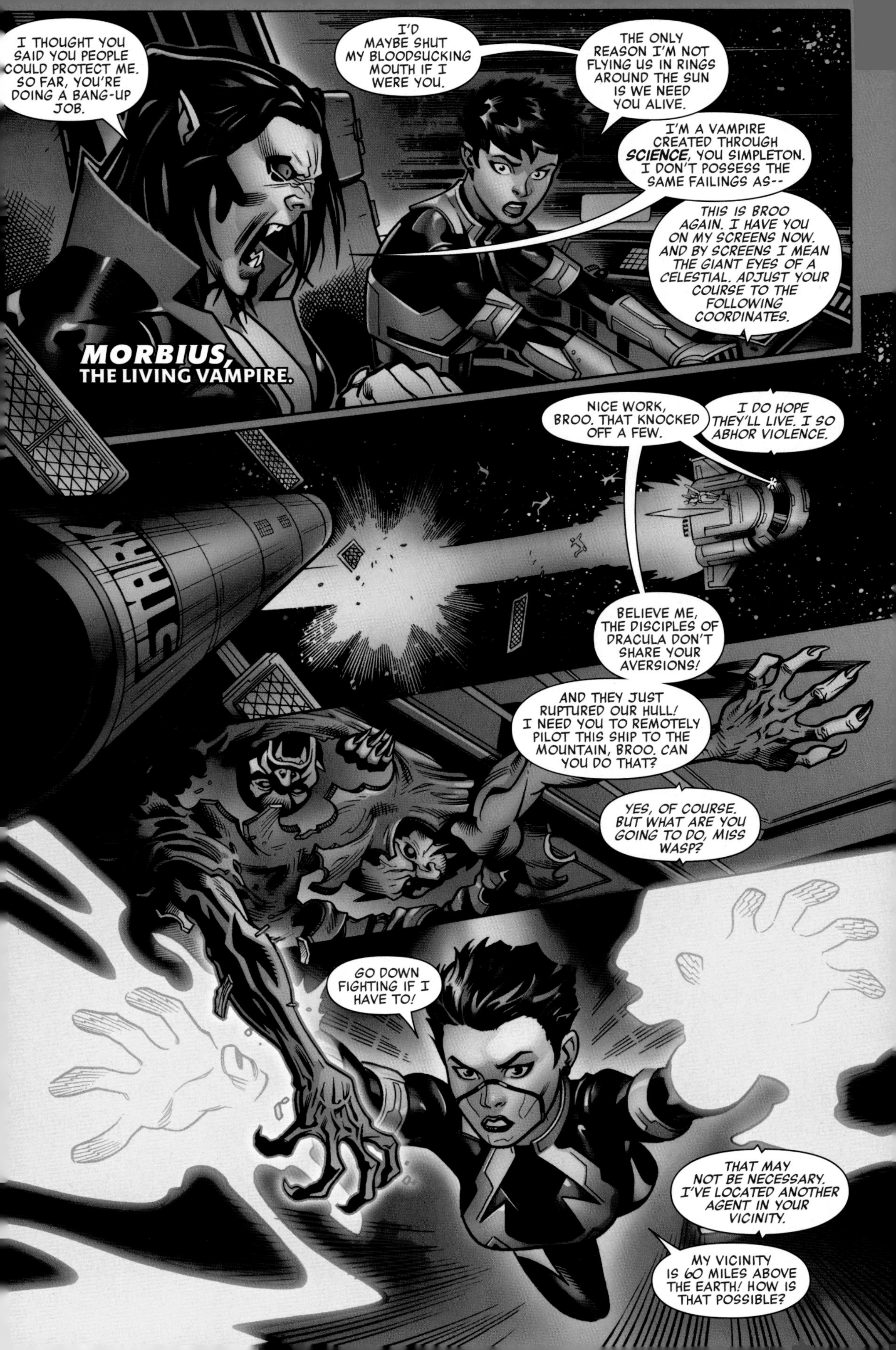
I THOUGHT YOU SAID YOU PEOPLE COULD PROTECT ME. SO FAR, YOU'RE DOING A BANG-UP JOB.
I'D MAYBE SHUT MY BLOODSUCKING MOUTH IF I WERE YOU.
THE ONLY REASON I'M NOT FLYING US IN RINGS AROUND THE SUN IS WE NEED YOU ALIVE.
I'M A VAMPIRE CREATED THROUGH SCIENCE, YOU SIMPLETON. I DON'T POSSESS THE SAME FAILINGS AS--
THIS IS BROO AGAIN. I HAVE YOU ON MY SCREENS NOW. AND BY SCREENS I MEAN THE GIANT EYES OF A CELESTIAL. ADJUST YOUR COURSE TO THE FOLLOWING COORDINATES.
MORBIUS, THE LIVING VAMPIRE.
NICE WORK, BROO. THAT KNOCKED OFF A FEW.
I DO HOPE THEY'LL LIVE. I SO ABHOR VIOLENCE.
BELIEVE ME, THE DISCIPLES OF DRACULA DON'T SHARE YOUR AVERSIONS!
AND THEY JUST RUPTURED OUR HULL! I NEED YOU TO REMOTELY PILOT THIS SHIP TO THE MOUNTAIN, BROO. CAN YOU DO THAT?
YES, OF COURSE. BUT WHAT ARE YOU GOING TO DO, MISS WASP?
GO DOWN FIGHTING IF I HAVE TO!
THAT MAY NOT BE NECESSARY. I'VE LOCATED ANOTHER AGENT IN YOUR VICINITY.
MY VICINITY IS 60 MILES ABOVE THE EARTH! HOW IS THAT POSSIBLE?

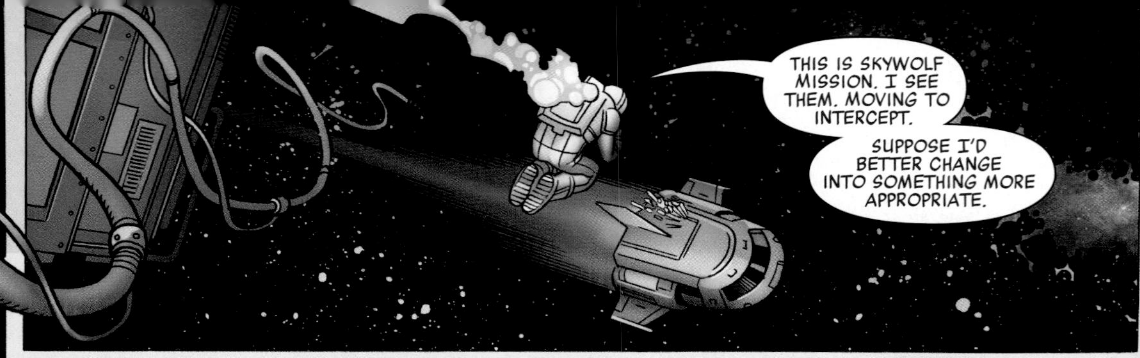
THIS IS SKYWOLF MISSION. I SEE THEM. MOVING TO INTERCEPT.
SUPPOSE I'D BETTER CHANGE INTO SOMETHING MORE APPROPRIATE.

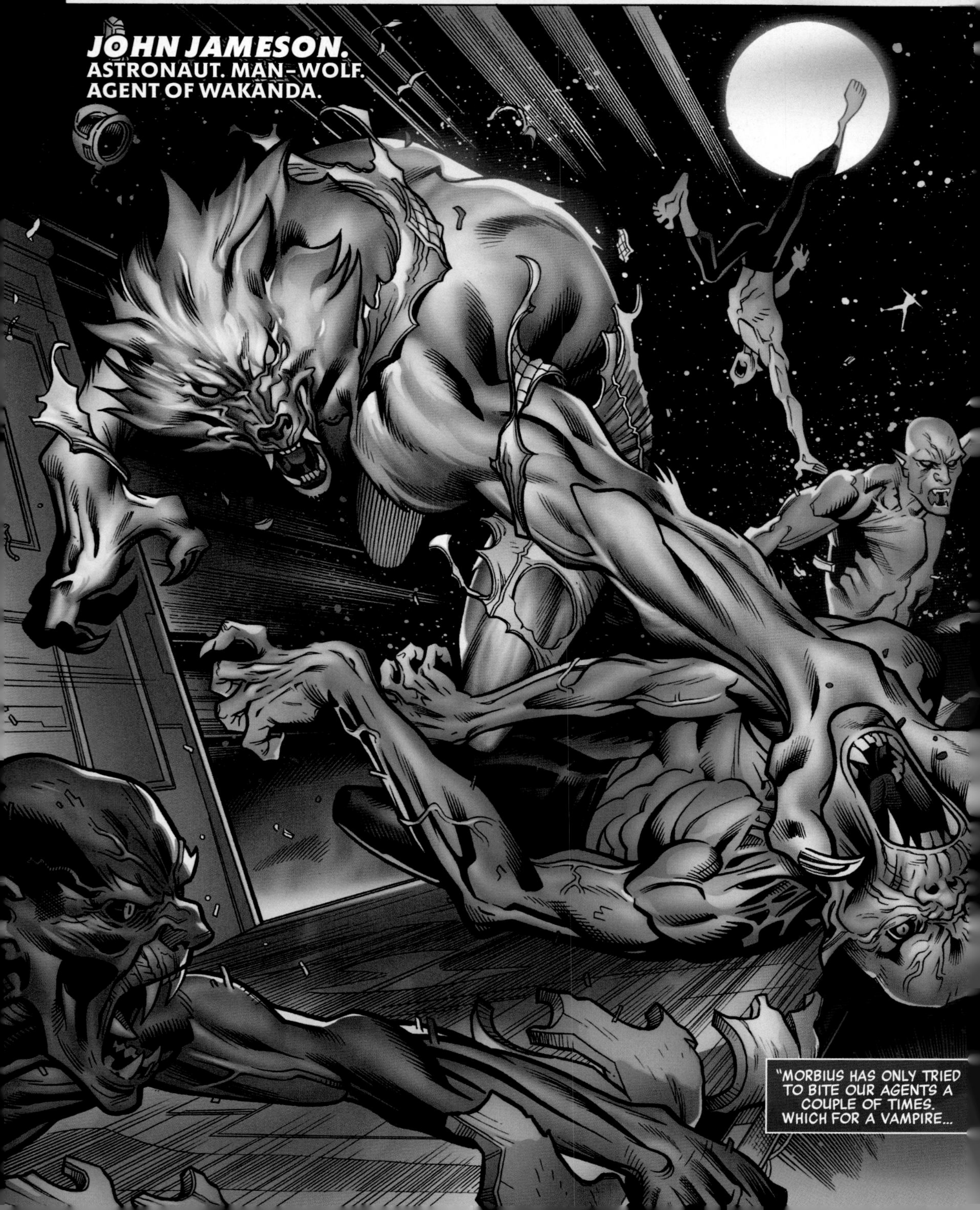
JOHN JAMESON.
ASTRONAUT. MAN-WOLF. AGENT OF WAKANDA.
"MORBIUS HAS ONLY TRIED TO BITE OUR AGENTS A COUPLE OF TIMES. WHICH FOR A VAMPIRE...

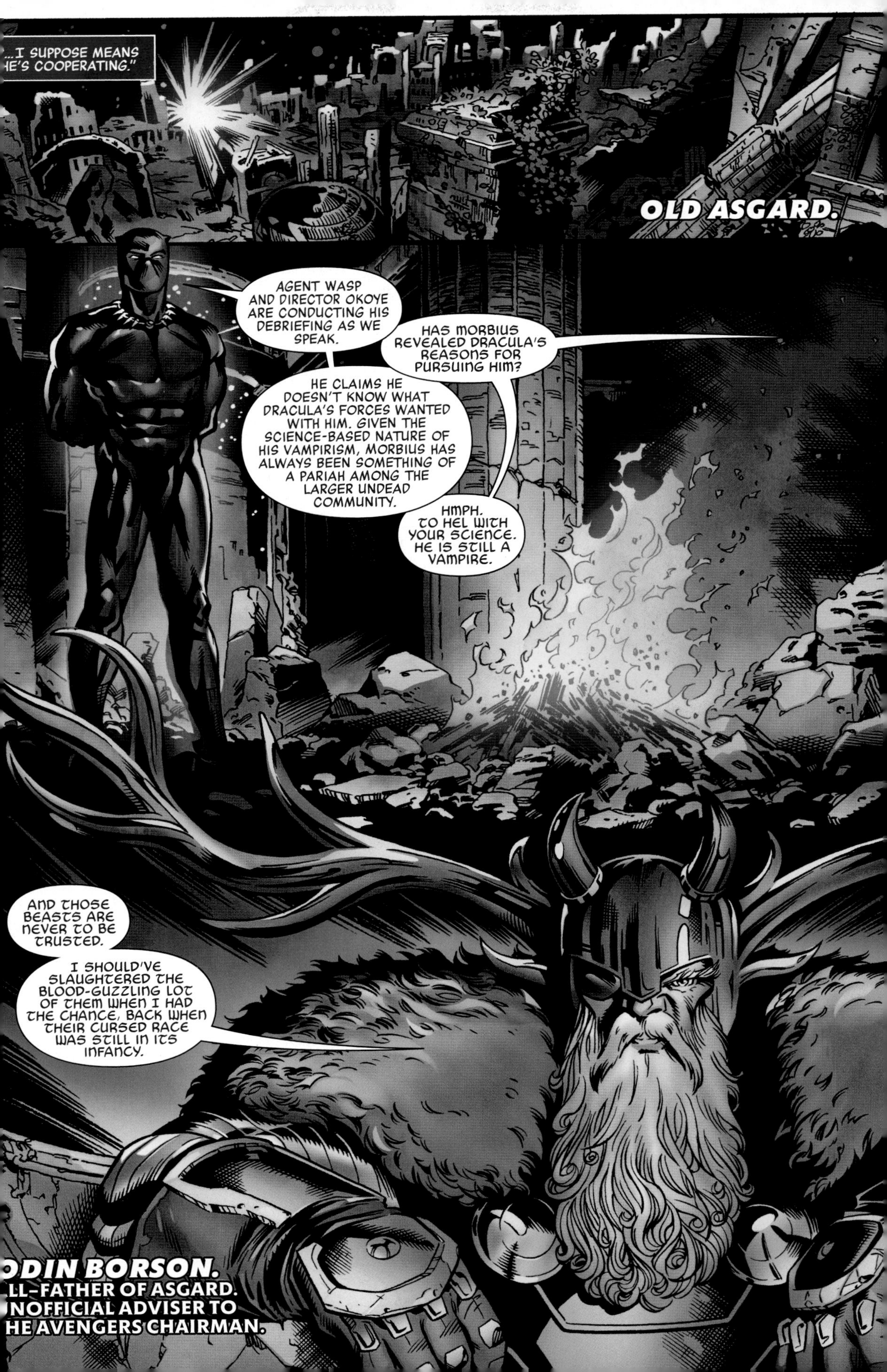
...I SUPPOSE MEANS
HE'S COOPERATING."
OLD ASGARD.
AGENT WASP AND DIRECTOR OKOYE ARE CONDUCTING HIS DEBRIEFING AS WE SPEAK.
HAS MORBIUS REVEALED DRACULA'S REASONS FOR PURSUING HIM?
HE CLAIMS HE DOESN'T KNOW WHAT DRACULA'S FORCES WANTED WITH HIM. GIVEN THE SCIENCE-BASED NATURE OF HIS VAMPIRISM, MORBIUS HAS ALWAYS BEEN SOMETHING OF A PARIAH AMONG THE LARGER UNDEAD COMMUNITY.
HMPH. TO HEL WITH YOUR SCIENCE. HE IS STILL A VAMPIRE.
AND THOSE BEASTS ARE NEVER TO BE TRUSTED.
I SHOULD'VE SLAUGHTERED THE BLOOD-GUZZLING LOT OF THEM WHEN I HAD THE CHANCE, BACK WHEN THEIR CURSED RACE WAS STILL IN ITS INFANCY.
ODIN BORSON.
LL-FATHER OF ASGARD.
NOFFICIAL ADVISER TO
HE AVENGERS CHAIRMAN.

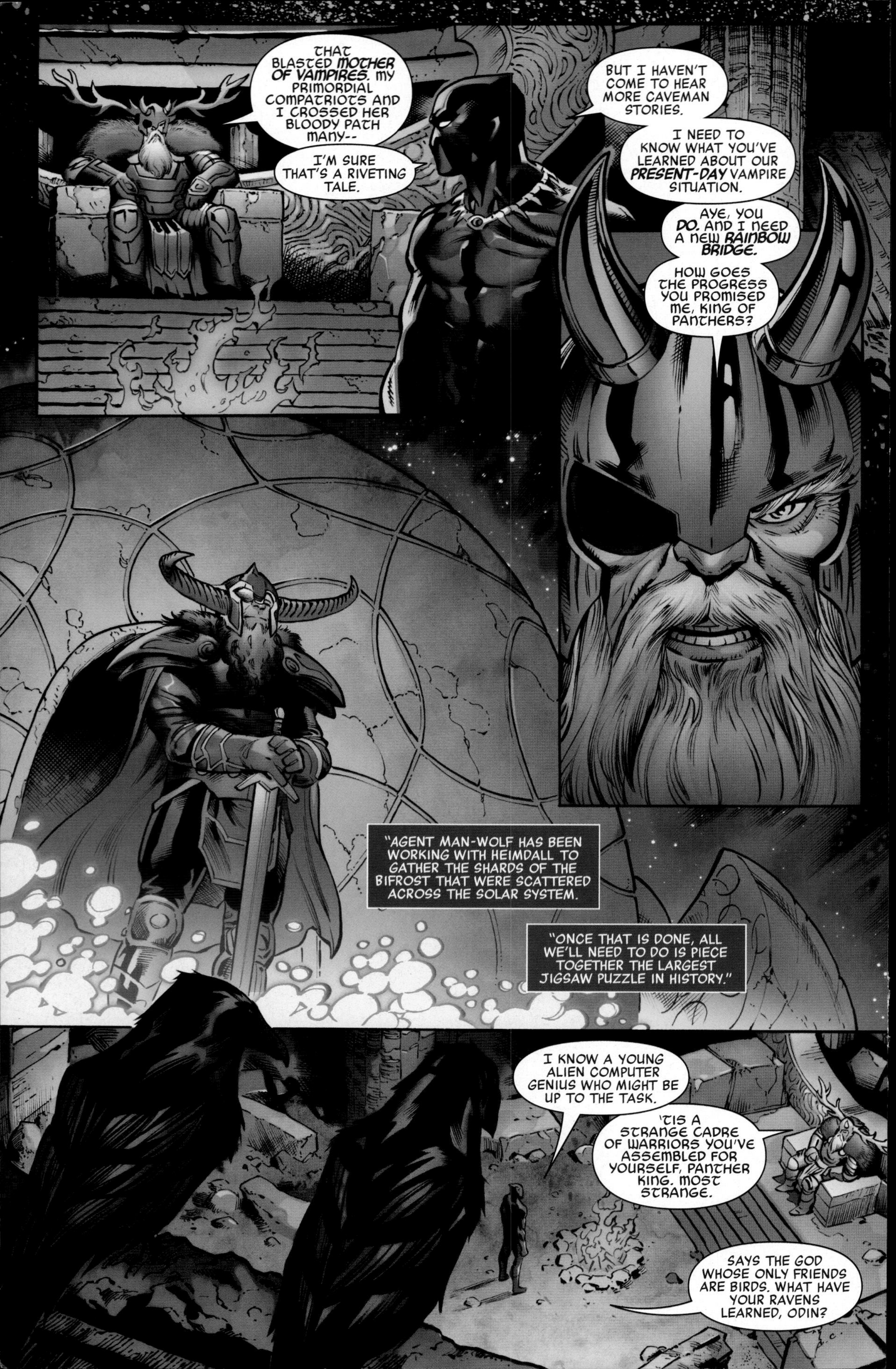

THAT BLASTED MOTHER OF VAMPIRES. MY PRIMORDIAL COMPATRIOTS AND I CROSSED HER BLOODY PATH MANY--
I'M SURE THAT'S A RIVETING TALE.
BUT I HAVEN'T COME TO HEAR MORE CAVEMAN STORIES.
I NEED TO KNOW WHAT YOU'VE LEARNED ABOUT OUR PRESENT-DAY VAMPIRE SITUATION.
AYE, YOU DO. AND I NEED A NEW RAINBOW BRIDGE.
HOW GOES THE PROGRESS YOU PROMISED ME, KING OF PANTHERS?
"AGENT MAN-WOLF HAS BEEN WORKING WITH HEIMDALL TO GATHER THE SHARDS OF THE BIFROST THAT WERE SCATTERED ACROSS THE SOLAR SYSTEM.
"ONCE THAT IS DONE, ALL WE'LL NEED TO DO IS PIECE TOGETHER THE LARGEST JIGSAW PUZZLE IN HISTORY."
I KNOW A YOUNG ALIEN COMPUTER GENIUS WHO MIGHT BE UP TO THE TASK.
'TIS A STRANGE CADRE OF WARRIORS YOU'VE ASSEMBLED FOR YOURSELF, PANTHER KING. MOST STRANGE.
SAYS THE GOD WHOSE ONLY FRIENDS ARE BIRDS. WHAT HAVE YOUR RAVENS LEARNED, ODIN?

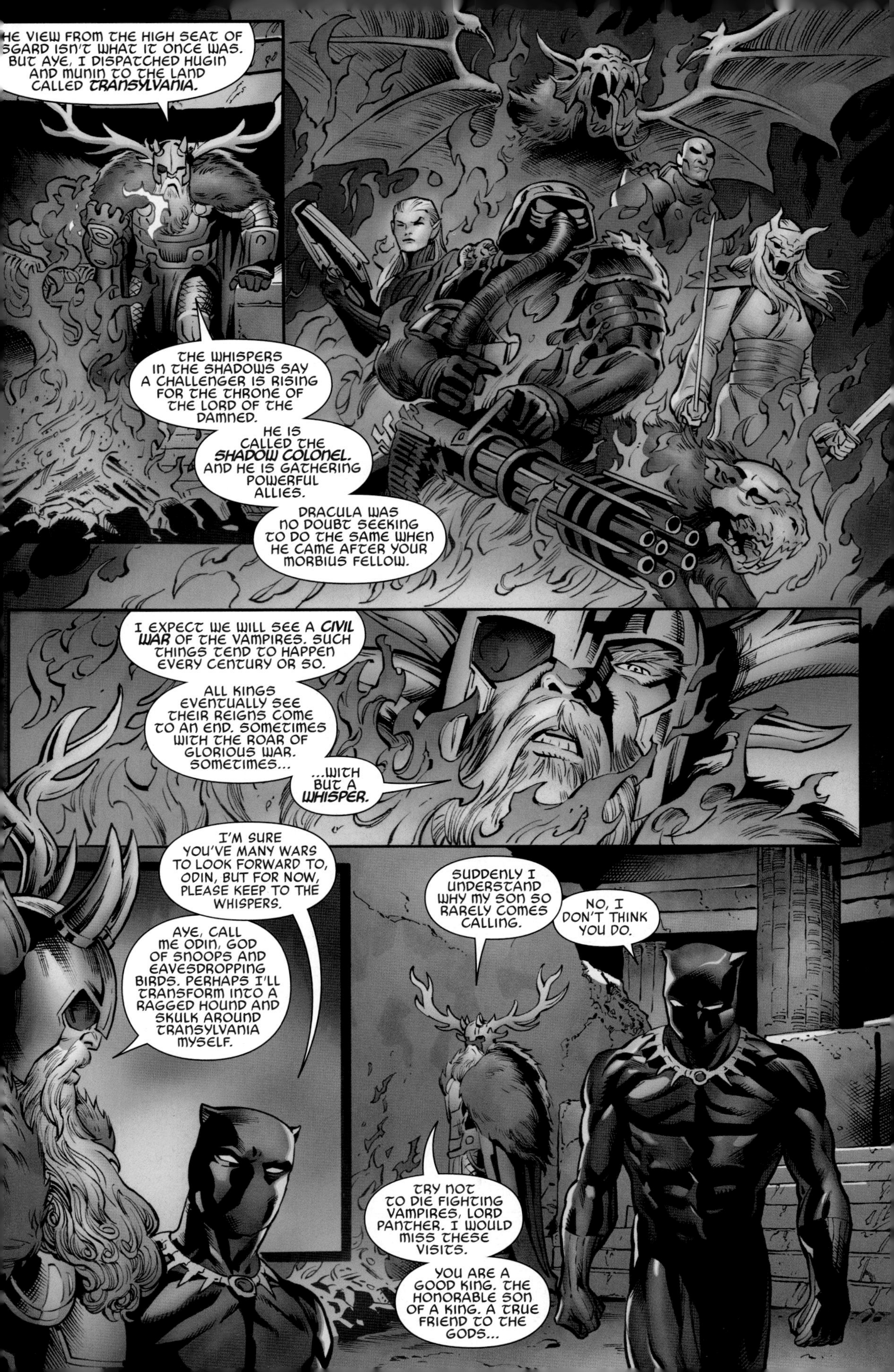
HE VIEW FROM THE HIGH SEAT OF
SGARD ISN'T WHAT IT ONCE WAS. BUT AYE, I DISPATCHED HUGIN AND MUNIN TO THE LAND CALLED TRANSYLVANIA.
THE WHISPERS IN THE SHADOWS SAY A CHALLENGER IS RISING FOR THE THRONE OF THE LORD OF THE DAMNED.
HE IS CALLED THE SHADOW COLONEL. AND HE IS GATHERING POWERFUL ALLIES.
DRACULA WAS NO DOUBT SEEKING TO DO THE SAME WHEN HE CAME AFTER YOUR MORBIUS FELLOW.
I EXPECT WE WILL SEE A CIVIL WAR OF THE VAMPIRES. SUCH THINGS TEND TO HAPPEN EVERY CENTURY OR SO.
ALL KINGS EVENTUALLY SEE THEIR REIGNS COME TO AN END. SOMETIMES WITH THE ROAR OF GLORIOUS WAR. SOMETIMES...
...WITH BUT A WHISPER.
I'M SURE YOU'VE MANY WARS TO LOOK FORWARD TO, ODIN, BUT FOR NOW, PLEASE KEEP TO THE WHISPERS.
AYE, CALL ME ODIN, GOD OF SNOOPS AND EAVESDROPPING BIRDS. PERHAPS I'LL TRANSFORM INTO A RAGGED HOUND AND SKULK AROUND TRANSYLVANIA MYSELF.
SUDDENLY I UNDERSTAND WHY MY SON SO RARELY COMES CALLING.
NO, I DON'T THINK YOU DO.
TRY NOT TO DIE FIGHTING VAMPIRES, LORD PANTHER. I WOULD MISS THESE VISITS.
YOU ARE A GOOD KING. THE HONORABLE SON OF A KING. A TRUE FRIEND TO THE GODS...

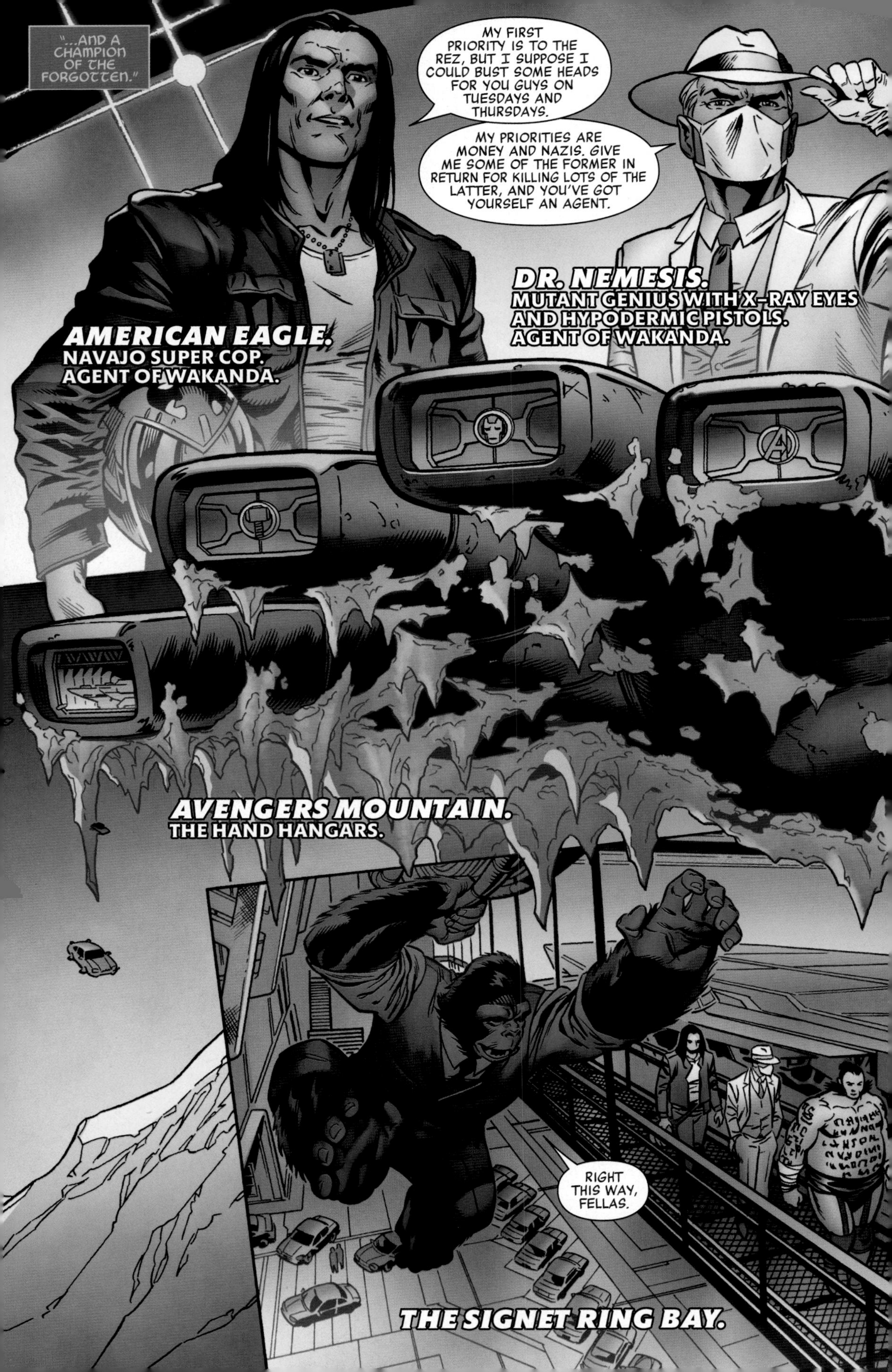
"...AND A CHAMPION OF THE FORGOTTEN."
MY FIRST PRIORITY IS TO THE REZ, BUT I SUPPOSE I COULD BUST SOME HEADS FOR YOU GUYS ON TUESDAYS AND THURSDAYS.
MY PRIORITIES ARE MONEY AND NAZIS. GIVE ME SOME OF THE FORMER IN RETURN FOR KILLING LOTS OF THE LATTER, AND YOU'VE GOT YOURSELF AN AGENT.
AMERICAN EAGLE.
NAVAJO SUPER COP.
AGENT OF WAKANDA.
DR. NEMESIS.
MUTANT GENIUS WITH X-RAY EYES AND HYPODERMIC PISTOLS.
AGENT OF WAKANDA.
AVENGERS MOUNTAIN.
THE HAND HANGARS.
RIGHT THIS WAY, FELLAS.
THE SIGNET RING BAY.

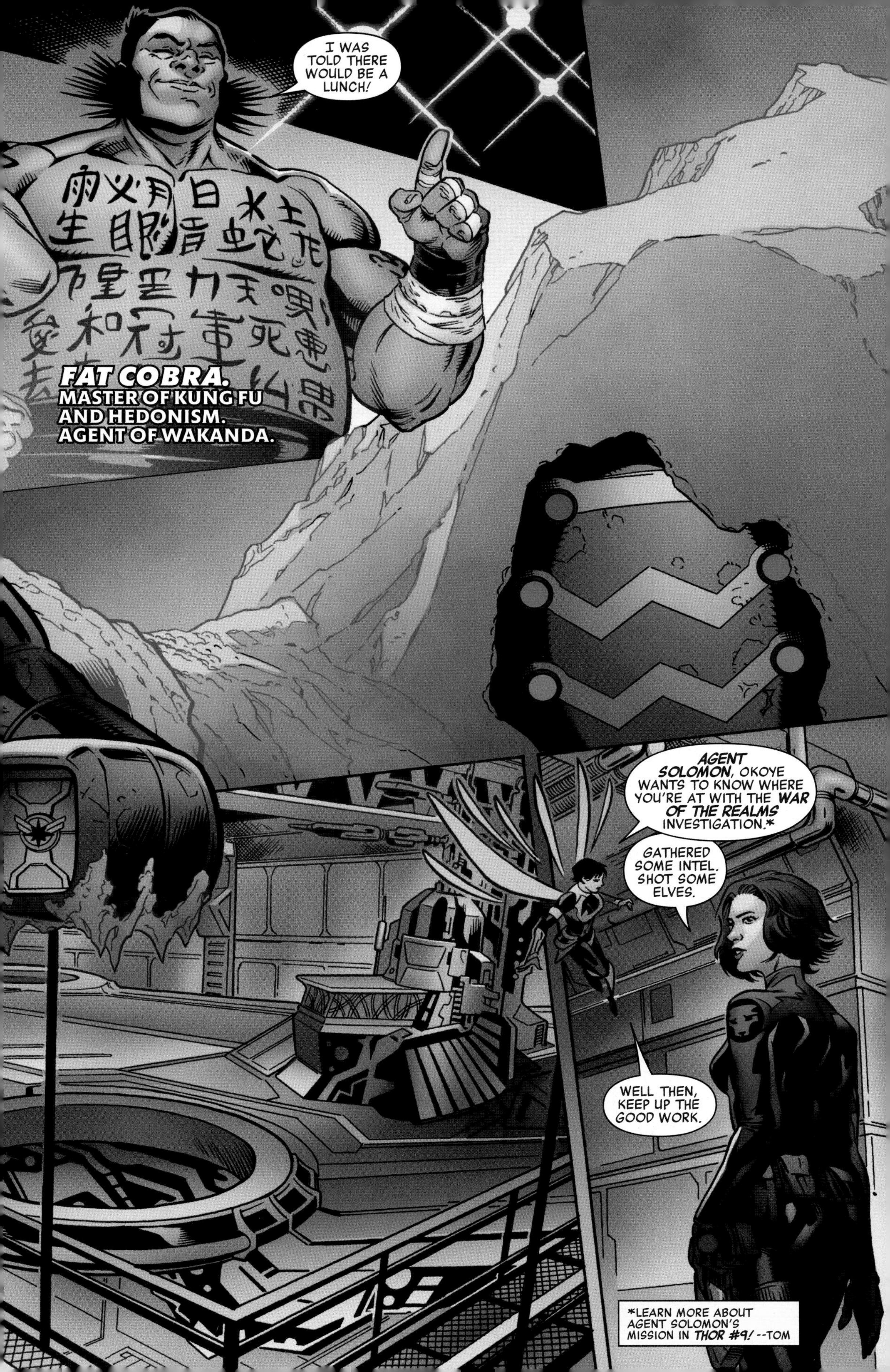
I WAS TOLD THERE WOULD BE A LUNCH!
FAT COBRA.
MASTER OF KUNG FU AND HEDONISM. AGENT OF WAKANDA.
AGENT SOLOMON, OKOYE WANTS TO KNOW WHERE YOU'RE AT WITH THE WAR OF THE REALMS INVESTIGATION.*
GATHERED SOME INTEL. SHOT SOME ELVES.
WELL THEN, KEEP UP THE GOOD WORK.
*LEARN MORE ABOUT AGENT SOLOMON'S MISSION IN THOR #9! --TOM

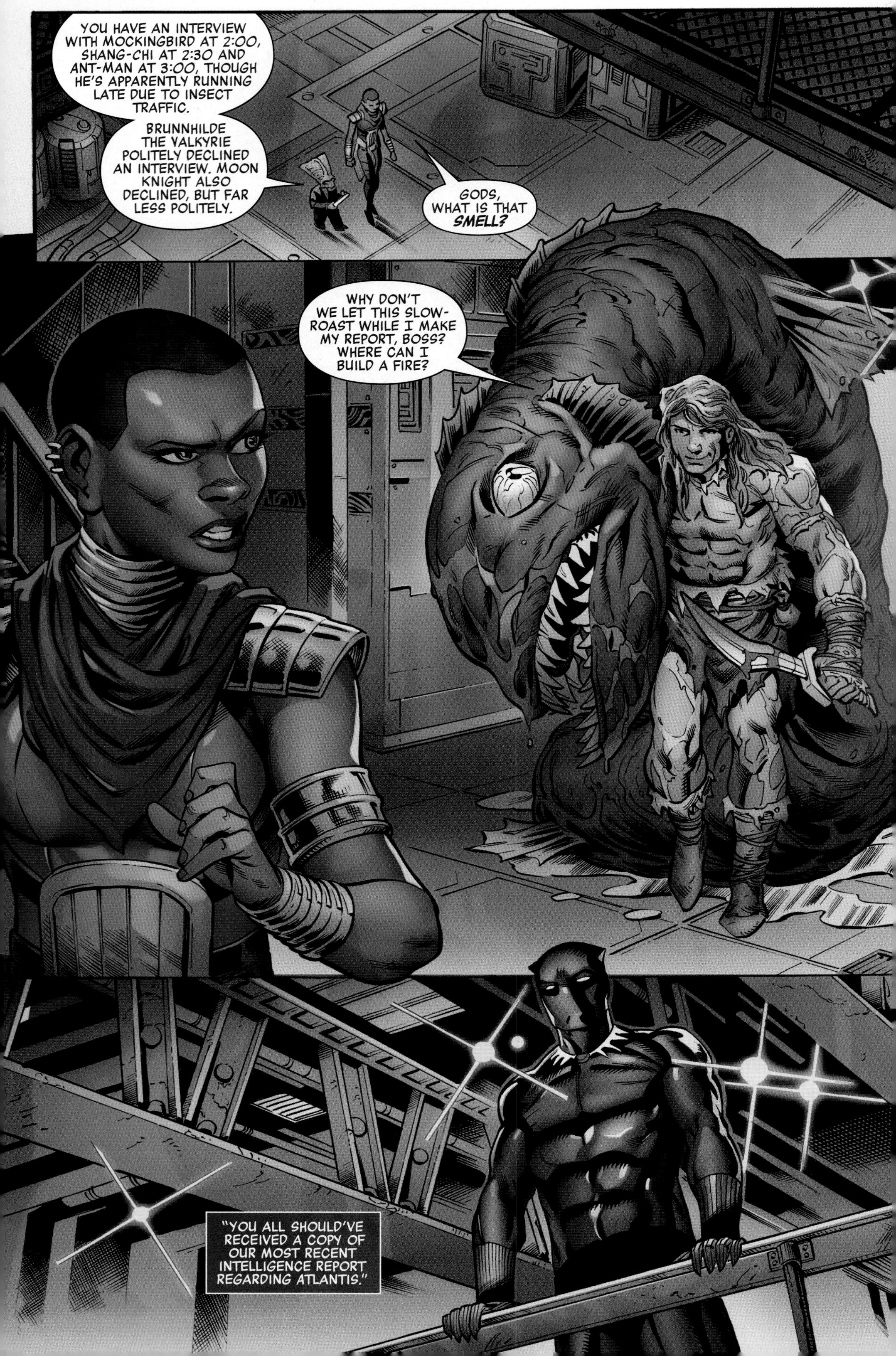
YOU HAVE AN INTERVIEW WITH MOCKINGBIRD AT 2:00, SHANG-CHI AT 2:30 AND ANT-MAN AT 3:00, THOUGH HE'S APPARENTLY RUNNING LATE DUE TO INSECT TRAFFIC.
BRUNNHILDE THE VALKYRIE POLITELY DECLINED AN INTERVIEW. MOON KNIGHT ALSO DECLINED, BUT FAR LESS POLITELY.
GODS, WHAT IS THAT SMELL?
WHY DON'T WE LET THIS SLOW-ROAST WHILE I MAKE MY REPORT, BOSS? WHERE CAN I BUILD A FIRE?
"YOU ALL SHOULD'VE RECEIVED A COPY OF OUR MOST RECENT INTELLIGENCE REPORT REGARDING ATLANTIS."

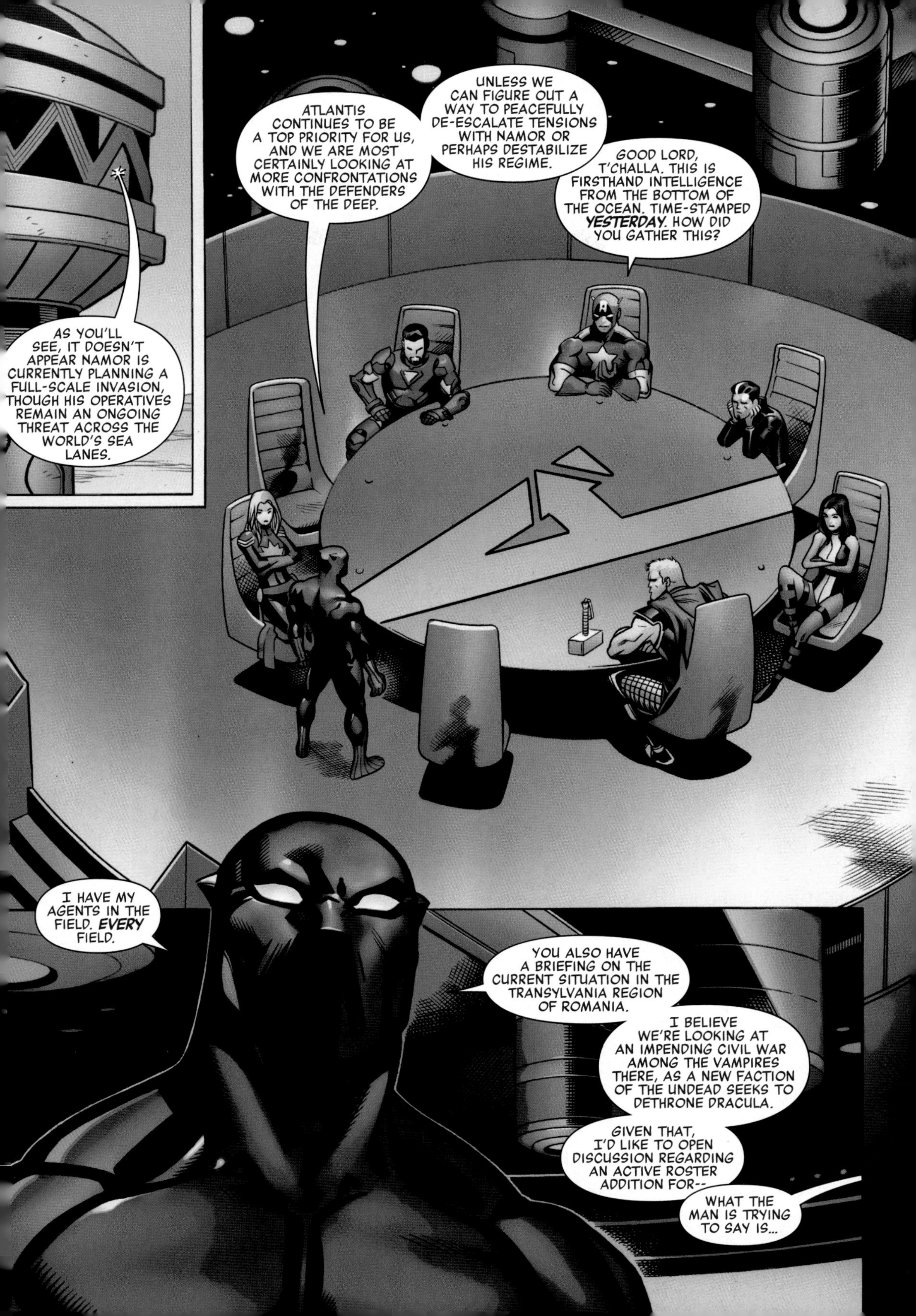
ATLANTIS CONTINUES TO BE A TOP PRIORITY FOR US, AND WE ARE MOST CERTAINLY LOOKING AT MORE CONFRONTATIONS WITH THE DEFENDERS OF THE DEEP.
UNLESS WE CAN FIGURE OUT A WAY TO PEACEFULLY DE-ESCALATE TENSIONS WITH NAMOR OR PERHAPS DESTABILIZE HIS REGIME.
AS YOU'LL SEE, IT DOESN'T APPEAR NAMOR IS CURRENTLY PLANNING A FULL-SCALE INVASION, THOUGH HIS OPERATIVES REMAIN AN ONGOING THREAT ACROSS THE WORLD'S SEA LANES.
GOOD LORD, T'CHALLA. THIS IS FIRSTHAND INTELLIGENCE FROM THE BOTTOM OF THE OCEAN. TIME-STAMPED ***YESTERDAY***. HOW DID YOU GATHER THIS?
I HAVE MY AGENTS IN THE FIELD. ***EVERY*** FIELD.
YOU ALSO HAVE A BRIEFING ON THE CURRENT SITUATION IN THE TRANSYLVANIA REGION OF ROMANIA.
I BELIEVE WE'RE LOOKING AT AN IMPENDING CIVIL WAR AMONG THE VAMPIRES THERE, AS A NEW FACTION OF THE UNDEAD SEEKS TO DETHRONE DRACULA.
GIVEN THAT, I'D LIKE TO OPEN DISCUSSION REGARDING AN ACTIVE ROSTER ADDITION FOR--
WHAT THE MAN IS TRYING TO SAY IS...

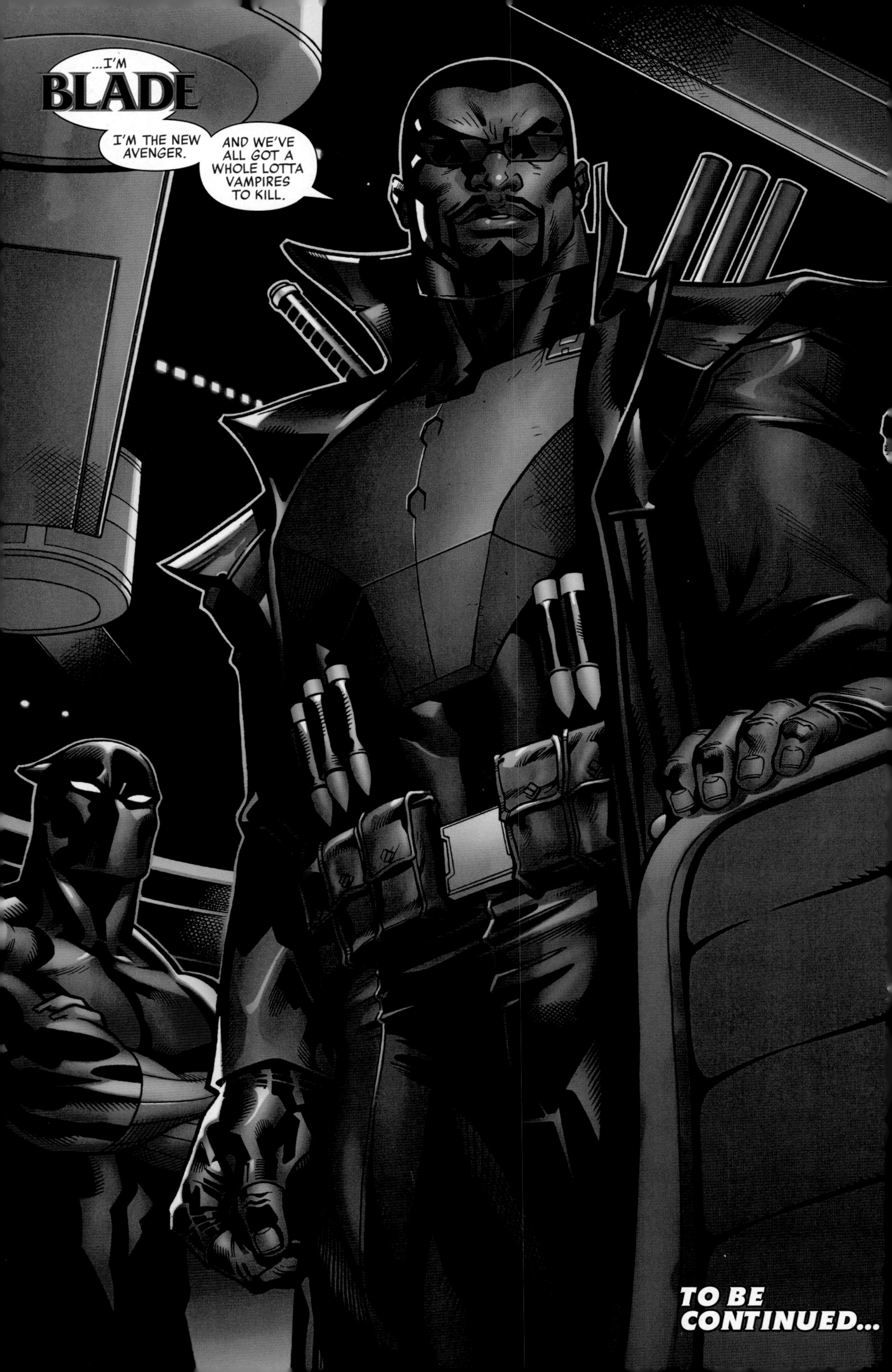
...I'M BLADE
I'M THE NEW AVENGER.
AND WE'VE ALL GOT A WHOLE LOTTA VAMPIRES TO KILL.
TO BE CONTINUED...

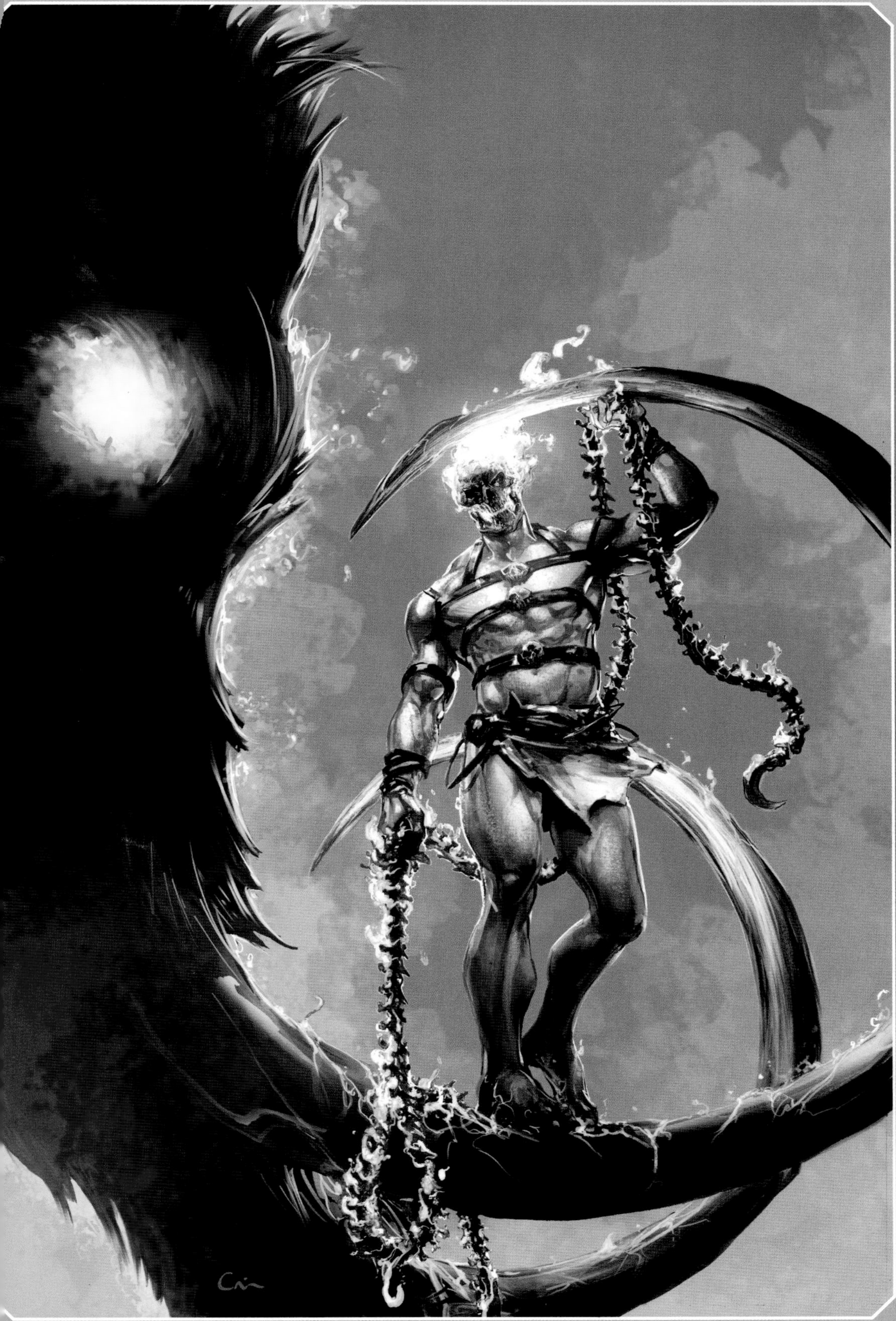

CLAYTON CRAIN
7 VARIANT

TRADD MOORE & FELIPE SOBREIRO
7 COSMIC GHOST RIDER VS. VARIANT

MIKE McKONE & CHRIS SOTOMAYOR
8 COSMIC GHOST RIDER VS. VARIANT

PHILIP TAN & MARTE GRACIA
8 VARIANT

DAVID FINCH & PETER STEIGERWALD
10 VARIANT

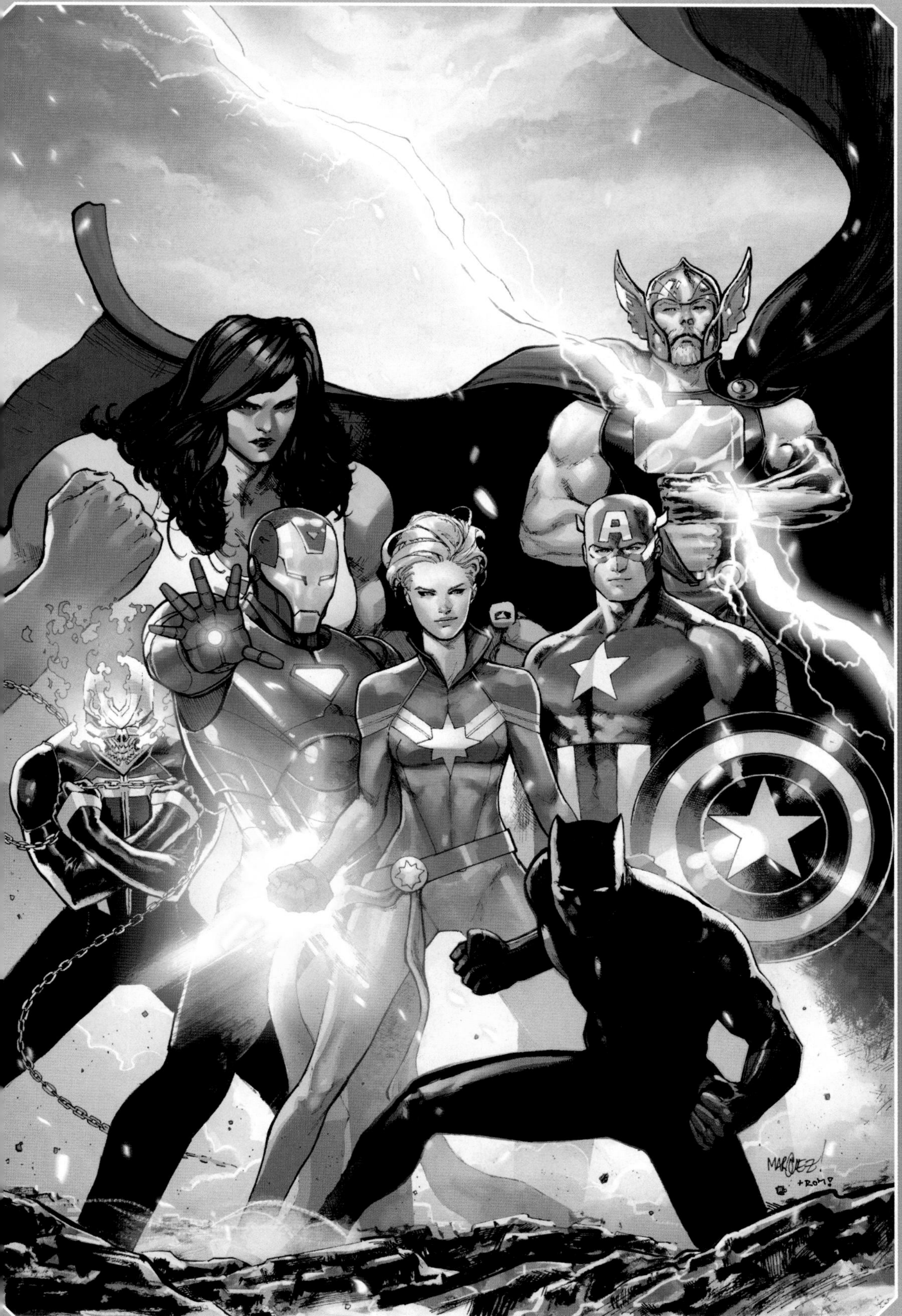
MARQUEZ!
+ROM!

DAVID MARQUEZ & ROMULO FAJARDO JR.
10 VARIANT

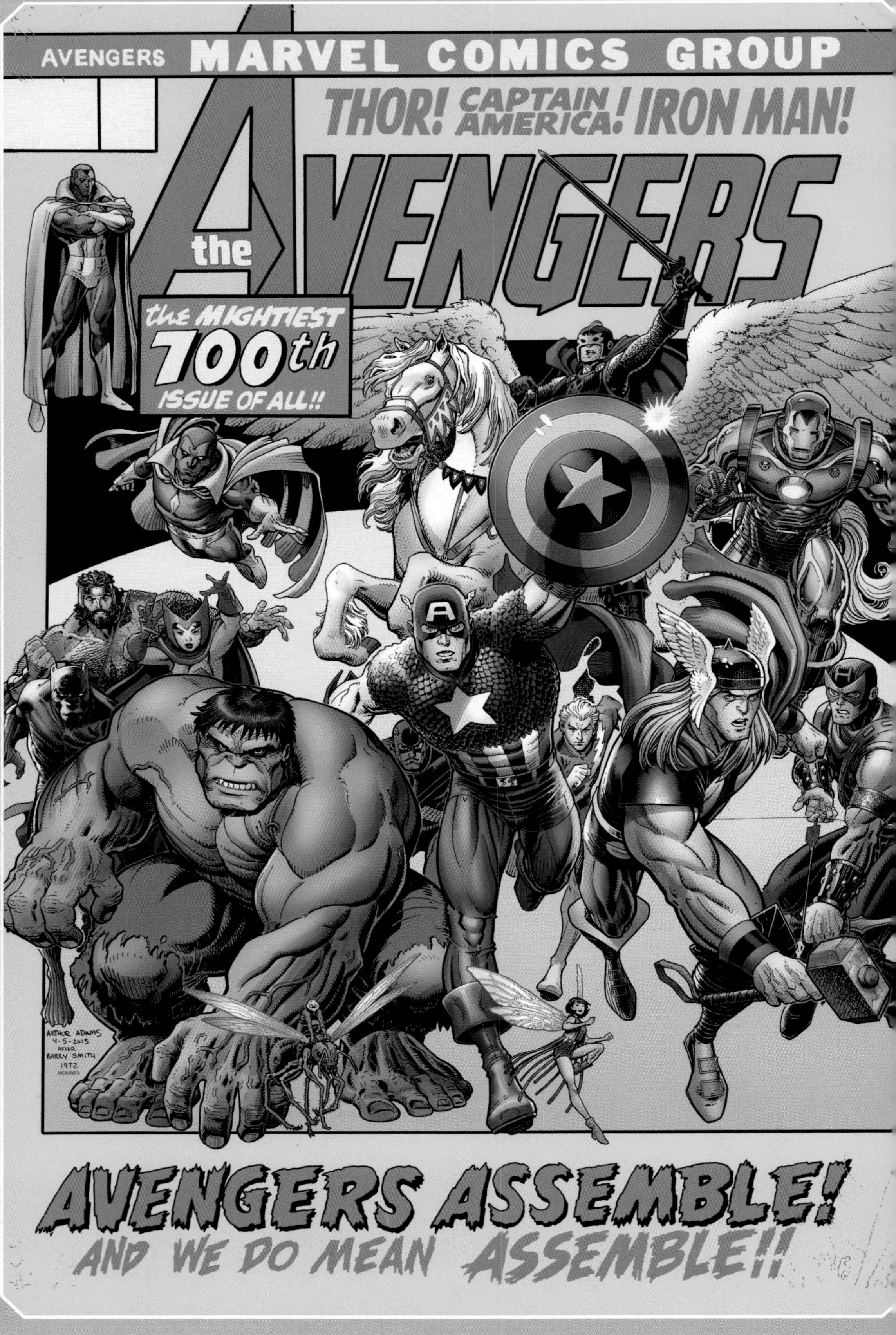
AVENGERS
MARVEL COMICS GROUP
THOR! CAPTAIN AMERICA! IRON MAN!
the AVENGERS
the MIGHTIEST 100th ISSUE OF ALL!!
ARTHUR ADAMS
4-5-2013
AFTER
BARRY SMITH
1972
AVENGERS ASSEMBLE!
AND WE DO MEAN ASSEMBLE!!

ARTHUR ADAMS & PAUL MOUNTS
10 VARIANT

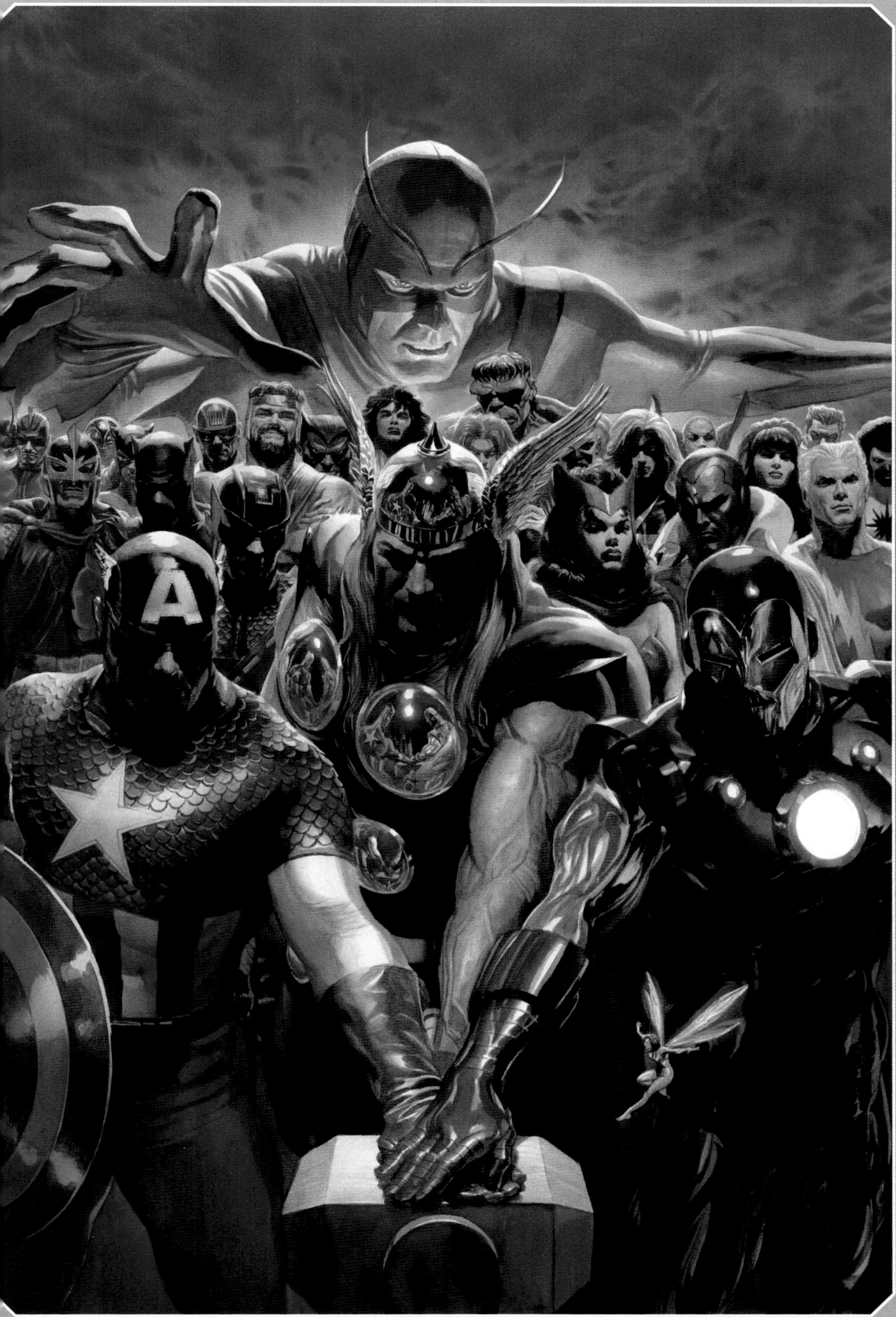

ALEX ROSS
10 VARIANT

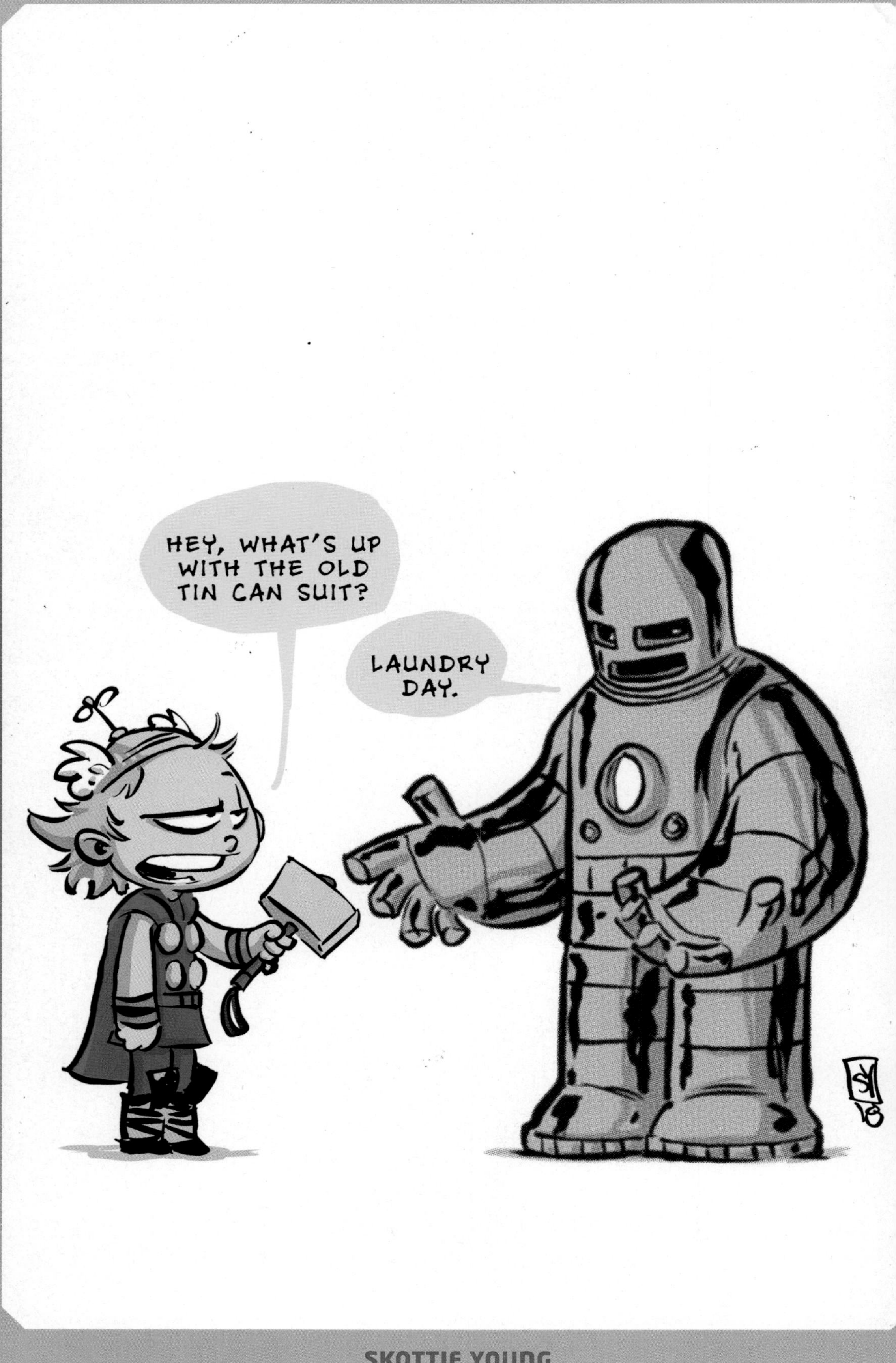
HEY, WHAT'S UP WITH THE OLD TIN CAN SUIT?
LAUNDRY DAY.

SKOTTIE YOUNG
10 VARIANT

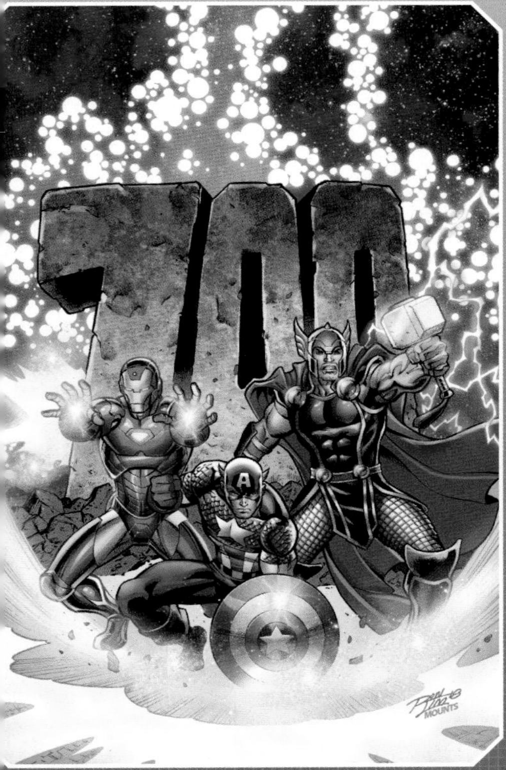
700

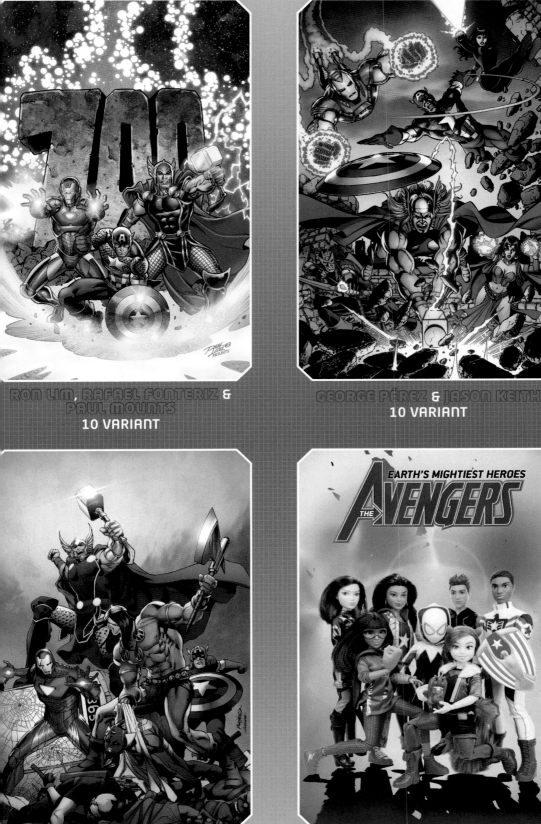

RON LIM, RAFAEL FONTERIZ & PAUL MOUNTS
10 VARIANT

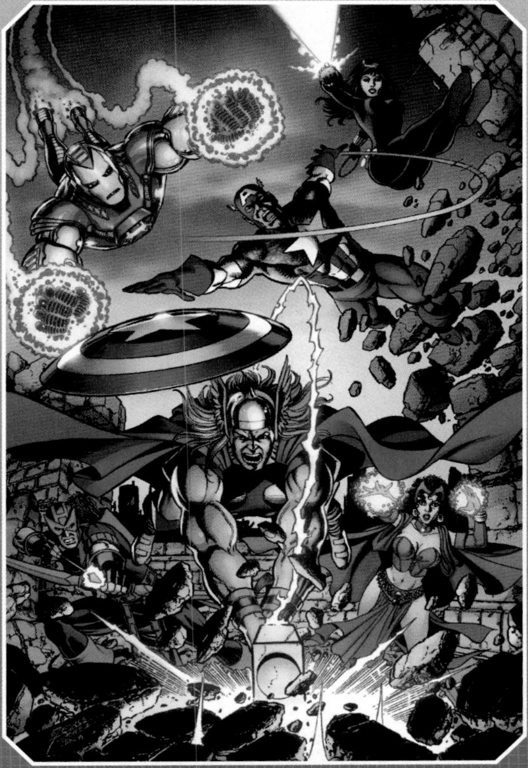

GEORGE PÉREZ & JASON KEITH
10 VARIANT

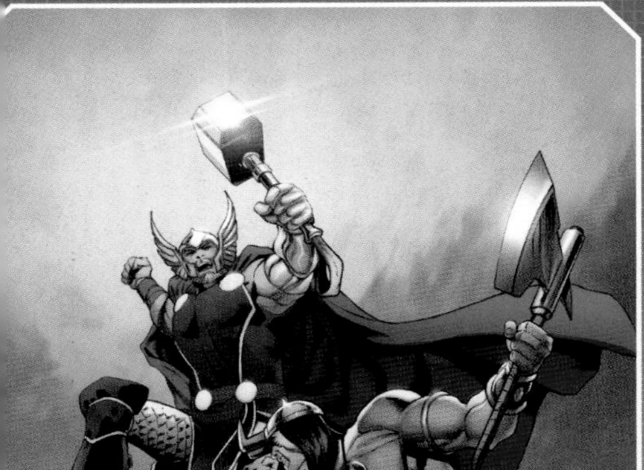

CARLOS PACHECO, ANEKE & JASON KEITH
11 CONAN VARIANT

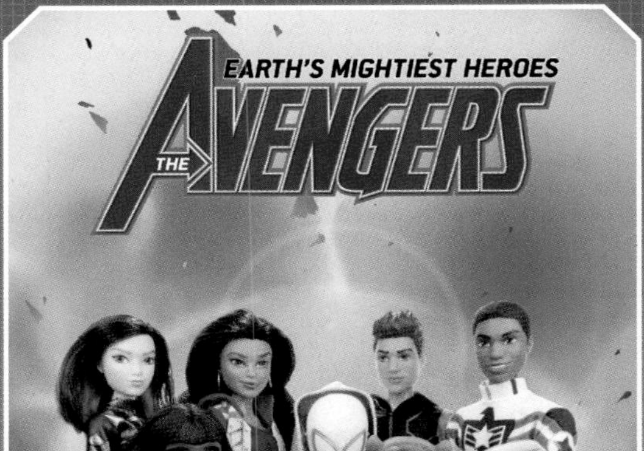
EARTH'S MIGHTIEST HEROES
THE AVENGERS

12 MARVEL RISING ACTION DOLL HOMAGE VARIANT

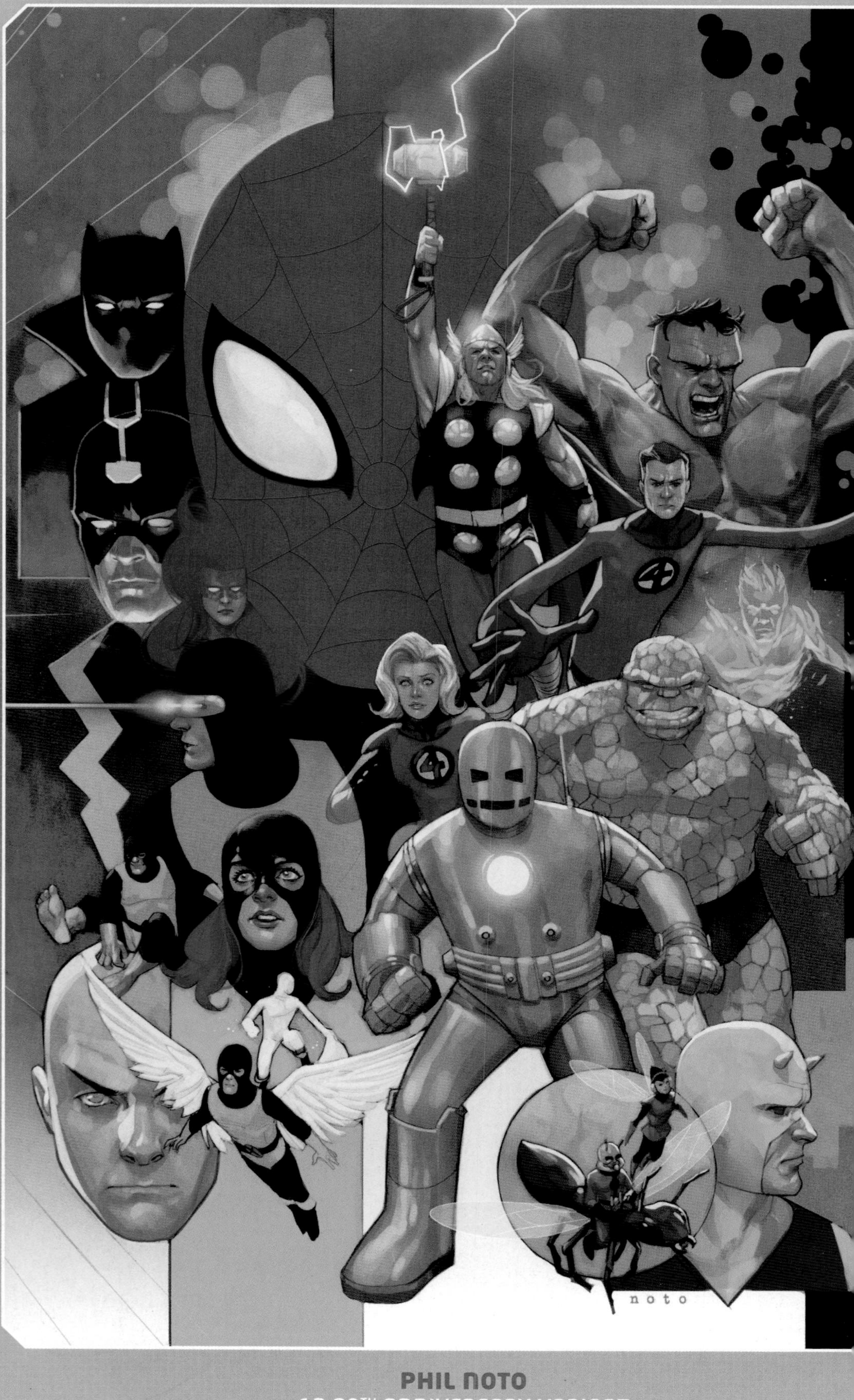
noto

PHIL NOTO
12 80TH ANNIVERSARY VARIANT